Biology 2

3.4 Humans and Their Environment

Reference

Controlled Assessment

Exam Help

Published by CGP

Editors:
Charlotte Burrows, Jane Ellingham, Rachael Rogers, Camilla Simson, Hayley Thompson.

Contributors:
Gemma Hallam, Adrian Schmit.

ISBN: 978 1 84762 220 4

With thanks to Janet Cruse-Sawyer, Glenn Rogers and Karen Wells for the proofreading.
With thanks to Laura Jakubowski for the copyright research.

Groovy website: www.cgpbooks.co.uk
Printed by Elanders Ltd, Newcastle upon Tyne.
Jolly bits of clipart from CorelDRAW®

How to use this book

Learning Objectives

- These tell you exactly what you need to learn, or be able to do, for the exam.

- There's a specification reference at the bottom that links to the AQA specification.

Examples

These are here to help you understand the theory.

Tips and Exam Tips

- There are tips throughout the book to help you understand the theory.

- There are also exam tips to help you with answering exam questions.

Learning Objectives:
- Know what an adaptation is.
- Understand how animals can be adapted to live in desert or arctic conditions, including the effect of surface area, insulation, body fat and camouflage.
- Understand how plants can be adapted to live in desert conditions, including the effect of surface area, water storage tissues and extensive roots.
- Know that some plants and animals have adaptations to help deter predators.
- Understand what is meant by the term 'extremophile'.
- Be able to identify adaptations in organisms and understand how they help the organism to survive.
- Understand that plants and animals need resources from their environment to survive and reproduce, and that they compete for these resources

Specification Reference
B1.4.1

1. Adaptations and Competition

Organisms survive in many different environments because they are adapted to them and can compete for resources.

Animal adaptations

Adaptations are characteristics which increase an organism's chance of survival in the environment in which it lives. Animals that live in different environments have different adaptations.

Desert animals

The desert is a very hot and dry environment. Desert animals need to be able to save water and keep cool. Desert animals are adapted to their environment in the following ways:

- They have a large surface area compared to volume. This lets them lose more body heat, which helps to stop them overheating.

Example

The fennec fox has very large ears. This is an adaptation which increases its surface area and helps it to lose heat in its desert environment.

Figure 1: A fennec fox.

- They are efficient with water — they lose less water by producing small amounts of concentrated urine and they also make very little sweat.

- They have thin layers of body fat and thin insulating coats — these adaptations help them to lose body heat.

- They have a sandy colour to give good camouflage — this helps them to avoid predators, or sneak up on prey.

Example

A camel is adapted to survive in desert conditions:

Camels are able to tolerate large changes in temperature, so they don't sweat much

Camels keep all their fat in their humps to help them lose heat from the rest of their body

Light-brown colour for camouflage

Exam Tip
You could also be asked to interpret data on rooting powders in the exam.

Figure 9: A gardener using rooting powder when planting cuttings.

Tip: Don't forget to refer to the experiment in your answer to Q1 a). Don't just talk about what you know about auxin.

2. Rooting powders

Plant cuttings won't always grow in soil. If you add rooting powder, which contains the plant hormone auxin, they'll produce roots rapidly and start growing as new plants. This helps growers to produce lots of clones of a really good plant very quickly.

Practice Questions — Fact Recall

Q1   What is gravitropism?

Q2   What effect does auxin have on cell elongation in a plant root?

Q3   Explain how plant roots grow in response to moisture in the soil.

Practice Questions — Application

Q1   A scientist conducted an experiment to study phototropism in cress seedlings. 12 cress seeds were planted in Petri dish A and left directly under a light source. Another 12 cress seeds were planted in Petri dish B and provided with a light source placed to one side. The growth of the seeds after two weeks is shown in the diagram:

light source

cress seedlings

A   B

a) Describe how the distribution of auxin in the shoots of the cress seedlings will differ between Petri dish A and Petri dish B.

b) i) Other than the position of the light source, the scientist tried to keep the conditions in both Petri dishes the same. Explain why she did this.

ii) Give two conditions that the scientist needed to keep the same during the experiment.

Q2   Dan grows plants for a garden centre. He is trying to work out the best rooting powder to use for his cuttings. From the same type of plant, he grows 50 cuttings in rooting powder A, 50 in rooting powder B and 50 without rooting powder. He grows all the cuttings under the same conditions. His results are shown in the table.

	Powder A	Powder B	No powder
Average increase in root length (mm) After 1 week	8	10	6
After 2 weeks	17	19	14
After 3 weeks	24	28	20

a) From these results, what can you conclude about which rooting powder is the best to use? Explain your answer.

b) Explain why Dan grew some cuttings without rooting powder.

Practice Questions

- There are a lot of facts to learn for GCSE Biology — fact recall questions test that you know them.

- Annoyingly, the examiners also expect you to be able to apply your knowledge to new situations — application questions give you plenty of practice at doing this.

- All the answers are in the back of the book.

How Science Works

- How Science Works is a big part of GCSE Biology. There's a whole section on it at the front of the book.

- How Science Works is also covered throughout the book wherever you see this symbol.

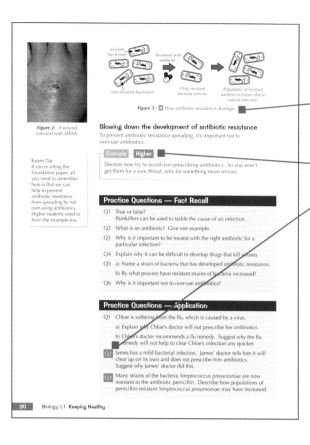

Figure 1: How antibiotic resistance develops.

Figure 2: A wound infected with MRSA.

Exam Tip
If you're sitting the Foundation paper, all you need to remember here is that we can help to prevent antibiotic resistance from spreading by not over-using antibiotics. Higher students need to learn the example too.

Slowing down the development of antibiotic resistance
To prevent antibiotic resistance spreading, it's important not to over-use antibiotics.

Example — Higher
Doctors now try to avoid over-prescribing antibiotics. So you won't get them for a sore throat, only for something more serious.

Practice Questions — Fact Recall

Q1 True or false?
Painkillers can be used to tackle the cause of an infection.

Q2 What is an antibiotic? Give one example.

Q3 Why is it important to be treated with the right antibiotic for a particular infection?

Q4 Explain why it can be difficult to develop drugs that kill viruses.

Q5 a) Name a strain of bacteria that has developed antibiotic resistance.
   b) By what process have resistant strains of bacteria increased?

Q6 Why is it important not to over-use antibiotics?

Practice Questions — Application

Q1 Chloe is suffering from the flu, which is caused by a virus.
   a) Explain why Chloe's doctor will not prescribe her antibiotics.
   b) Chloe's doctor recommends a flu remedy. Suggest why the flu remedy will not help to clear Chloe's infection any quicker.

Q2 James has a mild bacterial infection. James' doctor tells him it will clear up on its own and does not prescribe him antibiotics. Suggest why James' doctor did this.

Q3 Many strains of the bacteria *Streptococcus pneumoniae* are now resistant to the antibiotic penicillin. Describe how populations of penicillin-resistant *Streptococcus pneumoniae* may have increased.

Higher Exam Material

- Some of the material in this book will only come up in the exam if you're sitting the higher exam papers.

- This material is clearly marked with boxes that look like this:

  Higher **H** **Q1**

- If you're sitting the foundation papers, you don't need to learn it.

Section Checklist

Each section has a checklist at the end with boxes that let you tick off what you've learnt.

Glossary

There's a glossary at the back of the book full of all the definitions you need to know for the exam, plus loads of other useful words.

Exam-style Questions

- Practising exam-style questions is really important — there are some testing you on material from every section.

- They're the same style as the ones you'll get in the real exams.

- All the answers are in the back of the book, along with a mark scheme to show you how you get the marks.

- Higher-only questions are marked like this: **1** (b)

Controlled Assessment and Exam Help

There are sections at the back of the book stuffed full of things to help you with the controlled assessment and the exams.

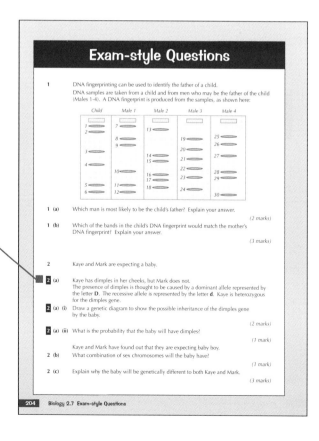

Exam-style Questions

1   DNA fingerprinting can be used to identify the father of a child.
     DNA samples are taken from a child and from men who may be the father of the child (Males 1-4). A DNA fingerprint is produced from the samples, as shown here:

1 (a)   Which man is most likely to be the child's father? Explain your answer.
        (2 marks)

1 (b)   Which of the bands in the child's DNA fingerprint would match the mother's DNA fingerprint? Explain your answer.
        (3 marks)

2   Kaye and Mark are expecting a baby.

2 (a)   Kaye has dimples in her cheeks, but Mark does not.
        The presence of dimples is thought to be caused by a dominant allele represented by the letter **D**. The recessive allele is represented by the letter **d**. Kaye is heterozygous for the dimples gene.

2 (a) (i)   Draw a genetic diagram to show the possible inheritance of the dimples gene by the baby.
            (2 marks)

2 (a) (ii) What is the probability that the baby will have dimples?
            (1 mark)

        Kaye and Mark have found out that they are expecting baby boy.

2 (b)   What combination of sex chromosomes will the baby have?
        (1 mark)

2 (c)   Explain why the baby will be genetically different to both Kaye and Mark.
        (3 marks)

1. The Scientific Process

Science is all about finding things out and learning things about the world we live in. This topic is all about the scientific process — how a scientist's initial idea turns into a theory that is accepted by the wider scientific community.

Hypotheses

Scientists try to explain things. Everything. They start by observing something they don't understand — it could be anything, e.g. planets in the sky, a person suffering from an illness, what matter is made of... anything.

Then, they come up with a **hypothesis** — a possible explanation for what they've observed. (Scientists can also sometimes form a model too — a simplified description or a representation of what's physically going on). The next step is to test whether the hypothesis might be right or not — this involves gathering evidence (i.e. data from investigations).

The scientist uses the hypothesis to make a **prediction** — a statement based on the hypothesis that can be tested. They then carry out an investigation. If data from experiments or studies backs up the prediction, you're one step closer to figuring out if the hypothesis is true.

Testing a hypothesis

Other scientists will use the hypothesis to make their own predictions, and carry out their own experiments or studies. They'll also try to reproduce the original investigations to check the results. And if all the experiments in the world back up the hypothesis, then scientists start to think it's true.

However, if a scientist somewhere in the world does an experiment that doesn't fit with the hypothesis (and other scientists can reproduce these results), then the hypothesis is in trouble. When this happens, scientists have to come up with a new hypothesis (maybe a modification of the old hypothesis, or maybe a completely new one).

Accepting a hypothesis

If pretty much every scientist in the world believes a hypothesis to be true because experiments back it up, then it usually goes in the textbooks for students to learn. Accepted hypotheses are often referred to as **theories**.

Our currently accepted theories are the ones that have survived this 'trial by evidence' — they've been tested many, many times over the years and survived (while the less good ones have been ditched). However... they never, never become hard and fast, totally indisputable fact. You can never know... it'd only take one odd, totally inexplicable result, and the hypothesising and testing would start all over again.

Learning Objectives:

- Know what a hypothesis and a prediction are and understand their roles in developing scientific ideas.

- Understand that scientists try to explain observations using evidence collected in investigations.

- Understand the importance of carrying out fair tests and collecting repeatable, reproducible and valid results.

- Understand why some decisions relating to science are not just based on scientific evidence but take other factors into account.

Specification Reference
How Science Works

Tip: Investigations include lab experiments and studies.

Tip: Sometimes it can take a really long time for a hypothesis to be accepted.

Over time scientists have come up with different hypotheses about how illnesses are caused:

- Hundreds of years ago, we thought demons caused illness.

- Then we thought it was caused by 'bad blood' (and treated it with leeches).

- Now we know most illnesses are due to microorganisms.

Figure 1: *Historical artwork of a woman using leeches to treat disease.*

Collecting evidence

If a hypothesis is going to get accepted, there needs to be good evidence for it. The way evidence is gathered can have a big effect on how trustworthy it is.

Results from experiments in laboratories are great. A lab is the easiest place to control variables so that they're all kept constant (except for the one you're investigating). This makes it easier to carry out a **fair test**. For things that you can't investigate in the lab (e.g. climate) you conduct scientific studies. As many of the variables as possible are controlled, to make it a fair test.

Old wives' tales, rumours, hearsay, "what someone said", and so on, should be taken with a pinch of salt. Without any evidence they're not scientific — they're just opinions.

Tip: See page 6 for more on fair testing and variables.

Figure 2: *A scientist doing a laboratory experiment.*

Sample size

Data based on small samples isn't as good as data based on large samples. A sample should be representative of the whole population (i.e. it should share as many of the various characteristics in the population as possible) — a small sample can't do that as well.

The bigger the sample size the better, but scientists have to be realistic when choosing how big.

If you were studying how lifestyle affects people's weight it'd be great to study everyone in the UK (a huge sample), but it'd take ages and cost a bomb. Studying a thousand people would be more realistic.

Quality of evidence

You can have confidence in the results if they can be repeated (during the same experiment) and other scientists can reproduce them too (in other experiments). If the results aren't **repeatable** or **reproducible**, you can't believe them.

In 1998, a scientist claimed that he'd found a link between the MMR vaccine (for measles, mumps and rubella) and autism. As a result, many parents stopped their children from having the vaccine — which led to a big rise in the number of children catching measles. However, no other scientist has been able to reproduce the results since. Health authorities have now concluded that the vaccine is safe to use.

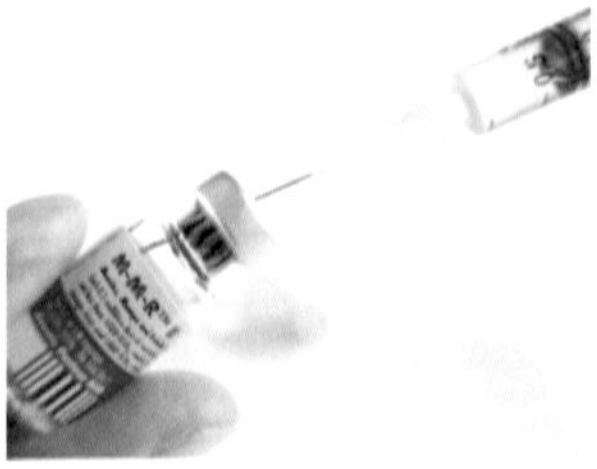

Figure 3: The MMR vaccine.

If results are repeatable and reproducible, they're said to be **reliable**.

Getting valid evidence

Evidence also needs to be **valid**. Valid means that the data answers the original question.

Do power lines cause cancer?

Some studies have found that children who live near overhead power lines are more likely to develop cancer. What they'd actually found was a **correlation** (relationship) between the variables "presence of power lines" and "incidence of cancer". They found that as one changed, so did the other.

But this evidence is not enough to say that the power lines cause cancer, as other explanations might be possible. For example, power lines are often near busy roads, so the areas tested could contain different levels of pollution from traffic. So these studies don't show a definite link and so don't answer the original question.

Tip: To be valid, a result must also be repeatable and reproducible.

Tip: See page 13 for more on correlation.

Communicating results

Once evidence is collected it can be shared with other people. It's important that the evidence isn't presented in a **biased** way. This can sometimes happen when people want to make a point, e.g. they overemphasise a relationship in the data. (Sometimes without knowing they're doing it.) And there are all sorts of reasons why people might want to do this.

- They want to keep the organisation or company that's funding the research happy. (If the results aren't what they'd like they might not give them any more money to fund further research.)
- Governments might want to persuade voters, other governments, journalists, etc.
- Companies might want to 'big up' their products. Or make impressive safety claims.
- Environmental campaigners might want to persuade people to behave differently.

There's also a risk that if an investigation is done by a team of highly-regarded scientists it'll be taken more seriously than evidence from less well known scientists. But having experience, authority or a fancy qualification doesn't necessarily mean the evidence is good — the only way to tell is to look at the evidence scientifically (e.g. is it repeatable, valid, etc.).

Issues created by science

Scientific knowledge is increased by doing experiments. And this knowledge leads to scientific developments, e.g. new technologies or new advice. These developments can create issues though. For example, particular scientific developments might be ignored if they could create political issues, or emphasised if they help a particular cause.

Tip: See page 278 for more on global warming.

> **Example**
>
> Some governments were pretty slow to accept the fact that human activities are causing global warming, despite all the evidence. This is because accepting it means they've got to do something about it, which costs money and could hurt their economy. This could lose them a lot of votes.

Scientific developments can cause a whole host of other issues too.

Figure 4: Dolly the sheep — the first mammal to be cloned. A great scientific advance but some people think that cloning animals is morally wrong.

> **Examples**
>
> - **Economic issues:** Society can't always afford to do things scientists recommend (e.g. investing heavily in alternative energy sources) without cutting back elsewhere.
>
> - **Social issues:** Decisions based on scientific evidence affect people — e.g. should junk food be taxed more highly (to encourage people to be healthy)? Should alcohol be banned (to prevent health problems)? Would the effect on people's lifestyles be acceptable?
>
> - **Environmental issues:** Genetically modified crops may help us produce more food — but some people think they could cause environmental problems.
>
> - **Ethical issues:** There are a lot of things that scientific developments have made possible, but should we do them? E.g. cloning humans.

2. Limitations of Science

Science has taught us an awful lot about the world we live in and how things work — but science doesn't have the answer for everything.

Questions science hasn't answered yet

We don't understand everything. And we never will. We'll find out more, for sure — as more hypotheses are suggested, and more experiments are done. But there'll always be stuff we don't know.

Examples

- Today we don't know as much as we'd like about the impacts of global warming. How much will sea level rise? And to what extent will weather patterns change?

- We also don't know anywhere near as much as we'd like about the Universe. Are there other life forms out there? And what is the Universe made of?

These are complicated questions. At the moment scientists don't all agree on the answers because there isn't enough repeatable, reproducible and valid evidence. But eventually, we probably will be able to answer these questions once and for all. All we need is more evidence. But by then there'll be loads of new questions to answer.

Questions science can't answer

There are some questions that all the experiments in the world won't help us answer — the "should we be doing this at all?" type questions.

Example

Think about embryo screening (which allows you to choose an embryo with particular characteristics). It's possible to do it, but does that mean we should?

Some people say it's good... couples whose existing child needs a bone marrow transplant, but who can't find a donor, will be able to have another child selected for its matching bone marrow. This would save the life of their first child — and if they want another child anyway... where's the harm?

Other people say it's bad... they say it could have serious effects on the new child. In this example, the new child might feel unwanted — thinking they were only brought into the world to help someone else. And would they have the right to refuse to donate their bone marrow (as anyone else would)?

The question of whether something is morally or ethically right or wrong can't be answered by more experiments — there is no "right" or "wrong" answer. The best we can do is get a consensus from society — a judgement that most people are more or less happy to live by. Science can provide more information to help people make this judgement, and the judgement might change over time. But in the end it's up to people and their conscience.

Learning Objectives:

- Know that there are some things that haven't yet been explained by science because we don't have enough good evidence.

- Understand why some questions can't ever be answered by science alone.

Specification Reference
How Science Works

Figure 1: *Global warming could cause weather patterns to change — which may result in longer, hotter droughts in some areas.*

Tip: It's important that scientists don't get wrapped up in whether they <u>can</u> do something, before stopping to think about whether they <u>should</u> do it. Some experiments have to be approved by ethics councils before scientists are allowed to carry them out.

Learning Objectives:
- Know how to design fair investigations that allow good quality data to be collected.

Specification Reference
How Science Works

3. Designing Investigations

To be a good scientist you need to know how to design a good experiment. That's what this topic is all about — how to make your experiment safe and how to make sure you get good quality results.

Making predictions from a hypothesis

Scientists observe things and come up with hypotheses to explain them (see page 1). To figure out whether a **hypothesis** might be correct or not you need to do an investigation to gather some evidence. The evidence will help support or disprove the hypothesis.

The first step is to use the hypothesis to come up with a **prediction** — a statement about what you think will happen that you can test.

Tip: Sometimes the words 'hypothesis' and 'prediction' are used interchangeably.

Example
If your hypothesis is "eating a diet containing a large amount of saturated fat causes a high blood cholesterol level", then your prediction might be "people who eat large amounts of saturated fats will have a high level of cholesterol in their blood".

Tip: See page 3 for more on valid evidence.

Investigations are used to see if there are patterns or relationships between two variables. For example, to see if there's a pattern or relationship between the variables 'amount of saturated fats eaten' and 'blood cholesterol level'. The investigation has to be a **fair test** to make sure the evidence is **valid**.

Ensuring it's a fair test

Tip: A variable is just something in the experiment that can change.

In a lab experiment you usually change one variable and measure how it affects the other variable. To make it a fair test everything else that could affect the results should stay the same (otherwise you can't tell if the thing you're changing is causing the results or not — the data won't be valid).

Example
You might change only the temperature of an enzyme-controlled reaction and measure how it affects the rate of reaction. You need to keep the pH the same, otherwise you won't know if any change in the rate of reaction is caused by the change in temperature, or the change in pH.

The variable you change is called the **independent variable**. The variable you measure is called the **dependent variable**. The variables that you keep the same are called **control variables**.

Example
In the enzyme-controlled reaction example above, temperature is the independent variable, the rate of the reaction is the dependent variable and the control variables are pH, volume of reactants, concentration of reactants, etc.

Figure 1: *A student investigating the rate of an enzyme-controlled reaction.*

Control experiments and control groups

To make sure no other factors are affecting the results, you also have to include a **control experiment** — an experiment that's kept under the same conditions as the rest of the investigation, but doesn't have anything done to it.

Example

You investigate antibiotic resistance in bacteria by growing cultures of bacteria on agar plates, then adding paper discs soaked in antibiotic.

If the bacteria are resistant to the antibiotic they will continue to grow. If they aren't resistant a clear patch will appear around the disc where they have died or haven't grown.

A disc that isn't soaked in antibiotic is included to act as a control. This makes sure any result is down to the antibiotic, not the presence of a paper disc.

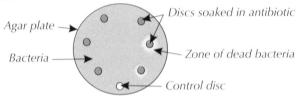

Agar plate

Bacteria

Discs soaked in antibiotic

Zone of dead bacteria

Control disc

Figure 2: *An investigation into antibiotic resistance.*

It's important that a study is a fair test, just like a lab experiment. It's a lot trickier to control the variables in a study than it is in a lab experiment though. Sometimes you can't control them all, but you can use a **control group** to help. This is a group of whatever you're studying (people, plants, lemmings, etc.) that's kept under the same conditions as the group in the experiment, but doesn't have anything done to it.

Tip: A study is an investigation that doesn't take place in a lab.

Example

If you're studying the effect of pesticides on crop growth, pesticide is applied to one field but not to another field (the control field). Both fields are planted with the same crop, and are in the same area (so they get the same weather conditions).

The control field is there to try and account for variables like the weather, which don't stay the same all the time, but could affect the results.

Tip: A pesticide is a chemical that can be used to kill insects.

Figure 3: *Crops being sprayed with pesticides.*

Trial runs

It's a good idea to do a **trial run** (a quick version of your experiment) before you do the proper experiment. Trial runs are used to figure out the range (the upper and lower limit) of variable values used in the proper experiment. If you don't get a change in the dependent variable at the upper values in the trial run, you might narrow the range in the proper experiment. But if you still get a big change at the upper values you might increase the range.

Example

For an experiment into the rate of an enzyme-controlled reaction, you might do a trial run with a temperature range of 10-50 °C. If there was no reaction at the upper end (e.g. 40-50 °C), you might narrow the range to 10-40 °C for the proper experiment.

Tip: If you don't have time to do a trial run, you could always look at the data other people have got doing a similar experiment and use a range and interval values similar to theirs.

Trial runs can also be used to figure out the intervals (gaps) between the values too. The intervals can't be too small (otherwise the experiment would take ages), or too big (otherwise you might miss something).

Example

If using 1 °C intervals doesn't give you much change in the rate of reaction each time, you might decide to use 5 °C intervals, e.g 10, 15, 20, 25, 30, 35, 40 °C.

Trial runs can also help you figure out whether or not your experiment is repeatable.

Tip: Consistently repeating the results is crucial for checking that your results are repeatable.

Example

If you repeat it three times and the results are all similar, the experiment is repeatable.

Ensuring your experiment is safe

To make sure your experiment is safe you must identify all the **hazards**. A hazard is something that can potentially cause harm. Hazards include:

Tip: You can find out about potential hazards by looking in textbooks, doing some internet research, or asking your teacher.

- Microorganisms: e.g. some bacteria can make you ill.
- Chemicals: e.g. sulfuric acid can burn your skin and alcohols catch fire easily.
- Fire: e.g. an unattended Bunsen burner is a fire hazard.
- Electricity: e.g. faulty electrical equipment could give you a shock.

Scientists need to manage the risk of hazards by doing things to reduce them.

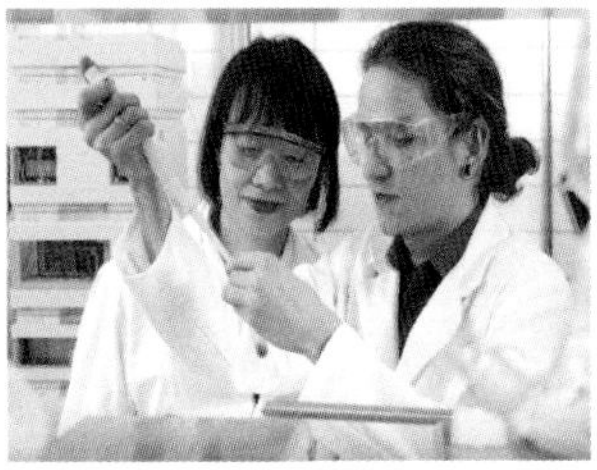

Figure 4: *Scientists wearing safety goggles to protect their eyes during an experiment.*

Examples

- If you're working with sulfuric acid, always wear gloves and safety goggles. This will reduce the risk of the acid coming into contact with your skin and eyes.
- If you're using a Bunsen burner, stand it on a heat proof mat. This will reduce the risk of starting a fire.

4. Collecting Data

Once you've designed your experiment, you need to get on and do it. Here's a guide to making sure the results you collect are good.

Learning Objectives:

- Know how to collect good quality data, taking repeatability, reproducibility, accuracy, precision and equipment selection and use into account.
- Understand what random errors, systematic errors and anomalous results are.

Specification Reference
How Science Works

Getting good quality results

When you do an experiment you want your results to be **repeatable**, **reproducible** and as **accurate** and **precise** as possible.

To check repeatability you need to repeat the readings — you should repeat each reading at least three times. To make sure your results are reproducible you can cross check them by taking a second set of readings with another instrument (or a different observer). Checking your results match with secondary sources, e.g. other studies, also increases the reliability of your data.

Your data also needs to be accurate. Really accurate results are those that are really close to the true answer. Collecting lots of data and calculating a mean will improve the accuracy of your results. Your data also needs to be precise. Precise results are ones where the data is all really close to the mean (i.e. not spread out).

Tip: For more on means see page 11.

Tip: Sometimes, you can work out what result you should get at the end of an experiment (the theoretical result) by doing a bit of maths. If your experiment is accurate there shouldn't be much difference between the theoretical results and the result you actually get.

Example

Look at the data in this table. Data set 1 is more precise than data set 2 because all the data in set 1 is really close to the mean, whereas the data in set 2 is more spread out.

Repeat	Data set 1	Data set 2
1	12	11
2	14	17
3	13	14
Mean	13	14

Choosing the right equipment

When doing an experiment, you need to make sure you're using the right equipment for the job. The measuring equipment you use has to be sensitive enough to measure the changes you're looking for.

Example

If you need to measure changes of 1 ml you need to use a measuring cylinder that can measure in 1 ml steps — it'd be no good trying with one that only measures 10 ml steps, it wouldn't be sensitive enough.

Figure 1: *Different types of measuring cylinder and glassware — make sure you choose the right one before you start an experiment.*

The smallest change a measuring instrument can detect is called its **resolution**. For example, some mass balances have a resolution of 1 g, some have a resolution of 0.1 g, and some are even more sensitive.

Tip: Calibration is a way of making sure that a measuring device is measuring things accurately — you get it to measure something you know has a certain value and set the device to say that amount.

Figure 2: *A mass balance that has been set to zero.*

Also, equipment needs to be calibrated so that your data is more accurate.

> **Example**
>
> Mass balances need to be set to zero before you start weighing things.

Errors

Random errors

The results of your experiment will always vary a bit because of **random errors** — tiny differences caused by things like human errors in measuring. You can reduce their effect by taking many readings and calculating the mean.

Systematic errors

If the same error is made every time, it's called a **systematic error**.

> **Example**
>
> If you measured from the very end of your ruler instead of from the 0 cm mark every time, all your measurements would be a bit small.

Tip: A zero error is a specific type of systematic error.

Tip: Repeating the experiment in the exact same way and calculating an average won't correct a systematic error.

Just to make things more complicated, if a systematic error is caused by using equipment that isn't zeroed properly it's called a **zero error**. You can compensate for some systematic and zero errors if you know about them though.

> **Example**
>
> If a mass balance always reads 1 gram before you put anything on it, all your measurements will be 1 gram too heavy. This is a zero error. You can compensate for this by subtracting 1 gram from all your results.

Anomalous results

Sometimes you get a result that doesn't seem to fit in with the rest at all. These results are called **anomalous results** (or outliers).

> **Example**
>
> Look at the data in this table. The entry that has been circled is an anomalous result because it's much larger than any of the other data values.
>
> | Experiment | A | B | C | D | E | F |
> |---|---|---|---|---|---|---|
> | Rate of reaction (cm³/s) | 10.5 | 11.2 | 10.8 | 85.4 | 10.6 | 11.1 |

Tip: There are lots of reasons why you might get an anomalous result, but usually they're due to human error rather than anything crazy happening in the experiment.

You should investigate anomalous results and try to work out what happened. If you can work out what happened (e.g. you measured something totally wrong) you can ignore them when processing your results.

5. Processing and Presenting Data

Once you've collected some data, you might need to process it, and then you'll need to present it in a way that you can make sense of.

Learning Objectives:
- Know why data is often organised into tables and understand the limitations of using tables to organise data.
- Be able to calculate ranges and means.
- Be able to select and draw an appropriate graph to display the data collected in an investigation.

Specification Reference
How Science Works

Organising data

It's really important that your data is organised. Tables are dead useful for organising data. When you draw a table use a ruler, make sure each column has a heading (including the units) and keep it neat and tidy.

Annoyingly, tables are about as useful as a chocolate teapot for showing patterns or relationships in data. You need to use some kind of graph for that.

Processing your data

When you've done repeats of an experiment you should always calculate the **mean**. To do this add together all the data values and divide by the total number of values in the sample.

You might also need to calculate the **range** (how spread out the data is). To do this find the largest number and subtract the smallest number from it.

Tip: You should ignore anomalous results when calculating the mean and the range — see previous page for more on anomalous results.

Example

Look at the data in the table below. The mean and range of the data for each test tube has been calculated.

Test tube	Repeat (g) 1	2	3	Mean (g)	Range (g)
A	28	37	32	$(28 + 37 + 32) \div 3 = 32.3$	$37 - 28 = 9$
B	47	51	60	$(47 + 51 + 60) \div 3 = 52.7$	$60 - 47 = 13$
C	68	72	70	$(68 + 72 + 70) \div 3 = 70.0$	$72 - 68 = 4$

Plotting your data on a graph

One of the best ways to present your data after you've processed it is to plot your results on a graph. There are lots of different types of graph you can use. The type of graph you use depends on the type of data you've collected.

Bar charts

If either the independent or dependent variable is **categoric** you should use a bar chart to display the data.

Tip: Categoric data is data that comes in distinct categories, for example, blood type, eye colour, sex (i.e. whether you're male or female).

You also use a bar chart if one of the variables is **discrete** (the data can be counted in chunks, where there's no in-between value, e.g. number of people is discrete because you can't have half a person).

There are some golden rules you need to follow for drawing bar charts:

Tip: These golden rules will make sure that your bar chart is clear, easy to read and easy to understand if someone else looks at it.

- Draw it nice and big (covering at least half of the graph paper).
- Leave a gap between different categories.
- Label both axes and remember to include the units.
- If you've got more than one set of data include a key.
- Give your graph a title explaining what it is showing.

Have a look at Figure 1 for an example of a pretty decent bar chart.

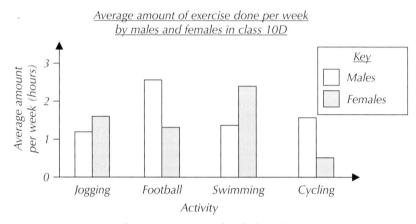

Figure 1: An example of a bar chart.

Line graphs

If the independent and the dependent variable are **continuous** (numerical data that can have any value within a range, e.g. length, volume, temperature) you should use a line graph to display the data. Here are the golden rules for drawing line graphs:

Exam Tip
You could be asked to draw a bar chart or a line graph in your exam. If so, make sure you follow the golden rules or you could end up losing marks.

- Draw it nice and big (covering at least half of the graph paper).
- Put the independent variable (the thing you change) on the x-axis (the horizontal one).
- Put the dependent variable (the thing you measure) on the y-axis (the vertical one).
- Label both axes and remember to include the units.
- To plot the points, use a sharp pencil and make a neat little cross.
- Don't join the dots up. You need to draw a line of best fit (or a curve of best fit if your points make a curve). When drawing a line (or curve), try to draw the line through or as near to as many points as possible, ignoring anomalous results.
- If you've got more than one set of data include a key.
- Give your graph a title explaining what it is showing.

See Figure 2 on the next page for an example of a pretty good line graph.

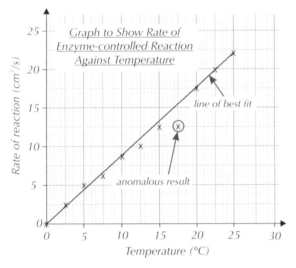

Figure 2: An example of a line graph.

Tip: If you're not in an exam, you can use a computer to plot your line graph and draw your line of best fit for you.

Scatter graphs

Scatter graphs are very similar to line graphs but they often don't have a line of best fit drawn on them. Like line graphs, scatter graphs can be used if the independent and dependent variables are continuous.

Tip: Scatter graphs can also be called scattergrams or scatterplots.

Correlations

Line graphs and scatter graphs are used to show the relationship between two variables (just like other graphs). Data can show three different types of **correlation** (relationship):

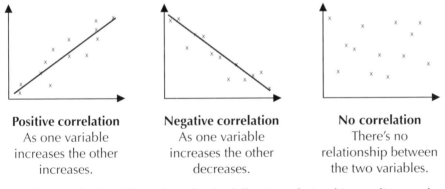

Positive correlation
As one variable increases the other increases.

Negative correlation
As one variable increases the other decreases.

No correlation
There's no relationship between the two variables.

Tip: If all of the points are very close to the line of best fit then it's said to be a strong correlation. If there is a general trend but all the points are quite far away from the line of best fit it's a weak correlation.

You also need to be able to describe the following relationships on line graphs.

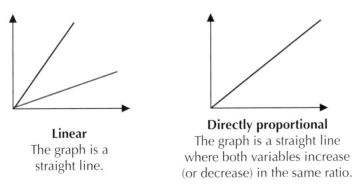

Linear
The graph is a straight line.

Directly proportional
The graph is a straight line where both variables increase (or decrease) in the same ratio.

Tip: On this graph the lines show positive linear relationships, but you can get linear relationships that show negative correlation too.

- Be able to draw conclusions based on the data available.
- Understand the difference between correlation and causation, and the possible reasons for correlation.
- Be able to evaluate investigations.

Specification Reference
How Science Works

6. Drawing Conclusions

So... you've planned an amazing experiment, you've done the experiment, collected some data and have processed and presented your data in a sensible way. Now it's time to figure out what your data actually tells you.

How to draw conclusions

Drawing conclusions might seem pretty straightforward — you just look at your data and say what pattern or relationship you see between the dependent and independent variables.

But you've got to be really careful that your conclusion matches the data you've got and doesn't go any further. You also need to be able to use your results to justify your conclusion (i.e. back up your conclusion with some specific data).

Example

The table shows the heights of pea plant seedlings grown for three weeks with different fertilisers.

Fertiliser	Mean growth (mm)
A	13.5
B	19.5
No fertiliser	5.5

You could conclude that fertiliser B makes pea plant seedlings grow taller over a three week period than fertiliser A.

The justification for this conclusion is that over the three week period, fertiliser B made pea plants grow 6 mm more on average than fertiliser A.

You can't conclude that fertiliser B makes any other type of plant grow taller than fertiliser A — the results could be totally different.

Tip: Causation just means one thing is causing another.

Tip: Lots of things are correlated without being directly related. E.g. the level of carbon dioxide (CO_2) in the atmosphere and the amount of obesity have both increased over the last 100 years, but that doesn't mean increased atmospheric CO_2 is causing people to become obese.

Correlation and causation

If two things are correlated (i.e. there's a relationship between them) it doesn't necessarily mean that a change in one variable is causing the change in the other — this is really important, don't forget it. There are three possible reasons for a correlation:

1. Chance

Even though it might seem a bit weird, it's possible that two things show a correlation in a study purely because of chance.

Example

One study might find a correlation between the number of people with breathing problems and the distance they live from a cement factory. But other scientists don't get a correlation when they investigate it — the results of the first study are just a fluke.

2. They're linked by a third variable

A lot of the time it may look as if a change in one variable is causing a change in the other, but it isn't — a third variable links the two things.

> **Example**
>
> There's a correlation between water temperature and shark attacks. This obviously isn't because warmer water makes sharks crazy. Instead, they're linked by a third variable — the number of people swimming (more people swim when the water's hotter, and with more people in the water you get more shark attacks).

3. Causation

Sometimes a change in one variable does cause a change in the other.

> **Example**
>
> There's a correlation between smoking and lung cancer. This is because chemicals in tobacco smoke cause lung cancer.

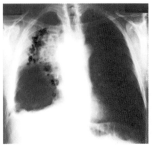

Figure 1: A coloured chest X-ray of a smoker who has lung cancer.

You can only conclude that a correlation is due to cause when you've controlled all the variables that could, just could, be affecting the result. (For the smoking example above this would include things like age and exposure to other things that cause cancer).

Evaluation

This is the final part of an investigation. Here you need to evaluate (assess) the following things about your experiment and the data you gathered.

- **Repeatability**: Did you take enough repeat readings of the measurements? Would you do more repeats if you were to do the experiment again? Do you think you'd get similar data if you did the experiment again?

- **Reproducibility**: Have you compared your results with other people's results? Were your results similar? Could other scientists gain data showing the same relationships that are shown in your data?

- **Validity**: Does your data answer the question you set out to investigate?

Once you've thought about these points you can decide how much confidence you have in your conclusion. For example, if your results are repeatable, reproducible and valid and they back up your conclusion then you can have a high degree of confidence in your conclusion.

1. Diet and Metabolic Rate

Learning Objectives:
- Understand the importance of a balanced diet.
- Know what carbohydrates, fats and proteins are used for by the body.
- Understand why the body needs small amounts of vitamins and mineral ions.
- Understand what is meant by the term 'metabolic rate'.
- Understand why metabolic rate varies between different people.
- Know that exercising increases the amount of energy you use.

Specification Reference B1.1.1

Your diet is important. It's where you get your energy from, as well as the nutrients your body needs to stay healthy.

The importance of a balanced diet

For good health, your diet must provide the energy you need (but not more) — see page 19. But that's not all. There are five important **nutrients** — carbohydrates, proteins, fats, vitamins and mineral ions. Each nutrient has different uses in the body — so you need to have the right balance of these too (see Figure 1). You need:

- enough carbohydrates to release energy,
- enough fats to keep warm and release energy,
- enough protein for growth, cell repair and cell replacement,
- tiny amounts of various vitamins and mineral ions to keep your skin, bones, blood and everything else generally healthy.

You also need enough fibre to keep everything moving smoothly through your digestive system.

Some sources of the main nutrients are shown in Figure 2.

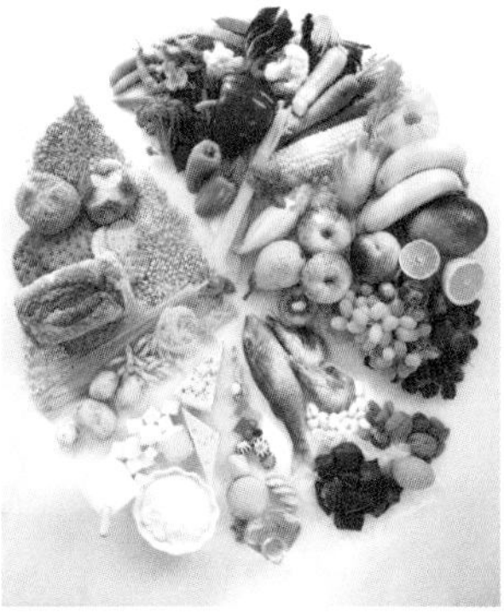

Figure 1: *This food wheel shows what the relative proportions of different foods should be in a healthy diet.*

Nutrient	Sources
Carbohydrates	Pasta, rice
Fats	Butter, oily fish
Protein	Meat, fish
Vitamins	Various, e.g. vitamin C is found in oranges. Vitamin D is in eggs.
Minerals	Various, e.g. calcium is found in milk. Iron is found in red meat.

Figure 2: *Table showing sources of the main nutrients.*

Varying energy needs

You need energy to fuel the chemical reactions in the body that keep you alive. These reactions are called your **metabolism**, and the speed at which they occur is your **metabolic rate**. There are slight variations in the resting metabolic rate of different people — take a look at the examples on the next page.

- Muscle needs more energy than fatty tissue, which means (all other things being equal) people with a higher proportion of muscle to fat in their bodies will have a higher metabolic rate.

- Physically bigger people are likely to have a higher metabolic rate than smaller people — the bigger you are, the more energy your body needs to be supplied with (because you have more cells).

- Men tend to have a slightly higher rate than women — they're slightly bigger and have a larger proportion of muscle. Other genetic factors may also have some effect.

- Regular exercise can boost your resting metabolic rate because it builds muscle.

Tip: Your resting metabolic rate is your metabolic rate when you're at rest (not doing very much).

Exercise and energy needs

When you exercise, you obviously need more energy — so your metabolic rate goes up during exercise and stays high for some time after you finish (particularly if the exercise is strenuous).

So people who have more active jobs need more energy on a daily basis — builders require more energy per day than office workers, for instance. Different activities need different amounts of energy — see Figure 4.

Figure 3: The more muscle you have, the higher your metabolic rate.

Activity	Average Amount of Energy Burned (kJ/min)
Sleeping	4.5
Watching TV	7
Cycling (5 mph)	21
Jogging (5 mph)	40
Climbing stairs	77
Swimming	35
Rowing	58
Slow walking	14

Figure 4: A table showing the average number of kilojoules burned per minute during different activities.

Tip: A kJ (kilojoule) is a unit of energy.

This means your activity level affects the amount of energy your diet should contain. If you do little exercise, you're going to need less energy, so less fat and carbohydrate in your diet, than if you're constantly on the go.

Practice Questions — Fact Recall

Q1 What does the body need carbohydrates for?

Q2 Why does the body need vitamins and mineral ions?

Q3 What is meant by the term 'metabolic rate'?

Q4 True or false? Everybody's metabolic rate is exactly the same.

Q5 Explain how your activity level affects the amount of energy you use.

Practice Questions — Application

Q1 Meat is a major source of protein. Explain why people who don't eat meat should still make sure they get enough protein in their diet.

Q2 Joe is a professional rower. He spends 35 hours a week in training. Paula is a graphic designer. She spends 40 hours a week in the office, but likes to go cycling at weekends.

a) Who would you expect to have the higher resting metabolic rate, Joe or Paula? Give a reason for your answer.

b) Who would you expect to have a higher energy intake? Explain your answer.

Q3 On an expedition across the Antarctic, a man dragging a sledge behind him can expect to burn between 6000 and 7000 calories a day. A man working inside one of the Antarctic research stations burns about 2750 calories per day.

a) Suggest why the man dragging the sledge burns so many more calories than the man in the research station.

b) Suggest two nutrients that someone on this type of expedition is likely to need in large amounts. Explain your answer.

Tip: Calories are a measure of the energy in food — see p. 21.

2. Factors Affecting Health

Our health can be affected by what we eat. But it can also be affected by things like how much we exercise and factors we inherit from our parents.

An unbalanced diet

People whose diet is badly out of balance are said to be **malnourished**. Malnourished people can be fat or thin, or unhealthy in other ways.

The effects of eating too much

Excess carbohydrate or fat in the diet can lead to **obesity**. Obesity is a common disorder in developed countries (e.g. the UK) — it's defined as being 20% (or more) over the maximum recommended body mass. Hormonal problems can lead to obesity, though the usual cause is a bad diet, overeating and a lack of exercise.

Health problems that can arise as a result of obesity include: arthritis (inflammation of the joints), **type 2 diabetes** (inability to control blood sugar level), high blood pressure and heart disease. It's also a risk factor for some kinds of cancer.

Eating too much can also lead to other health problems. Too much saturated fat in your diet can increase your blood cholesterol level (see next page). Eating too much salt can cause high blood pressure and heart problems.

The effects of eating too little

Some people suffer from lack of food, particularly in developing countries (e.g. Ethiopia). The effects of this type of malnourishment vary depending on what foods are missing from the diet. But problems commonly include slow growth (in children), fatigue, poor resistance to infection, and irregular periods in women. A lack of vitamins or minerals in the diet can cause **deficiency diseases**.

> **Examples**
>
> - A lack of vitamin C can cause scurvy, a deficiency disease that causes problems with the skin, joints and gums (see Figure 1).
>
>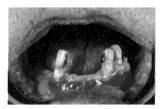
>
>   *Figure 1: Scurvy can cause the gums to swell and the teeth to fall out.*
>
> - A lack of iron (a mineral) can cause iron deficiency anaemia, a deficiency disease that affects the red blood cells, making you feel tired and weak.

Learning Objectives:

- Understand that by not eating a balanced diet, you can become malnourished.
- Understand that malnourished people can be overweight or underweight.
- Understand that an unbalanced diet can cause health problems such as type 2 diabetes and deficiency diseases.
- Understand how exercise helps to keep you healthy.
- Understand that inherited factors can affect your metabolic rate, as well as your health (e.g. your blood cholesterol level).

Specification Reference B1.1.1

Tip: Malnourishment is different from starvation, which is not getting enough food of any sort. And remember, you can also become malnourished by eating too much — it just means that your diet is badly out of balance.

Exam Tip
You don't need to learn the effects of any specific deficiency diseases for the exam — these examples are just to help your understanding.

A lack of exercise

Exercise is important for good health as well as diet — people who exercise regularly are usually healthier than those who don't. Exercise increases the amount of energy used by the body and decreases the amount stored as fat. It also builds muscle so it helps to boost your metabolic rate (see pages 16-17). So people who exercise are less likely to suffer from health problems such as obesity.

However, sometimes people can be fit but not healthy — e.g. you can be physically fit and slim, but malnourished at the same time because your diet isn't balanced.

Inherited factors

It's not just about what you eat and how much exercise you do — your health can depend on inherited factors too.

Tip: Your thyroid gland is in your neck. It makes hormones (see page 47) that regulate your metabolic rate.

Some people may inherit factors that affect their metabolic rate, e.g. some inherited factors cause an underactive thyroid gland, which can lower the metabolic rate and cause obesity.

Other people may inherit factors that affect their **blood cholesterol level**. Cholesterol is a fatty substance that's essential for good health — it's found in every cell in the body. But you don't want too much of it because a high cholesterol level in the blood has been linked to an increased risk of various problems, including coronary heart disease. Some inherited factors increase blood cholesterol level, which increases the risk of heart disease.

Tip: Coronary heart disease can result in things like angina (chest pain) and heart attacks.

Example

The liver is really important in controlling the amount of cholesterol in the body. It makes new cholesterol and removes any that isn't used from the blood so that it can be eliminated from the body. The amount the liver makes depends partly on inherited factors.

Practice Questions — Fact Recall

Q1 What does it mean if someone is malnourished?

Q2 How can an unbalanced diet lead to obesity?

Q3 Give one health problem that can be caused by obesity.

Q4 True or false? A lack of certain minerals in the diet can lead to deficiency diseases.

Q5 Explain why people who exercise on a regular basis are usually healthier than those who don't.

Q6 Give two ways in which inherited factors can affect health.

3. Evaluating Food, Lifestyle and Diet

This topic is all about using your scientific knowledge to evaluate information about (yep, you've guessed it) food, lifestyle and diet. Don't panic though, I'll explain everything over the next three pages...

Evaluating information on food

In the exam, you may get asked to evaluate information about how food affects health.

Here are some of the things that might make you classify a food as being unhealthy:

- A high saturated fat content — eating too much saturated fat can raise your blood cholesterol level (see previous page).

- A high sodium or salt content — eating too much salt (usually in the form of sodium) can lead to health problems such as high blood pressure.

- A high energy content — the energy in food is usually measured in kilojoules (kJ) or calories. Eating too many high energy foods could lead to obesity.

On the other hand, a food that is low in calories but high in protein, fibre or important vitamins and minerals may be considered fairly healthy.

Example

Look at the two food labels shown below. Which food is healthier? Explain your answer.

A

NUTRITIONAL INFORMATION	
	per serving
Energy	388 kJ
Protein	6 g
Carbohydrate	14 g
of which sugars	6 g
Fat	4.2 g
of which saturates	2.2 g
Fibre	3.5 g
Calcium	200 mg
Sodium	250 mg

B

NUTRITIONAL INFORMATION	
	per serving
Energy	305 kJ
Protein	3 g
Carbohydrate	9 g
of which sugars	8 g
Fat	2.1 g
of which saturates	0.5 g
Fibre	3 g
Calcium	500 mg
Sodium	125 mg

Looking at the two food labels above, food A has a higher protein content than food B, but it also has a higher energy content, a much higher saturated fat content and double the sodium content of food B. Food B also provides more calcium than food A. So food B is the healthier food.

Learning Objectives:
- Be able to evaluate information about food and health.
- Be able to evaluate information about how lifestyle affects health and disease.
- Understand that to lose weight, you need to take in less energy than you use up.
- Be able to evaluate claims made about slimming products.

Specification Reference
B1.1, B1.1.1

Tip: A high energy food isn't necessarily bad for you — but if you take in more energy than you use up, you could end up becoming overweight.

Exam Tip
The information you get in the exam could also be in the form of a table, chart or graph.

Figure 1: This food label shows levels of sugar, fat and salt as a percentage of an adult's guideline daily amount.

Evaluating information on lifestyle

You might also get asked to evaluate information about how lifestyle affects health. Your lifestyle includes what you eat and what you do.

> **Example**
>
> A person who eats too much fat or carbohydrate and doesn't do much exercise will increase their risk of obesity. This means they'll also increase their risk of developing the health problems associated with obesity — like type 2 diabetes and heart disease (see p. 19).

Remember, you'll need to use your knowledge of how diet and exercise affect health to answer exam questions — make sure all the facts on pages 16-20 are well lodged in your memory.

Evaluating slimming claims

There are loads of slimming products (e.g. diet pills, slimming milkshakes) and slimming programmes (e.g. the Atkins Diet™) around — and they all claim they'll help you lose weight. But it can be difficult to know whether or not they actually work. In the exam, you could be asked to evaluate a claim made about a slimming product. If so, it's a good idea to look out for these things:

Is the report a scientific study, published in a reputable journal?

Before results are published in a scientific journal, they're reviewed by other scientists (in a process called peer review) to make sure they were obtained in a scientific way. This doesn't guarantee that the results are correct, just that they seem reasonable to the experts.

Tip: A reputable journal is one with a good reputation. Reputable scientific journals include Nature, Science, and the British Medical Journal.

Was it written by a qualified person, not connected with the people selling it?

Someone who works for the company that makes the slimming product might present their results in a **biased** way to make the product sound better than it really is (see page 3). Results from an independent study are less likely to be biased.

Tip: In this case, an independent study is one which is carried out by scientists with no connection to the product or who don't stand to gain from it.

Was the sample of people asked/tested large enough?

Large samples are generally better than small samples as they're more representative of the population as a whole (see page 2).

> **Example**
>
> A common way to promote a new diet is to say, "Celebrity A has lost x pounds using it". But effectiveness in one person doesn't mean much. Only a large survey can tell if a diet is more or less effective than just eating less and exercising more — and these aren't done often.

Have there been other studies which found similar results?

Results that can be reproduced by other scientists are more likely to be believable (see pages 2-3).

Misleading slimming claims

Really, all you need to do to lose weight is to take in less energy than you use. So diets and slimming products will only work if you...

- eat less fat or carbohydrate (so that you take in less energy), or
- do more exercise (so that you use more energy).

So some claims may be true but a little misleading.

> **Example**
>
> Low-fat bars might be low in fat, but eating them without changing the rest of your diet doesn't necessarily mean you'll lose weight — you could still be taking in too much energy.

Practice Questions — Application

Q1 Two food labels are shown below. Both labels use a "traffic light" system to show the levels of fat, salt and sugar present in the food. Red means "high", orange means "medium" and green means "low".

Food A

Food B

a) i) Which food has the highest level of fat?

   ii) Why might a food that is high in fat be considered unhealthy?

b) The maximum recommended daily salt intake for an adult is 6 g. What percentage of this intake would you get from Food B?

c) Which of the two foods shown above is healthiest? Give a reason for your answer.

Q2 The manufacturers of a slimming milkshake make the following claim:

   "8 out of 10 people lose weight using our milkshake".

The claim is based on the results of a trial carried out by the manufacturers. The trial involved 20 women, all of whom drank the same slimming milkshake for one month. 16 women said they lost weight. No other data was collected and the women weren't independently weighed.

Do you think the manufacturers have enough evidence to make their claim? Give two reasons for your answer.

4. Fighting Disease

Part of being healthy means being free from disease.
But that's easier said than done...

Pathogens

Microorganisms that enter the body and cause disease are called **pathogens**. Pathogens cause **infectious diseases** — diseases that can easily spread. There are two main types of pathogen — bacteria and viruses.

Bacteria

Bacteria are very small living cells (about 1/100th the size of your body cells), which can reproduce rapidly inside your body. They make you feel ill by doing two things:

- producing **toxins** (poisons)
- damaging your cells

> **Example**
>
> *Vibrio cholerae* — these bacteria cause cholera (a nasty diarrhoeal disease). They make you feel ill by releasing a toxin into the small intestines.

Viruses

Viruses are not cells. They're tiny, about 1/100th the size of a bacterium. They replicate themselves by invading your cells and using the cells' machinery to produce many copies of themselves. The cell will usually then burst, releasing all the new viruses (see Figure 1). This cell damage is what makes you feel ill.

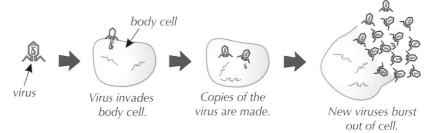

body cell

virus

Virus invades body cell.　*Copies of the virus are made.*　*New viruses burst out of cell.*

Figure 1: *A virus replicating in a human cell.*

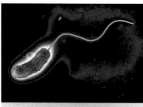

Figure 2: *A* Vibrio cholerae *bacterium (top). HIV particles (blue) infecting a white blood cell (bottom).*

> **Example**
>
> HIV — this virus infects and destroys cells that normally help to defend the body against disease (like white blood cells, see next page). This makes HIV sufferers more likely to get ill from infection by other pathogens.

Your body's defences

In order to cause disease, pathogens first need to enter the body.
Luckily your body has a few ways to stop them doing just that, including:

1. The skin

Your skin stops a lot of nasties getting inside your body. If you cut yourself
though, pathogens can get into your bloodstream through the wound. To try
and prevent this from happening, small fragments of cells (called platelets)
help blood clot quickly to seal wounds. If the blood contains low numbers of
platelets then it will clot more slowly.

2. Mucus in the respiratory tract

Your respiratory tract (breathing pipework) is lined with sticky mucus. This
traps pathogens that are in the air and stops them from reaching the lungs.
Tiny hairs in the respiratory tract beat to move the mucus away from the
lungs, back towards the mouth.

*Figure 3: Bacteria
(yellow) sticking to mucus
(blue) on microscopic
hairs in the nose.*

The immune system

If something does make it through your defences, your immune system kicks
in. The most important part is the **white blood cells**. They travel around
in your blood and crawl into every part of you, constantly patrolling for
pathogens. When they come across an invading pathogen
they have three lines of attack:

1. Consuming them

White blood cells can
engulf pathogens and digest
them (see Figure 4).

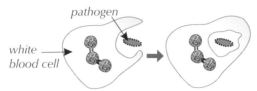

Figure 4: A white blood cell engulfing a pathogen.

2. Producing antitoxins

These counteract toxins produced by the invading bacteria.

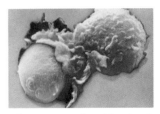

*Figure 5: A white blood cell
(blue/pink) engulfing a
pathogen (yellow/green).
Seen under a microscope.*

3. Producing antibodies

Every invading cell has unique molecules (called **antigens**) on its surface.
When your white blood cells come across a foreign antigen (i.e. one they
don't recognise), they will start to produce proteins called **antibodies**.
The antibodies then lock onto the foreign antigens and kill the invading
pathogens (see Figure 6).

Exam Tip
Don't be tempted to
write 'white blood cells
engulf disease' in the
exam — white blood
cells engulf pathogens
(which cause disease).

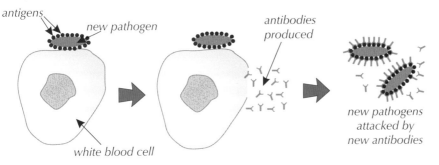

Figure 6: Diagram showing the production of antibodies.

The antibodies produced are specific to that type of antigen — they won't lock on to any others. Antibodies are then produced rapidly and carried around the body to kill all similar bacteria or viruses (i.e. ones with the same antigens).

If the person is infected with the same pathogen again the white blood cells will rapidly produce the antibodies to kill it — the person is naturally **immune** to that pathogen and won't get ill.

Example

Say you're infected with the mumps virus. When your white blood cells come across the foreign antigens on the surface of the virus, they'll start to produce the antibodies to destroy it. Eventually they'll produce enough antibodies to overcome the infection — but, in the meantime, you'll feel ill.

If you ever get infected with the mumps virus again though, your white blood cells will 'remember' and rapidly produce the antibodies to destroy it — so you shouldn't get sick again. You're immune to mumps.

Practice Questions — Fact Recall

Q1 Name two types of pathogen and explain how each one makes you feel ill.

Q2 Give three ways in which white blood cells help to defend the body against disease.

Q3 What does it mean if a person is immune to a particular pathogen?

Practice Questions — Application

Q1 As a child, John suffered from measles. Measles are caused by a virus.

a) Explain why John is unlikely to get ill with measles again.

b) German measles are caused by a different virus, which John has never had before. Explain why John could still become ill from German measles.

Q2 *Clostridium tetani* is the bacterium that causes tetanus. It usually enters the body through deep cuts.

a) Suggest two ways in which *Clostridium tetani* bacteria may make you feel ill.

b) Suggest one way in which the body tries to prevent *Clostridium tetani* from entering the bloodstream.

5. Fighting Disease — Vaccination

Vaccinations have changed the way we fight disease.
We don't always have to deal with the problem once it's happened —
we can prevent it happening in the first place.

What are vaccinations?

When you're infected with a new microorganism, it takes your white blood cells a few days to learn how to deal with it. But by that time, you can be pretty ill. Vaccinations can stop you feeling ill in the first place.

Vaccinations involve injecting small amounts of dead or inactive microorganisms. These carry antigens, which cause your white blood cells to produce antibodies to attack them — even though the microorganism is harmless (since it's dead or inactive).

> **Example**
>
> The **MMR vaccine** is given to children. It contains weakened versions of the viruses that cause measles, mumps and rubella (German measles) all in one vaccine.

If live microorganisms of the same type then appear at a later date, the white blood cells can rapidly mass-produce antibodies to kill off the pathogen. The vaccinated person is now immune to that pathogen and won't get ill (see Figure 1).

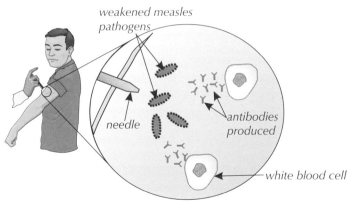

weakened measles pathogens

needle

antibodies produced

white blood cell

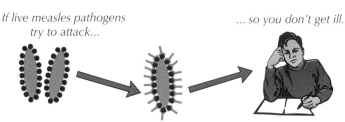

If live measles pathogens try to attack...

... so you don't get ill.

... they are quickly recognised and attacked by antibodies...

Figure 1: *A diagram to show how vaccination works.*

Learning Objectives:
- Understand how vaccinations work.
- Know what the MMR vaccine is used for.
- Understand that if enough people are immune to a particular pathogen, the spread of the pathogen is reduced.
- Be able to evaluate the pros and cons of vaccinations.

Specification Reference B1.1.2

Exam Tip
You need to learn this example for your exam.

Tip: The 'weakened' viruses in the MMR vaccine are still alive, but aren't able to cause disease.

Tip: Remember, antibodies are specific to a particular type of pathogen (see p. 26). So a vaccination against the typhoid virus will only protect you against typhoid — it won't make you immune to anything else.

Tip: Some vaccinations "wear off" over time. So booster injections may need to be given to increase levels of antibodies again.

Vaccinations — pros and cons

You need to be able to weigh up the pros and cons of vaccinations.

Exam Tip
In the exam, you might get asked to 'evaluate' the pros and cons of vaccinations. This means giving a balanced account of both the advantages and the disadvantages, before trying to come up with an overall judgement.

Pros

- Vaccines have helped control lots of infectious diseases that were once common in the UK (e.g. polio, measles, whooping cough, rubella, mumps, tetanus...). Smallpox no longer occurs at all, and polio infections have fallen by 99%.

- Big outbreaks of disease — called **epidemics** — can be prevented if a large percentage of the population is vaccinated. That way, even the people who aren't vaccinated are unlikely to catch the disease because there are fewer people able to pass it on. But if a significant number of people aren't vaccinated, the disease can spread quickly through them and lots of people will be ill at the same time.

Cons

- Vaccines don't always work — sometimes they don't give you immunity.

- You can sometimes have a bad reaction to a vaccine (e.g. swelling, or maybe something more serious like a fever or seizures). But bad reactions are very rare.

Figure 2: *A baby being given the MMR vaccine.*

Balancing the risks

Deciding whether to have a vaccination means balancing risks — the risk of catching the disease if you don't have a vaccine, against the risk of having a bad reaction if you do. As always, you need to look at the evidence.

> **Example**
>
> If you get measles (the disease), there's about a 1 in 15 chance that you'll get complications (e.g. pneumonia) — and about 1 in 500 people who get measles actually die. However, the number of people who have a problem with the vaccine is more like 1 in 1 000 000.

Practice Question — Application

Q1 Whooping cough is a severe cough that can cause serious breathing difficulties in young babies.

In 2012, the US state of Washington declared a whooping cough epidemic. The Department of Health encouraged all adults to get booster vaccinations against the disease, to help protect babies who were too young to receive the vaccination.

a) What is a 'whooping cough epidemic'?

b) Suggest how a whooping cough vaccination might work.

c) Explain how a large-scale vaccination of adults could help to protect babies who haven't been vaccinated.

6. Fighting Disease — Drugs

There aren't vaccinations against every pathogen (not just yet, anyway) so you're still going to get ill sometimes. And that's when drugs come in...

Different types of drugs

Painkillers (e.g. aspirin) are drugs that relieve pain. However, they don't actually tackle the cause of the disease, they just help to reduce the symptoms. Other drugs do a similar kind of thing — reduce the symptoms without tackling the underlying cause. For example, lots of "cold remedies" don't actually cure colds — they have no effect on the cold virus itself.

Antibiotics (e.g. **penicillin**) work differently — they actually kill (or prevent the growth of) the bacteria causing the problem without killing your own body cells. Different antibiotics kill different types of bacteria, so it's important to be treated with the right one.

But antibiotics don't destroy viruses (e.g. flu or cold viruses). Viruses reproduce using your own body cells, which makes it very difficult to develop drugs that destroy just the virus without killing the body's cells.

Antibiotic resistance

Bacteria can **mutate** — in other words, their genetic material can change. Sometimes the mutations cause them to be resistant to (not killed by) an antibiotic. Resistant strains ('types') of bacteria like **MRSA** (see below) have increased as a result of a process known as **natural selection**.

Examples

- MRSA (methicillin-resistant *Staphylococcus aureus*) causes serious wound infections and is resistant to the powerful antibiotic, methicillin.

- Some strains of the bacteria that cause TB (a lung disease) are now resistant to several of the antibiotics that would normally be used to fight them.

How antibiotic resistance develops [Higher]

If you have an infection, some of the bacteria might be resistant to antibiotics. This means that when you treat the infection, only the non-resistant strains of bacteria will be killed. The individual resistant bacteria will survive and reproduce, and the population of the resistant strain will increase (see Figure 1, next page). This is an example of natural selection. The resistant strain could cause a serious infection that can't be treated by antibiotics (like MRSA).

Learning Objectives:

- Understand that some drugs reduce the symptoms of a disease, but don't destroy the pathogens.
- Understand that antibiotics (e.g. penicillin) are drugs used to kill bacteria.
- Understand that different antibiotics kill different bacteria and that antibiotics have no effect on viruses.
- Understand why it's hard to produce drugs to kill viruses.
- Understand that bacteria can mutate and that this can lead to the development of antibiotic-resistant strains, e.g. MRSA, by natural selection.
- **H** Understand in more detail how populations of antibiotic-resistant bacteria develop.
- Understand that by avoiding over-use of antibiotics, we can slow down the spread of antibiotic resistance.
- **H** Understand why antibiotics are now usually only used to treat more serious infections.

Specification Reference B1.1.2

Tip: There's more on natural selection on pages 110-111.

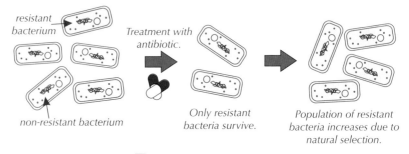

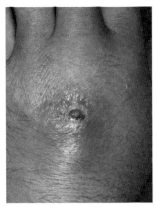

Figure 2: *A wound infected with MRSA.*

resistant bacterium

non-resistant bacterium

Treatment with antibiotic.

Only resistant bacteria survive.

Population of resistant bacteria increases due to natural selection.

Figure 1: **H** *How antibiotic resistance develops.*

Slowing down the development of antibiotic resistance

To prevent antibiotic resistance spreading, it's important not to over-use antibiotics.

Example — Higher

Doctors now try to avoid over-prescribing antibiotics. So you won't get them for a sore throat, only for something more serious.

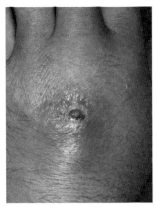

Exam Tip
If you're sitting the Foundation paper, all you need to remember here is that we can help to prevent antibiotic resistance from spreading by not over-using antibiotics. Higher students need to learn the example too.

Practice Questions — Fact Recall

Q1 True or false?
Painkillers can be used to tackle the cause of an infection.

Q2 What is an antibiotic? Give one example.

Q3 Why is it important to be treated with the right antibiotic for a particular infection?

Q4 Explain why it can be difficult to develop drugs that kill viruses.

Q5 a) Name a strain of bacteria that has developed antibiotic resistance.

b) By what process have resistant strains of bacteria increased?

Q6 Why is it important not to over-use antibiotics?

Practice Questions — Application

Q1 Chloe is suffering from the flu, which is caused by a virus.

a) Explain why Chloe's doctor will not prescribe her antibiotics.

b) Chloe's doctor recommends a flu remedy. Suggest why the flu remedy will not help to clear Chloe's infection any quicker.

Q2 James has a mild bacterial infection. James' doctor tells him it will clear up on its own and does not prescribe him antibiotics. Suggest why James' doctor did this.

Q3 Many strains of the bacteria *Streptococcus pneumoniae* are now resistant to the antibiotic penicillin. Describe how populations of penicillin-resistant *Streptococcus pneumoniae* may have increased.

7. Fighting Disease — Investigating Antibiotic Action

Scientists developing new antibiotics or disinfectants need to be able to test whether or not they actually work. That means setting up bacterial cultures...

Culturing microorganisms

You can test the action of antibiotics or disinfectants by growing **cultures** of microorganisms in the lab. Microorganisms are grown (cultured) on a "culture medium". This is usually agar jelly containing the carbohydrates, minerals, proteins and vitamins the microorganisms need to grow. Here's how to test the action of antibiotics:

- Agar jelly is heated to kill any unwanted microorganisms. The hot agar jelly is then poured into shallow round plastic dishes called Petri dishes.

- When the jelly's cooled and set, inoculating loops (wire loops) are used to transfer microorganisms to the culture medium. The microorganisms then multiply.

- Paper discs are soaked in different types of antibiotics and placed on the jelly. Antibiotic-resistant bacteria will continue to grow around them but non-resistant strains will die (see Figures 1 and 2).

- A paper disc not soaked in antibiotic can be included as a control — this should show that any results are down to the antibiotic, not the disc itself.

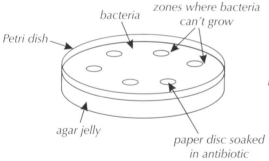

Petri dish
bacteria
zones where bacteria can't grow
agar jelly
paper disc soaked in antibiotic

Figure 1: *Diagram to show how antibiotic action can be investigated in the lab.*

Avoiding contamination

The Petri dishes, culture medium and inoculating loops must be **sterilised** before use, e.g. the inoculating loops are passed through a flame. If equipment isn't sterilised, unwanted microorganisms in the culture medium will grow and affect the result.

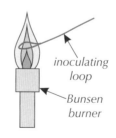

inoculating loop
Bunsen burner

The Petri dish must also have a lid to stop any microorganisms in the air contaminating the culture. The lid should also be taped on.

Learning Objectives:

- Know that bacteria can be cultured in the lab to investigate the action of antibiotics and disinfectants.

- Know how to prevent contamination of bacterial cultures.

- Understand why bacterial cultures are kept at 25 °C in schools, but at higher temperatures in industry.

Specification Reference B1.1.2

Tip: You can test the action of disinfectants in exactly the same way as antibiotics — just soak the paper discs in disinfectants instead.

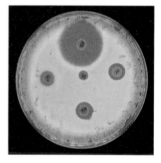

Figure 2: *Antibiotic discs on a bacterial culture. You can see clear zones around the discs where the bacteria can't grow.*

Tip: You can sterilise equipment in a machine called an autoclave — it basically steams equipment at high pressure. Your school might have an autoclave.

Incubation temperatures

In the lab at school, cultures of microorganisms are kept at about 25 °C because harmful pathogens aren't likely to grow at this temperature. In industrial conditions, cultures are incubated at higher temperatures so that they can grow a lot faster.

Practice Question — Application

Q1   Giles is investigating the action of different antibiotics against a strain of bacteria. He cultures the bacteria on a dish containing agar jelly.

a) Giles transfers the bacteria to the jelly using a sterile inoculating loop.

   i) How could Giles have sterilised the loop?

   ii) Why did Giles need to sterilise the inoculating loop?

Once Giles has transferred the bacteria to the dish, he places 6 paper discs, each soaked in a different antibiotic, onto the jelly. He then tapes a lid on the dish and leaves it for a few days.

His results are shown in the diagram below.

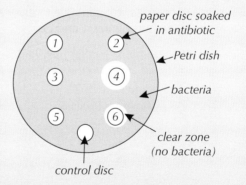

b) i) Which antibiotics were the bacteria resistant to? Explain your answer.

   ii) Which antibiotic was most effective against the bacteria? Explain your answer.

   iii) Give one variable Giles should have controlled in order to make this a fair test.

c) Explain why Giles put a lid on the Petri dish before leaving it overnight?

d) Giles was working in a school laboratory. Explain why his cultures had to be kept at 25 °C.

Tip: There's more on variables and fair tests in the How Science Works section at the start of this book. See page 6.

8. Fighting Disease — Past & Future

The way we deal with diseases now is very different to a hundred years ago. And it's changing all the time...

The work of Semmelweis

Ignaz Semmelweis was a doctor who worked in Vienna General Hospital (in Austria) in the 1840s. While he was there, he saw that women were dying in huge numbers after childbirth from a disease called puerperal fever.

He believed that doctors were spreading the disease on their unwashed hands. By telling doctors entering his ward to wash their hands in an antiseptic solution, he cut the death rate from 12% to 2%.

The antiseptic solution killed bacteria on doctors' hands, though Semmelweis didn't know this (the existence of bacteria and their part in causing disease wasn't discovered for another 20 years). So Semmelweis couldn't prove why his idea worked, and his methods were dropped when he left the hospital (allowing death rates to rise once again — d'oh).

Nowadays we know that basic hygiene is essential in controlling disease (though recent reports have found that a lack of it in some modern hospitals has helped the disease MRSA spread). In fact, a better understanding of things like immunity and how antibiotics work has changed the way we treat disease too.

Learning Objectives:

- Understand how Semmelweis reduced deaths through hand-washing and how this affects infection control in hospitals today.
- Understand why the way we treat disease has changed over time.
- Understand that antibiotics have reduced deaths from bacterial diseases.
- Understand why antibiotic resistance is increasing and that new antibiotics need to be developed as a result.
- Understand how mutations in bacteria and viruses could lead to epidemics and pandemics — and be able to evaluate the consequences.

Specification Reference B1.1.2

The spread of antibiotic resistance

For the last few decades, we've been able to deal with bacterial infections pretty easily using antibiotics. As a result of this, the death rate from infectious bacterial diseases has fallen dramatically.

> **Example**
>
> During the First World War, nearly 20% of US soldiers who caught pneumonia (a bacterial infection) died as a result. During World War II, this figure dropped to less than 1% thanks to treatment with penicillin.

But bacteria evolve antibiotic resistance, e.g MRSA bacteria are already resistant to certain antibiotics. And over-use of antibiotics has made this problem worse — by increasing the likelihood of people being infected by antibiotic-resistant strains (see pages 29-30). As a result, bacteria that are resistant to most known antibiotics ('superbugs') are becoming more common.

People who become infected with these bacteria can't easily get rid of them (because antibiotics don't work) and may pass on the infection to others. So antibiotic resistance is a big problem and it's encouraged drug companies to work on developing new antibiotics that are effective against these resistant strains.

Figure 1: *Photograph of the doctor, Ignaz Semmelweis.*

New and emerging dangers

We face new and scary dangers from pathogens all the time...

Bacteria

As you know, bacteria can mutate to produce new strains (see page 29). A new strain could be antibiotic-resistant, so current treatments would no longer clear an infection. Or a new strain could be one that we've not encountered before, so no-one would be immune to it. This means a new strain of bacteria could spread rapidly in a population of people and could even cause an **epidemic** — a big outbreak of disease.

Tip: TB is a very serious lung disease caused by a bacterial infection.

> **Example**
>
> Multi-drug-resistant TB (also known as MDR-TB) is a form of TB that has developed resistance to multiple antibiotics, making it hard to treat. Scientists in China have reported an MDR-TB epidemic there — over one hundred thousand Chinese people develop MDR-TB each year and a third of all new TB cases in China are antibiotic-resistant.

Viruses

Tip: White blood cells recognise pathogens by their antigens (see p. 25) — so even if you've been vaccinated against a virus, if its antigens change, your white blood cells won't recognise it and you won't be immune.

Viruses also tend to mutate often. This makes it hard to develop vaccines against them because the changes to their DNA can lead to them having different antigens. There'd be a real problem if a virus evolved so that it was both deadly and very infectious. (Flu viruses, for example, evolve quickly so this is quite possible.)

If this happened, precautions could be taken to stop the virus spreading in the first place (though this is hard nowadays — millions of people travel by plane every day). And vaccines and antiviral drugs could be developed (though these take time to mass produce). But in the worst-case scenario, a flu **pandemic** (when a disease spreads all over the world) could kill billions of people.

> **Example**
>
> Between 1918 and 1920, a mutated strain of the H1N1 flu virus caused a pandemic that is thought to have killed up to 50 million people.

Practice Questions — Fact Recall

Q1 What did the doctor Ignaz Semmelweis discover in relation to infectious disease?

Q2 How have antibiotics affected death rates from infectious diseases?

Q3 Explain why drug companies are trying to develop new antibiotics.

Practice Question — Application

Q1 In 2009, a mutated version of the H1N1 virus appeared, causing a flu pandemic. Suggest how the appearance of the mutated virus might have led to the pandemic.

Section Checklist – Make sure you know...

Diet and Metabolic Rate

- ☐ That for good health, you need a balanced diet — this provides the energy you need (but not more), as well as the right balance of nutrients.
- ☐ That carbohydrates and fats are needed by the body to provide energy and that proteins are needed for growth, cell repair and cell replacement.
- ☐ That the body needs tiny amounts of vitamins and mineral ions to keep healthy.
- ☐ That your metabolic rate is the speed at which the chemical reactions in your body occur.
- ☐ How things like muscle mass and exercise habits affect resting metabolic rate.
- ☐ That the more exercise you do, the more energy you use.

Factors Affecting Health

- ☐ That you can become malnourished by eating an unbalanced diet and that malnourished people can be underweight or overweight.
- ☐ That an unbalanced diet can lead to obesity, which increases your risk of type 2 diabetes.
- ☐ That an unbalanced diet can result in a lack of vitamins or minerals, which can cause deficiency diseases.
- ☐ That exercise keeps you healthy by increasing the amount of energy used by the body and decreasing the amount stored as fat.
- ☐ That inherited factors can affect your metabolic rate, overall health and blood cholesterol level.

Evaluating Food, Lifestyle and Diet

- ☐ How to evaluate information about how food and lifestyle affect health, and how lifestyle affects disease.
- ☐ That to lose weight you need to take in less energy than you use up, so you need to eat less or exercise more.
- ☐ How to evaluate claims made about slimming products.

Fighting Disease

- ☐ That pathogens are microorganisms that enter the body and cause disease, e.g. bacteria and viruses.
- ☐ That bacteria make you feel ill by producing toxins and causing cell damage, and that viruses make you feel ill through cell damage.
- ☐ How the body defends itself against pathogen entry (e.g. through the skin and respiratory tract).
- ☐ How white blood cells help to defend the body against pathogens — by engulfing pathogens, producing antitoxins and producing antibodies.
- ☐ That antibodies only lock onto and kill specific pathogens.
- ☐ How the production of antibodies leads to immunity — if you're infected with a pathogen for a second time, white blood cells will rapidly produce antibodies to kill it and you won't get ill. **cont...**

Fighting Disease — Vaccination

☐ How vaccinations work — dead or inactive pathogens are used to trigger the production of antibodies by white blood cells.

☐ That the MMR vaccine is given to children to protect them against measles, mumps and rubella.

☐ That if enough people are immune to a particular pathogen, it can reduce the spread of the pathogen, preventing an epidemic.

☐ The pros and cons of vaccinations and how to evaluate them.

Fighting Disease — Drugs

☐ That drugs (such as painkillers) reduce the symptoms of a disease, but don't kill pathogens.

☐ That antibiotics (such as penicillin) are drugs that kill the bacteria which cause infectious diseases.

☐ That antibiotics are specific, so it's important to be treated with the right one.

☐ That antibiotics don't destroy viruses.

☐ That viruses reproduce inside body cells, making it difficult to develop drugs against them.

☐ That bacteria can mutate, leading to the development of antibiotic resistance by natural selection and that MRSA is an example of a strain of antibiotic-resistant bacteria.

☐ H How populations of antibiotic-resistant bacteria develop — when you treat an infection, only resistant bacteria will survive and reproduce, increasing the population of the resistant strain.

☐ That to prevent antibiotic resistance spreading, it's important not to over-use antibiotics.

☐ H That doctors won't usually prescribe antibiotics for a mild infection, e.g. a sore throat.

Fighting Disease — Investigating Antibiotic Action

☐ That the effectiveness of antibiotics and disinfectants can be tested by growing cultures in the lab.

☐ How to prevent the contamination of bacterial cultures — by passing inoculating loops through a flame to sterilise them, by sterilising Petri dishes and culture media, and by taping lids onto Petri dishes.

☐ Why bacterial cultures are kept at 25 °C in schools, but at higher temperatures in industry.

Fighting Disease — Past & Future

☐ How Semmelweis reduced deaths from infectious disease through hand-washing and how this still applies in modern hospitals.

☐ That increased understanding of immunity and antibiotic action has changed how we treat disease.

☐ That antibiotics have reduced deaths from bacterial diseases such as pneumonia.

☐ Why antibiotic resistance in bacteria is increasing (e.g. the over-use of antibiotics).

☐ That new antibiotics are being developed as a result of increasing antibiotic resistance.

☐ How mutations in bacteria and viruses could lead to epidemics and pandemics.

☐ What the consequences of these epidemics and pandemics might be and how to evaluate them.

Exam-style Questions

1   The Body Mass Index (BMI) can be used to determine whether people are overweight or underweight.

1 (a)   The formula given below can be used to calculate BMI.
The table shows how BMI can be used to classify people's weight.

$$BMI = \frac{body\ mass\ (in\ kg)}{height^2\ (in\ m)}$$

BMI	Weight Description
below 18.5	underweight
18.5 - 24.9	normal
25 - 29.9	overweight
30 - 40	moderately obese
above 40	severely obese

1 (a) (i)   Kate is 1.56 m tall. She weighs 64 kg. Use the formula to calculate Kate's BMI.

(1 mark)

1 (a) (ii)   According to the table, what is Kate's weight description?

(1 mark)

1 (b)   An excess of carbohydrate or fat in the diet can cause weight gain.
What are both carbohydrate and fat needed for by the body?

(1 mark)

1 (c)   Explain how exercise can help you to lose weight.

(2 marks)

2   Robin is going on holiday. His doctor advises him to get a vaccination against the hepatitis A virus. The virus causes a type of liver disease.

2 (a)   Suggest how the hepatitis A virus makes you feel ill.

(1 mark)

2 (b) (i)   The vaccination should make Robin immune to hepatitis A.
Suggest how it will work.

(4 marks)

2 (b) (ii)   The vaccination against hepatitis A will not make Robin immune to the hepatitis B virus. Explain why.

(2 marks)

2 (c)   There are currently no drugs available which will cure hepatitis A.
Suggest why scientists may have had difficulty developing a drug that will get rid of a hepatitis A infection.

(2 marks)

3   The graph below shows the number of measles cases reported each year worldwide, along with the estimated vaccine coverage.

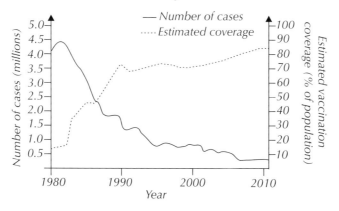

3 (a)   Measles is caused by a pathogen. What is a pathogen?

(1 mark)

3 (b)   Describe the trends shown in the graph.
Use data from the graph to support your answer.

(4 marks)

3 (c)   Evaluate how far this data supports the case for vaccinating people against measles.

(3 marks)

4   A doctor needs to find out which antibiotics will treat a patient's infection, so she sends a sample of bacteria taken from the patient to be cultured in the lab.

A lab technician fills a Petri dish with agar jelly. When this has set, he transfers the bacterial sample to the dish using an inoculating loop.

4 (a)   Describe **two** steps the lab technician should take during this process to avoid contamination of the bacterial culture.

(2 marks)

Once the lab technician has transferred the bacteria, he places 5 different paper discs, each soaked in a different antibiotic, onto the agar. He also puts one paper disc that hasn't been soaked in antibiotic onto the agar. He leaves the Petri dish overnight. The diagram shows the dish a few days later.

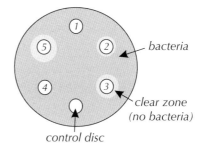

4 (b)   From these results, which antibiotic (1-5) is the best one to use to treat the patient's infection? Explain your answer.

(2 marks)

4 (c)   The bacteria that caused the infection are resistant to some of the antibiotics tested. Explain how the bacteria may have developed resistance to these antibiotics.

(5 marks)

1. The Nervous System

First up in this section, an overview of the nervous system...

What is the nervous system?

Your nervous system is what allows you to respond to changes in your environment. It also allows you to coordinate your actions. The nervous system is made up of all the **neurones** (nerve cells) in your body — there's more on these on the next page.

Stimuli and receptors

A change in your environment that you might need to respond to is called a **stimulus** (the plural is 'stimuli'). A stimulus can be light, sound, touch, pressure, pain, chemical, or a change in position or temperature.

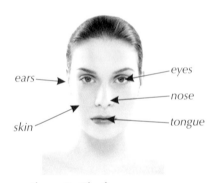

ears — eyes
nose
skin — tongue

Figure 1: *The five sense organs.*

Stimuli are detected by groups of cells called **receptors**. They change stimulus energy (e.g. light energy) into electrical impulses.

Many receptors are found in **sense organs**. You have five different sense organs — eyes, ears, nose, tongue and skin (see Figure 1). They all contain different receptors.

The sense organs and their receptors

- **Eyes** — contain light receptors which are sensitive to light. Like most animal cells, light receptors have a structure called a **nucleus**, which contains their genetic material (see page 96). They're also filled with a jelly-like substance called **cytoplasm** and are surrounded by a **cell membrane** (see Figure 2).

- **Ears** — contain sound receptors which are sensitive to sound. They also contain "balance" receptors which are sensitive to changes in position.

- **Nose** — contains smell receptors which are sensitive to chemical stimuli.

- **Tongue** — contains taste receptors which are sensitive to chemical stimuli. The taste receptors can detect bitter, salt, sweet and sour, plus the taste of savoury things like monosodium glutamate (MSG).

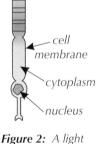

cell membrane
cytoplasm
nucleus

Figure 2: *A light receptor cell.*

Learning Objectives:

- Know that the nervous system allows humans to respond to their environment and coordinate actions.
- Know that changes in the environment (stimuli) are detected by receptor cells.
- Know that light is detected by receptor cells in our eyes, and how these receptor cells have the same structure as most other animal cells.
- Know the types of stimuli receptors in our ears, nose, tongue and skin detect.
- Know that information from receptors travels via neurones to the brain, where a response is coordinated.
- Know that muscles and glands are effectors.
- Know how muscles and glands respond to nervous impulses.

Specification Reference B1.2.1

Tip: Nerve impulses are electrical signals that pass along neurones. They carry information around the body at a very high speed.

- **Skin** — contains receptors that are sensitive to touch, pressure, pain and temperature change.

- **Skin** — contains receptors that are sensitive to touch, pressure, pain and temperature change.

Tip: Don't get sense organs and receptors mixed up. The eye is a sense organ — it contains light receptors. The ear is a sense organ — it contains sound receptors.

The central nervous system (CNS)

The central nervous system (CNS) is where all the information from the receptors is sent, and where reflexes (see p. 43) and actions are coordinated.

The central nervous system consists of the brain and spinal cord only (see Figure 3). Neurones transmit information as electrical impulses to and from the CNS. This happens very quickly.

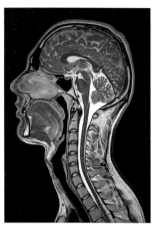

Figure 3: *Scan of the head and neck. The brain and upper spinal cord can be seen in orange/red.*

Effectors

'Instructions' from the CNS are sent along neurones to **effectors**. Effectors are **muscles** or **glands** which respond to nervous impulses and bring about a response to a stimulus. Muscles and glands respond to nervous impulses in different ways:

- Muscles contract.

- Glands secrete chemical substances called hormones (see page 47).

Different types of neurone

Different types of neurone are involved in the transfer of information to and from the CNS:

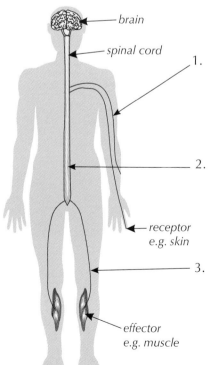

brain

spinal cord

receptor e.g. skin

effector e.g. muscle

1. **Sensory neurones**
   The nerve cells that carry signals as electrical impulses from the receptors in the sense organs to the central nervous system.

2. **Relay neurones**
   The nerve cells that carry signals from sensory neurones to motor neurones. They are found in the central nervous system.

3. **Motor neurones**
   The nerve cells that carry signals from the central nervous system to the effectors.

Exam Tip
The exam isn't just a test of what you know — it's also a test of how well you can apply what you know. For instance, you might have to take what you know about a human and apply it to a horse (e.g. sound receptors in its ears send information to the brain via sensory neurones). The key is not to panic — just think carefully about the information that you are given.

The transmission of information to and from the CNS is summarised in Figure 4:

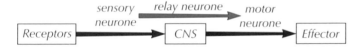

Figure 4: *Flow diagram showing the transmission of information to and from the CNS.*

Practice Questions — Fact Recall

Q1   What is a stimulus?

Q2   What are cells called that detect stimuli?

Q3   The diagram on the right is a light receptor cell.
     What is the object labelled X?

Q4   Which two sense organs are sensitive to chemical stimuli?

Q5   Which type of effector secretes hormones?

Q6   A sensory neurone is a type of neurone.
     Name two other types of neurone.

Practice Questions — Application

Q1   A dog hears a cat moving in the garden, so runs towards it.

   a) i) What is the stimulus in this situation?

   ii) What detects the stimulus in this situation?

   iii)What name is given to the type of neurone that transmits
       information about the stimulus to the central nervous system?

   The dog's brain sends an impulse to the dog's muscles which
   act as an effector.

   b) i) What type of neurone transmits information from the central
          nervous system to an effector?

   ii) How do the dog's muscles respond to the nerve impulse?

Q2   Complete the table to show how each stimulus is detected.

Stimulus	Sense Organ	Receptors Sensitive To
A loud bang		
A moving object		
Walking on a slanted floor		
Touching a hot object		
An unpleasant smell		
Standing on a pin		

Exam Tip
Make sure you know
which type of neurone
transfers information
to which place in the
nervous system — it's
easy to get the different
types of neurones
confused and they often
come up in exams.

Learning Objectives:

- Know that synapses are connections between neurones.
- Understand that chemicals are released at the synapses, which allows information to be transferred from one neurone to the next.
- Know that reflexes are fast, automatic responses to stimuli.
- Know that sensory neurones, relay neurones and motor neurones are all involved in reflexes.
- Know the order of events in a simple reflex action and understand the roles of receptors, effectors, sensory neurones, relay neurones, motor neurones and synapses.

Specification Reference
B1.2.1

2. Synapses and Reflexes

Reflexes are rapid responses to stimuli that happen without you having to think about them — they're automatic. The neurones involved in a reflex aren't all joined together though — they have gaps between them called synapses.

Synapses

The connection between two neurones is called a synapse. The nerve signal is transferred by chemicals which diffuse (move) across the gap. These chemicals then set off a new electrical signal in the next neurone. This is shown in Figure 1.

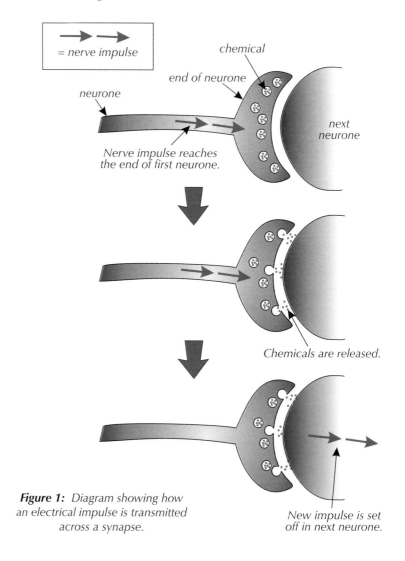

Figure 1: *Diagram showing how an electrical impulse is transmitted across a synapse.*

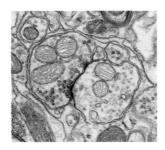

Figure 2: *A synapse viewed under a microscope. The neurones are shown in green. The red dots contain the chemicals that diffuse between the neurones.*

Neurones deliver information really quickly because the signal is transmitted by electrical impulses. Synapses slow down the transmission of a nervous impulse because the diffusion of chemicals across the gap takes time (it's still pretty fast though).

Reflexes

Reflexes are fast, automatic responses to certain stimuli. They bypass your conscious brain completely when a quick response is essential — your body just gets on with things. Reflexes can reduce your chance of being injured, although they have other roles as well.

Tip: 'Automatic' means done without thinking.

Examples

- If someone shines a bright light in your eyes, your pupils automatically get smaller. This means that less light gets into your eyes, which stops them getting damaged.

- Adrenaline is a hormone (see p. 47), which gets your body ready for action. If you get a shock, your body releases adrenaline automatically — it doesn't wait for you to decide that you're shocked.

- The knee-jerk reflex helps maintain posture and balance. Doctors test this reflex by tapping just below the knee with a small hammer. This stimulates pressure receptors, making a muscle in the upper leg contract, which causes the lower leg to rise up.

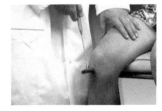

Figure 3: *The knee-jerk reflex. Doctors often use this test to see if a patient's reflexes are working properly.*

Reflex arcs

The passage of information in a reflex (from receptor to effector) is called a reflex arc. The neurones in reflex arcs go through the spinal cord or through an unconscious part of the brain. Here are the main stages in a reflex arc:

1. When a stimulus is detected by receptors, impulses are sent along a sensory neurone to the CNS.

Tip: Flick back to page 40 for more on sensory, relay and motor neurones.

2. When the impulses reach a synapse between the sensory neurone and a relay neurone, they trigger chemicals to be released (see previous page). These chemicals cause impulses to be sent along the relay neurone.

3. When the impulses reach a synapse between the relay neurone and a motor neurone, the same thing happens. Chemicals are released and cause impulses to be sent along the motor neurone.

4. The impulses then travel along the motor neurone to the effector.

Tip: Remember, electrical impulses pass between the different neurones via diffusion of chemicals at the synapse. They don't just jump between the neurones.

5. If the effector is a muscle, it will respond to the impulse by contracting. If it's a gland, it will secrete a hormone.

Because you don't have to think about the response (which takes time) a reflex is quicker than normal responses. Figure 4 summarises a reflex arc:

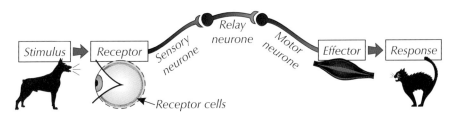

Figure 4: *Block diagram of a reflex arc.*

If a bee stings a person's finger, the reflex response is that the hand moves away from the source of pain. Here's the pathway taken by this reflex arc:

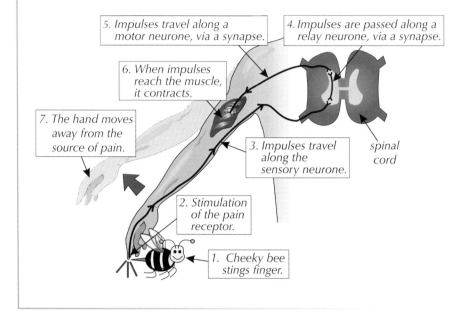

5. Impulses travel along a motor neurone, via a synapse.

4. Impulses are passed along a relay neurone, via a synapse.

6. When impulses reach the muscle, it contracts.

7. The hand moves away from the source of pain.

3. Impulses travel along the sensory neurone.

spinal cord

2. Stimulation of the pain receptor.

1. Cheeky bee stings finger.

Tip: The important things to remember about reflexes are that they're <u>automatic</u> (you don't have to think about them) and <u>rapid</u> (so they're often able to prevent or reduce the chance of injury).

Practice Questions — Fact Recall

Q1 a) What is the connection between two neurones called?

b) How do nerve impulses travel between two neurones?

Q2 What is a reflex?

Q3 Do reflex arcs travel through conscious parts of the brain?

Q4 What neurone comes after the sensory neurone in a reflex arc?

Q5 If the effector in a reflex arc is a gland, what will the response of that reflex arc be?

Practice Question — Application

Exam Tip
Questions on reflex arcs are quite common in the exam. Make sure you know the general pathway they take really well, and you'll be able to apply it to any reflex response you're given.

David steps on a drawing pin and immediately pulls his foot up off the pin.

Q1 a) What is the stimulus in this response?

b) What is the effector in this response? How does it respond?

c) Complete the pathway taken by this reflex arc.

Stimulus → Receptor → Sensory neurone...

3. Homeostasis

The internal conditions in the body must be kept constant — it stops cell damage that could happen if we didn't keep on top of things. Luckily there are some clever systems in place to keep everything plodding along steadily.

Learning Objectives:

- Know that the internal conditions in the body must be carefully controlled.
- Know why body temperature must be controlled.
- Know that the ion content of the body is controlled and that ions leave the body via the skin in sweat and via the kidneys in urine.
- Know that the water content of the body is controlled and how water leaves the body via the lungs, the skin and the kidneys.
- Know why the blood glucose level needs carefully regulating.

Specification Reference B1.2.2

What is homeostasis?

To keep all your cells working properly, certain things must be kept at the right level — not too high, and not too low. Homeostasis is the way in which this happens. The posh way of saying it is that "homeostasis is the maintenance of a constant internal environment".

Bodily levels that need to be controlled include:

> **Examples**
>
> - Temperature
> - Ion content of the body
> - Water content of the body
> - Blood glucose content

There's a bit more on each of these examples in the rest of this topic.

Controlling body temperature

All of your metabolic reactions (the chemical reactions that go on inside your body to keep you alive) are controlled by proteins called **enzymes**. The enzymes within the human body work best at about 37 °C — and so this is the temperature your body tries to maintain.

A part of the brain acts as your own personal thermostat. It's sensitive to the blood temperature in the brain, and it receives messages from receptors in the skin that provide information about skin temperature.

Body temperature needs to be controlled to within a few degrees. If it becomes too high or too low it can be very dangerous.

Controlling ion content

Ions (e.g. sodium, Na^+) are taken into the body in food, then absorbed into the blood. If the food contains too much of any kind of ion then the excess ions need to be removed. E.g. a salty meal will contain far too much Na^+.

Some ions are lost in sweat (which tastes salty, you'll have noticed). The kidneys (see Figure 1) will remove the excess from the blood — this is then got rid of in urine.

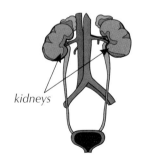

kidneys

Figure 1: *Diagram of the kidneys*

Controlling water content

There's also a need for the body to constantly balance the water coming in against the water going out. Water is taken into the body as food and drink and is lost from the body in these ways:

Tip: Some water is also lost in faeces. Lovely.

- through the skin as sweat.
- via the lungs in breath.
- via the kidneys as urine.

The balance between sweat and urine can depend on what you're doing, or what the weather's like...

Examples

- On a cold day, or when you're not exercising, you don't sweat much, so you'll produce more urine, which will be pale (since the waste carried in the urine is more diluted).

- On a hot day, or when you're exercising, you sweat a lot, and so you will produce less urine, but this will be more concentrated (and hence a deeper colour). You will also lose more water through your breath when you exercise because you breathe faster.

Figure 2: *During exercise water is lost through sweating, and this has to be replaced.*

Tip: For more on metabolism, have a look back at page 16.

Controlling blood glucose

Eating foods containing carbohydrate puts glucose (a sugar) into the blood from the gut. The normal **metabolism** of cells removes glucose from the blood. But if you do a lot of vigorous exercise, then much more glucose is removed.

That's because glucose is used by your cells as an energy source. A hormone called **insulin** helps to maintain the right level of glucose in your blood, so your cells get a constant supply of energy.

Practice Questions — Fact Recall

Q1 What is homeostasis?

Q2 Why must body temperature be kept constant?

Q3 Give two ways in which ions are lost from the body.

Q4 Give three ways in which water is lost from the body.

Q5 Name a hormone involved in the regulation of the blood glucose level.

Q6 Why must the blood glucose level be carefully controlled?

4. Hormones

Along with the nervous system, hormones allow us to react to changes in the environment and in our bodies in order to keep everything ticking over nicely.

What are hormones?

Hormones are chemicals released directly into the blood to regulate bodily processes. They are carried in the **blood plasma** (the liquid part of the blood) to other parts of the body, but only affect particular cells (called **target cells**) in particular places. Hormones control things in organs and cells that need constant adjustment.

Examples

- Follicle stimulating hormone (FSH), luteinising hormone (LH) and oestrogen are hormones involved in the regulation of the menstrual cycle (see pages 49-51).

- Insulin is a hormone that helps control the glucose content of the blood.

Make sure you learn this definition:

> Hormones are chemical messengers which travel in the blood to activate target cells.

Glands

Hormones are produced in (and secreted by) various **glands**.

Examples

1. The **pituitary gland** — this produces many important hormones including FSH and LH.

2. The **ovaries** (females only). The ovaries produce oestrogen.

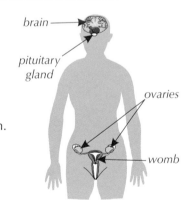

Figure 1: Diagram showing the location of the pituitary and ovaries in the body.

As hormones are carried in the blood, they tend to travel around the body relatively slowly (compared to nervous impulses anyway). They also tend to have relatively long-lasting effects.

Learning Objectives:
- Know that hormones are chemical substances which control many functions in organs and cells.
- Know that hormones are carried in the blood to their target organs.
- Know that glands secrete hormones.
- Know that the pituitary gland secretes follicle stimulating hormone (FSH) and the ovaries secrete oestrogen.

Specification Reference B1.2.2

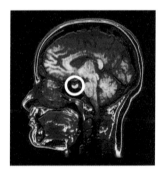

Figure 2: Scan of the brain. The pituitary gland (green structure) is circled in white.

Exam Tip
The pituitary gland and the ovaries are the two examples of glands that you need to learn for the exam. There are loads more glands in the body though, each doing its own thing.

Comparing nerves and hormones

Hormones and nerves do similar jobs in the body, but with a few differences. These are summarised in Figure 3.

Nerves	Hormones
Fast action	Slower action
Act for a short time	Act for a long time
Acts on a very precise area	Acts in a more general way

Figure 3: *Table summarising the differences between nerves and hormones.*

If you're not sure whether a response is nervous or hormonal, have a think...

- If the response is really quick, it's probably nervous.
  Some information needs to be passed to effectors really quickly (e.g. pain signals, or information from your eyes telling you about a car heading your way), so it's no good using hormones to carry the message — they're too slow.
- If a response lasts for a long time, it's probably hormonal.
  For example, when you get a shock, a hormone called adrenaline is released into the body (causing the fight-or-flight response, where your body is hyped up ready for action). You can tell it's a hormonal response (even though it kicks in pretty quickly) because you feel a bit wobbly for a while afterwards.

Exam Tip
Try and learn to spell difficult words like 'pituitary'. In some questions you'll be marked on your spelling and, even when you're not, you still need to make sure the examiner knows what you're talking about.

Practice Questions — Fact Recall

Q1 How are hormones carried around the body?

Q2 True or false? Hormones affect all cells.

Q3 Name a hormone secreted from the pituitary gland.

Q4 Name a hormone secreted from the ovaries.

Q5 Which produces a faster response — nerves or hormones?

5. The Menstrual Cycle

Hormones secreted by the ovaries and the pituitary gland are responsible for controlling the changes that occur during a woman's menstrual cycle.

What is the menstrual cycle?

The menstrual cycle is the monthly sequence of events in which the female body releases an egg and prepares the **uterus** (womb) in case it receives a fertilised egg. This includes:

- The build-up of the protective lining in the uterus ready for the implantation of a fertilised egg.

- The release of an egg from the woman's ovaries.

- The breakdown of the uterus lining if a fertilised egg does not implant. This results in bleeding, which is known as menstruation (a period).

The four stages of the menstrual cycle

The menstrual cycle has four stages. These are shown in Figure 1 and are explained below.

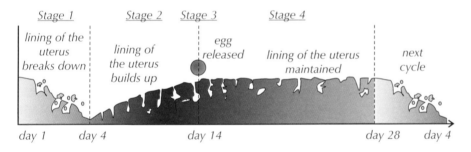

Figure 1: Diagram showing the four stages of the menstrual cycle.

- **Stage 1**
  Day 1 is when the bleeding starts.
  The uterus lining breaks down for about four days.

- **Stage 2**
  The lining of the uterus builds up again, from day 4 to day 14, into a thick spongy layer full of blood vessels, ready to receive a fertilised egg.

- **Stage 3**
  An egg is released from the ovary at day 14.

- **Stage 4**
  The wall is then maintained for about 14 days, until day 28.
  If no fertilised egg has landed on the uterus wall by day 28, the spongy lining starts to break down again and the whole cycle starts again.

Learning Objectives:

- Know that hormones secreted by the ovaries and pituitary gland control the menstrual cycle.

- Know that follicle stimulating hormone (FSH), luteinising hormone (LH) and oestrogen are all involved in the menstrual cycle.

- Know that FSH promotes egg maturation and causes the ovaries to produce hormones such as oestrogen.

- Know that LH stimulates the release of an egg.

- Know that oestrogen inhibits FSH production.

Specification Reference B1.2.2

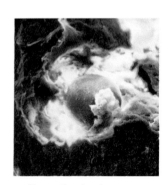

Figure 2: A microscope image showing an egg (pink oval) being released from an ovary (brown).

Hormonal control of the menstrual cycle

You need to know about these three hormones that are involved in the menstrual cycle:

1. FSH (Follicle Stimulating Hormone)

Exam Tip
Make sure you don't talk about egg 'production' or 'development' if you're asked about the menstrual cycle in the exam. Eggs already exist in a woman's ovaries at birth. FSH causes these eggs to <u>mature</u> and LH (see below) causes them to be <u>released</u>.

- Produced by the pituitary gland.
- Causes an egg to mature in one of the ovaries and stimulates the ovaries to produce oestrogen (see Figure 3).

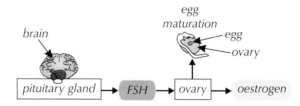

Figure 3: *Diagram showing the role of FSH in the menstrual cycle.*

2. Oestrogen

- Produced in the ovaries.
- Causes the pituitary gland to produce LH (see below) and inhibits the further release of FSH (see Figure 4).

Tip: The inhibition of FSH by oestrogen makes sure that no more eggs mature during that month's cycle.

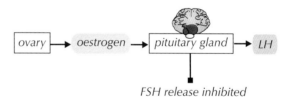

Figure 4: *Diagram showing the role of oestrogen in the menstrual cycle.*

3. LH (Luteinising Hormone)

Tip: Progesterone is another hormone involved in the menstrual cycle — it's produced by the ovaries.

- Produced by the pituitary gland.
- Stimulates the release of an egg at around the middle (day 14) of the menstrual cycle (see Figure 5).

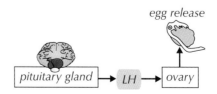

Figure 5: *Diagram showing the role of LH in the menstrual cycle.*

Levels of FSH, oestrogen and LH change throughout the menstrual cycle. So the level of one hormone can be used to predict the level of another hormone:

Example

FSH stimulates the ovaries to produce oestrogen, so if the FSH level rises, you'd expect the oestrogen level to rise too. The increasing oestrogen level will then inhibit FSH release, causing the FSH level to drop.

Practice Questions — Fact Recall

Q1 What is the hormone FSH responsible for in the menstrual cycle?

Q2 Which hormone inhibits the release of FSH?

Q3 What is the function of LH?

Q4 Which two glands secrete the hormones that control the menstrual cycle?

Practice Question — Application

Q1 The graph below shows the level of a hormone measured in the bloodstream of one woman during her 28 day menstrual cycle.

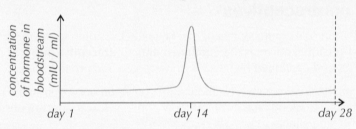

a) Which hormone do you think is shown on the graph? Give a reason for your answer.

b) Where is the hormone you gave in part a) produced?

c) The graph below shows the level of the same hormone measured in another woman during her 28 day menstrual cycle. This woman is struggling to have children. Suggest why this might be.

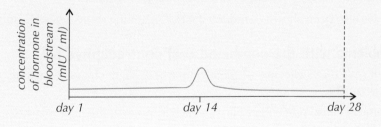

Tip: Think about what happens around the middle of the menstrual cycle.

Tip: Both graphs are drawn to the same scale.

Learning Objectives:
- Understand that hormones can be used to control fertility.
- Know that oestrogen and progesterone can be taken in oral contraceptives to inhibit FSH production, which prevents eggs from maturing, therefore reducing fertility.
- Know why oral contraceptives used to cause more significant side effects and how the number of side effects has now been reduced.
- Know that FSH and LH can be taken to increase fertility in women whose FSH levels are too low.
- Understand the steps involved in In Vitro Fertilisation (IVF).
- Be able to evaluate the use of IVF and hormones to control fertility.

Specification Reference
B1.2.2

6. Controlling Fertility

The hormones involved in the menstrual cycle can be used to increase or decrease a woman's fertility. This is useful for a whole load of reasons...

Reducing fertility

Contraceptives are used to prevent pregnancy. The hormones oestrogen and progesterone can be taken by women to reduce their **fertility** (their ability to get pregnant) and so are often used as contraceptives.

Oestrogen

Oestrogen can be used to prevent egg release. This may seem kind of strange (since naturally oestrogen helps stimulate the release of eggs — see page 50). But if oestrogen is taken every day to keep the level of it permanently high, it inhibits FSH production, and after a while egg maturation and therefore egg release stop.

Progesterone

Progesterone (another hormone involved in the menstrual cycle) also reduces fertility, e.g. by stimulating the production of thick cervical mucus which prevents any sperm getting through and reaching an egg. It can inhibit egg maturation and therefore the release of an egg too.

Oral contraceptives

The pill is an oral contraceptive (it can be taken by mouth to decrease fertility). The first version (known as the **combined oral contraceptive pill**) was made in the 1950s and contained high levels of oestrogen and progesterone.

However, there were concerns about a link between oestrogen in the pill and side effects like blood clots. The pill now contains lower doses of oestrogen so has fewer side effects.

There's also a **progesterone-only pill** — it has fewer side effects than the combined pill (but it's not as effective).

There are both positives and negatives associated with using the pill:

Benefits of the combined oral contraceptive pill
- The pill's over 99% effective at preventing pregnancy.
- It's also been shown to reduce the risk of getting some types of cancer.

Problems with the combined oral contraceptive pill
- It isn't 100% effective — there's still a very slight chance of getting pregnant.
- It can cause side effects like headaches, nausea, irregular menstrual bleeding, and fluid retention.
- It doesn't protect against STDs (sexually transmitted diseases).

Figure 1: *The contraceptive pill is used to reduce fertility, decreasing the risk of pregnancy.*

Tip: Oral contraceptives are sometimes called birth-control pills.

Increasing fertility

Hormones can also be taken by women to increase their fertility.
For example, some women have an FSH level that is too low to cause their eggs to mature. This means that no eggs are released and the women can't get pregnant.

The hormones FSH and LH can be injected by these women to stimulate egg maturation and release in their ovaries. These 'fertility drugs' can help a lot of women to get pregnant when previously they couldn't. They are often used during IVF too — see below.

Tip: Flick back to page 50 for a reminder of what the hormones FSH and LH do.

Problems with fertility drugs

Using fertility drugs like FSH and LH has its problems:

▪ They don't always work — some women may have to use the treatment many times, which can be expensive.

▪ Too many eggs could be stimulated, resulting in unexpected multiple pregnancies (twins, triplets etc.).

Tip: As well as being hard work, having multiple births puts a bigger stress on the mother and embryos' health during pregnancy.

In Vitro Fertilisation (IVF)

IVF is a process that can be used to help couples who are having difficulty having children.

IVF involves the following steps:

1. FSH and LH are given to the woman to stimulate the maturation of multiple eggs.

2. Eggs are then collected from the woman's ovaries.

3. The eggs are fertilised in a lab using the man's sperm.

4. The fertilised eggs then grow into embryos (small balls of cells).

5. Once the embryos have formed, one or two of them are transferred to the woman's uterus. Transferring more than one improves the chance of pregnancy.

This is summarised in Figure 2.

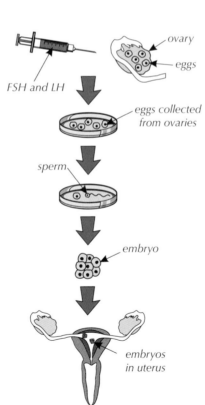

FSH and LH
ovary
eggs
eggs collected from ovaries
sperm
embryo
embryos in uterus

Figure 2: Diagram showing the steps involved in IVF.

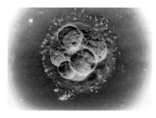

Figure 3: An embryo ready for transfer into a uterus.

The pros and cons of IVF

The main benefit of IVF is that it can give an infertile couple a child — a pretty obvious benefit. However there are negative sides to the treatment:

- Some women have a strong reaction to the hormones — e.g. abdominal pain, vomiting, dehydration.

- There have been some reports of an increased risk of cancer due to the hormonal treatment (though others have reported no such risk — the position isn't really clear at the moment).

- Multiple births can happen if more than one embryo grows into a baby — these are risky for the mother and babies (there's a higher risk of miscarriage, stillbirth...).

Practice Questions — Fact Recall

Q1 Explain the function of oestrogen in the combined contraceptive pill.

Q2 Apart from oestrogen, what hormone is found in the combined pill?

Q3 Why does the modern pill only contain small amounts of oestrogen?

Q4 FSH and LH can be given to women to stimulate egg maturation and release. Give a problem associated with using hormones in this way.

Q5 What is the next step after egg collection in IVF?

Q6 When are embryos transferred into the uterus during IVF?

Practice Question — Application

Q1 Jenny is 28 and is considering IVF as she and her partner are struggling to have children.

a) At the fertility clinic, the doctors discover that Jenny has an extremely low level of the hormone FSH. Explain how this may be preventing her from becoming pregnant.

b) The table shows some data about women aged 18-34 undergoing IVF in the UK in 2009 and 2010 using their own fresh eggs.

Year	Number of embryo transfers during IVF	Number of IVF pregnancies
2009	15813	6433
2010	16652	6695

Calculate the percentage of embryo transfers that resulted in pregnancy for 18-34 year olds undergoing IVF in 2010.

c) The average multiple pregnancy rate of women undergoing IVF in 2010 in the UK with their own fresh eggs was 22.2%. The multiple pregnancy rate of normal pregnancies was lower than this. Give a reason why this might be.

Tip: IVF can be done using a woman's own fresh eggs (eggs freshly collected from the woman), frozen eggs (eggs which have been extracted at an earlier date and frozen until needed), or using eggs from another woman.

Exam Tip
Read any data given to you carefully. In this question, make sure you're using the correct numbers from the table.

7. Plant Hormones

Like animals, plants have to respond to stimuli. Plant hormones control and coordinate the response of plants to light, moisture and gravity.

A plant's needs

Plants need to be able to detect and respond to stimuli (changes in the environment) in order to survive:

Examples

- Plants need light to make their own food. Plants can sense light, and grow towards it in order to maximise the amount of light they receive.

- Plants also need water to survive. They can sense moisture in the soil, so their roots grow towards it.

- Plants can sense and respond to gravity. This makes sure that their roots and shoots grow in the right direction.

Auxin

Auxin is a plant hormone that controls growth near the tips of shoots and roots. It controls the growth of a plant in response to different stimuli.

> Auxin controls:
>
> - **Phototropism** — plant growth in response to light.
>
> - **Gravitropism** (also known as **geotropism**) — plant growth in response to gravity.
>
> - Plant growth in response to moisture.

Auxin is produced in the tips of roots and shoots and moves backwards to stimulate the **cell elongation** process which occurs in the cells just behind the tips (see Figure 2). If the tip of a shoot is removed, no auxin is available and the shoot may stop growing.

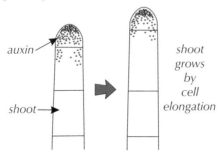

auxin

shoot

shoot grows by cell elongation

Figure 2: *Auxin release from the tips of shoots results in cell elongation and shoot growth.*

Learning Objectives:

- Understand that the hormone auxin controls phototropism and gravitropism (geotropism) in plants.

- Know that plants respond to light, gravity and moisture, because of the uneven distribution of auxin, which causes uneven growth rates in the shoots and roots.

- Know that plants' shoots grow towards light and away from gravity.

- Know that plants' roots grow towards moisture and gravity.

- Know that plant hormones are used as rooting compounds and weedkillers in agriculture and horticulture and be able to evaluate their use.

Specification Reference B1.2.3

Figure 1: *A plant displaying phototropism — its shoot is growing towards the light.*

Tip: Cell elongation just means that the cells of the plant get bigger (longer).

Shoot and root growth

Extra auxin promotes growth in the shoot but inhibits growth in the root. This, coupled with the unequal distribution of auxin in the shoot or root tip, produces the following results:

1. Shoots grow towards light

When a shoot tip is exposed to light, more auxin accumulates on the side that's in the shade than the side that's in the light. This makes the cells grow (elongate) faster on the shaded side, so the shoot bends towards the light (see Figure 3).

Tip: In <u>shoots</u>, more auxin on one side means that the cells on that side will <u>grow faster</u>. This will cause the plant to bend <u>away</u> from that side, e.g.

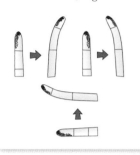

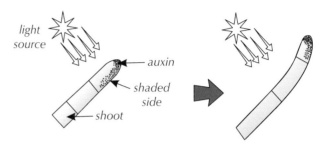

Figure 3: *Diagram to show how auxin causes shoot growth towards the light.*

2. Shoots grow away from gravity

When a shoot is growing sideways, gravity produces an unequal distribution of auxin in the tip, with more auxin on the lower side. This causes the lower side to grow faster, bending the shoot upwards, as shown in Figure 5.

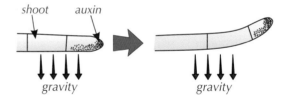

Figure 5: *Diagram to show how auxin causes shoot growth away from gravity.*

Figure 4: *A plant displaying gravitropism — its shoots are growing away from gravity.*

The distribution of auxin in response to gravity means that the shoot should always grow in the right direction (i.e. upwards), even in the absence of light.

3. Roots grow towards gravity

When a root is growing sideways, more auxin will accumulate on its lower side. In a root the extra auxin inhibits growth. This means the cells on top elongate faster, and the root bends downwards (see Figure 6).

Tip: In <u>roots</u>, more auxin on one side means that the cells on that side will <u>grow slower</u>. This will cause the plant to bend <u>towards</u> that side, e.g.

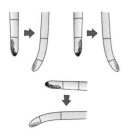

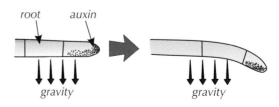

Figure 6: *Diagram to show how auxin causes root growth towards gravity.*

4. Roots grow towards moisture

An uneven amount of moisture either side of a root produces more auxin on the side with more moisture. This inhibits growth on that side, causing the root to bend in that direction, towards the moisture (see Figure 7).

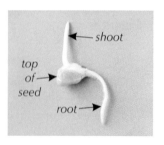

Figure 8: This seed was grown sideways (not upright) and in the dark, but its shoot is growing upwards and its root downwards (i.e. in the right directions) because of gravitropism.

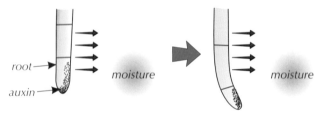

Figure 7: Diagram to show how auxin causes root growth towards moisture.

Uses of plant hormones

Plant hormones can be extracted and used by people in agriculture (farming) and horticulture (gardening). Artificial versions can also be made.

1. Selective weedkillers

Most weeds in crop fields are broad-leaved, unlike grasses and cereals which have very narrow leaves. Selective weedkillers are made of plant growth hormones — they only affect the broad-leaved plants. They disrupt their normal growth patterns, which soon kills them, but leave the crops untouched. You could be asked to interpret data on selective weedkillers in the exam:

Example

A farmer was studying the effect of selective weedkillers on barley yield. He grew the same type of barley in three fields of the same size and soil type. He used one type of selective weedkiller in Field A, another type in Field B, and left Field C untreated. He measured the crop yield of each field after one year. The results are shown in the graph.

Tip: Crop yield is a way of measuring the amount of crop produced by an area of land.

You could be asked to draw conclusions from the data...
From this graph, you can conclude that the crop yield for Field B was higher than the yields for Fields A and C. This could be because the weedkiller used to treat Field B was the most effective at removing weeds, which meant the crops had less competition, so the yield was greater.

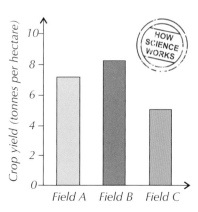

You could be asked why Field C was left untreated...
It was a control (see page 7) — the conditions were the same in Field C as the other fields (e.g. same sized field, same soil type, etc.) but no weedkiller was applied. This shows that the increased crop yield displayed in the other fields was likely to be due to the presence of weedkiller and nothing else.

Tip: Weeds compete with crops for resources, e.g. light and nutrients. If you remove the weeds, you remove the competition — so the crop will have more resources. This should mean that the crop grows more and produces a bigger yield. There's more on competition on p. 77.

Figure 9: *A gardener using
rooting powder when
planting cuttings.*

Tip: Don't forget to
refer to the experiment
in your answer to
Q1 a). Don't just talk
about what you know
about auxin.

2. Rooting powders

Plant cuttings won't always grow in soil. If you add rooting powder,
which contains the plant hormone auxin, they'll produce roots rapidly
and start growing as new plants. This helps growers to produce lots of
clones of a really good plant very quickly.

Practice Questions — Fact Recall

Q1 What is gravitropism?

Q2 What effect does auxin have on cell elongation in a plant root?

Q3 Explain how plant roots grow in response to moisture in the soil.

Practice Questions — Application

Q1 A scientist conducted an experiment to study phototropism in cress
seedlings. 12 cress seeds were planted in Petri dish A and left
directly under a light source. Another 12 cress seeds were planted in
Petri dish B and provided with a light source placed to one side.
The growth of the seeds after two weeks is shown in the diagram:

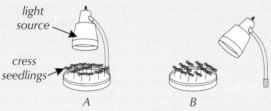

a) Describe how the distribution of auxin in the shoots of the cress
seedlings will differ between Petri dish A and Petri dish B.

b) i) Other than the position of the light source, the scientist tried to
keep the conditions in both Petri dishes the same.
Explain why she did this.

ii) Give two conditions that the scientist needed
to keep the same during the experiment.

Q2 Dan grows plants for a garden centre. He is trying to work out the
best rooting powder to use for his cuttings. From the same type
of plant, he grows 50 cuttings in rooting powder A, 50 in rooting
powder B and 50 without rooting powder. He grows all the cuttings
under the same conditions. His results are shown in the table.

		Powder A	Powder B	No powder
Average increase in root length (mm)	After 1 week	8	10	6
	After 2 weeks	17	19	14
	After 3 weeks	24	28	20

a) From these results, what can you conclude about which rooting
powder is the best to use? Explain your answer.

b) Explain why Dan grew some cuttings without rooting powder.

Section Checklist — Make sure you know...

The Nervous System

☐ That the nervous system allows humans to respond to changes in the environment (stimuli) and to coordinate their behaviour.

☐ That receptor cells detect stimuli.

☐ That light receptor cells in the eyes contain a nucleus and cytoplasm, and are surrounded by a cell membrane, like most other animal cells.

☐ That receptor cells in the ears detect sound and aid balance, that chemical receptors in our nose and tongue allow us to smell and taste, and that receptors in our skin respond to touch, pressure, pain and changes in temperature.

☐ That information from receptors travels via neurones to the brain, where a response is coordinated.

☐ That effectors are muscles and glands, and that muscles respond to nervous impulses by contracting, and glands respond by secreting hormones.

Synapses and Reflexes

☐ That the connections between neurones are called synapses and that a nerve signal is transferred across a synapse by chemicals that diffuse across the gap.

☐ That reflexes are fast, automatic responses involving receptors, sensory neurones, relay neurones, motor neurones, synapses and effectors.

☐ That in a simple reflex, stimuli are detected by receptors and transmitted to the central nervous system as nervous impulses via sensory neurones. The impulses are then transferred via a relay neurone in the CNS to a motor neurone, which sends impulses to an effector. The effector then produces a response.

Homeostasis

☐ That internal conditions within the body, including body temperature, ion content, water content and blood glucose level need to be carefully controlled.

☐ That body temperature must be controlled to allow the enzymes involved in bodily processes to work at their best.

☐ That ions are removed from the body via the skin in sweat and via the kidneys in urine.

☐ That water leaves the body via the lungs in breath, the skin in sweat and the kidneys in the urine.

☐ That blood glucose must be regulated to ensure our cells get enough energy.

Hormones

☐ That hormones are chemical messengers which travel in the blood to activate target cells.

☐ That hormones are secreted by glands, e.g. follicle stimulating hormone (FSH) by the pituitary gland and oestrogen by the ovaries.

cont...

The Menstrual Cycle

☐ That the menstrual cycle (the monthly sequence of events in which the female body releases an egg and prepares the uterus in case it receives a fertilised egg) is controlled by hormones. These are secreted by the ovaries (e.g. oestrogen) and the pituitary gland (e.g. FSH and LH).

☐ That FSH causes eggs to mature and the ovaries to produce oestrogen, that luteinising hormone (LH) stimulates egg release and that oestrogen inhibits FSH production.

Controlling Fertility

☐ How the hormones oestrogen and progesterone can be used to decrease fertility.

☐ That oral contraceptives containing large doses of oestrogen used to cause many side effects, so oral contraceptives now contain lower doses of oestrogen or just progesterone.

☐ That progesterone-only pills cause fewer side effects than oral contraceptives containing oestrogen.

☐ How the hormones FSH and LH can be used as 'fertility drugs' to increase fertility.

☐ The pros and cons of using fertility drugs such as FSH and LH to control fertility, e.g. they may help women to get pregnant, but don't always work. They also increase the risk of multiple pregnancies.

☐ The basic process involved in In Vitro Fertilisation (IVF) — women are given FSH and LH to stimulate egg maturation and release. The eggs are collected and fertilised using sperm. The resulting embryos are grown until they are tiny balls of cells, at which point they are transferred into a uterus.

☐ The pros and cons associated with IVF, e.g. it can give a childless couple a child, but some women can react badly to the hormones and it's possible that the hormones may increase the risk of cancer. It also increases the risk of multiple births.

Plant Hormones

☐ That the plant hormone auxin is responsible for plant growth in response to light (phototropism), plant growth in response to gravity (gravitropism) and plant growth in response to moisture.

☐ How the uneven distribution of auxin leads to uneven rates of cell elongation, allowing plant shoots to grow towards light and away from gravity, and plant roots to grow towards moisture and gravity.

☐ That plant hormones are used as rooting compounds and weedkillers in agriculture and horticulture, and be able to evaluate their use.

1   A scientist conducted an experiment on reaction time.

Subjects had an electrode placed on their upper arm to detect when their muscle contracted. The subjects were asked to place their finger on a metal disc, which gave out a small electric shock at random. This shock caused the muscle in the upper arm to contract.

The scientist measured reaction time as the time it took between the initiation of the shock and the contraction of the muscle in the upper arm.

The diagram shows the pathway taken in this reflex response.

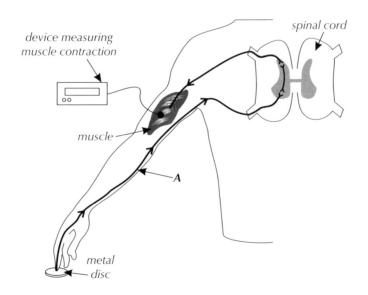

1 (a) (i)   What is the effector in this response?

(1 mark)

1 (a) (ii) Name the neurone labelled **A** in the diagram.

(1 mark)

1 (b)   The average reaction time measured during the experiment was 0.024 s.

After he had recorded their reaction times, the scientist gave the subjects a drug which is known to increase the amount of chemical released at the synapses. He then repeated the experiment.

What do you think would happen to the average reaction time after administration of the drug? Explain your answer.

(2 marks)

1 (c)   Reflexes often help to protect us from injury.
Suggest and explain **two** features of reflexes that help them do this.

(4 marks)

2   The diagram shows a plant that has been kept in a cupboard for one week.
While it was in the cupboard, it had three possible light sources (labelled **A**, **B** and **C** in the diagram).

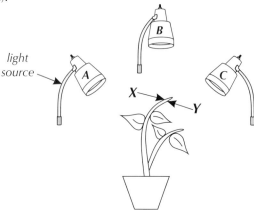

2 (a) (i)   The plant only had one light source on during the week.
Which light source do you think it was, **A**, **B** or **C**? Explain your answer.

(1 mark)

2 (a) (ii)   Samples of the plant shoot are taken from point **X** and point **Y** and analysed for the presence of auxin. Which sample do you think will contain most auxin, sample **X** or sample **Y**? Explain your answer.

(3 marks)

2 (b)   This plant was produced by taking a cutting from another plant and applying rooting powder to it before planting it in a pot. Explain why rooting powder was used.

(2 marks)

3   The combined pill (which contains both oestrogen and progesterone) and the progesterone-only pill are two types of oral contraceptive. Read the following information about them.

> The combined oral contraceptive pill is reported to have a failure rate of just 0.1%, if taken correctly and consistently. It should be taken around the same time every day, but is still effective if taken up to 12 hours late. The combined oral contraceptive pill increases the risk of blood clots and cannot be taken if the woman is breast feeding. It is taken by some women to control their periods if they experience heavy bleeding.
>
> The progesterone-only pill has to be taken at the same time everyday or within up to three hours, to be effective. If it is taken correctly the failure rate is reported to be 0.5%. The progesterone-only pill can lead to irregular bleeding, but it can be taken if breast feeding and can be taken by some women who have a history of blood clots.

In this question you will be assessed on the quality of your English, the organisation of your ideas and your use of appropriate specialist vocabulary.

Evaluate the use of the two types of oral contraceptive pill.

(6 marks)

1. Drugs and Drug Claims

Drugs can have positive effects on the body, e.g. they can help cure illness. But you have to be careful when looking at what drugs claim to do...

What are drugs?

Drugs are substances that alter what goes on in your body. Your body's essentially a seething mass of chemical reactions — drugs can interfere with these reactions, sometimes for the better, sometimes not.

Some of the chemical changes caused by drugs can lead to the body becoming **addicted to** (dependent on) the drug. If the drug isn't taken, an addict can suffer **withdrawal symptoms**.

Examples

Heroin, **cocaine**, nicotine and caffeine are all very addictive drugs and can all cause withdrawal symptoms. E.g. heroin withdrawal can cause symptoms of restlessness, muscle pain, vomiting and cold flushes. Caffeine withdrawal can cause headaches and drowsiness.

Types of drugs

There are many different types of drugs, including:

- **Medicinal drugs** — drugs that are medically useful, like antibiotics (see p. 29). For some of these drugs you don't need a prescription (e.g. paracetamol), but for others you do (e.g. morphine, a strong painkiller) because they can be dangerous if misused.

- **Recreational drugs** — drugs used for fun (see pages 69-70).

- **Performance-enhancing drugs** — drugs that can improve a person's performance in sport (see below).

Performance-enhancing drugs

Some athletes take performance-enhancing drugs to make them better at sport. There are different types of performance-enhancing drugs.

Examples

- **Anabolic steroids** — these increase muscle size, so the athlete is stronger.

- **Stimulants** — these increase heart rate, so glucose and oxygen are transported to the athlete's muscles faster (giving them more energy).

Learning Objectives:

- Understand what drugs do and how they can lead to addiction and withdrawal symptoms.
- Know that heroin and cocaine are very addictive drugs.
- Know what performance-enhancing drugs are.
- Understand why anabolic steroids and stimulants are used as performance-enhancing drugs.
- Know that some performance-enhancing drugs are illegal and some can be prescribed legally, but that all are banned by sporting bodies.
- Be able to evaluate the use of performance-enhancing drugs, including the ethical issues around them.
- Know what statins do and be able to evaluate their effect.
- Be able to evaluate claims about prescribed and non-prescribed drugs.

Specification Reference
B1.3.1

Exam Tip
You need to learn these two examples of performance-enhancing drugs for the exam.

But these drugs can have negative health effects, e.g. steroids can cause high blood pressure and high doses of stimulants can cause an irregular heartbeat. Some performance-enhancing drugs are banned by law, some are prescription-only, but all are banned by sporting bodies.

Evaluating the use of performance-enhancing drugs

There are also ethical problems with taking performance-enhancing drugs:

<u>Against drugs...</u>	<u>For drugs...</u>
It's unfair if people gain an advantage by taking drugs, not just through training.	Athletes have the right to make their own decision about whether taking drugs is worth the risk or not.
Athletes may not be fully informed of the serious health risks of the drugs they take.	Drug-free sport isn't really fair anyway — different athletes have access to different training facilities, coaches, equipment, etc. You could argue that taking drugs makes things fairer.
It's unfair if athletes from wealthy countries can afford to buy the drugs and athletes from poorer countries can't.	It avoids a situation where athletes who take a banned substance without knowing are penalised (punished).

Evaluating drug claims

You might have to evaluate claims about prescribed or non-prescribed drugs in the exam. If so, you need to look at these claims critically.

> **Example**
>
> **Statins** are prescribed drugs used to lower the risk of heart and circulatory disease.
>
> There's evidence that statins lower blood cholesterol and significantly lower the risk of heart disease in diabetic patients.
>
> The original research was done by government scientists with no connection to the manufacturers. And the sample was big — 6000 patients.
>
> It compared two groups of patients — those who had taken statins and those who hadn't (a control group, see p. 7). Other studies have since backed up these findings, so the results were reproducible (see pages 2-3).

HOW SCIENCE WORKS

But research findings aren't always so clear cut...

> **Example**
>
> In 2012, it was claimed that taking a low dose of aspirin each day could help to prevent cancer.
>
> But taking aspirin can have serious side-effects — for example, it can increase the risk of internal bleeding. And the data the claim was based on came from studies that weren't originally designed to look at the effect of aspirin on cancer risk.
>
> So until more specific studies are done, there's not enough evidence to say whether the possible benefits of taking aspirin to prevent cancer outweigh the dangers.

Practice Questions — Fact Recall

Q1 Why may a person become addicted to a drug?

Q2 Give two examples of drugs that are very addictive.

Q3 a) Give one example of a performance-enhancing drug.

   b) Describe one effect that the drug in part a) has on the body.

Q4 What are statins prescribed to do?

Practice Question — Application

Q1 Beth is an athlete. She is considering taking amphetamines. Amphetamines are a type of drug that increase heart rate and may help Beth to perform better.

   a) i) What type of drug are amphetamines?

      ii) Briefly explain how using amphetamines may help Beth to perform better.

   Beth is due to take part in an international competition and has to have a drug test beforehand.

   b) Suggest one reason why sporting bodies carry out drug testing.

   Beth is not aware that the side effects of using amphetamines include increased blood pressure, reduced appetite, hallucinations and even heart attacks. These are serious health risks and are one reason why some people are against the use of these drugs in sport.

   c) Give another reason why people may be against the use of amphetamines in sport.

   d) Give one reason why people may support the use of performance-enhancing drugs in sport.

Exam Tip
Don't be put off if you're given a question in the exam about a drug you haven't heard of — just read the question carefully and apply what you know about drugs in general to answer the question.

- Know that scientists are always developing new drugs.

- Understand why new medicinal drugs have to be tested before becoming available to the public (to check effectiveness, toxicity and dosage).

- Understand what happens when testing drugs in the laboratory and in clinical trials.

- Know what the terms 'optimum dose', 'placebo' and 'double-blind trials' mean.

- Know what the drug thalidomide was developed as.

- Understand what happened when thalidomide was used to relieve morning sickness in pregnant women without being tested for that use.

- Know how drug testing changed after the problems thalidomide caused.

- Know what thalidomide is used to treat today.

Specification Reference
B1.3.1

2. Testing Medicinal Drugs

Pharmacies stock lots of medicines that can prevent or cure diseases. But before they make it onto the pharmacy shelves the drugs have to be tested...

Laboratory testing

New drugs are constantly being developed. But before they can be given to the general public, they have to go through a thorough testing procedure — starting in the laboratory.

Cells and tissues

First of all, drugs are tested on human cells and tissues in the lab. However, you can't use human cells and tissues to test drugs that affect whole or multiple body systems, e.g. testing a drug for blood pressure must be done on a whole animal because it has an intact circulatory system.

Live animals

The next step is to test the drug on live animals. This is to see whether the drug works (produces the effect you're looking for), to find out about its **toxicity** (how harmful it is) and the best dosage (the dose at which it's most effective).

The law in Britain states that any new drug must be tested on two different live mammals. Some people think it's cruel to test on animals, but others believe this is the safest way to make sure a drug isn't dangerous before it's given to humans. Other people think that animals are so different from humans that testing on animals is pointless.

Clinical trials

If the drug passes the tests on animals then it's tested on human volunteers in a clinical trial.

First, the drug is tested on healthy volunteers. This is to make sure that it doesn't have any harmful side effects when the body is working normally. At the start of the trial, a very low dose of the drug is given and this is gradually increased.

If the results of the tests on healthy volunteers are good, the drugs can be tested on people suffering from the illness. The **optimum dose** is found — this is the dose of drug that is the most effective and has few side effects.

Placebos

To test how well the drug works, patients are put into two groups. One is given the new drug, the other is given a placebo (a substance that's like the drug being tested but doesn't do anything). This is so the doctor can see the actual difference the drug makes — it allows for the placebo effect (when the patient expects the treatment to work and so feels better, even though the treatment isn't doing anything).

Example

A pharmaceutical company has developed a drug, Drug X, to help people with high blood cholesterol to lower their cholesterol level. The drug was tested on 1500 patients with high cholesterol. The patients were divided into two groups and over six months each patient had one tablet per day. One group had a tablet containing Drug X and the other group had a tablet without Drug X — the placebo.

Tip: People in the control group of a clinical trial should be similar to people in the treatment group, e.g. of a similar age, gender, etc. This helps to make sure the study is a fair test — see How Science Works pages 6-7 for more on making a study a fair test.

HOW SCIENCE WORKS

Blind and double-blind trials

Clinical trials are blind — the patient in the study doesn't know whether they're getting the drug or the placebo. In fact, they're often double-blind — neither the patient nor the doctor knows until all the results have been gathered (see Figure 1). This is so the doctors monitoring the patients and analysing the results aren't subconsciously influenced by their knowledge.

	Blind trial	Double-blind trial
Does the **patient** know whether they're getting the drug or the placebo?	no	no
Does the **doctor** know whether the patient is getting the drug or the placebo?	yes	no

Figure 1: *Table summarising blind and double-blind trials.*

The importance of drug testing

It's really important that drugs are tested thoroughly before being used to make sure they're safe. An example of what can happen when drugs are not thoroughly tested is the case of **thalidomide**...

Example

Thalidomide is a drug that was developed in the 1950s. It was intended as a sleeping pill, and was tested for that use. But later it was also found to be effective in relieving morning sickness in pregnant women.

Unfortunately, thalidomide hadn't been tested as a drug for morning sickness, and so it wasn't known that it could pass through the placenta and affect the fetus, causing abnormal limb development. In some cases, babies were born with no arms or legs at all. About 10 000 babies were affected by thalidomide, and only about half of them survived.

The drug was banned, and more rigorous testing procedures were introduced. More recently thalidomide has been used in the treatment of leprosy and other diseases, e.g. some cancers.

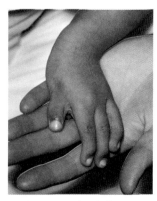

Figure 2: *This baby was born with a deformed hand due to thalidomide.*

Practice Questions — Fact Recall

Q1 Which comes first during drug testing — laboratory testing or clinical trials?

Q2 In the laboratory, what may drugs be tested on?

Q3 Give two reasons why drugs need to be tested in the laboratory.

Q4 a) In a clinical trial, what type of volunteer is the drug tested on first — healthy volunteers or people suffering from the illness?

b) Describe the dosage of drug that is first used in a clinical trial.

Q5 What is a placebo?

Q6 Briefly explain what is involved in a double-blind trial.

Exam Tip
If you're asked what a placebo is in the exam, remember that it's <u>not</u> a drug — this is because it doesn't actually do anything.

Practice Questions — Application

Q1 For each of the drugs below, suggest what would have been given as a placebo when that drug went through clinical trials.

a) a paracetamol capsule   b) a steroid inhaler

c) a cortisone injection

Q2 A new weight-loss pill has been developed called Drug X. The pill was tested in a double-blind clinical trial. It involved three groups of obese volunteers (50 per group), all of whom wanted to lose weight.
Each group member took a pill three times a day for a year, alongside diet and exercise. The first group took Drug X, the second group took a similar weight-loss pill already available (Drug Y) and the third group took a placebo. The average weight loss per person after one year is shown on the graph.

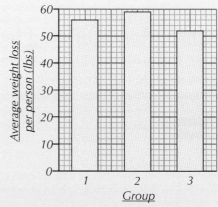

a) i) Would the doctors involved in this trial have known which patients were being given the placebo? Explain your answer.

ii) Suggest what could have been used as a placebo in this trial.

b) Why do you think Group 2 was included in the trial?

c) From these results, what can you conclude about Drug X? Use data from the graph to support your answer.

Exam Tip
When answering a question about a clinical trial in the exam, make sure you read all the information you're given. Here you need to have spotted that it's a double-blind trial — this will help you answer Q2 a) i).

3. Recreational Drugs

Some drugs are just used for fun. But with fun comes risk...

What are recreational drugs?

Recreational drugs are drugs used for fun. They can be legal or illegal.

Illegal recreational drugs

Illegal drugs are often divided into two main classes — soft and hard. Hard drugs are usually thought of as being seriously addictive and generally more harmful than soft drugs. But the terms "soft" and "hard" are a bit vague — they're not scientific descriptions, and you can certainly have problems with soft drug use.

> **Examples**
>
> - **Heroin** and **ecstasy** (hard drugs) and **cannabis** (a soft drug) can all cause heart and circulatory system problems.
>
> - Recent studies suggest that for young people who are already more at risk of developing mental health problems because of their genes, using cannabis may increase this risk even further.

Reasons for using recreational drugs

So if all these recreational drugs are so dangerous, why do so many people use them? There are various reasons why...

> **Example**
>
> When asked why they use cannabis, most users quote either simple enjoyment, relaxation or stress relief. Some say they do it to get stoned or for inspiration. Some multiple sclerosis sufferers say cannabis can relieve pain.
>
> But very often this turns out to be not the whole story. There may be other factors in the user's background or personal life which influence them in choosing to use drugs. It's a personal thing, and often pretty complicated.

Progression from soft drugs to hard drugs

Almost all users of hard drugs have tried cannabis first (though most users of cannabis do not go on to use hard drugs). The link between cannabis and hard drugs isn't clear, but three opinions are common...

1. Cannabis is a "stepping stone" — the effects of cannabis create a desire to try harder drugs.

2. Cannabis is a "gateway drug" — cannabis use brings people into contact with drug dealers.

3. It's all down to genetics — certain people are more likely to take drugs generally, so cannabis users will also try other drugs.

Learning Objectives:

- Know that heroin, ecstasy and cannabis are illegal recreational drugs and understand the health problems they cause.

- Be able to evaluate different types of drugs and know why some people use illegal recreational drugs.

- Understand why people might progress from using soft recreational drugs to using hard recreational drugs.

- Know that nicotine and alcohol are legal recreational drugs and understand that they can cause health problems.

- Be able to compare the overall impact on people's health of legal recreational drugs and illegal recreational drugs.

Specification Reference B1.3.1

Legal recreational drugs

Legal recreational drugs can have a massive impact on people's health.

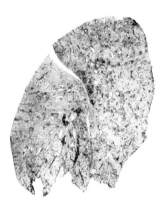

Figure 1: A diseased lung from a smoker.

> ## Examples
>
> **Nicotine** (the drug found in tobacco smoke) and **alcohol** are both legal recreational drugs. Smoking and drinking alcohol can have the following effects on a person's health:
>
> | Smoking | Alcohol |
> |---|---|
> | <ul><li>Causes disease of the heart, blood vessels and lungs.</li><li>Tobacco smoke also causes cancer.</li><li>Nicotine is addictive so it's hard to stop smoking.</li></ul> | <ul><li>Affects the nervous system and slows down the body's reactions.</li><li>Too much alcohol leads to impaired judgement, poor coordination and unconsciousness.</li><li>Excessive drinking can cause liver disease and brain damage.</li><li>Alcohol is also addictive.</li></ul> |

Tip: Nicotine and alcohol are not prescribed drugs, but some legal drugs are prescribed by doctors. These can also have a massive impact on health if people misuse them, e.g. people can become addicted to prescribed painkillers if they're overused.

Legal recreational drugs can also have a massive impact on society.

> ## Examples
>
> Smoking and alcohol have the following effects on our society:
>
> - The National Health Service spends loads on treating people with lung diseases caused by smoking. Add to this the cost to businesses of people missing days from work, and the figures get pretty scary.
>
> - The same goes for alcohol. The costs to the NHS are huge, but are pretty small compared to the costs related to crime (police time, damage to people/property) and the economy (lost working days etc.).
>
> - And in addition to the financial costs, alcohol and smoking cause sorrow and anguish to people affected by them, either directly or indirectly.

Legal drugs, like nicotine and alcohol, have a bigger impact in the UK than illegal drugs, as so many people take them.

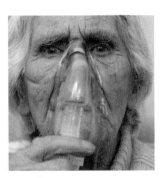

Figure 2: A woman receiving oxygen therapy — a treatment for lung disease caused by smoking.

Practice Questions — Fact Recall

Q1 Name two illegal and two legal recreational drugs.

Q2 Describe two opinions about the link between cannabis and hard drug use.

Q3 Do legal or illegal drugs have the biggest impact on people and society in the UK? Explain your answer.

Section Checklist — Make sure you know...

Drugs and Drug Claims

- ☐ That drugs cause chemical changes in the body, which can lead to addiction.
- ☐ That people addicted to drugs may suffer withdrawal symptoms without them.
- ☐ That heroin and cocaine are really addictive drugs.
- ☐ That performance-enhancing drugs are drugs that can improve a person's performance in sport.
- ☐ That anabolic steroids increase muscle growth and stimulants increase heart rate and how these can make a person better at sport.
- ☐ That some performance-enhancing drugs are illegal, some can be prescribed legally but that all are banned by sporting bodies.
- ☐ The issues surrounding the use of performance-enhancing drugs and how to evaluate them.
- ☐ That statins reduce the risk of heart and circulatory diseases and how to evaluate data on them.
- ☐ How to evaluate claims about prescribed and non-prescribed drugs.

Testing Medicinal Drugs

- ☐ That scientists are developing new drugs all the time, which have to be tested before use.
- ☐ That new medicinal drugs are first tested in the laboratory on human cells, tissues and animals.
- ☐ That drugs have to be tested to make sure they work, are safe and that the best dosage is known.
- ☐ That after lab testing, drugs are tested in clinical trials on healthy volunteers at low doses. They're then tested on ill volunteers to find the optimum dose of a drug (the dose the drug works best at).
- ☐ What a placebo is (a substance that's similar to the drug being tested but that doesn't do anything) and why they are used in clinical trials (to make sure the drug works).
- ☐ That in a double-blind trial neither the doctors nor the volunteers know which volunteers have been given the drug and who has been given the placebo.
- ☐ That the drug thalidomide was made for use as a sleeping pill. However, it was also used to relieve morning sickness in pregnant women without being tested for that use. As a result the drug caused abnormal limb development in many babies and even death. The drug was banned and now drug testing is much more thorough. Thalidomide is now used to treat leprosy and some cancers.

Recreational Drugs

- ☐ That heroin, ecstasy and cannabis are all illegal recreational drugs which can cause heart and circulatory system problems, and that cannabis may increase the risk of developing mental health problems in some people.
- ☐ That people use illegal recreational drugs for many reasons.
- ☐ The main opinions on why some people who use cannabis (a soft drug) may progress to using hard drugs.
- ☐ That nicotine and alcohol are legal recreational drugs and can cause many health problems.
- ☐ That legal drugs have a greater impact on people and society because far more people use them.

Exam-style Questions

1   Heroin is an illegal recreational drug.

1 (a)   Which of the following are also illegal drugs? Tick **two** boxes.

            Cannabis   ☐

            Nicotine   ☐

            Statins   ☐

            Ecstasy   ☐

(2 marks)

            Alcohol is a legal recreational drug.

1 (b) (i) Long-term, heavy drinkers of alcohol can feel nervous, depressed or irritable if they suddenly stop drinking. They may also be sick or sweat a lot.

            What are these symptoms and why do they occur?

(2 marks)

    (ii) Excessive drinking of alcohol can lead to liver disease and brain damage. Suggest **one** negative effect this may have on society.

(1 mark)

2   The drug thalidomide was developed in the 1950s.

2 (a)   What type of drug was thalidomide developed as?

(1 mark)

            Thalidomide was given to pregnant women to stop morning sickness.

2 (b) (i) Describe the effect this had on the women's babies and explain why this effect was not already known.

(2 marks)

2 (b) (ii) Describe the consequences your answer to part **(b) (i)** had on the use of thalidomide and the future of drug testing.

(2 marks)

3   *In this question you will be assessed on the quality of your English, the organisation of your ideas and your use of appropriate specialist vocabulary.*

            Scientists are developing new drugs all the time. Before the public can use these drugs they have to be thoroughly tested in the laboratory and in clinical trials.

            Describe the process of testing a new medicinal drug, both in the laboratory and in clinical trials, and explain why the different testing procedures must be carried out.

(6 marks)

4   A study was done to find out if taking aspirin will reduce the risk of colorectal cancer in people who already have an increased risk of developing the disease (due to genetic factors).

Patients in the study were randomly put into two groups — a treatment group and a control group. The treatment group were given a 600 mg aspirin tablet per day. The control group were given a placebo.

4 (a) (i)   Suggest what was used as a placebo in this study.

(1 mark)

4 (a) (ii)   Explain why a placebo was included in this trial.

(1 mark)

The graph shows some of the results from the study:

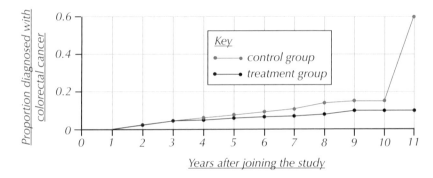

4 (b)   How do the results from the control group compare to those from the treatment group? Use data from the graph to support your answer.

(3 marks)

Not everyone who took part in the trial continued to take the tablets they were given for the same length of time. The scientists behind the study decided to see what sort of effect this had on the likelihood of the participants developing cancer.

To do this, they split data from the treatment group and the control group into two further groups. The scientists then looked at the risk of developing cancer for each new group. The results are shown in the table:

	Treatment group		Control group	
	Aspirin taken daily for 2 years or more	Aspirin taken daily for less than 2 years	Placebo taken daily for 2 years or more	Placebo taken daily for less than 2 years
Risk of developing colorectal cancer (incidence rate per 100 person-years).	0.06	0.13	0.14	0.10

4 (c)   A newspaper headline reported the study and wrote:
'An aspirin a day will halve your risk of cancer'.

Give **three** reasons why this headline is inaccurate.

(3 marks)

Learning Objectives:
- Know what an adaptation is.
- Understand how animals can be adapted to live in desert or arctic conditions, including the effect of surface area, insulation, body fat and camouflage.
- Understand how plants can be adapted to live in desert conditions, including the effect of surface area, water storage tissues and extensive roots.
- Know that some plants and animals have adaptations to help deter predators.
- Understand what is meant by the term 'extremophile'.
- Be able to identify adaptations in organisms and understand how they help the organism to survive.
- Understand that plants and animals need resources from their environment to survive and reproduce, and that they compete for these resources.

Specification Reference
B1.4.1

1. Adaptations and Competition

Organisms survive in many different environments because they are adapted to them and can compete for resources.

Animal adaptations

Adaptations are characteristics which increase an organism's chance of survival in the environment in which it lives. Animals that live in different environments have different adaptations.

Desert animals

The desert is a very hot and dry environment. Desert animals need to be able to save water and keep cool. Desert animals are adapted to their environment in the following ways:

- They have a large surface area compared to volume. This lets them lose more body heat, which helps to stop them overheating.

> **Example**
>
> The fennec fox has very large ears. This is an adaptation which increases its surface area and helps it to lose heat in its desert environment.
>
>
>
> **Figure 1:** A fennec fox.

- They are efficient with water — they lose less water by producing small amounts of concentrated urine and they also make very little sweat.

- They have thin layers of body fat and thin insulating coats — these adaptations help them to lose body heat.

- They have a sandy colour to give good camouflage — this helps them to avoid predators, or sneak up on prey.

> **Example**
>
> A camel is adapted to survive in desert conditions:
>
> Camels are able to tolerate large changes in temperature, so they don't sweat much.
>
>
>
> Camels keep all their fat in their humps to help them lose heat from the rest of their body.
>
> Light-brown colour for camouflage.

Arctic animals

The Arctic is a very cold environment. Arctic animals need to be able to reduce their heat loss. Arctic animals are adapted to their environment in the following ways:

- They have a small surface area compared to volume — they have a compact (rounded) shape to keep their surface area to a minimum, which reduces heat loss.

- They are well insulated — they have a thick layer of blubber (body fat) for insulation, which also acts as an energy store when food is scarce. They also have thick hairy coats to keep body heat in, and greasy fur which sheds water (this prevents cooling due to evaporation).

- They have white fur for good camouflage — this helps them to avoid predators, or sneak up on prey.

Tip: Generally, animals with a larger body mass will have a small surface area compared to volume and vice versa. This is why animals with larger body masses (e.g. polar bears) are found in cold environments.

Example

A polar bear is adapted to survive in arctic conditions. It has a rounded shape, which gives it a small surface area to volume ratio. It has a thick layer of blubber and a thick hairy coat for insulation. A polar bear also has white fur, for camouflage against the snowy conditions.

Figure 2: *Polar bears are adapted for their arctic environment.*

Plant adaptations

Plants also have adaptations to help them survive in their environment.

Desert plants

Desert plants have adapted to having little water in the following ways:

- They have a small surface area compared to volume. Plants lose water vapour from the surface of their leaves, so some desert plants have spines or smaller leaves to reduce water loss (by reducing the surface area). The total surface area of some desert plants is about 1000 times smaller than normal plants, which also reduces water loss.

- They have water storage tissues — this means they can save water for use during very dry periods.

- They maximise water absorption — some desert plants have shallow but extensive roots to absorb water quickly over a large area. Others have deep roots to access underground water.

Figure 3: *The spines on a desert plant help to reduce water loss.*

Example

A cactus is adapted to survive in desert conditions. It has:

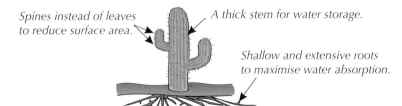

Spines instead of leaves to reduce surface area.

A thick stem for water storage.

Shallow and extensive roots to maximise water absorption.

Adaptations to deter predators

Some plants and animals have adaptations to help protect them against being eaten by other organisms.

Figure 4: The aquatic coral snake has vibrant colours, warning predators that it is poisonous and shouldn't be eaten.

> ## Examples
>
> - Some plants and animals have thorns (like roses) or sharp spines (like cacti and porcupines), which can hurt organisms that try to eat them.
>
> - Some produce poisons — like poison ivy and some tropical tree frogs. Tree frog poison can make a predator ill or even kill them. Predators soon learn to avoid eating similar organisms.
>
> - Some have amazing warning colours to signal to predators that they are dangerous — like wasps and aquatic coral snakes (see Figure 4).

Adaptations in microorganisms

Microorganisms have a huge variety of adaptations so that they can live in a wide range of environments. For example, some microorganisms (e.g. bacteria) are known as **extremophiles** — they're adapted to live in seriously extreme conditions like super hot volcanic vents, in very salty lakes or at high pressure on the sea bed.

Tip: A hydrothermal vent is an opening in the sea bed which sends out extremely hot water.

> ## Example
>
> *Thermococcus litoralis* is an extremophile. It's a bacterium that's found in deep sea hydrothermal vents. It's adapted to survive and reproduce at temperatures between 85 and 88 °C, which is much higher than most bacteria can tolerate.

Identifying and explaining adaptations

In the exam you might be given information about any organism and its environment and be asked to identify or explain its adaptations. Here's an example to show you how to do it...

Exam Tip
In the exam you could be asked to identify an animal's adaptations from explanations given. Therefore you need to think about what body features it needs. For example, if you're told that an adaptation helps an animal keep its balance when hopping then it will probably need to have a tail.

> ## Example
>
> **The Weddell seal lives in cold antarctic conditions and hunts fish in water covered by ice. Use this information and the diagram, to explain how the seal is adapted to live in the antarctic.**
>
>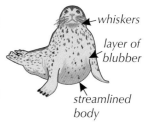
>
> *whiskers*
> *layer of blubber*
> *streamlined body*
>
> You need to look at the adaptations labelled on the diagram and think about how they allow the seal to keep warm and hunt fish, for example:
>
> - Its whiskers help it to detect fish in the dark conditions under water.
>
> - Its layer of blubber helps insulate it in the cold water.
>
> - Its streamlined body helps reduce resistance from the water, so it can swim fast to catch fish.

Competition

Organisms need things from their environment and from other organisms in order to survive and reproduce. Plants need light, space, water and minerals (nutrients) from the soil to survive. Animals need space (territory), food, water and mates to be able to survive and reproduce. Organisms compete with other species (and members of their own species) for the same resources.

Tip: Organisms that are better adapted to their environment are better at competing for resources and will be more likely to survive than those that aren't as well adapted.

Examples

- Red and grey squirrels live in the same habitat and eat the same food. Competition with the grey squirrels for these resources means there's not enough food for the reds — so the population of red squirrels is decreasing.

- Weeds compete with crop plants for light and nutrients. Farmers use weedkillers to kill weeds so there is less competition and the crops get all the light and nutrients, which enables them to grow better.

Figure 5: *The population size of red squirrels in Britain is decreasing due to increased competition from grey squirrels.*

Practice Questions — Fact Recall

Q1 What is an adaptation?

Q2 How does having water storage tissues help a desert plant to survive?

Q3 Give two examples of adaptations that would help an organism to deter predators.

Q4 a) What is an extremophile?

 b) Give two examples of the type of conditions in which you might find an extremophile.

Q5 What resources do plants compete for?

Q6 What resources do animals compete for?

Practice Question — Application

Q1 The table below gives descriptions of two different species of animal.

Species	Description
Equus assinus	Long ears, short fur and a grey or brown colour.
Alopex lagopus	Short ears and muzzle and a thick, white coat.

For each species, say whether you think they live in arctic or desert conditions. Explain your choices.

Tip: The muzzle is the mouth and nose area of an animal.

- Understand that changes in the environment are caused by living and non-living factors.
- Understand how changes in the environment can affect organisms.
- Be able to evaluate data showing the effect of environmental changes on organisms.

Specification Reference B1.4.2

Tip: A change could be an increase or a decrease.

Tip: A population is all the organisms of one species living in the same area.

2. Environmental Change

Changes in the environment can have a big impact on living organisms...

Causes of environmental change

The environment in which plants and animals live changes all the time. These changes are caused by living and non-living factors.

Environmental changes caused by **living factors** include things such as:

- A change in the occurrence of infectious diseases.
- A change in the number of predators.
- A change in the number of prey or the availability of food sources.
- A change in the number or types of competitors.

Environmental changes caused by **non-living factors** include things such as:

- A change in average temperature.
- A change in average rainfall.
- A change in the level of air or water pollution.

How environmental change affects organisms

Environmental changes can affect animals and plants in these three ways:

1. Population size increases

An environmental change may cause the number of organisms of a particular species living in an area to increase.

> **Example**
>
> If the number of mice increases (an environmental change), then there's more food available for owls, so more owls survive and reproduce, and their numbers increase too.

2. Population size decreases

An environmental change may also cause the number of organisms of a particular species living in an area to decrease.

> **Example**
>
> The number of bees in the US is falling rapidly. Experts aren't sure why but it could be due to a number of different environmental changes such as:
>
> - Some pesticides (chemicals that kill pests) may be having a negative effect on bees.
> - There's less food available — there aren't as many nectar-rich plants around any more.
> - There's more disease — bees are being killed by new pathogens or parasites.

Figure 1: *The population size of bees is decreasing in the US due to environmental changes.*

3. Population distribution change

The distribution of an organism is where the organism is found.
Many different environmental changes can cause the distribution of a population to change.

> **Example**
>
> The European Bee-Eater bird is a Mediterranean bird species. However, this bird is now present in parts of Germany due to a rise in the average temperature there.

Tip: Average temperatures are usually warmer in the Mediterranean than in Germany.

Practice Questions — Fact Recall

Q1 Give three examples of environmental changes caused by living factors.

Q2 Give three examples of environmental changes caused by non-living factors.

Practice Questions — Application

Q1 An environmental study was done on a lake over a number of years. Over the course of the study the pH of the lake gradually decreased due to the effect of acid rain. Mayfly cannot survive in water with a low pH, whereas frogs which prey on mayfly can.

   a) The population size of mayfly changed during the study.

     i) Suggest how the population size changed.

     ii) Was this change due to a living or non-living factor?

   b) The population size of the frogs also changed during the study. Suggest how and why the population size changed.

Q2 The graph shows the extent of arctic sea ice measured every December between 1995 and 2012.

   a) Calculate the percentage change in the extent of sea ice between 1995 and 2012.

   b) Suggest what has caused the change and say whether this is a living or non-living factor.

   c) Polar bears depend on sea ice for survival. Suggest how the change in the extent of sea ice has affected the polar bear population.

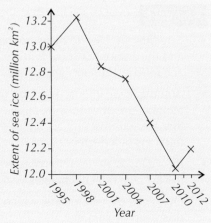

Learning Objectives:
- Understand that lichens are living indicators and how they can be used to monitor air pollution.
- Understand that some invertebrate animals are living indicators and how they can be used to monitor water pollution.
- Understand that non-living indicators can be used to measure environmental changes such as temperature, rainfall and dissolved oxygen concentration.

Specification Reference
B1.4.2

Tip: An invertebrate animal is just an animal that does not have a backbone.

3. Measuring Environmental Change

Scientists can get some idea of how much our environment is changing using living and non-living indicators.

Living indicators

Some organisms are very sensitive to changes in their environment and so can be studied to see the effect of environmental change — these organisms are known as **living indicators**. They can be used to monitor pollution.

Air pollution

Air pollution can be monitored by looking at particular types of **lichen** that are very sensitive to the concentration of sulfur dioxide in the atmosphere (and so can give a good idea about the level of pollution from car exhausts, power stations, etc.). The number and type of lichen at a particular location will indicate how clean the air is (e.g. the air is clean if there are lots of lichen).

Water pollution

If raw sewage is released into a river, the bacterial population in the water increases and uses up the oxygen. Some **invertebrate animals**, like mayfly larvae, are good indicators for water pollution because they're very sensitive to the concentration of dissolved oxygen in the water. If you find mayfly larvae in a river, it indicates that the water is clean.

Other invertebrate species have adapted to live in polluted conditions — so if you see a lot of them you know there's a problem. For example, rat-tailed maggots and sludgeworms indicate a very high level of water pollution.

Non-living indicators

A non-living indicator is something that is not alive, but can be measured or monitored to give information about environmental change, e.g. temperature. Scientists use different methods and equipment to collect data about non-living indicators.

> **Examples**
>
> - Satellites are used to measure the temperature of the sea surface and the amount of snow and ice cover. These are modern, accurate instruments and give us a global coverage.
> - Automatic weather stations are used to tell us the atmospheric temperature at various locations. These contain thermometers that are sensitive and accurate — they can measure to very small fractions of a degree.
> - Rain gauges are used to measure rainfall, to find out how much the average rainfall changes year on year.
> - Dissolved oxygen meters, which measure the concentration of dissolved oxygen in water, are used to discover how the level of water pollution is changing.

Figure 1: *An automatic weather station can monitor temperature.*

Practice Questions — Fact Recall

Q1   What is a living indicator?

Q2   What gas in the atmosphere are lichen sensitive to?

Q3   What type of organisms can be used to monitor water pollution?

Q4   Give three examples of non-living indicators of environmental change.

Practice Questions — Application

Q1   Lichen grow on tree trunks. One way of investigating the amount of lichen in an area is to measure how much of a sample of tree trunks are covered in lichen (percentage cover). In an experiment, scientists recorded the percentage cover of lichen on trees outside their laboratory (0 km) and at different locations up to a distance of 100 km away. A graph produced from their results is shown below.

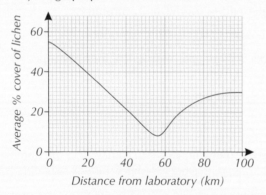

Figure 2: Lichen is commonly found growing on trees.

There is a power station somewhere within the area the scientists studied. By looking at the graph, how far from the laboratory would you expect the power station to be? Explain your answer.

Q2   The table below shows the levels of three types of invertebrate animals found in different areas of a river.

Organism	Area A	Area B	Area C
Stonefly larvae	High	Low	Low
Water louse	Low	High	Moderate
Sludgeworms	Low	High	High

Stonefly larvae can't tolerate a low concentration of dissolved oxygen in water.

a) Use the information available to explain which area of the river is the cleanest.

b) Which organism is most well adapted to live in polluted water? Explain your answer.

Exam Tip
Make sure you write concentration of dissolved oxygen in the exam — you could be throwing away marks if you write the 'amount' or 'level'.

Section Checklist — Make sure you know...

Adaptations and Competition

☐ That an adaptation is a characteristic which helps an organism to survive in its environment.

☐ That desert animals have adaptations including a large surface area compared to volume, a thin layer of body fat, a thin insulating coat and camouflage.

☐ That arctic animals have adaptations including a small surface area compared to volume, a thick layer of body fat (blubber), a thick insulating coat and camouflage.

☐ That desert plants have adaptations including a small surface area compared to volume, water storage tissues and a wide or deep root system.

☐ That some plants and animals have adaptations to deter predators, such as thorns or spines, poisons and warning colours.

☐ That an extremophile is an organism that is adapted to survive in extreme conditions (e.g. at very high temperatures, in very high salt levels or at high pressure).

☐ How to identify adaptations of a given organism and explain how the adaptations help the organism to survive in its environment, e.g. help it to find food.

☐ That plants need light, space, water and nutrients to survive and reproduce.

☐ That animals need space, food, water and mates to survive and reproduce.

☐ That plants and animals compete with other species and members of their own species for the resources they need to survive and reproduce.

Environmental Change

☐ That environmental changes can be caused by living factors (e.g. a change in the number of competitors) and non-living factors (e.g. a change in average temperature or rainfall).

☐ That environmental changes can cause an increase or decrease in population size, or a change in the distribution of populations.

☐ How to evaluate data showing the effect of environmental changes on organisms.

Measuring Environmental Change

☐ That lichens are living indicators that can be used to monitor air pollution because they are sensitive to the concentration of sulfur dioxide in the atmosphere.

☐ That some invertebrate animals are living indicators that can be used to monitor water pollution because they are affected by the concentration of dissolved oxygen in water.

☐ That non-living indicators are not alive, but can be measured or monitored to give information about environmental change, e.g. sea surface temperature can be monitored by satellites, rainfall can be measured using rain gauges.

1. Pyramids of Biomass

Learning Objectives:
- Know what 'biomass' is.
- Understand that biomass decreases at each trophic level moving up a food chain.
- Know how to draw a pyramid of biomass.
- Know how to interpret a pyramid of biomass.

Specification Reference B1.5.1

Information about food chains can be shown on pyramid diagrams...

Food chains

A food chain shows what eats what. The first organism in a food chain is called a producer (i.e. a plant). The animal that eats the plant is called a primary consumer, and the animal that eats the primary consumer is called a secondary consumer.

Example

A food chain:

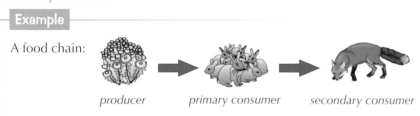

producer   primary consumer   secondary consumer

Each stage of a food chain is called a **trophic level**. There's less energy and less **biomass** (mass of living material) every time you move up a trophic level in a food chain. There are usually fewer organisms every time you move up a level too, although this isn't always true.

Tip: The reasons for there being less energy and biomass as you go up a food chain are shown on page 86.

Example

In this food chain, the number of organisms increases as you move up the chain until the last stage — there 500 fleas feed on one fox.

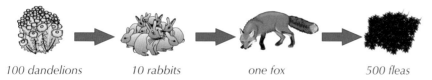

100 dandelions   10 rabbits   one fox   500 fleas

So a better way to look at the food chain is often to think about biomass instead of number of organisms. Biomass means the mass of living material.

Pyramids of biomass

Information about biomass can be used to construct a **pyramid of biomass** to represent the food chain. Each bar on a pyramid of biomass shows the mass of living material at that stage of the food chain — basically how much all the organisms at each level would "weigh" if you put them all together. The big bar along the bottom of the pyramid always represents the producer. The next bar will be the primary consumer, then the secondary consumer and so on up the food chain. Most of the biomass at each level is lost, so does not become biomass in the next level up. This is why biomass pyramids are practically always pyramid-shaped.

A pyramid of biomass of the 'fox' food chain:

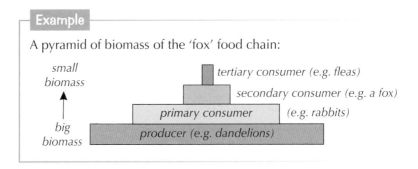

small biomass

↑

big biomass

tertiary consumer (e.g. fleas)

secondary consumer (e.g. a fox)

primary consumer (e.g. rabbits)

producer (e.g. dandelions)

Constructing a pyramid of biomass

You need to be able to construct pyramids of biomass. Luckily it's pretty simple — they'll give you all the information you need to do it in the exam.

A great tit feeds on 20 caterpillars, which in turn feed on a rose bush. Draw and label a pyramid of biomass to represent this food chain.

Here's what you need to remember when drawing a pyramid like this:

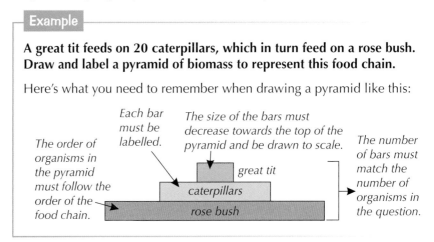

The order of organisms in the pyramid must follow the order of the food chain.

Each bar must be labelled.

The size of the bars must decrease towards the top of the pyramid and be drawn to scale.

The number of bars must match the number of organisms in the question.

great tit

caterpillars

rose bush

Interpreting a pyramid of biomass

You also need to be able to look at pyramids of biomass and explain what they show about the food chain.

Look at the pyramid of biomass below:

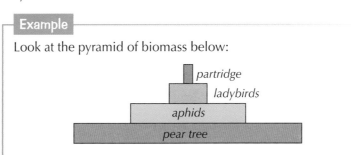

partridge

ladybirds

aphids

pear tree

Even if you know nothing about the natural world, you're probably aware that a tree is quite a bit bigger than an aphid. So what's going on here is that lots (probably thousands) of aphids are feeding on a few great big trees. Quite a lot of ladybirds are then eating the aphids, and a few partridges are eating the ladybirds.

Biomass and energy are still decreasing as you go up the levels — it's just that one tree can have a very big biomass, and can fix a lot of the Sun's energy using all those leaves.

Tip: Remember, pyramids of biomass represent food chains, so if the number of organisms in one trophic level changes (e.g. if their population size decreases), this will affect their biomass and the biomass of organisms elsewhere in the food chain.

Tip: Plants fix the Sun's energy during photosynthesis (the process by which plants make their own food).

You could also be expected to do a bit of maths, such as working out the ratio of the biomass at different levels.

Example

You might be given a pyramid of biomass like this one and be asked to work out the ratio of the biomass of ladybirds to the biomass of aphids.

So you need to count how many squares wide the ladybird and aphid bars are and then work out the ratio. Like this:

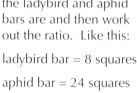

ladybird bar = 8 squares

aphid bar = 24 squares

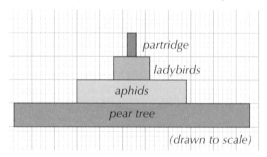

(drawn to scale)

So the ratio of the ladybirds' biomass to the aphids' biomass is 8:24, which is the same as 1:3.

Practice Questions — Fact Recall

Q1 What is biomass?

Q2 Why is a pyramid of biomass nearly always pyramid shaped?

Practice Questions — Application

Q1 Caterpillars feed on cabbage plants.
Small birds eat the caterpillars and a bigger bird eats the small birds.
Draw and label a pyramid of biomass to represent this food chain.

Q2 Look at this pyramid of biomass.

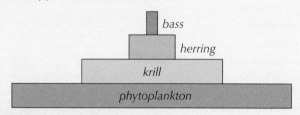

a) Which organism is the producer?

b) Which organism has the smallest biomass?

c) Why is the bar representing the herring smaller than the bar representing the krill?

- Understand that the source of energy for most food chains is the Sun.
- Understand how green plants and algae absorb light energy and convert it to chemical energy.
- Know that this chemical energy is stored in the cells of plants and algae.
- Understand the ways in which biomass and energy are lost at each stage of a food chain.

Specification Reference B1.5.1

2. Energy Transfer in Food Chains

Energy is transferred along a food chain, but lots is lost along the way...

How does energy get into a food chain?

Energy from the Sun is the source of energy for nearly all life on Earth. Green plants and algae use a small percentage of the light energy from the Sun to convert carbon dioxide (from the air) and water (from the soil) into chemical energy (food) during **photosynthesis**. This energy's stored in the substances which make up the cells of plants and algae (biomass), and then works its way through the food chain as animals eat them and each other (see Figure 1).

Light energy from the sun...   *... is absorbed and converted to chemical energy in photosynthesis...*   *... which is then eaten...*   *... and passed along the food chain.*

Figure 1: *Light energy from the Sun is the source of all energy in a food chain.*

Tip: Most of the light energy from the Sun is not transferred to chemical energy in plants. There are a few reasons for this, e.g. some of it isn't absorbed by the leaf and some of it is the wrong wavelength to be used in photosynthesis.

Biomass and energy loss in food chains

Both biomass and energy are lost at each stage of the food chain. Biomass and energy are lost for a number of different reasons:

Respiration

Every organism in the food chain respires. Respiration supplies the energy for all life processes, including movement. Most of the energy released by respiration is eventually lost to the surroundings as heat. This is especially true for mammals and birds, whose bodies must be kept at a constant temperature which is normally higher than their surroundings.

Tip: Think of all the food (energy) you've eaten in your life. If someone ate you they wouldn't get all that energy — most of it will have been used up just keeping you alive or has passed out of your body as waste products.

Uneaten material

Some of the material which makes up plants and animals is inedible (e.g. bone), so it doesn't pass to the next stage of the food chain. Also some organisms die before they're eaten, so their remains are left to decay and their energy doesn't get passed along the food chain (instead the energy gets passed to the microorganisms that break down the remains).

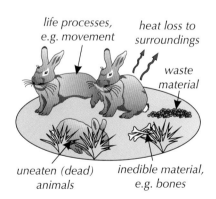

life processes, e.g. movement   *heat loss to surroundings*   *waste material*   *uneaten (dead) animals*   *inedible material, e.g. bones*

Figure 2: *Ways that biomass and energy are lost at each stage in a food chain.*

Tip: There's more on microorganisms and decay on page 88.

Waste products

Material and energy are also lost from the food chain in the organisms' waste materials, such as faeces (poo) and urine, which are generally not eaten — see Figure 2.

Length of food chains

The loss of energy at each stage of a food chain explains why you hardly ever get food chains with more than about five trophic levels. So much energy is lost at each stage that there's not enough left to support more organisms after four or five stages.

Practice Questions — Fact Recall

Q1　What sort of energy is at the start of nearly all food chains?

Q2　What sort of energy is stored in the cells of green plants and algae?

Q3　Explain how energy from the Sun gets passed along a food chain.

Q4　True or False? Energy is only lost between the first and second trophic levels of a food chain.

Practice Question — Application

Q1　In a food chain, duckweed is eaten by ducks, which are then eaten by a fox. Explain why not all of the energy the ducks get from the duckweed is passed on to the fox.

Section Checklist — Make sure you know...

Pyramids of Biomass

☐ That biomass is the mass of living material.

☐ That as you move up a food chain, there's less biomass at each level.

☐ That to draw a pyramid of biomass you need to draw a separate bar for each trophic level of a food chain, the size of the bars needs to decrease towards the top of the pyramid and be drawn to scale, the order of the bars must match the order in the food chain and all the bars must be labelled.

☐ How to interpret a pyramid of biomass, e.g. use one to explain what is happening in a food chain.

Energy Transfer in Food Chains

☐ That the source of energy at the start of most food chains is light energy from the Sun.

☐ That green plants and algae absorb some of the Sun's light energy and convert it into chemical energy when they photosynthesise.

☐ That green plants and algae store chemical energy from photosynthesis in their cells, and this is passed along a food chain when animals eat the plants and algae.

☐ That biomass and energy are lost at each stage of a food chain. This is because organisms respire and the energy released from respiration is used to fuel life processes or lost as heat. Also some of the organisms' material is not eaten (e.g. bones are inedible and some organisms die before being eaten) and some energy is lost in waste products (e.g. faeces and urine).

Learning Objectives:

- Know that living organisms take in materials from their environment and use them for life processes.

- Understand how the materials that an organism takes in are returned to the environment.

- Know that microorganisms decay material.

- Know the conditions in which microorganisms work best to decay material.

- Know that the decay process releases materials back into the soil which plants can reuse.

- Know what is meant by the term, 'stable community'.

- Be able to evaluate schemes that recycle kitchen and garden waste.

Specification Reference
B1.6.1

1. Decay

The process of decay is essential for keeping nature's cycle of nutrients going...

The cycle of elements

Living things are made of materials they take from the world around them. They need to take in materials for growth and other life processes. Plants take elements like carbon, oxygen, hydrogen and nitrogen from the soil or the air. They turn these elements into the complex compounds (carbohydrates, proteins and fats) that make up living organisms, and these compounds then pass through the food chain.

These elements are returned to the environment in waste products produced by the organisms, or when the organisms die. These materials decay because they're broken down (digested) by microorganisms — that's how the elements get put back into the soil.

Microorganisms work best in warm, moist conditions (and slower in cold or dry conditions). Many microorganisms also break down material faster when there's plenty of oxygen available for respiration. Respiration produces heat, which increases the temperature of their environment further.

All the important elements are thus recycled — they return to the soil, ready to be used by new plants and put back into the food chain again. In a **stable community** the materials taken out of the soil and used are balanced by those that are put back in. There's a constant cycle happening.

Compost

Kitchen waste (e.g. food peelings) and garden waste (e.g. dead leaves) can be made into compost. Compost is decayed remains of animal and plant matter that can be used as fertiliser. It recycles nutrients back into the soil — giving you a lovely garden.

Compost bins recreate the ideal conditions for decay — see Figure 1. Compost bins come in many shapes and sizes. There are also council recycling schemes that collect kitchen and garden waste and do the composting for you.

Extra decomposers added (compost maker)

Finely shredded waste is best

Warmth generated by microorganisms helps it all along

Mesh sides to let air in

Figure 1: *A compost bin provides the right conditions for microorganisms to work.*

Tip: Some compost bins can be rotated so that the microorganisms get more oxygen. This means they'll respire more (which means they'll work faster).

Council-run composting schemes can be beneficial as they help to reduce the amount of space taken up by landfill sites. They can also make money for the council by producing compost, which can then be sold.

Tip: 'Landfill site' is just the posh term for a rubbish dump or tip.

Practice Questions — Fact Recall

Q1   Why do living organisms take in materials from their environment?

Q2   Elements are returned to the environment when an organism dies.

   a) Describe how this happens.

   b) Give one other way in which elements are returned to the environment.

Q3   Describe the conditions in which microorganisms are most active.

Q4   What is a stable community?

Q5   Compost is the decayed remains of animal and plant matter. Why is compost used on gardens?

Practice Question — Application

Gary recycles his garden waste by making it into compost. He does this in his garden using this compost bin:

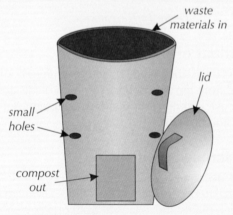

Figure 2: Compost bins can come in lots of different shapes and sizes.

Q1   Suggest why the compost bin has small holes in it.

Q2   Gary has found that compost is made more quickly if he puts his compost bin in a sunny area of the garden. Explain why this is.

Q3   Gary's neighbour told him that he should always keep the lid on his compost bin to stop water vapour escaping out of the bin. Explain how the presence of water vapour would help compost to be made.

- Know what is meant by 'the carbon cycle'.
- Understand that carbon dioxide is removed from the atmosphere by photosynthesis and the carbon is used to make carbon compounds.
- Understand how carbon is passed along food chains.
- Understand the role of detritus feeders and microorganisms in decay.
- Understand how carbon is returned to the atmosphere as carbon dioxide by respiration.
- Understand how carbon is returned to the atmosphere as carbon dioxide by combustion.

Specification Reference B1.6.2

2. The Carbon Cycle

Carbon is one of the elements in our environment that is constantly being recycled...

What is the carbon cycle?

Carbon is constantly being cycled — from the air, through food chains and eventually back out into the air again. The carbon cycle shows how carbon is recycled — see Figure 1.

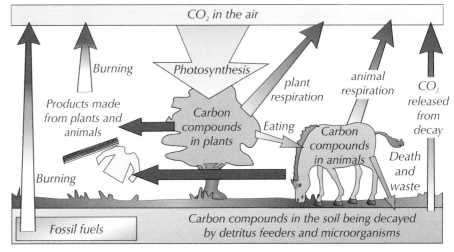

Figure 1: The carbon cycle.

Carbon is taken out of the air

The whole carbon cycle is "powered" by **photosynthesis**. CO_2 (carbon dioxide) is removed from the atmosphere by green plants and algae, and the carbon is used to make carbon compounds in the plants and algae, such as carbohydrates, fats and proteins.

Carbon moves through food chains

Some of the carbon becomes part of the fats and proteins in animals when the plants and algae are eaten. The carbon then moves through the food chain. The energy that green plants and algae get from photosynthesis is transferred up the food chain.

When plants, algae and animals die, other animals (called **detritus feeders**) and microorganisms feed on their remains. Animals also produce waste, and this too is broken down by detritus feeders and microorganisms. Compounds in the waste are taken up from the soil by plants as nutrients — they're put back into the food chain again.

Figure 2: Woodlice are detritus feeders.

Tip: Fossil fuels are made of decayed plant and animal matter.

Carbon is returned to the air

Some carbon is returned to the atmosphere as CO_2 when the plants, algae, animals (including detritus feeders) and microorganisms **respire**. Also CO_2 is released back into the air when some useful plant and animal products, e.g. wood and fossil fuels, are burnt (**combustion**).

Q1   What process removes carbon dioxide from the atmosphere?

Q2   What do plants use carbon for?

Q3   What happens to the carbon in green plants when the plants are eaten by animals?

Q4   How do detritus feeders put carbon back into the atmosphere?

Q5   How does the carbon contained within fossil fuels get back into the atmosphere?

Section Checklist — Make sure you know...

Decay

☐ That living things take the materials they need (e.g. carbon and nitrogen) from the environment and use them for growth and other life processes.

☐ That these materials are returned to the environment in the organism's waste products or when the organism dies.

☐ That when an organism dies, its remains are broken down by microorganisms and the elements it contains are returned to the soil where they can be used by new plants.

☐ That microorganisms are most active in warm, moist conditions with a good oxygen supply.

☐ That a stable community is one in which the materials taken out of the soil and used are balanced by those that are put back in — there's a constant cycle of materials.

☐ How to evaluate schemes for recycling kitchen and garden waste.

The Carbon Cycle

☐ That the carbon cycle shows how carbon is constantly recycled (from the air, through food chains, and back into the air again).

☐ That carbon is removed from the air as carbon dioxide when green plants and algae photosynthesise.

☐ That green plants and algae use the carbon in carbon dioxide to make carbohydrates, fats and proteins.

☐ That carbon is passed along the food chain when animals eat other organisms and in this way the energy that green plants and algae get from photosynthesis is transferred up the food chain.

☐ That animals use carbon to make fats and proteins in their body.

☐ That detritus feeders and microorganisms break down dead organisms and animal waste, which puts compounds back into the soil that can be taken up by plants as nutrients.

☐ That when green plants, algae, animals (including detritus feeders) and microorganisms respire, carbon dioxide is put back into the air.

☐ That the burning (combustion) of products made from plants and animals (e.g. wood) and fossil fuels puts carbon dioxide back into the air.

Exam-style Questions

1   The diagram below shows how a particular food chain is part of the carbon cycle.

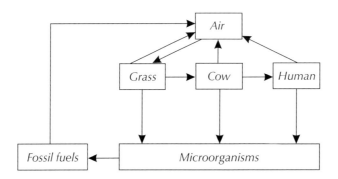

*In this question you will be assessed on the quality of your English,
the organisation of your ideas and your use of appropriate specialist vocabulary.*

Use the information in the diagram and your own knowledge to describe
the processes in which carbon is cycled between this food chain, other living
organisms and the air.

(6 marks)

2   Below is a pyramid of biomass.
It represents a food chain involving algae, fish and birds.

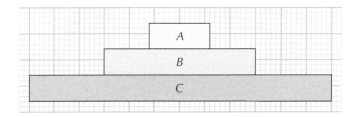

2 (a)   Explain why the Sun is needed at the start of all food chains.

(4 marks)

2 (b)   Which bar on the pyramid (A-C) represents the algae? Explain your answer.

(1 mark)

2 (c) (i)   The ratio of bar C to bar B is 2:1.
Calculate the ratio of bar B to bar A.

(2 marks)

2 (c) (ii)   Neither of the ratios in part (c) (i) are 1:1 because biomass is lost
as you go up a food chain. Explain how biomass is lost from a food chain.

(3 marks)

3 Scientists have been studying a species of wolf. The wolf lives in rocky mountains where the temperature at night can drop as low as –15°C. Its main source of prey is rodents that live in burrows beneath the ground. The wolf has adaptations to help it survive in the rocky mountains as shown on the diagram below.

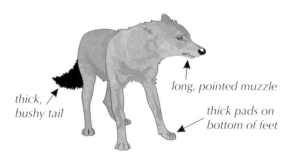

thick,
bushy tail

long, pointed muzzle

thick pads on
bottom of feet

3 (a) (i) What is an adaptation?

(1 mark)

3 (a) (ii) Use the information and the diagram above to suggest how the wolf is
adapted to survive in the rocky mountains.

(3 marks)

3 (b) Scientists have been recording the total population size of the wolf over a number of
years. Their findings and some other data are shown in the table and graph below.

Year	Total population size of wolf	Total population size of one type of prey (million)	Rabies outbreak in this year
2007	401	1.96	No
2008	327	2.01	Yes
2009	330	2.09	No
2010	341	2.06	No
2011	265	2.01	Yes
2012	269	1.99	No

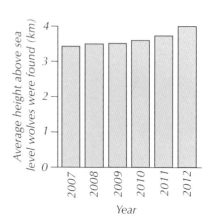

3 (b) (i) Describe the overall trend in the total population size of the wolf species studied.

(1 mark)

3 (b) (ii) Suggest the environmental change that's responsible for this trend.
Use data from the table to support your answer.

(3 marks)

3 (b) (iii) Since 2007, the land higher than 3.5 km above sea level has gradually
been taken over as farmland. Use data from the graph to suggest how this
has affected the distribution of the wolf population.

(2 marks)

Learning Objectives:

- Understand why plants and animals have characteristics which are similar to their parents.
- Understand that differences between organisms can be due to their genes, their environment or both.

Specification Reference B1.7.1

1. Variation

These pages are all about the differences between you, me, and well... everyone else really. It's fascinating stuff...

What is variation?

Different species look... well... different — my dog definitely doesn't look like a daisy. But even organisms of the same species will usually look at least slightly different — e.g. in a room full of people you'll see different colour hair, individually shaped noses, a variety of heights, etc.

These differences are called the variation within a species — and there are two types of variation: **genetic variation** and **environmental variation**.

Genetic variation

All plants and animals have characteristics that are in some ways similar to their parents' (e.g. I've got my dad's nose, apparently). This is because an organism's characteristics are determined by the **genes** inherited from their parents. Genes are the codes inside your cells that control how you're made (there's more about genes on page 97). These genes are passed on in **sex cells** (**gametes**), which the offspring develop from (see page 98).

Most animals (and quite a lot of plants) get some genes from the mother and some from the father. This combining of genes from two parents causes genetic variation — no two of the species are genetically identical (other than identical twins).

Some characteristics are determined only by genes.

Figure 1: *Identical twins have exactly the same genes, which is why they look so alike.*

> **Examples**
>
> - Violet flower colour.
> - Eye colour, blood group and inherited disorders (e.g. haemophilia or cystic fibrosis) in animals.

Environmental variation

The environment that organisms live and grow in also causes differences between members of the same species — this is called environmental variation.

Environmental variation covers a wide range of differences — from losing your toes in a piranha attack, to getting a suntan, to having yellow leaves and so on. Basically, any difference that has been caused by the conditions something lives in, is an environmental variation.

Example

A plant grown on a nice sunny windowsill would grow luscious and green.

The same plant grown in darkness would grow tall and spindly and its leaves would turn yellow — these are environmental variations.

Tip: Plants are strongly influenced by environmental factors, e.g. sunlight, moisture level, temperature and soil mineral content.

Genetic and environmental variation

Most characteristics are determined by a mixture of genetic and environmental factors.

Examples

- Height — the maximum height that an animal or plant could grow to is determined by its genes. But whether it actually grows that tall depends on its environment, e.g. how much food it gets.

- Intelligence — one theory is that although your maximum possible IQ might be determined by your genes, whether or not you get to it depends on your environment, e.g. your upbringing and school life.

- Health — some people are more likely to get certain diseases (such as cancer or heart disease) because of their genes. But lifestyle also affects the risk, e.g. whether you smoke or how much junk food you eat.

Tip: Environmental factors aren't just the physical things around you. They can include things like the way you were brought up too.

Practice Questions — Application

Q1 Your sporting ability may be affected by your genes and your environment. Suggest one environmental factor that may affect your sporting ability.

Q2 Identical twins have exactly the same genes. Non-identical twins don't. Studies have shown that:

- identical twins tend to have more similar IQs than non-identical twins (Study 1).

- identical twins who are brought up together tend to have more similar IQs than identical twins who are brought up separately (Study 2).

What do the results of Studies 1 and 2 suggest about the influence of genes and the environment on IQ? Explain your answer.

- Know that chromosomes are found in the cell nucleus.
- Know that chromosomes carry genes.
- Understand that genes control an organism's characteristics.

Specification Reference B1.7.1

2. Genes, Chromosomes and DNA

Well, this is it. Probably the most important topic in the whole of biology — genes. It's certainly one of the most important topics in this section, so make sure you've got your head around it before you move on.

The cell nucleus

Most cells in your body have a structure called a **nucleus**. The nucleus contains your genetic material (the instructions you need to grow and develop). This material is stored in the form of chromosomes — see Figure 1.

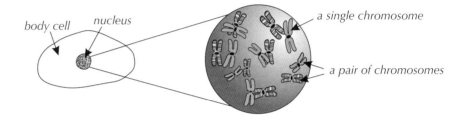

Figure 1: *Diagram to show that a cell nucleus contains chromosomes.*

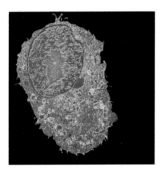

Figure 2: *A human cell (blue) and its nucleus (orange and green), seen under a microscope.*

In mammals, chromosomes come in pairs. The human cell nucleus contains 23 pairs of chromosomes. There are two No. 19 chromosomes, two No. 12s, two No. 3s, etc.

Chromosomes and DNA

Chromosomes are long lengths of a molecule called **DNA**. The DNA is coiled up to form the arms of the chromosome (see Figure 4).

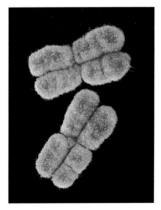

Figure 3: *A pair of human chromosomes seen under a microscope. (In fact, it's pair No. 3.)*

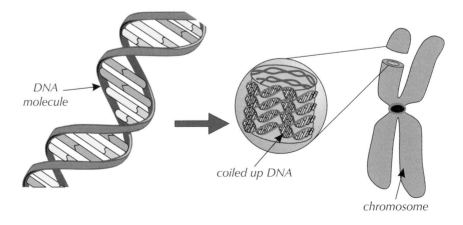

Figure 4: *Diagram to show how DNA coils up to form a chromosome.*

Chromosomes and genes

Chromosomes carry genes (see Figure 5). These are short sections of DNA. Genes control our characteristics. Different genes control the development of different characteristics, e.g. hair colour, eye colour.

Tip: A chromosome contains thousands of genes, not just one. This diagram is just to help show you what's going on.

gene for brown hair colour

gene for green eye colour

brown hair colour

green eye colour

Figure 5: *Diagram showing relationship between chromosomes, genes and characteristics.*

There can be different versions of the same gene, which give different versions of a characteristic, like blue or brown eyes. The different versions of the same gene are called **alleles** instead of genes — it's more sensible than it sounds!

Tip: You might sometimes see chromosomes drawn like this:

That's because chromosomes only look like this:

just before a cell divides for reproduction and growth (see p. 99).

Practice Questions — Fact Recall

Q1 Where in the cell are chromosomes found?

Q2 a) What are genes?

b) What do we need different genes for?

Practice Questions — Application

The photograph on the right was taken under a microscope. It shows a cell, its nucleus and chromosomes.

Q1 Which arrow is pointing to:

a) the cell?

b) the nucleus?

c) a chromosome?

Q2 Suggest why it is not possible to see individual genes in this photograph.

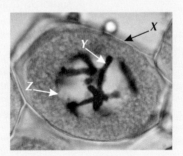

Exam Tip
Make sure you don't get genes and chromosomes mixed up in the exam if you have to label them — chromosomes are long lengths of DNA and they carry genes.

- Understand that sexual reproduction involves the fusion of gametes and creates genetic variation in the offspring.
- Understand that asexual reproduction does not involve the fusion of gametes and creates genetically identical offspring (clones).

Specification Reference B1.7.2

3. Reproduction

Organisms make more of themselves through reproduction.
There are two types: sexual and asexual. You need to know about both.

Sexual reproduction

Sexual reproduction is where genetic information from two organisms (a father and a mother) is combined to produce offspring which are genetically different to either parent.

Gametes

In sexual reproduction the mother and father produce gametes — e.g. egg and sperm cells in animals (see Figure 1). In humans, each gamete contains 23 chromosomes — half the number of chromosomes in a normal cell. (Instead of having two of each chromosome, a gamete has just one of each.)

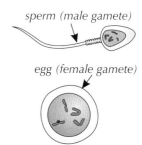

sperm (male gamete)

egg (female gamete)

Figure 1: *The sperm and egg cells.*

Fertilisation

The egg (from the mother) and the sperm cell (from the father) fuse together to form a cell with the full number of chromosomes (half from the father, half from the mother). The fusion of gametes is known as fertilisation (see Figure 3).

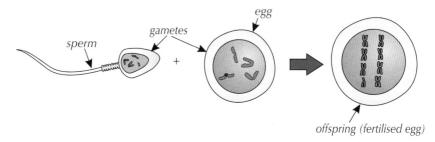

sperm   *gametes*   *egg*

offspring (fertilised egg)

Figure 3: *Diagram showing fertilisation.*

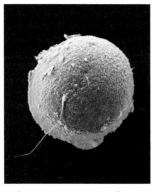

Figure 2: *A sperm (shown in blue) fertilising an egg (shown in yellow) as seen under a microscope.*

This is why the offspring inherits features from both parents — it's received a mixture of chromosomes from its mum and its dad (and it's the chromosomes that decide how you turn out). This mixture of genetic material produces variation in the offspring. Pretty cool, eh.

Here's the main thing to remember about sexual reproduction:

> Sexual reproduction involves the fusion of male and female gametes. Because there are two parents, the offspring contain a mixture of their parents' genes and are genetically different to their parents.

Exam Tip
You need to know the definition of sexual reproduction for the exam. The really important bit is that it involves the fusion of gametes.

Asexual reproduction

An ordinary cell can make a new cell by simply dividing in two. The new cell has exactly the same genetic information (i.e. genes) as the parent cell — this is known as asexual reproduction.

Here's how it works:

1. X-shaped chromosomes have two identical halves.

2. Each chromosome splits down the middle to form two identical sets of 'half chromosomes' (i.e. two sets of DNA strands). A membrane forms around each set.

3. The DNA then replicates (copies) itself to form two identical cells with complete sets of X-shaped chromosomes (ready to divide again).

This is how all plants and animals grow and produce replacement cells.

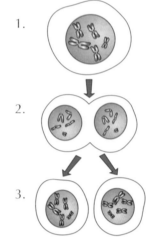

Figure 4: *Diagram showing the three main stages of asexual reproduction.*

Some organisms also produce offspring using asexual reproduction, e.g. bacteria and certain plants.

Here's the main thing to remember about asexual reproduction:

> In asexual reproduction there's only one parent. There's no fusion of gametes, no mixing of chromosomes and no genetic variation between parent and offspring. The offspring are genetically identical to the parent — they're **clones**.

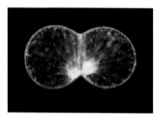

Figure 5: *A single-celled organism called a 'sea sparkle' undergoing asexual reproduction.*

Tip: There's more on clones on the next few pages.

Practice Question — Application

Q1 For each of the following examples, write down whether it's a case of sexual or asexual reproduction, and explain your answer.

a) A single-celled amoeba splits in two to form two genetically identical offspring.

b) Gametes from a male pea plant are crossed with gametes from a female pea plant to produce genetically varied offspring.

c) A lion and a tiger mate to produce an animal known as a 'liger'. The liger shares features with both its parents.

d) A single Brahminy blind snake lays a batch of unfertilised eggs. The offspring that hatch are clones of the mother snake.

Tip: To answer these questions, you need to think about the main differences between sexual and asexual reproduction — look back at the green summary boxes if you need clues.

- Know that plants can be cloned by taking cuttings — and why this is beneficial.

- Know that plants can also be cloned through tissue culture.

- Understand the process by which animals can be cloned using embryo transplants.

- Understand the process by which animals can be cloned using adult cell cloning.

- Be able to interpret information about cloning methods.

- Be able to give informed opinions on the issues surrounding cloning.

Specification Reference B1.7.2

4. Cloning

This topic is all about how humans can control reproduction. Read on...

What is cloning?

Cloning means making an exact (genetically identical) copy of an organism. It's basically just another term for asexual reproduction (see previous page). Plants which reproduce asexually are able to clone themselves naturally. Cloning can also be done artificially (by humans) — which is what the next few pages are all about.

Cloning plants

It's pretty easy to clone plants. Gardeners have been doing it for years. There are two ways of doing it:

1. Cuttings

Gardeners can take cuttings from good parent plants, and then plant them to produce genetically identical copies (clones) of the parent plant. These plants can be produced quickly and cheaply.

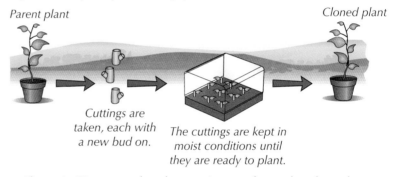

Parent plant

Cloned plant

Cuttings are taken, each with a new bud on.

The cuttings are kept in moist conditions until they are ready to plant.

Figure 1: *Diagram to show how cuttings can be used to clone plants.*

2. Tissue culture

This is a more modern method of cloning plants. A few plant cells are put in a growth medium with hormones, and they grow into new plants — clones of the parent plant. These plants can be made very quickly, in very little space, and be grown all year.

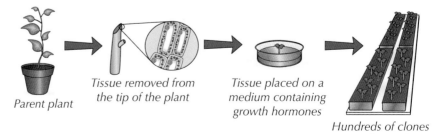

Parent plant

Tissue removed from the tip of the plant

Tissue placed on a medium containing growth hormones

Hundreds of clones can be made

Figure 2: *A tobacco plant being grown by tissue culture (top). A room full of tissue cultures (bottom).*

Figure 3: *Diagram to show how tissue culture can be used to clone plants.*

Embryo transplants

You can produce animal clones using embryo transplants. An embryo is created, then split many times in the early stages to form clones. The cloned embryos are then implanted (inserted) into host mothers to continue developing.

> **Tip:** Once an egg cell has been fertilised and starts dividing, it becomes an embryo. The embryo grows and develops into a baby.

> **Example**
>
> Farmers can use embryo transplants to produce cloned offspring from their best bull and cow:
>
> 1. Sperm cells are taken from a prize bull and egg cells are taken from a prize cow. The sperm are then used to artificially fertilise an egg cell.
>
> 2. The embryo that develops is then split many times (to form clones) before any cells become specialised.
>
> 3. These cloned embryos can then be implanted into lots of other cows...
>
> 4. ...where they grow into calves (which will all be genetically identical to each other).
>
> This is shown in Figure 4.
>
>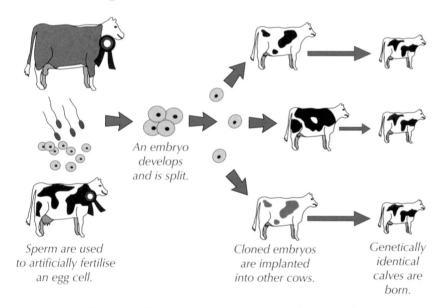
>
> *An embryo develops and is split.*
>
> *Sperm are used to artificially fertilise an egg cell.*
>
> *Cloned embryos are implanted into other cows.*
>
> *Genetically identical calves are born.*
>
> **Figure 4:** *Diagram to show how genetically identical calves can be produced through embryo transplants.*

> **Tip:** A specialised cell is one that performs a specific function, e.g. a white blood cell defends against pathogens.

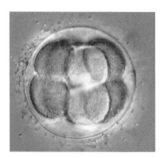

Figure 5: *An early embryo under the microscope — each ball is an individual cell. It's at this stage that the cells are separated in an embryo transplant.*

> **Tip:** The calves here are clones of each other and of the original embryo — but they're not clones of the original bull and cow. Instead, they contain a mixture of genes from both parents.

Adult cell cloning

Adult cell cloning can also be used to make animal clones. Adult cell cloning involves taking an unfertilised egg cell and removing its genetic material (the nucleus). A complete set of chromosomes from an adult body cell (e.g. a skin cell) is inserted into the 'empty' egg cell. The egg cell is then stimulated by an electric shock — this makes it divide, just like a normal embryo.

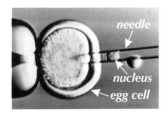

Figure 6: *A nucleus being injected into an egg cell during adult cell cloning.*

When the embryo is a ball of cells, it's implanted into the uterus (womb) of an adult female (the surrogate mother). Here the embryo grows into a genetically identical copy (clone) of the original adult body cell (see Figure 7). This technique was used to create Dolly — the famous cloned sheep.

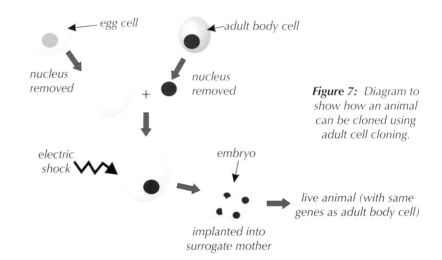

Figure 7: *Diagram to show how an animal can be cloned using adult cell cloning.*

Tip: Remember, it's only the <u>nucleus</u> from the adult body cell that gets inserted into the empty egg cell.

Figure 8: *Dolly, the world's first cloned sheep, and the scientist who made her (he's the one on the right).*

Issues surrounding cloning

There are many social, economic and ethical issues surrounding cloning — you need to know what they are for your exam.

Benefits

- Cloning quickly gets you lots of "ideal" offspring with known characteristics. This can benefit farmers, e.g. if a farmer has a cow that produces lots of milk, he could clone it and create a whole herd of cows that all produce lots of milk relatively quickly.

- The study of animal clones could lead to greater understanding of the development of the embryo, and of ageing and age-related disorders.

- Cloning could be used to help preserve endangered species.

Concerns

Tip: Alleles are different forms of a gene (see page 97).

- Cloning gives you a "reduced gene pool" — this means there are fewer different alleles in a population. If a population are all closely related and a new disease appears, they could all be wiped out — there may be no allele in the population giving resistance to the disease.

- It's possible that cloned animals might not be as healthy as normal ones, e.g. Dolly the sheep had arthritis, which tends to occur in older sheep (but the jury's still out on if this was due to cloning).

Tip: It's currently illegal to clone a human in the UK.

- Some people worry that humans might be cloned in the future. If it was allowed, any success may follow many unsuccessful attempts, e.g. children born severely disabled. Also, you'd need to consider the human rights of the clone — the clone wouldn't have a say in whether it wanted to be a clone or not, so is it fair to produce one?

Practice Questions — Fact Recall

Q1 Plants can be cloned by taking cuttings.

a) Give two benefits of taking cuttings to clone plants.

b) Give one other way of cloning plants.

Q2 Name two methods of animal cloning.

Practice Questions — Application

Read the following passage and then answer the questions that follow.

Scientists in the US have been experimenting with cloning the African black-footed cat — an animal classed as 'threatened' on endangered species lists. Their aim is to take a skin cell nucleus from an adult black-footed cat and implant it into an empty egg cell provided by a domestic cat. Once dividing, the embryo will be implanted in the domestic cat in order to develop.

Q1 Once the black-footed cat nucleus has been implanted into the egg cell of the domestic cat, how will it be stimulated to divide?

Q2 Would an embryo created by the scientists' method share any genetic material with the domestic cat? Explain your answer.

Although no black-footed kittens have yet been born as a result of this method, the US team behind the project are confident that it will help to save endangered species.

Q3 Suggest how each of the following could help to save the black-footed cat:

a) using common domestic cats as surrogate mothers rather than black-footed cats.

b) being able to take skin cells from black-footed cats that have already died as well as ones that are still alive.

Many wildlife conservationists are against using cloning to save endangered species. Some argue that the money would be better spent on conserving the places in which endangered species live.

Q4 Suggest two more concerns people may have of using cloning to save an endangered species.

Figure 9: *The African black-footed cat.*

Tip: Think about the number of domestic cats compared to how many black-footed cats there are likely to be.

5. Genetic Engineering

Tip: Remember, DNA is what makes up chromosomes (see page 96).

Humans are able to change an organism's genes through a process called genetic engineering. It's really quite clever...

What is genetic engineering?

The basic idea is to copy a useful gene from one organism's chromosome into the cells of another.

How genetic engineering works:

1. A useful gene is "cut" from one organism's chromosome using enzymes.

2. Enzymes are then used to cut another organism's chromosome and then to insert the useful gene.

Scientists use this method to do all sorts of things.

Example

The human insulin gene can be inserted into bacteria to produce human insulin:

1. The insulin gene is first cut out of human DNA using enzymes.

2. The same enzymes are then used to cut the bacterial DNA and different enzymes are used to insert the human insulin gene.

3. The bacteria are then allowed to multiply. The insulin they produce while they grow is purified and used by people with diabetes.

This is summarised in Figure 1.

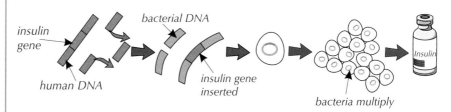

Figure 1: *Diagram showing how bacteria can be genetically engineered to produce insulin.*

Genetic engineering of plants and animals

Useful genes can be transferred into animals and plants at the very early stages of their development (i.e. shortly after fertilisation). This means they'll develop useful characteristics.

- **Genetically modified (GM) crops** are crops which have had their genes modified, e.g. to make them resistant to viruses, insects or herbicides (chemicals used to kill weeds).

- Sheep have been genetically engineered to produce substances, like drugs, in their milk that can be used to treat human diseases.

- Genetic disorders like cystic fibrosis are caused by faulty genes. Scientists are trying to treat these disorders by inserting working genes into sufferers. This is called gene therapy.

Tip: Herbicides kill weeds, but they can also end up killing crops. 'Selective herbicides' are usually used to stop this from happening, but they don't always kill all the weeds. If a crop is herbicide-resistant, more effective herbicides can be used to get rid of weeds — without risk to the crop.

The issues surrounding genetic engineering

Genetic engineering is an exciting new area in science which has the potential for solving many of our problems (e.g. treating diseases, more efficient food production etc.) but not everyone thinks it's a great idea.

There are worries about the long-term effects of genetic engineering — that changing a person's genes might accidentally create unplanned problems, which could then get passed on to future generations.

It's the same with GM crops...

The issues surrounding GM crops

HOW SCIENCE WORKS

Benefits

- On the plus side, GM crops can increase the yield of a crop, making more food. For example, insect-resistant crops shouldn't get eaten by insects so much — leaving more food for us.

- People living in developing nations often lack nutrients in their diets. GM crops could be engineered to contain the nutrient that's missing. For example, they're testing 'golden rice' that contains beta-carotene — a lack of this substance causes blindness.

Tip: 'Yield' just means the amount of product made. So the yield of a wheat field would be the amount of wheat produced. Insects eating the crop, disease, and competition with weeds all reduce crop yield.

Concerns

- Some people say that growing GM crops will affect the number of weeds and flowers (and so the population of insects) that live in and around the crops — reducing farmland biodiversity (the variety of living organisms on the farmland).

- Not everyone is convinced that GM crops are safe. People are worried they may develop allergies to the food — although there's probably no more risk for this than for eating usual foods.

- A big concern is that transplanted genes may get out into the natural environment. For example, the herbicide resistance gene may be picked up by weeds, creating a new 'superweed' variety.

Tip: GM crops are already being grown elsewhere in the world (not the UK) often without any problems.

Practice Questions — Fact Recall

Q1 In genetic engineering, useful genes are transferred into animals and plants in the early stages of their development. Explain why.

Q2 a) What does the 'GM' stand for in 'GM crop'?

b) Some GM crops are resistant to viruses. What else can they be made resistant to? Give two examples.

Practice Questions — Application

B. thuringiensis is a species of bacteria. It produces a crystal protein, which is poisonous to insects when eaten. Some crop plants, including cotton and potatoes, have been genetically engineered to produce the *Bt* crystal protein.

Q1 Explain how enzymes would be used to make a cotton plant that can produce the *Bt* crystal protein.

Q2 Suggest a benefit of genetically engineering crop plants to produce the *Bt* crystal protein. Explain your answer.

Q3 Suggest a possible risk of growing crop plants that have been genetically engineered to produce the *Bt* crystal protein.

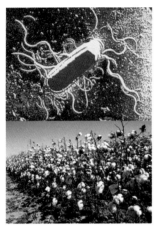

Figure 2: *A B. thuringiensis bacterium (top). GM cotton which produces the* Bt *crystal protein (bottom).*

Section Checklist — Make sure you know...

Variation

☐ That plants and animals have similar characteristics to their parents because an organism's characteristics are carried by genes, which are passed on from parents to their offspring in gametes.

☐ That differences between organisms can be determined by their genes, their environment or both.

Genes, Chromosomes and DNA

☐ That chromosomes are found in the cell nucleus and carry genes.

☐ That genes control characteristics in an organism and that different genes control different characteristics.

Reproduction

☐ That sexual reproduction involves the fusion of male and female gametes (e.g. sperm and egg cells) from two parents and creates offspring which contain a mixture of their parents' genes.

☐ That asexual reproduction involves no fusion of gametes, only one parent and no mixing of genes which creates offspring that are genetically identical to the parent (clones).

cont...

Cloning

☐ That plants can be cloned using cuttings and that this allows plants to be produced quickly and cheaply.

☐ That plants can also be cloned through tissue culture (a method of producing whole plants from plant cells grown on a growth medium).

☐ How cloned animals can be produced using embryo transplants — sperm is used to fertilise an egg, creating an embryo. The embryo is then split many times to produce clones before any cells become specialised. The cloned embryos are implanted into host mothers.

☐ How animals can be cloned using adult cell cloning — a nucleus from an adult body cell is inserted into an 'empty' egg cell. The egg cell is then stimulated to divide by electric shock and the embryo is implanted into the uterus of a surrogate mother.

☐ How to interpret information about cloning methods.

☐ The issues surrounding cloning and how to make judgements about them.

Genetic Engineering

☐ How genetic engineering works — enzymes are used to cut out useful genes from one organism's chromosome and then insert them into another's.

☐ That 'new' genes are often transferred into plants and animals at an early stage of their development, so that the plant or animal develops useful characteristics.

☐ How to interpret information about cloning methods.

☐ That GM (genetically modified) crops are examples of genetically engineered organisms and that some GM crops are resistant to insects or herbicides.

☐ The issues surrounding genetic engineering and how to make judgements about them.

☐ The issues surrounding GM crops, including: GM crops can increase yields; some people are concerned that they could negatively affect the weeds and insects that grow around GM crops; some people are concerned they could negatively affect human health.

Exam-style Questions

1 (a) Complete the paragraph below, using the correct words from the box.
You may only use each word once.

> chromosomes   gametes   variation   cloning   characteristics

Genes are found on .... Genes control an organism's

.... Genes are passed on from parents to offspring in the

.... The combining of genes from two parents creates genetic

.... in the offspring.

(4 marks)

1 (b) The girls shown below are identical twins. They have exactly the same genes.

1 (b) (i) Both twins have blue eyes. What determines the twins' eye colour?

(1 mark)

1 (b) (ii) The twin on the left is taller than the twin on the right.
Suggest **one** possible explanation for this difference in height.

(1 mark)

1 (c) The twins were born as a result of sexual reproduction.
Explain what sexual reproduction is.

(4 marks)

2 Cloned pigs may be created using embryo transplants.
The diagram below shows the creation of a pig embryo for this purpose.

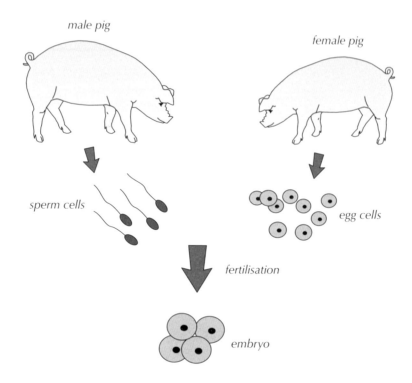

2 (a) (i) Describe how genetically identical pigs will now be created using this embryo.

(3 marks)

2 (a) (ii) Is this an example of sexual or asexual reproduction?
Give **two** reasons for your answer.

(2 marks)

2 (b) The pigs that are born as a result of this process will share characteristics with
both the male pig and the female pig. Explain why.

(2 marks)

2 (c) *In this question you will be assessed on the quality of your English,*
the organisation of your ideas and your use of appropriate specialist vocabulary.

Certain groups of people (e.g. farmers, scientists) may want to clone pigs.
However, other people may have concerns about the cloning of pigs.

Using your scientific knowledge, discuss the possible benefits and concerns of
cloning pigs.

(6 marks)

Learning Objectives:

- Understand the theory of evolution — life on Earth began more than 3 billion years ago as simple organisms from which all more complex organisms evolved.

- Know that natural selection explains how evolution occurs.

- Know that Charles Darwin came up with the idea of natural selection.

- Understand the three main stages involved in natural selection.

- Know that mutations can result in new forms of a gene and how this can lead to changes in a species.

Specification Reference B1.8.1

Figure 1: *Charles Darwin.*

Tip: Genetic differences are caused by sexual reproduction (see page 98) and mutations (see next page).

1. Evolution and Natural Selection

This is it. The 'Big One' — how life on Earth began, and, um, kept on going...

The theory of evolution

The theory of evolution is this:

> More than 3 billion years ago, life on Earth began as simple organisms from which all the more complex organisms evolved.

It means that rather than just popping into existence, complex organisms like animals and plants 'developed' over billions of years from simpler single-celled organisms, such as bacteria.

Natural selection

Natural selection explains how evolution occurs. The scientist **Charles Darwin**, came up with the idea of natural selection in the 1800s. It works like this:

1. Individuals within a species show variation because of the differences in their genes.

   Example

   Some rabbits have big ears and some have small ones.

2. Individuals with characteristics that make them better adapted to the environment have a better chance of survival and so are more likely to breed successfully.

   Example

   Big-eared rabbits are more likely to hear a fox approaching them, and so are more likely to survive and have lots of offspring. Small-eared rabbits are more likely to get eaten.

   FOX!

3. So, the genes that are responsible for the useful characteristics are more likely to be passed on to the next generation.

Tip: Remember, it's the <u>genes</u> that get passed on to the next generation (not the characteristics themselves).

> **Example**
>
> All the baby rabbits are born with big ears.

Over time, the gene for a useful characteristic will become more common (accumulate) in a population. This will lead to changes in a species. The gradual changing of a species over time is evolution. Eventually, if the changes are great enough, a new species will evolve.

Mutations

Evolution can occur due to mutations.

> A mutation is a change in an organism's DNA (genes).

Most of the time mutations have no effect, but occasionally they can be beneficial by producing a useful characteristic. This characteristic may give the organism a better chance of surviving and reproducing — especially if the environment changes in some way. If so, the beneficial mutation is more likely to be passed on to future generations by natural selection. Over time, the beneficial mutation will accumulate in a population, sometimes changing a whole species.

Exam Tip
Don't get natural selection and evolution mixed up. Natural selection is when a useful characteristic (i.e. one that gives a better chance of survival) becomes more common in a population. Evolution is the gradual changing of a species over time (which happens as a result of natural selection).

> **Example**
>
> A mutation may make a bacterium resistant to an antibiotic (see page 29). If the antibiotic appears in the bacterium's environment (e.g. a person with a bacterial infection starts taking antibiotics), the mutation may give the bacterium a better chance of surviving, reproducing and passing the beneficial mutation on to future generations. Over time, the mutation will accumulate in the bacterial population.

Practice Questions — Fact Recall

Q1 According to the theory of evolution, how long ago did life on Earth begin?

Q2 According to the theory of evolution, how did complex organisms come to exist on Earth?

Q3 a) What is natural selection?

b) Who came up with the idea of natural selection?

Q4 a) What is a mutation?

b) Explain how a mutation can lead to changes in a species.

Exam Tip
Facts like how long ago life on Earth began and who came up with natural selection are dead easy to learn — and they could mean dead easy marks in the exam.

Practice Questions — Application

Q1 Warfarin is a chemical that was commonly used to kill rats. It is now used less often as many rats have become resistant to it.

Use the theory of evolution by natural selection to explain how most rats have become warfarin-resistant.

Q2 In 1810, a herd of reindeer were taken from the Arctic to an area with a warmer climate. The herd were then left to live and reproduce in the area and were revisited in 1960. Some information about the herd is shown in the graph.

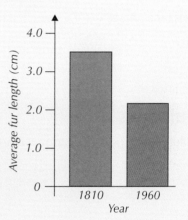

a) By roughly how much did the average fur length of the herd change between 1810 and 1960?

b) Explain this change in terms of natural selection.

Tip: To help you answer Q2 b), think about how the change in fur length might affect the reindeer in their new environment.

2. Ideas About Evolution

Darwin's ideas about natural selection are now pretty well established. But when they were first published, there wasn't as much evidence to support them.

Controversy

Darwin's theory of evolution by natural selection is widely accepted today. But Darwin's idea was very controversial at the time — for various reasons...

1.   It went against common religious beliefs about how life on Earth developed — it was the first plausible explanation for our own existence without the need for a "Creator" (God).

2.   Darwin couldn't give a good explanation for why these new, useful characteristics appeared or exactly how individual organisms passed on their beneficial characteristics to their offspring. But then he didn't know anything about genes or mutations — they weren't discovered 'til 50 years after his theory was published.

3.   There wasn't enough evidence to convince many scientists, because not many other studies had been done into how organisms change over time.

For these reasons, Darwin's idea was only accepted gradually, as more and more evidence came to light.

Lamarck

Darwin wasn't the only person who tried to explain evolution. There were different scientific **hypotheses** around at the same time, such as Lamarck's:

Lamarck (1744-1829) argued that if a characteristic was used a lot by an organism then it would become more developed during its lifetime. E.g. if a rabbit used its legs to run a lot (to escape predators), then its legs would get longer.

Lamarck believed that these acquired characteristics would be passed on to the next generation, e.g. the rabbit's offspring would have longer legs.

Proving or disproving hypotheses

Often scientists come up with different hypotheses to explain similar observations. Scientists might develop different hypotheses because they have different beliefs (e.g. religious) or they have been influenced by different people (e.g. other scientists and their way of thinking)... or they just think differently.

The only way to find out whose hypothesis is right is to find evidence to support or disprove each one.

Learning Objectives:

*   Know the reasons why Darwin's theory of evolution by natural selection wasn't accepted straight away.
*   Understand that there have been other hypotheses about evolution, including Lamarck's — which was based on the idea that 'acquired characteristics' could be inherited.
*   Know the differences between Darwin's theory and other hypotheses that try to explain evolution.
*   Be able to suggest why scientists come up with different hypotheses based on the same observations.
*   Understand that we now know Lamarck's hypothesis was wrong.
*   Be able to interpret data about the development of evolutionary hypotheses.

Specification Reference B1.8.1

***Figure 1:** Lamarck.*

Tip: There's more about hypotheses on page 1.

Example

Lamarck and Darwin both had different hypotheses to explain how evolution happens.

In the end Lamarck's hypothesis was rejected because experiments didn't support his hypothesis. You can see it for yourself, e.g. if you dye a hamster's fur bright pink (not recommended), its offspring will still be born with the normal fur colour because the new characteristic won't have been passed on.

The discovery of genetics supported Darwin's idea because it provided an explanation of how organisms born with beneficial characteristics can pass them on (i.e. via their genes).

There's now so much evidence for Darwin's idea that it's an accepted hypothesis (a theory).

Practice Questions — Application

Q1 Kyra is a geneticist — her work involves looking at how our genes affect us. Neil is a psychologist — his work involves looking at how our experiences influence our behaviour.

Kyra believes that alcohol addiction is down to the genes you inherit. Neil believes that alcohol addiction develops as a result of your upbringing and environment. Suggest a reason why Kyra and Neil have different opinions on the reasons for an alcohol addiction.

Q2 A farmer clips the flight feathers on the wings of his chickens. This makes the feathers shorter and stops the birds being able to fly. The offspring of these birds develop normal flight feathers and are able to fly. Explain how this scenario helps to disprove Lamarck's hypothesis about evolution.

Q3 Anteaters feed on insects such as ants. They have evolved extremely long tongues, which help them to reach inside ant nests and get at the ants.

a) Suggest how Lamarck may have explained the evolution of long tongues in anteaters.

b) How would scientists explain the evolution of long tongues in anteaters using the idea of natural selection?

3. Classification

Classification means sorting things into groups. Like organisms, for example...

Classifying organisms

Looking at the similarities and differences between organisms allows us to classify them into groups.

> **Examples**
>
> - **Plants** make their own food (by a process called photosynthesis) and are fixed in the ground.
>
> - **Animals** move about the place and can't make their own food.
>
> - **Microorganisms** are different to plants and animals, e.g. bacteria are single-celled.

Studying the similarities and differences between organisms also help us to understand how all living things are related (**evolutionary relationships**) and how they interact with each other (**ecological relationships**).

Studying evolutionary relationships

Species with similar characteristics often have similar genes because they share a **recent common ancestor**. This makes them closely related. They often look very alike and tend to live in similar types of habitat.

> **Example**
>
> Whales and dolphins are closely related mammals that live in the sea.

Occasionally, genetically different species might look alike too.

> **Example**
>
> Dolphins and sharks look pretty similar because they've both adapted to living in the same habitat. But they're not closely related — they've evolved from different ancestors.

Evolutionary trees

Evolutionary trees show common (shared) ancestors and relationships between organisms. The more recent the common ancestor, the more closely related the two species. There are some examples of evolutionary trees on the next page.

Learning Objectives:

- Know that looking at the similarities and differences between organisms allows us to classify them into groups, e.g. plants, animals and microorganisms.

- Know that looking at the similarities and differences between organisms allows us to understand their evolutionary relationships.

- Understand how evolutionary trees show the relationships between organisms.

- Know that looking at the similarities and differences between organisms allows us to understand their ecological relationships.

Specification Reference B1.8.1

Tip: All organisms are related in some way, even if only distantly. That's because all life on Earth evolved from the same simple organisms.

Figure 1: *This shark (top) and dolphin (bottom) have similar streamlined bodies to help them move through the water, but aren't closely related.*

Example 1

This evolutionary tree shows that whales and dolphins have a recent common ancestor so are closely related. They're both more distantly related to sharks:

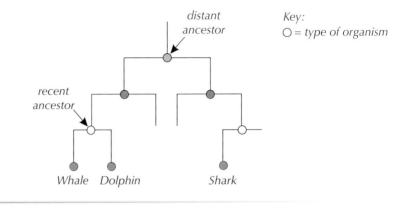

Example 2

This evolutionary tree shows the relationships between humans and some of the great apes. Each point at which the lines meet, indicates a common ancestor.

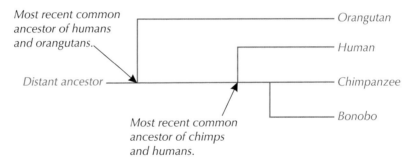

You can see that humans are more closely related to chimpanzees than to orangutans because they share a more recent common ancestor.

Studying ecological relationships

If we see organisms in the same environment with similar characteristics, it suggests they might be in competition.

Example

Dolphins and sharks often compete for the same food source (fish).

Differences between organisms in the same environment can show predator-prey relationships.

Dolphins swim in small groups, but herring swim in giant shoals —
this is because dolphins hunt herring, so the herring move around in
large groups for protection.

Figure 2: *A group of
dolphins hunting a shoal of
fish. The fish bunch together
in a large ball for protection.*

Practice Questions — Fact Recall

Q1 How are we able to classify organisms into animals, plants and
microorganisms?

Q2 Organisms in the same environment, often have similar
characteristics, e.g. dolphins and sharks. What can this tell us
about their ecological relationship?

Practice Questions — Application

Q1 The picture below is of a sea cucumber.

The sea cucumber crawls along the sea bed feeding on the dead
material it finds there (its only source of food). Is the sea cucumber
an animal or a plant? Give two reasons for your answer.

Q2 The tree below shows the evolutionary relationships
between some of the big cats.

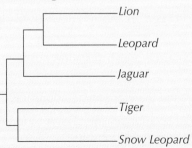

— Lion

— Leopard

— Jaguar

— Tiger

— Snow Leopard

a) Which animal is most closely related to:

i) the leopard?   ii) the tiger?

b) Which animal evolved first, the jaguar or the lion?

c) Do the lion and the snow leopard share a common ancestor?

Evolution and Natural Selection

☐ The theory of evolution — life on Earth began more than 3 billion years ago as simple organisms from which all more complex organisms evolved.

☐ That Charles Darwin came up with the idea of natural selection to explain how evolution occurs.

☐ How natural selection works — individuals show variation, some individuals have characteristics that make them more likely to survive and breed, the genes for these characteristics are more likely to be passed onto the next generation.

☐ That a change in a gene is called a mutation.

☐ That a mutation may give rise to a beneficial characteristic, which helps the organism to survive and reproduce (especially if the environment changes).

☐ That a beneficial mutation can accumulate in a population and lead to a change in a species.

Ideas About Evolution

☐ The reasons why Darwin's theory of evolution by natural selection wasn't accepted straight away — it went against common religious beliefs; Darwin couldn't explain how characteristics were inherited (genes wouldn't be discovered for another 50 years); there wasn't enough evidence to support his theory.

☐ That there have been other hypotheses to explain how evolution occurs, including Lamarck's (which was based on the idea that 'acquired characteristics' could be inherited).

☐ The reasons why scientists might come up with different hypotheses based on the same observations, e.g. religious beliefs, personal backgrounds.

☐ How we came to reject Lamarck's hypothesis (experimental evidence didn't support it) and accept Darwin's (the discovery of genetics explained how characteristics could be inherited).

☐ How to interpret evidence about evolutionary hypotheses.

Classification

☐ How looking at the similarities and differences between organisms allows us to classify them as plants, animals and microorganisms.

☐ How looking at the similarities and differences between organisms allows us to understand their evolutionary relationships.

☐ How evolutionary trees show common ancestors and therefore the relationships between organisms.

☐ How looking at the similarities and differences between organisms allows us to understand their ecological relationships, e.g. competition, predator-prey relationships.

Exam-style Questions

1   The evolutionary tree shows how some groups of animals, including snakes, are related.

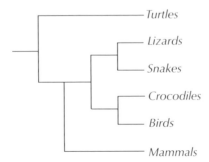

1 (a)   Which of the following groups of animals are most closely related?
Tick the correct box below.

Turtles and lizards ☐   Snakes and crocodiles ☐

Crocodiles and birds ☐   Birds and mammals ☐

(1 mark)

1 (b)   According to the tree, which group of animals evolved first?

(1 mark)

The picture shows a type of snake called a Sinaloan milk snake.

The milk snake is relatively harmless,
but it has evolved to have a very
similar pattern and colouring to
the deadly poisonous coral snake,
which lives in the same environment.
The coral snake's colouring warns
predators that it is dangerous to eat.

1 (c)   Using the idea of natural selection, explain how the milk snake may have evolved to have a similar colouring to the coral snake.

(3 marks)

1 (d)   The theory of evolution by natural selection was proposed by Charles Darwin.
Darwin's ideas about natural selection were only gradually accepted.
Give **three** reasons why this was the case.

(3 marks)

1. Cell Structure

All living things are made of cells — they're the building blocks of every organism on the planet. But different organisms have different cell structures...

Animal cells

Most animal cells, including most human cells, have the following parts — make sure you know them all. The parts are labelled in Figure 1.

- **Nucleus** — contains genetic material that controls the activities of the cell.

- **Cytoplasm** — a gel-like substance where most of the chemical reactions happen. It contains enzymes (see p. 156) that control these chemical reactions.

- **Cell membrane** — holds the cell together and controls what goes in and out.

- **Mitochondria** — these are where most of the reactions for respiration take place (see p. 167). Respiration releases energy that the cell needs to work.

- **Ribosomes** — these are where proteins are made in the cell.

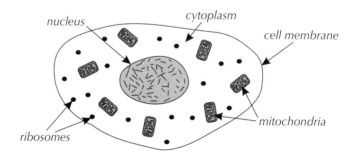

Figure 1: *The structure of a typical animal cell.*

Plant cells

Plant cells usually have all the bits that animal cells have, plus a few extra:

- **Cell wall** — a rigid structure made of cellulose. It supports and strengthens the cell. The cells of algae (e.g. seaweed) also have a rigid cell wall.

- **Permanent vacuole** — contains cell sap, a weak solution of sugar and salts.

- **Chloroplasts** — these are where photosynthesis occurs, which makes food for the plant (see page 136). They contain a green substance called **chlorophyll**, which absorbs the light energy needed for photosynthesis.

The parts of a typical plant cell are shown in Figure 3.

Learning Objectives:

- Know that most human and other animal cells have a nucleus, cytoplasm, cell membrane, mitochondria and ribosomes, and know the function of each of these parts.

- Know that plant and algal cells have the same parts as animal cells, plus a cell wall made of cellulose to strengthen the cell.

- Know that plant cells also usually have chloroplasts and a permanent vacuole.

- Know that yeast is a single-celled microorganism, and know the structure of a yeast cell.

- Know the structure of a bacterial cell.

Specification Reference B2.1.1

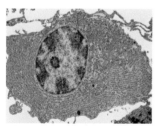

Figure 2: *A human cell seen under a microscope — the blue and yellow oval is the nucleus.*

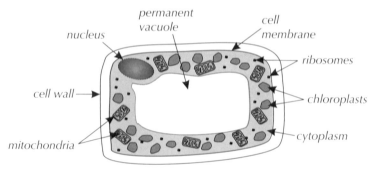

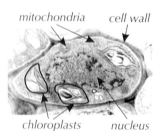

Figure 3: The structure of a typical plant cell.

Figure 4: A cross-section of a plant cell seen under a microscope.

Yeast cells

Yeast is a single-celled microorganism. A yeast cell has a nucleus, cytoplasm, and a cell membrane surrounded by a cell wall (see Figure 5).

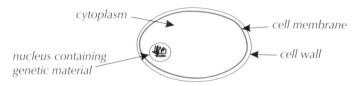

Figure 5: The structure of a yeast cell.

Tip: 'Genetic material' is just another word for 'genes', 'DNA' or 'chromosomes'.

Bacterial cells

Bacteria are also single-celled microorganisms. A bacterial cell has cytoplasm and a cell membrane surrounded by a cell wall. The genetic material floats in the cytoplasm because bacterial cells don't have a nucleus (see Figure 6).

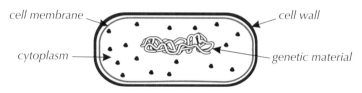

Figure 6: The structure of a typical bacterial cell.

Tip: The diagrams on this page and the previous one all show 'typical' cells.
In reality the structure of a cell varies according to what job it does, so most cells won't look exactly like these.

Practice Questions — Fact Recall

Q1 Which part of an animal cell controls its activity?

Q2 Where do most of the chemical reactions take place in a cell?

Q3 What are mitochondria needed for in a cell?

Q4 Name three things that a plant cell usually has, that an animal cell doesn't.

Q5 Describe the structure of a yeast cell.

Q6 Give one difference between the structure of a yeast cell and the structure of a bacterial cell.

Exam Tip
You need to learn the functions of the cell parts, not just their names.

Learning Objectives:
- Understand that many cells are specialised — they perform a specific function.
- Be able to relate the structure of a cell to its function.

Specification Reference
B2.1.1

2. Specialised Cells

Not all cells in an organism do the same job. A cell's structure is related to the job it does, so cell structure can vary...

What is a specialised cell?

A specialised cell is one that performs a specific function. Most cells in an organism are specialised. A cell's structure (e.g. its shape and the parts it contains) helps it to carry out its function — so depending on what job it does, a specialised cell can look very different to the cells you saw on pages 120-121.

Examples of specialised cells

In the exam, you could be asked to relate the structure of a cell to its function. The idea is that you apply your knowledge of cell structure (see previous topic) to the information you're given about the role of the cell in an organism. Don't panic — it's easier than it sounds. Here are a few examples to help you understand how cell structure and function are related:

1. Sperm and egg cells (animals)

Sperm and egg cells are specialised for reproduction. The main functions of an egg cell are to carry the female DNA and to nourish the developing embryo in the early stages, so the egg cell contains huge food reserves to feed the embryo.

The function of a sperm is to get the male DNA to the female DNA. It has a long tail and a streamlined head to help it swim to the egg. There are also lots of **mitochondria** (see p.120) in the cell to provide the energy it needs to do this.

Exam Tip
Energy is released by respiration, which mostly takes place in the mitochondria.
So <u>any cell</u> that needs lots of energy to do its job will have lots of mitochondria.

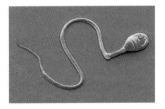

Figure 1: *A microscope image of a sperm cell. It's easy to see the streamlined head and tail.*

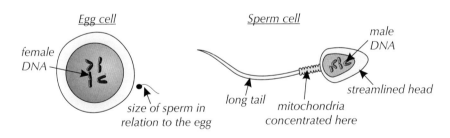

Figure 2: *An egg cell and a sperm cell.*

Tip: Similar to sperm cells, bacterial cells sometimes have long tail-like structures to help them swim.

2. Red blood cells (animals)

Red blood cells are an important part of the blood — they are adapted to carry oxygen to every cell in the body. They have a biconcave shape (both sides of the cell curve inwards) which gives them a big surface area for absorbing oxygen — see Figure 3 (next page). This shape also helps them pass smoothly along capillaries (tiny blood vessels) to reach the body cells.

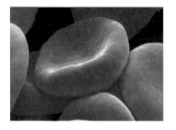

Figure 3: *A microscope image of red blood cells (left) and a cross-section through a red blood cell (right).*

biconcave shape

Red blood cells are packed with haemoglobin — the pigment that absorbs the oxygen. And unlike a typical animal cell (see page 120), red blood cells have no nucleus to leave even more room for haemoglobin.

3. Palisade leaf cells (plants)

Palisade leaf cells are adapted for photosynthesis. They are grouped together at the top of a leaf where most of the photosynthesis happens (see Figure 4a).

They're packed with **chloroplasts** (see page 120), which absorb the light energy needed for photosynthesis. There are more chloroplasts crammed at the top of the cell, so they're nearer the light (see Figure 4b).

They're tall with long sides, which means there's more surface area exposed for absorbing carbon dioxide from the air in the leaf. They're also thin, which means that you can pack loads of them in at the top of a leaf.

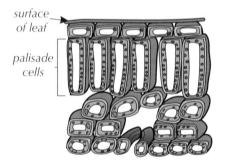

surface of leaf

palisade cells

Figure 4a: *Cross section through a leaf showing the position of palisade cells.*

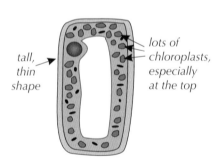

tall, thin shape

lots of chloroplasts, especially at the top

Figure 4b: *The structure of a palisade cell.*

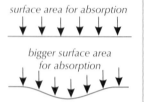

> **Exam Tip**
> The concave shape of a red blood gives it a bigger surface area than if the cell was flat. Look:
>
> surface area for absorption
>
> ↓ ↓ ↓ ↓ ↓ ↓
>
> bigger surface area for absorption
>
> ↓ ↓ ↓ ↓ ↓ ↓
>
> Folds or projections in the cell membrane would do the same thing. <u>Any cell</u> that absorbs molecules through its surface needs a <u>big surface area</u> — this helps it to absorb lots of molecules at once.

> **Tip:** Photosynthesis is the process in which plants use light energy from the sun to convert carbon dioxide and water into oxygen and glucose (food) — see page 136 for more.

Practice Questions — Application

Q1   The function of gastric chief cells is to secrete enzymes (proteins) into the stomach during digestion. Comment on the amount of ribosomes you'd expect to find in a gastric chief cell.

> **Tip:** Think about the function of ribosomes — see page 120.

Tip: To help with Q2 a), think about the job carried out by root hair cells and where they're found in the plant.

Q2 Root hair cells are specialised plant cells.
They absorb water and mineral ions from soil.

a) Which of the following diagrams (A-C) is most likely to show the correct structure of a root hair cell? Explain your answer.

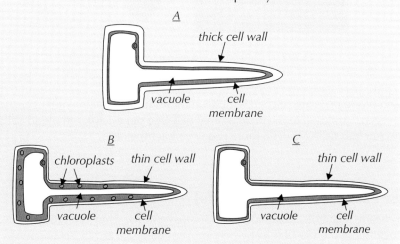

Tip: You're not expected to actually <u>know</u> the answer to these questions — just make sensible suggestions using the information given and your knowledge about cell structure from pages 120-121.

b) Suggest how the shape of a root hair cell makes it well adapted to its function.

Q3 A diagram of an epithelial cell from the small intestine is shown here:

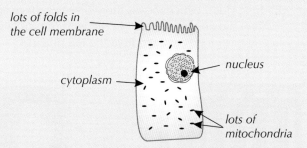

Tip: Look back at the examples on the last couple of pages if you're struggling with this one — the function of some of those cells involves absorption too.

These cells line the inner surface of the small intestine and their function is to absorb food molecules as they move through the intestine. Sometimes this process requires energy.

Use this information and the diagram to suggest two ways in which the structure of these cells helps them to carry out their function.

3. Diffusion

Particles tend to move about randomly and end up evenly spaced. This is important when it comes to getting substances in and out of cells.

What is diffusion?

"Diffusion" is simple. It's just the gradual movement of particles from places where there are lots of them to places where there are fewer of them. That's all it is — just the natural tendency for stuff to spread out.

Unfortunately you also have to learn the fancy way of saying the same thing, which is this:

> Diffusion is the spreading out of particles from an area of high concentration to an area of low concentration.

Diffusion happens in both solutions and gases — that's because the particles in these substances are free to move about randomly. The simplest type is when different gases diffuse through each other.

Example

When you spray perfume, the smell of perfume diffuses through the air in a room:

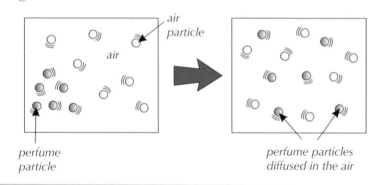

perfume particle

air particle

air

perfume particles diffused in the air

Diffusion across cell membranes

Cell membranes are clever because they hold the cell together but they let stuff in and out as well. **Dissolved substances** can move in and out of cells by diffusion.

Only very small molecules can diffuse through cell membranes though — things like **oxygen** (needed for respiration — see page 167), glucose, amino acids and water. Big molecules like starch and proteins can't fit through the membrane (see Figure 2 on the next page).

Learning Objectives:

- Know the definition of 'diffusion'.
- Know that dissolved substances (such as oxygen) can move in and out of a cell by diffusion.
- Understand that during diffusion, the net movement of substances will be from an area of higher concentration to an area of lower concentration.
- Understand that the rate of diffusion is faster when there is a greater difference in the concentration of particles.

Specification Reference B2.1.2

Figure 1: *The ink particles in this flask are diffusing into the water — they're moving from an area of high concentration (at the bottom of the flask) to an area of low concentration (higher up).*

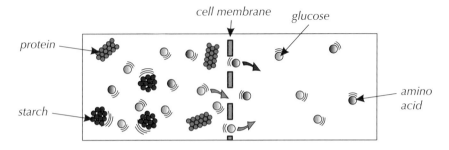

protein

starch

amino
acid

Figure 2: *Diagram to show diffusion across a cell membrane.*

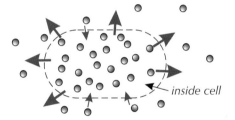

Just like with diffusion in air, particles flow through the cell membrane from where there's a high concentration (a lot of them) to where there's a low concentration (not such a lot of them).

They're only moving about randomly of course, so they go both ways — but if there are a lot more particles on one side of the membrane, there's a **net** (overall) movement from that side.

Particles are diffusing both in and out of this cell. However, the concentration of particles is higher inside the cell than outside, so the net movement of particles is out of the cell.

inside cell

The rate of diffusion

The rate of diffusion is affected by the difference in concentration of the particles — the bigger the difference in concentration, the faster the diffusion rate.

There will be a net movement of particles out of both Cell 1 and Cell 2 (shown below). However, the rate of diffusion will be faster out of Cell 1, because there's a bigger difference in the concentration of particles on either side of the cell membrane.

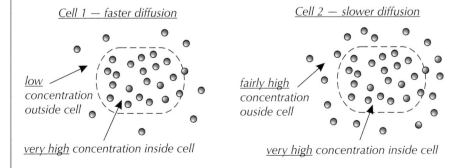

Cell 1 — faster diffusion

low concentration outside cell

very high concentration inside cell

Cell 2 — slower diffusion

fairly high concentration ouside cell

very high concentration inside cell

If you're struggling to remember which way the particles move in diffusion, think of it like this: if you were in a really crowded place, you'd probably want to get out of there to somewhere with a bit more room. It's the same with particles — they always diffuse from an area of high concentration to an area of low concentration.

Q1 When cells respire they produce carbon dioxide as a waste product. The carbon dioxide diffuses from the cells into the bloodstream, so it can be removed from the body.
Is carbon dioxide concentration greater in the bloodstream or inside respiring cells? Explain your answer.

Q2 At a disco in a school hall, a DJ releases a short blast of smoke from a smoke machine at the front of the stage.

a) Explain how the smoke reaches the people standing at the opposite end of the hall from the stage.

b) Five minutes later the DJ sets the smoke machine off for a second time. Explain how the rate of diffusion of the smoke is now different from the first time the DJ set the smoke machine off.

Section Checklist — Make sure you know...

Cell Structure

☐ That most human and animals cells have: a nucleus (which contains the genetic material that controls the activities of a cell), cytoplasm (where most of the chemical reactions happen), a cell membrane (which controls what goes in and out of the cell), mitochondria (where most of the reactions for respiration happen), and ribosomes (where proteins are made in the cell).

☐ That in addition to all the parts that animal cells have, plant and algal cells have a cell wall made of cellulose to strengthen the cell.

☐ That most plant cells also have a permanent vacuole containing cell sap and chloroplasts which absorb the light energy needed for photosynthesis.

☐ That yeast is a single-celled organism, and that a yeast cell has a nucleus, cytoplasm, cell membrane and a cell wall.

☐ That a bacterial cell has cytoplasm, a cell membrane and a cell wall, and that its genetic material is not in a nucleus.

Specialised Cells

☐ That many cells are specialised to carry out a specific function.

☐ How to relate a cell's structure (its shape and the parts it contains) to its function.

Diffusion

☐ That diffusion is the spreading out of particles from an area of high concentration to an area of low concentration.

☐ That dissolved substances such as oxygen (which is needed for respiration) move in and out of a cell by diffusion, and that the net (overall) movement will be to an area of lower concentration.

☐ That the bigger the difference in concentration, the faster the diffusion rate.

Learning Objectives:

- Know that large multicellular organisms have systems that allow them to exchange substances.

- Understand that, as a multicellular organism is developing, cells differentiate to produce specialised cells.

- Know what a tissue is and understand the roles of muscular, glandular and epithelial tissue.

- Know what an organ is and understand why the stomach contains muscular, glandular and epithelial tissue.

- Know what an organ system is and understand the roles of the organs (the pancreas, salivary glands, stomach, small intestine, liver and large intestine) that make up the digestive system.

Specification Reference
B2.2.1

1. Cell Organisation

Multicellular organisms (like humans) can have trillions of cells. To keep the organism going, those cells have to work together — which needs organisation.

How are cells organised?

Large **multicellular organisms** have different systems inside them for exchanging and transporting materials.

> **Example**
>
> Mammals have a breathing system — this includes the airways and lungs. The breathing system is needed to take air into and out of the lungs, so that oxygen and carbon dioxide can be exchanged between the body and the environment.

Exchange systems are made up of **specialised cells** (see page 122).   The process by which cells become specialised for a particular job is called **differentiation**. Differentiation occurs during the development of a multicellular organism.

Specialised cells are organised to form tissues, which form organs, which form organ systems — there's more about each of these over the next few pages.

Tissues

You need to know what a tissue is:

> A tissue is a group of similar cells that work together to carry out a particular function.

A tissue can include more than one type of cell. Mammals (like humans), have several different types of tissue:

> **Examples**
>
> - **Muscular tissue**, which contracts (shortens) to move whatever it's attached to.
>
> - **Glandular tissue**, which makes and secretes substances like enzymes (proteins that control chemical reactions, see p.156) and hormones (chemical messengers).
>
> - **Epithelial tissue**, which covers some parts of the body, e.g. the inside of the gut.

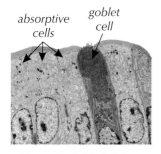

absorptive cells   *goblet cell*

Figure 1: *Epithelial tissue in the small intestine. It contains absorptive cells and goblet cells.*

Organs

Tissues are organised into organs:

> An organ is a group of different tissues that work together to perform a certain function.

Mammals have many different organs, which are made up of different tissues.

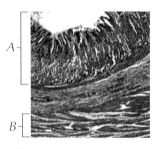

Figure 2: *A cross-section through part of the stomach. There's glandular tissue at the top (A) and muscular tissue at the bottom (B).*

Example

The **stomach** is an organ made of these tissues:

- **Muscular tissue**, which moves the stomach wall to churn up the food.
- **Glandular tissue**, which makes digestive juices to digest food.
- **Epithelial tissue**, which covers the outside and inside of the stomach.

Tip: Digestive juices are secretions from the digestive system that help to break down food. They contain enzymes (see page 156).

Organ systems

Organs are organised into organ systems:

> An organ system is a group of organs working together to perform a particular function.

Example

The **digestive system** is the organ system that breaks down food in humans and other mammals. It's also an exchange system — it exchanges materials with the environment by taking in nutrients and releasing substances such as bile (see page 161).

Tip: There's more on the digestive system on pages 159-161.

The digestive system (see Figure 3) is made up of these organs:

- **Glands** (e.g. the **pancreas** and **salivary glands**), which produce digestive juices.
- The **stomach**, where food is digested.
- The **liver**, which produces bile.
- The **small intestine**, where food is digested and soluble food molecules are absorbed.
- The **large intestine**, where water is absorbed from undigested food, leaving faeces.

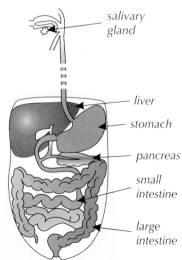

Figure 3: *A diagram of the human digestive system.*

Exam Tip
You need to learn the examples of muscular, glandular and epithelial tissue (see previous page), the stomach and the digestive system for your exam.

Size and scale

You need to have an understanding of the size and scale of all the structures that make up an organ system — from the tiny individual specialised cells to the organ system as a whole.

Exam Tip
You don't need to learn the lengths given in this example — they're just to give you an idea of size.

Tip: The digestive tract is the big long 'tube' which food passes through, including the small and large intestines. The intestines are all folded up, which is part of the reason why the digestive tract can be so long and yet still fit inside you.

Example

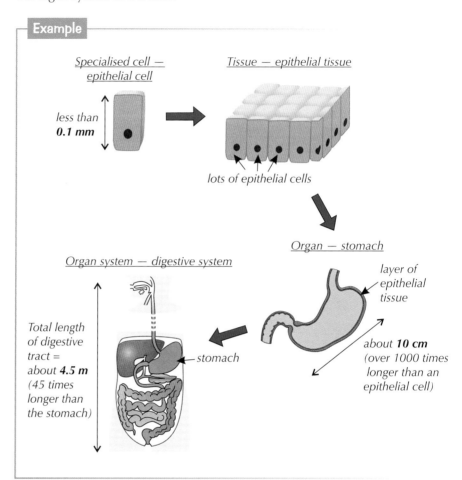

Specialised cell — epithelial cell

less than **0.1 mm**

Tissue — epithelial tissue

lots of epithelial cells

Organ — stomach

layer of epithelial tissue

about **10 cm** (over 1000 times longer than an epithelial cell)

Organ system — digestive system

*Total length of digestive tract = about **4.5 m** (45 times longer than the stomach)*

stomach

Practice Questions — Fact Recall

Q1 a) Name the process by which cells become specialised for a particular function.

b) True or false? Cells become specialised for a particular function during the development of a multicellular organism.

Q2 a) What is a tissue?

b) Describe the role of glandular tissue.

c) Other than glandular tissue, name two types of tissue found in mammals.

Q3 What is an organ?

Q4 What term describes a group of organs which work together to perform a particular function?

Q5 Look at the diagram of the digestive system.

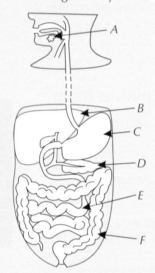

Write down the names of the organs labelled A-F and briefly say what each one does.

Exam Tip
You need to know where the organs of the digestive system are on a diagram for your exam, so make sure you can get them all right in Q5.

Practice Questions — Application

Q1 Cells in the hypophysis secrete thyroid-stimulating hormone into the blood. What type of tissue must the hypophysis contain? Explain your answer.

Q2 Blood is made up of specialised red blood cells and several different types of white blood cells. Is blood an example of a cell, tissue, organ or organ system? Explain your answer.

Q3 The fallopian tubes and uterus are part of the female reproductive system. A fallopian tube contains muscular and epithelial tissue. These work together to move a fertilised egg cell along the fallopian tube to the uterus (an organ).

a) Suggest why a fallopian tube has muscular tissue.

b) Is a fallopian tube a cell, tissue, organ or organ system? Explain your answer.

c) Rewrite the following list of structures in order of size. Start with the smallest:

uterus   reproductive system   egg cell   muscular tissue

Tip: The definitions of a tissue, an organ and an organ system should be really clear in your head. Take a look back at pages 128-129 if you're not sure of them.

Learning Objectives:
- Know that plants have organs including stems, roots and leaves.
- Understand the roles of epidermal tissue, mesophyll tissue, and xylem and phloem tissue in plants.

Specification Reference B2.2.2

2. Plant Tissues and Organs

You've just learnt about tissues and organs (see pages 128-129), but don't go thinking it's only animal cells that are organised this way — plant cells are organised into tissues and organs too.

What organs do plants have?

Plants are made of organs such as stems, roots and leaves — see Figure 1.

- **Stems** support the plant, and assist in the transport of water and nutrients between the roots and the leaves.

- **Roots** absorb water and mineral ions for the plant, and hold the plant in place.

- **Leaves** are the main site of photosynthesis in a plant.

Figure 1: *A photograph showing the three types of plant organs.*

Tip: Photosynthesis is the process by which plants make their own food. See page 136 for more.

What tissues do plants have?

Plant organs are made of tissues such as:

- **Mesophyll tissue** — this is where most of the photosynthesis in a plant occurs.

- **Xylem** and **phloem** — these tissues transport things like water, mineral ions and sucrose around the plant.

- **Epidermal tissue** — this covers the whole plant.

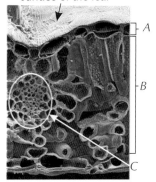

Figure 2: *A cross-section through a leaf, seen under a microscope. It shows the epidermal tissue (A), mesophyll tissue (B) and xylem and phloem tissue (C).*

Example

Leaves are made up of mesophyll tissue, xylem and phloem, and epidermal tissue as shown in Figures 2 and 3.

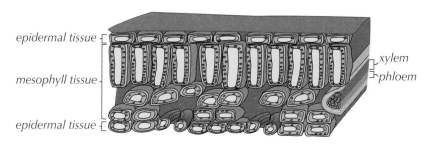

Figure 3: *Diagram showing the main tissues in a leaf.*

Q1   Name three plant organs.

Q2   Name the plant tissue where photosynthesis occurs.

Q3   What is the function of xylem and phloem tissue?

Q4   What type of tissue covers a plant?

Section Checklist — Make sure you know...

Cell Organisation

☐ That large multicellular organisms contain systems that allow them to exchange substances.

☐ That when a multicellular organism is developing, its cells differentiate into specialised cells.

☐ That a tissue is a group of similar cells that work together to carry out a particular function and that a tissue can include more than one type of cell.

☐ That muscular tissue contracts (shortens) to make things move, glandular tissue makes and secretes enzymes and hormones, and epithelial tissue covers some parts of the body, e.g. the gut.

☐ That an organ is a group of different tissues that work together to perform a certain function.

☐ That the stomach is an organ which contains muscular tissue to churn food and glandular tissue to make digestive juices. It is covered with epithelial tissue on the inside and outside.

☐ That an organ system is a group of organs working together to perform a particular function.

☐ That the digestive system is an organ system containing glands such as the salivary glands and the pancreas (which produce digestive juices), the stomach (where food is digested), the small intestine (where food is digested and soluble food molecules are absorbed), the liver (which produces bile), and the large intestine (which absorbs water from undigested food leaving faeces).

Plant Tissues and Organs

☐ That plants have organs such as stems, roots and leaves.

☐ That plants have tissues such as mesophyll tissue (for photosynthesis), xylem and phloem (to transport water and other substances around the plant) and epidermal tissue (to cover the plant).

Exam-style Questions

1   This diagram shows the single-celled microorganism, *S. cerevisiae*.

1 (a)   Look at the structures labelled A-D on the diagram.
Draw lines below to match each of the structures to
the correct name.

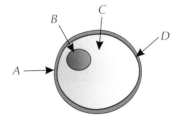

A	nucleus
B	cytoplasm
C	cell membrane
D	cell wall

(4 marks)

1 (b)   Is *S. cerevisiae* a yeast or a bacterium? Give a reason for your answer.

(1 mark)

2   Some people with stomach cancer have an operation to completely remove their
stomach.

2 (a)   The diagram shows part of the digestive system of someone who has had their stomach
removed.

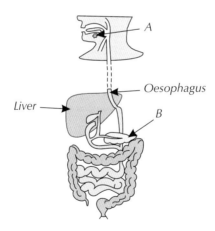

2 (a) (i)   Name the organ that the oesophagus (food pipe) now joins directly on to.

(1 mark)

2 (a) (ii)   Name the organs labelled **A** and **B** on the diagram and describe their role.

(3 marks)

2 (b)   The stomach is made up of several different tissue types.
Name and describe the functions of **two** types of tissue in the stomach.

(4 marks)

3   The diagram shows three different types of neurone. These neurones work together to carry electrical signals around the body. The electrical signals travel along the neurones to body cells — they're passed onto the body cells at the branched endings of the motor neurones.

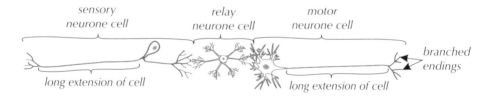

3 (a)   A neurone is a specialised cell. What is a specialised cell?

(1 mark)

3 (b)   Does the diagram as a whole represent a tissue, an organ or an organ system? Explain your answer.

(2 marks)

3 (c)   By reading the information above and looking at the diagram, suggest **one** way in which the structure of a **motor neurone cell** helps it to carry out its function.

(1 mark)

4   The photograph below shows a cross section through a leaf.

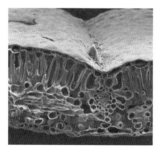

4 (a)   What name is given to the tissue that covers the leaf?

(1 mark)

4 (b)   Some of the cells in the photograph contain lots of chloroplasts. What plant tissue are these cells part of? Explain your answer.

(3 marks)

4 (c) (i)   Carbon dioxide diffuses into leaf cells from the air spaces surrounding them. What does this tell you about the concentration of carbon dioxide inside the cells compared to in the air spaces? Explain your answer.

(2 marks)

4 (c) (ii)   Throughout the day, the rate at which carbon dioxide diffuses into the leaf cells changes. Explain how a change in the concentration of carbon dioxide in the air spaces outside the cells could slow down the rate of diffusion.

(2 marks)

Learning Objectives:

- Know that the chloroplasts of plant cells and algae contain chlorophyll — a green substance which absorbs light energy.
- Know that during photosynthesis, the light energy absorbed by chlorophyll is used to convert carbon dioxide and water into glucose, and that oxygen is produced as a by-product.
- Know the word equation for photosynthesis.

Specification Reference B2.3.1

1. The Basics of Photosynthesis

Plants and algae make their own food using just light energy, a substance called chlorophyll, carbon dioxide from the air and water from the soil.

What is photosynthesis?

Photosynthesis is the process that produces 'food' in plants and algae. The 'food' it produces is **glucose** (a sugar). Plants use this glucose for a number of things, such as making cell walls and proteins (see page 145).

Where does photosynthesis happen?

Photosynthesis happens inside the **chloroplasts** in plant cells and algae. Chloroplasts contain a green substance called **chlorophyll**, which absorbs sunlight and uses its energy to convert carbon dioxide (from the air) and water (from the soil) into glucose. Oxygen is also produced as a by-product.

You need to learn the equation for photosynthesis:

$$\text{carbon dioxide} + \text{water} \xrightarrow{\text{light energy}} \text{glucose} + \text{oxygen}$$

Photosynthesis happens in the leaves of all green plants — this is largely what the leaves are for. Figure 2 shows a cross-section of a leaf showing the four raw materials (carbon dioxide, water, light energy and chlorophyll) needed for photosynthesis.

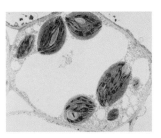

Figure 1: *Microscope image of a plant cell. The chloroplasts (green structures) can be seen clearly.*

Tip: Xylem is the tissue that transports water around a plant (see page 132).

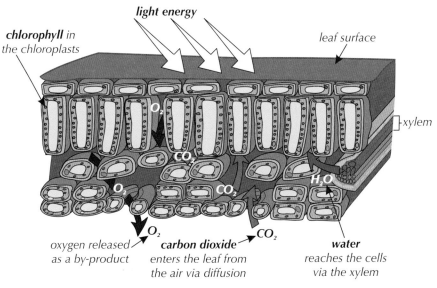

Figure 2: *Diagram of a cross-section through a leaf, showing the four raw materials required for photosynthesis.*

Q1 Which product produced by photosynthesis is 'food' for the plant?

Q2 a) Name the parts of a plant cell that contain chlorophyll.

b) What role does chlorophyll play in photosynthesis?

Q3 Write out the word equation for photosynthesis.

Q4 Which gas is used in photosynthesis?

Q5 What is the by-product of photosynthesis?

Practice Questions — Application

Q1 Three identical plants were grown for a week. They were treated in exactly the same way, except they each received different amounts of sunlight per day, as shown in this table:

Plant	Hours of sunlight received per day
A	3
B	7
C	10

The plants didn't have any source of light other than sunlight.

Which plant do you think will have produced the most glucose after one week? Explain your answer.

Q2 A scientist studied three different types of plant cell (taken from the same plant) under a microscope. She recorded the average number of chloroplasts she found in each type of cell, as shown in this table:

Type of plant cell	Average number of chloroplasts
1	20
2	0
3	51

Suggest which type of plant cell (1-3) is likely to have the highest rate of photosynthesis. Explain your answer.

Learning Objectives:
- Understand that light intensity, the availability of carbon dioxide and temperature all interact to affect the rate of photosynthesis, and that any one of these can be the limiting factor of photosynthesis.
- Understand that a low light intensity, low carbon dioxide level and low temperature can all limit the rate of photosynthesis.
- Be able to interpret data showing factors affecting the rate of photosynthesis.

Specification Reference
B2.3.1

Tip: Plants also need water for photosynthesis, but when a plant is so short of water that it becomes the limiting factor in photosynthesis, it's already in such trouble that this is the least of its worries.

Figure 1: *Pondweed giving off oxygen bubbles as a by-product of photosynthesis.*

2. The Rate of Photosynthesis

Photosynthesis doesn't always happen at the same rate — factors such as light intensity, carbon dioxide level and temperature can all affect the rate.

Limiting factors in photosynthesis

The rate of photosynthesis is affected by the intensity of light, the volume of carbon dioxide (CO_2), and the temperature. All three of these things need to be at the right level to allow a plant to photosynthesise as quickly as possible. If any one of these factors is too high or too low, it will become the **limiting factor**. This just means it's the factor which is stopping photosynthesis from happening any faster.

Which factor is limiting at a particular time depends on the environmental conditions:

Examples

- At night there's much less light than there is during the day, so light intensity is usually the limiting factor at night.
- In winter it's usually cold, so a low temperature is often the limiting factor.
- If it's warm enough and bright enough, the amount of CO_2 is usually limiting.

Investigating the rate of photosynthesis

To investigate the effect of different factors on photosynthesis, the rate of photosynthesis needs to be measured. There are different ways to do this:

Example

You can investigate the rate of photosynthesis of a water plant like Canadian pondweed. With this type of plant you can easily measure the amount of oxygen produced in a given time to show how fast photosynthesis is happening (remember, oxygen is made during photosynthesis). You could either count the bubbles given off, or if you want to be a bit more accurate you could collect the oxygen in a gas syringe as shown in Figure 2.

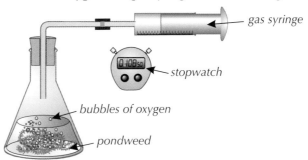

gas syringe

stopwatch

bubbles of oxygen

pondweed

Figure 2: *Diagram showing the experimental set up used to measure the rate of photosynthesis in water plants.*

Controlling variables

Generally, you'll only be investigating one factor that affects the rate of photosynthesis at a time, so you have to try and keep all the other variables constant, so that it's a fair test.

Tip: The variables in these experiments include all of the limiting factors of photosynthesis.

Examples

- Use a bench lamp to control the intensity of the light (careful not to block the light with anything).

- If your plant's in a flask, keep the flask in a water bath to help keep the temperature constant.

- There's not much you can do to keep the carbon dioxide level constant — you may just have to use a large container for your plant, and do the experiments as quickly as you can, so that the plant doesn't use up too much of the carbon dioxide in the container.

Tip: For more on designing investigations and controlling variables see pages 6-7.

Interpreting data on the rate of photosynthesis

You need to be able to interpret data showing how different factors affect the rate of photosynthesis.

1. Effect of light intensity

Light provides the energy needed for photosynthesis. As you can see from Figure 3, as the light level is raised, the rate of photosynthesis increases steadily — but only up to a certain point. Beyond that, it won't make any difference because then it'll be either the temperature or the carbon dioxide level which is the limiting factor.

Tip: If you're using a bench lamp to control light intensity and you just plot the rate of photosynthesis against "distance of lamp from the beaker", you get a weird-shaped graph. To get a graph like the one in Figure 3, you either need to measure the light intensity at the beaker using a light meter or do a bit of nifty maths with your results.

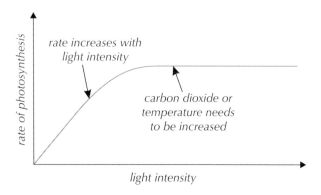

Figure 3: Graph showing how light intensity affects the rate of photosynthesis.

Remember, photosynthesis hasn't stopped when the graph levels off — it's just not increasing anymore.

2. Effect of carbon dioxide level

Carbon dioxide is one of the raw materials needed for photosynthesis.
As with light intensity the amount of carbon dioxide will only increase the rate of photosynthesis up to a point. After this the graph flattens out showing that carbon dioxide is no longer the limiting factor (see Figure 4).

Tip: If you're investigating the rate of photosynthesis using a plant in water, you can increase the CO_2 level by dissolving sodium hydrogen carbonate in the water. This gives off carbon dioxide.

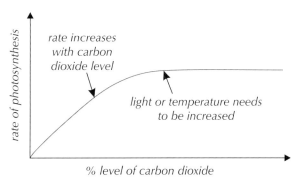

Figure 4: *Graph showing how carbon dioxide level affects the rate of photosynthesis.*

As long as light and carbon dioxide are in plentiful supply then the factor limiting photosynthesis must be temperature.

3. Effect of temperature

Tip: You can read more about enzymes on pages 156-158.

Enzymes are proteins which increase the speed of chemical reactions in living things — so enzymes increase the rate of photosynthesis in plant and algal cells. The speed at which enzymes work is affected by temperature.

Usually, if the temperature is the limiting factor in photosynthesis it's because it's too low — the enzymes needed for photosynthesis work more slowly at low temperatures. But if the plant gets too hot, the enzymes it needs for photosynthesis and its other reactions will be damaged. This happens at about 45 °C (which is pretty hot for outdoors, although greenhouses can get that hot if you're not careful). Figure 5 shows the effect of temperature on the rate of photosynthesis.

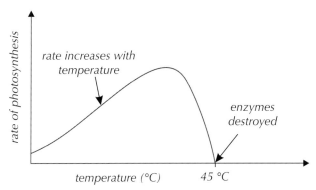

Figure 5: *Graph showing how temperature affects the rate of photosynthesis.*

Practice Question — Fact Recall

Q1 The rate of photosynthesis is affected by limiting factors.

a) What is meant by a 'limiting factor' of photosynthesis?

b) Give three factors that can affect the rate of photosynthesis.

Practice Questions — Application

Q1 Complete the table to show what is most likely to be the limiting factor of photosynthesis in the environmental conditions listed.

Environmental conditions	Most likely limiting factor
Outside on a cold winter's day.	
In an unlit garden at 1:30 am, in the UK, in summer.	
On a windowsill on a warm, bright day.	

Q2 Peter was investigating the rate of photosynthesis in pondweed. He put equally sized samples of pondweed from the same plant in two separate flasks containing different solutions. The solution in flask A had a lower carbon dioxide concentration than the solution in flask B. Peter put the flasks an equal distance away from a light source and gradually increased the intensity of the light throughout the experiment. He kept both flasks at a constant temperature of 25 °C. During the experiment Peter measured the amount of gas produced in each flask using a gas syringe. His results are shown on the graph:

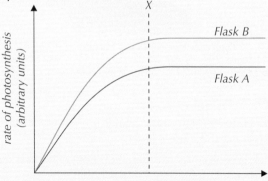

a) What gas did Peter collect in order to measure the rate of photosynthesis?

b) Give two things that Peter did to make the experiment a fair test.

c) Peter thinks that the limiting factor before point X in his experiment is light. Why does he think this?

d) Both graphs level off after point X. Suggest why Flask A levels off at a lower point than Flask B. Explain your answer.

Exam Tip
μmoles/m²/s is a unit used to measure light intensity. Don't panic if you see unfamiliar units in the exam — just focus on what the axis is showing you, e.g. here it's light intensity.

3. Artificially Controlling Plant Growth

As you've read on the last few pages, different factors affect the rate of photosynthesis. Farmers and other plant growers can use this knowledge to try and increase the rate of growth in their plants.

Greenhouses

If you know the ideal conditions for photosynthesis, then you can create an environment which maximises the rate of photosynthesis, which in turn maximises the rate of plant growth, (plants use some of the glucose produced by photosynthesis for growth — see page 145). The most common way to artificially create the ideal environment for plants is to grow them in a greenhouse. Commercial growers (people who grow plants to make money, such as farmers) often grow large quantities of plants in commercial greenhouses. The following conditions can easily be managed in a greenhouse:

1. Temperature

Greenhouses help to trap the Sun's heat, (see Figure 2) and make sure that the temperature doesn't become limiting.

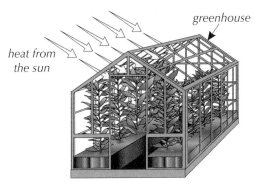

Figure 2: Greenhouses trap the Sun's heat.

Temperature can be controlled in other ways too:

> **Examples**
> - In winter, a farmer might use a heater in their greenhouse to keep the temperature at the ideal level.
> - In summer, greenhouses could get too hot, so farmers might use shades and ventilation to cool things down.

2. Light

Light is always needed for photosynthesis, so farmers often supply artificial light after the Sun goes down to give their plants more quality photosynthesis time.

3. Carbon dioxide concentration

Farmers can also increase the level of carbon dioxide in the greenhouse. A fairly common way is to use a paraffin heater to heat the greenhouse. As the paraffin burns, it makes carbon dioxide as a by-product.

Figure 1: Lettuces growing in a commercial greenhouse.

Figure 3: Lamps in greenhouses supply light so plants can continue to photosynthesise at night.

4. General health of plants

Keeping plants enclosed in a greenhouse also makes it easier to keep them free from pests and diseases. The farmer can add fertilisers to the soil as well, to provide all the minerals needed for healthy growth.

Greenhouse costs

Controlling the conditions in a greenhouse costs money — but if the farmer can keep the conditions just right for photosynthesis, the plants will grow much faster and a decent crop can be harvested much more often, which can then be sold.

It's important that a farmer supplies just the right amount of heat, light, etc. — enough to make the plants grow well, but not more than the plants need, as this would just be wasting money.

Interpreting data on artificial environments

In the exam you could be given some data about controlling photosynthesis in artificial environments (like greenhouses) and asked questions about it.

Example

A farmer normally grows his plants outside when the average air temperature is between 9 and 11 °C. The farmer wants to increase the growth rate of his plants, so he is considering getting a greenhouse. He finds some data on how temperature affects the rate of photosynthesis for the type of plants he grows. This is shown in the graph:

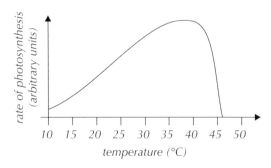

You could be asked to evaluate the benefits of growing plants in an artificial environment...
By looking at the graph you can see that the plants could photosynthesise faster if they were grown at temperatures higher than the average temperatures outside. If the farmer had a greenhouse he could control the temperature the plants were kept at, therefore increasing their rate of photosynthesis and growth. However, he would have to weigh up the cost of buying and running a greenhouse against this increased rate of growth.

You could be asked to make suggestions based on data from the graph...
For instance, you could be asked to suggest the best temperature for the farmer to keep his plants at and to explain why. Based on the graph, suggesting 37 °C would be a good idea, as this is the minimum temperature at which the rate of photosynthesis is highest. Keeping them at temperatures higher than this would just be a waste of money.

Exam Tip
If you get a question like this in the exam, remember that the aim of commercial farming is to make money. Farmers try to create conditions to increase photosynthesis (and therefore growth) but at a minimum cost.

Q1   Explain why some farmers grow plants in an artificial environment.

Q2   Farmers can control the light and temperature in a greenhouse. Give one other condition they can control in a greenhouse.

Practice Questions — Application

Exam Tip
In the exam you might see experiments using rate of plant growth or increase in plant mass as an indirect way of measuring the rate of photosynthesis. This is because some of the glucose produced by photosynthesis is used for growth in plants (see page 145).

A farmer grew the same type of plant in two greenhouses, A and B. He used a paraffin heater in Greenhouse A and an electric heater in Greenhouse B. Electric heaters don't release any carbon dioxide, whereas carbon dioxide is released when paraffin is burnt.

For 8 weeks the farmer recorded the average height of the plants in each greenhouse. He also monitored the temperature in both greenhouses. Plants in both greenhouses were exposed to the same amount of light and given the same amount of water and nutrients. His results are shown below:

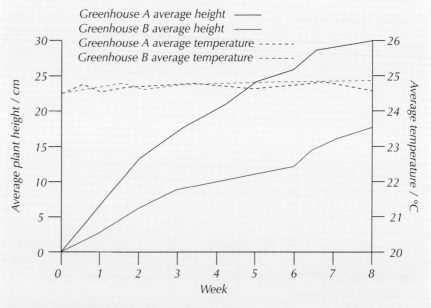

Greenhouse A average height ——
Greenhouse B average height ——
Greenhouse A average temperature ------
Greenhouse B average temperature ------

Q1   a) What was the average growth rate per week for the plants in Greenhouse A?

b) What was the average growth rate per week for the plants in Greenhouse B?

Tip: If you're stuck on Q2, have a look back at the pages on limiting factors of photosynthesis (138-140).

Q2   What factor do you think is responsible for the difference between the average growth rates of the plants in Greenhouse A compared to Greenhouse B. Explain your answer.

Q3   The farmer is trying to decide which type of heater to use on a permanent basis. Other than the effect on growth rate, suggest what else the farmer will need to consider when choosing a heater.

4. How Plants and Algae Use Glucose

As you know plants and algae photosynthesise to make 'food' in the form of glucose. They make use of this glucose in a number of ways...

What is glucose used for?

During photosynthesis, plants and algae convert carbon dioxide and water into glucose (see page 136). They use the glucose they produce for the following things:

1. Respiration

Plants and algae use some of the glucose they make for respiration. Respiration is a process which occurs in all living organisms — it's where energy is released from the breakdown of glucose (see page 167). Plants and algae use this energy to convert the rest of the glucose into various other useful substances, which they can use to build new cells and grow. To produce some of these substances plants also need to gather a few minerals from the soil (e.g. nitrates — see below).

2. Making cell walls

Glucose is converted into **cellulose** for making strong cell walls (see page 120), especially in a rapidly growing plant. These cell walls support and strengthen the cells.

3. Making proteins

Plant cells and algae use glucose to make **amino acids**. Amino acids are the building blocks which make up proteins. When amino acids are joined together in a particular sequence they make up a particular protein.

In plant cells, glucose is combined with **nitrate ions** (which are absorbed from the soil) to make amino acids, which are then made into proteins.

Storage of glucose

Glucose can be converted into other substances for storage:

Lipids

Plants and algae can convert some of the glucose they produce into lipids (fats and oils). Plants store lipids in seeds and algae store oil droplets in their cells.

> **Example**
>
> Sunflower seeds contain a lot of oil — we get cooking oil and margarine from them.

Learning Objectives:

- Know that the glucose produced by photosynthesis can be used for respiration.
- Know that plants and algae can also use this glucose to make cellulose and proteins.
- Know that plants need to take nitrate ions from the soil to make proteins.
- Know that plants and algae use glucose to make lipids, which are stored.
- Know that plants can also store glucose as starch.

Specification Reference B2.3.1

Figure 1: *Microscope image of a plant cell wall made up of strands of cellulose.*

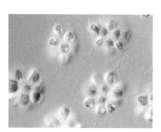

Figure 2: *Algal cells as seen under a microscope. The red dots are oil droplets.*

Starch

Plants and algae can convert glucose into starch. Glucose is stored as starch so it's ready for use when photosynthesis isn't happening as much, like in the winter. In plants starch is stored in roots, stems, seeds and leaves.

> **Example**
>
> Potato and parsnip plants store a lot of starch underground over the winter so a new plant can grow from it the following spring. We eat the swollen storage organs (see Figure 3).

Figure 3: *Potato plants that have just been dug up — the potatoes that we eat are starch stores for the plant.*

Starch is **insoluble** which makes it much better for storing than glucose — a cell with lots of glucose in would draw in loads of water and swell up.

Practice Questions — Fact Recall

Q1 By what process do plants and algae break down glucose in order to release energy?

Q2 What do plants and algae use cellulose for?

Q3 What do plants absorb from the soil to make proteins with?

Q4 Glucose can be stored as starch in plants and algae. How else is glucose stored?

Q5 Why is starch better for storage than glucose?

Section Checklist — Make sure you know...

The Basics of Photosynthesis

☐ That chlorophyll is a green substance found within the chloroplasts of plant cells and algae.

☐ That during photosynthesis, chlorophyll absorbs light energy, which is used to convert carbon dioxide (from the air) and water (from the soil) into glucose (a sugar).

☐ Know that oxygen is produced as a by-product of photosynthesis.

☐ That the word equation for photosynthesis is:

$$carbon\ dioxide\ +\ water\ \xrightarrow{light\ energy}\ glucose\ +\ oxygen.$$

The Rate of Photosynthesis

☐ That the rate of photosynthesis is affected by the interaction of light intensity, carbon dioxide concentration and temperature, and that any one of these three things can become the limiting factor of photosynthesis (the thing that stops it from happening any faster).

☐ That the rate of photosynthesis can be limited by low levels of light, low carbon dioxide levels or a low temperature.

☐ How to interpret data showing factors which affect the rate of photosynthesis.

Artificially Controlling Plant Growth

☐ That factors which affect the rate of photosynthesis (light intensity, carbon dioxide concentration and temperature) can be managed artificially (e.g. in a greenhouse) and that this is done in order to increase the rate of photosynthesis of plants.

☐ How to evaluate the benefits of growing plants in artificial environments.

How Plants and Algae Use Glucose

☐ That plants and algae use the glucose produced by photosynthesis for respiration, making cellulose (to strengthen cell walls) and for producing proteins.

☐ That plants need to absorb nitrate ions from the soil to make proteins.

☐ That plants and algae can store glucose as lipids (fats and oils) or as starch (which is insoluble).

Tip: Not all organisms are affected by all of these factors. For example, the availability of carbon dioxide and light doesn't really affect animals, but it does affect plants.

Figure 1: *The distribution of daisies is affected by the amount of light available — so they grow well in an open field like this one.*

1. Distribution of Organisms

Different environments will suit some organisms better than others. If the conditions within these environments change, then the type and number of organisms living there could change too...

Habitats and distribution

A **habitat** is the place where an organism lives, e.g. a playing field. **Distribution** is where organisms are found in a particular area, e.g. in a part of the playing field.

Factors affecting distribution

The distribution of organisms is affected by environmental factors such as:

- Temperature
- Availability of water
- Availability of oxygen

- Availability of carbon dioxide
- Availability of nutrients
- Amount of light

An organism might be more common in one area than another due to differences in environmental factors between the two areas.

> **Example**
>
> - In a field, you might find that daisies are more common in the open, than under trees. This is because there's more light available in the open and daisies need light to survive (they use it for photosynthesis — see page 136).
>
> - Some types of mayfly are more common in colder parts of a stream, as they can't tolerate the warmer temperatures in other parts of the stream.

Practice Questions — Fact Recall

Q1 What is meant by the 'distribution' of organisms?

Q2 List six factors which could affect the distribution of organisms.

2. Studying Distribution

Some scientists are interested in studying the distribution of organisms, so that they can see how environmental changes affect it. Right, enough talk — time to get your quadrat out...

Ways to study distribution

There are a couple of ways to study the distribution of organisms:

1. You can measure how common an organism is in two or more sample areas and compare them.

2. You can study how the distribution changes across an area e.g. from one edge of a field to another.

The data you collect can be used to provide evidence for environmental change. For instance, if the distribution of organisms across an area changes over time, this could be due to changes in the environment.

> **Example**
>
> The Dartford warbler is a species of bird. It has become more widely distributed in the UK in recent years — partly because warmer winters have allowed it to move further north and partly because there are now more areas of protected heathland for it to live in.

Studying distribution often involves the use of **quadrats** (see below) and **transects** (see page 151).

Studying distribution often involves the use of **quadrats** (see below) and **transects** (see page 151).

Using quadrats

Quadrats are really useful for studying the distribution of small organisms that are slow-moving or that don't move around. A quadrat is a square frame enclosing a known area, e.g. 1 m² (see Figure 1). To compare how common an organism is in two sample areas, you can collect data using random sampling with a quadrat. Just follow these simple steps:

1. Place a quadrat on the ground at a random point within the first sample area.

2. Count all the organisms within the quadrat and record the results.

3. Repeat steps 1 and 2 as many times as you can.

4. Repeat steps 1 to 3 in the second sample area.

5. Finally compare the two sets of results. To do this you'll need to work out the average result for each sample area, which involves a bit of maths...

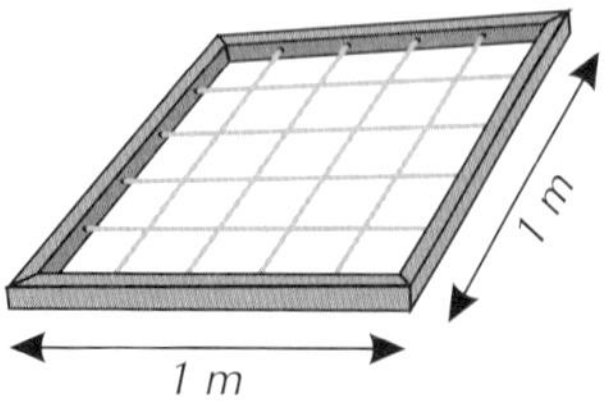

1 m

1 m

Figure 1: *A diagram of a 1 m² quadrat.*

Tip: It's really important that the quadrats are placed <u>randomly</u> within the sample area (see page 152 for how to do this). Taking random samples improves the validity of the study.

Figure 2: *A student using a quadrat to gather data on the distribution of organisms.*

Working out averages

There are three averages you need to know how to work out — the mean, the mode and the median:

> - **Mean** — you calculate this by adding together all the values in the data, and dividing that total by the number of values that you have.
> - The **mode** is the most common value in a set of data.
> - The **median** is the middle value in a set of data, when they're in order of size.

Examples

John counted the number of daffodils in 9 quadrats.
He recorded the following results: 5, 8, 2, 5, 9, 4, 11, 3, 7.

- **Mean:** work out the mean with this formula: $\dfrac{\text{total number of organisms}}{\text{number of quadrats}}$

  So the mean here is:

  $$\frac{5 + 8 + 2 + 5 + 9 + 4 + 11 + 3 + 7}{9} \ = \ \frac{54}{9} \ = \ \textbf{6 daffodils per quadrat.}$$

- **Mode:** count how often each value occurs in the data to find the value that is most common — **5**, 8, 2, **5**, 9, 4, 11, 3, 7. 5 occurs most often in the data, so **5** is the mode.

- **Median:** put the numbers in order of size — 2, 3, 4, 5, **5**, 7, 8, 9, 11, then find the middle value. Here the middle value is **5**, so that's the median.

Tip: If there are two middle numbers in a list of data, you just add them together and then divide by 2 to get the median. E.g. if you had the numbers 3, 4, 10, 19, the median would be **7**. (4 + 10 = 14, and then 14 ÷ 2 = **7**).

Population size

You can use the data you've gathered about an organism to work out the population size of the organism in the sample area. You need to:

1. Work out the mean number of organisms per m^2. (If your quadrat has an area of 1 m^2, this is the same as the mean number of organisms per quadrat.)

2. Then multiply the mean by the total area (in m^2) of the habitat.

Example

A field has an area of 800 m^2 and the mean number of daisies per m^2 is 22.
Calculate the population size of daisies in the field.

Size of the daisy population = mean number of daisies per m^2 × the total area
= 22 × 800
= **17 600 daisies**

Using transects

You can use lines called transects (see Figure 3) to help find out how organisms (like plants) are distributed across an area — e.g. if an organism becomes more or less common as you move from a hedge towards the middle of a field.

Tip: Transects can be used in any type of habitat, not just fields. For example, along a beach or in a stream.

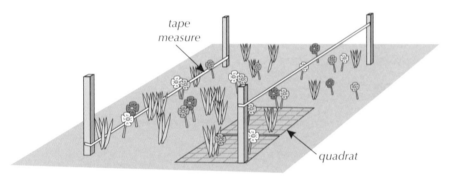

tape measure

quadrat

Figure 3: A diagram showing two transects.

Here's what to do:

1. Mark out a line in the area you want to study using a tape measure.

2. Then collect data along the line. You can do this by just counting all the organisms you're interested in that touch the line. Or, you can collect data by using quadrats. These can be placed next to each other along the line or at intervals, for example, every 2 m.

Figure 4: Students using a quadrat along a transect.

Reproducibility and validity

The environmental data you gather when using quadrats and transects can provide evidence for environmental change. But you need to think carefully about the reproducibility and validity of your study:

Tip: By collecting data about the distribution of organisms you are collecting environmental data.

Reproducibility

You need to be confident that the results of your study could be reproduced. This means that someone else should be able to carry out the same study and get similar results to you.

Tip: For more on reproducibility see page 2 and page 9 in 'How Science Works'.

One way to make your results more reproducible is to take a large sample size, e.g. use as many quadrats and transects as possible in your sample area. Bigger samples are more representative of the whole population (see page 2).

Validity

For your results to be valid they must be repeatable and reproducible, and answer the original question (what you are trying to find out).

Tip: Repeatable means that if you conduct the experiment again, using the same method and equipment as in your original experiment, then you'll get the same results again.

Tip: Have a look at page 3 for more information on validity.

To answer the original question, you need to control all the variables. The question you want to answer is whether a difference in distribution between two sample areas (or across one area) is due to a difference in one environmental factor. If you've controlled all the other variables that could be affecting the distribution, you'll know whether a difference in distribution is caused by the environmental factor or not.

If you don't control the other variables you won't know whether any correlation (relationship) you've found is because of chance, because of the environmental factor you're looking at or because of a different variable — the study won't give you valid data.

Exam Tip
In the exam you could be given an experiment and asked what variables were controlled. Think about what the experiment is trying to find out, and think of possible factors that could affect the results — these are the variables which need to be controlled.

> **Example**
>
> A student found a correlation between the number of daisies in an area and the amount of light.
>
> He found that there were more daisies growing in an area which received more light, than in an area where there was less light. However, he couldn't conclude that the amount of light caused the difference in the number of daisies because other variables, e.g. the availability of water, could have affected the results.
>
> Unless the student could control these variables too, his results wouldn't be valid.

Tip: You must put your quadrat down in a random place before you start counting — don't just plonk it down on the first big patch of organisms that you see.

Another way you can improve the validity of your results is to use random samples, e.g. randomly put down or mark out your quadrat or transect. You can do this by dividing the area you are going to study into a grid and using a random number generator, or drawing numbers out of a hat, to pick the coordinates of where you will place your quadrats or transect. If all your samples are in one spot, and everywhere else is different, the results you get won't be valid.

Practice Questions — Fact Recall

Q1 Describe how you would use random sampling with a quadrat to compare the distribution of organisms in two sample areas.

Q2 How do you calculate the mean of a set of data?

Q3 What is the mode value in a set of data?

Q4 What is the median value in set of data?

Q5 Describe one way in which a transect can be used to measure the distribution of organisms across an area.

Q6 Give one way you could increase the reproducibility of a study that involves collecting environmental data.

Q1 Joanne read that bulrushes grow best in moist soil or in shallow water. She wanted to find out whether this was true, so she investigated the distribution of bulrushes in her garden. She used a transect (as shown in the diagram) and recorded the number of bulrushes in each quadrat as shown in the table.

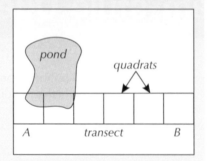

Quadrat	1	2	3	4	5	6
Number of Bulrushes	1	5	5	20	43	37

a) i) Calculate the mean number of bulrushes per quadrat.

ii) Calculate the modal number of bulrushes per quadrat.

iii) Calculate the median number of bulrushes per quadrat.

b) Joanne started counting at quadrat 1 and moved along the transect in order, to quadrat 6. Assuming that the information Joanne read was correct, do you think quadrat 1 is at end A or end B of the transect? Explain your answer.

c) Joanne didn't control any of the variables which may have affected the growth of bulrushes in her garden. Explain how this affects the validity of her study.

d) A change to the drainage system in Joanne's garden means that the area of the pond is gradually decreasing in size. Suggest how the distribution of bulrushes in the garden may change in the future if the size of the pond continues to decrease.

Tip: If you're asked to find the 'modal number' you need to find the mode.

HOW SCIENCE WORKS

Section Checklist — Make sure you know...

Distribution of Organisms

☐ That there are a number of environmental factors which can affect the distribution of organisms, including temperature and the availability of water, oxygen, carbon dioxide, nutrients and light.

☐ That the distribution of organisms varies in a habitat, and how to suggest reasons for this variation (often it's due to differences in environmental factors between different areas of the habitat).

Studying Distribution

☐ How random sampling with quadrats can be used to study the distribution of organisms.

☐ How to calculate the mean, mode and median of a set of data.

☐ How sampling along a transect can be used to show the distribution of organisms across an area.

☐ How to evaluate the methods used to collect environmental data, in terms of the validity of the methods used and the reproducibility of the data, as evidence of environmental change.

Exam-style Questions

1   A biology class were studying the distribution of organisms on a rocky shore line. Three students each set up a transect which ran from the water's edge up the shore, as shown in the diagram. All three students counted the number of limpets in each of the 50 cm × 50 cm quadrats. The number of limpets counted by each student are shown in the table.

Student A   Student B   Student C

Quadrat number	1	2	3	4	5	6	7
Student A Number of Limpets	18	65	70	55	30	10	0
Student B Number of Limpets	6	72	76	41	21	18	3
Student C Number of Limpets	14	83	84	57	26	16	1

shore

sea

quadrat

1 (a) (i)   Calculate the mean number of limpets found in quadrat 4.
Show your working.

(2 marks)

1 (a) (ii)   Limpets need to stay moist in order to survive, but they are able to survive for a period of time without water by clamping down onto the surface of rocks — this helps to prevent them from drying out. Close to the water's edge, limpets have lots of competition from other species for space.

Use this information and the data above to describe the distribution of limpets along the shore line and suggest reasons for it.

(3 marks)

1 (a) (iii)   One of the students thinks that they need to gather more data by setting up more transects. Explain why this would increase the reproducibility of their results.

(2 marks)

1 (b)   During the class study, another group of students investigated the distribution of a type of starfish. They divided the area of shoreline they were interested in studying into two sample areas (A and B), and placed 20 quadrats at random in each area. The students' results showed that sample area A contained a higher number of starfish.

1 (b) (i)   Why did the students place their quadrats randomly?

(1 mark)

1 (b) (ii)   Suggest **two** environmental factors that could explain the difference in the distribution of starfish in the two sample areas.

(2 marks)

2   Tim read the following information in a science magazine:

> You can measure the rate of photosynthesis in plants by doing the following:
>
> Cut discs from a plant leaf and put them in a 0.2% sodium hydrogen carbonate solution (which serves as a source of carbon dioxide). Put the solution and leaf discs in a syringe and then remove all the air from the syringe — this removes any gases out of the air spaces in the leaf, which will cause the leaf discs to sink.
>
> Then put the syringe containing the leaf discs under a light source. As the leaf discs photosynthesise, their cells produce oxygen. The oxygen will fill the air spaces in the leaf — with enough oxygen in the air spaces they'll begin to float. You can use the time this takes as a measure of the rate of photosynthesis.

2 (a) (i)   Where in a plant cell does photosynthesis take place?

(1 mark)

2 (a) (ii)   Complete the word equation for photosynthesis:

carbon dioxide + ... $\xrightarrow{\text{..........................}}$ glucose + oxygen

(2 marks)

Tim decided to use the method described in the science magazine to investigate the effect of light intensity on the rate of photosynthesis. He conducted the experiment at three different light intensities. For each light intensity he cut 10 equally sized discs from a leaf, and set up the experiment as described in the magazine article. He then timed how long it took for all of the leaf discs to float to the surface in the syringe. His results are shown in this table:

Light intensity	Time it took for all discs to float (minutes)
A	18
B	9
C	11

2 (b) (i)   Which light intensity do you think was the highest, A, B or C? Explain your answer.

(2 marks)

2 (b) (ii)   Tim thinks that if he keeps increasing the light intensity, he will keep increasing the rate of photosynthesis. Is he right? Explain your answer.

(4 marks)

2 (b) (iii)   Tim conducts the experiment again using light intensity A. This time he uses a solution containing 0.8% sodium hydrogen carbonate. Do you think it will take more or less than 18 minutes for all of the discs to float? Explain your answer.

(2 marks)

2 (c)   *In this question you will be assessed on the quality of your English, the organisation of your ideas and your use of appropriate specialist vocabulary.*

The process of photosynthesis produces glucose. Describe as fully as you can how this glucose may be used by a plant.

(6 marks)

Tip: All enzymes are proteins, but not all proteins are enzymes.

Tip: 'Biological' means related to living things. (Enzymes are biological catalysts because they're made by living things.)

1. Proteins and Enzymes

Proteins are involved in all the processes and chemical reactions that keep us ticking over, so it's really important that you learn what they're all about...

What are proteins?

Proteins are large biological molecules, which are made up of long chains of smaller molecules called **amino acids**. These chains are folded into unique shapes that other molecules can fit into, allowing proteins to do their jobs.

Proteins have a variety of functions. They can act as:

- **Structural components of tissue**, like muscles.
  For example, myosin and actin are proteins that make up muscles.

- **Hormones**, for example insulin is a protein that works as a hormone.

- **Antibodies** — these lock onto foreign antigens (the unique molecules on a pathogen's surface) and kill invading cells.

- **Catalysts** — better known as enzymes. All enzymes are proteins.

Enzymes

Living things have thousands of different chemical reactions going on inside them all the time. These reactions need to be carefully controlled — to get the right amounts of substances.

You can usually make a reaction happen more quickly by raising the temperature. This would speed up the useful reactions but also the unwanted ones too... not good. There's also a limit to how far you can raise the temperature inside a living creature before its cells start getting damaged.

So... living things produce enzymes that act as **biological catalysts**. Enzymes reduce the need for high temperatures and we only have enzymes to speed up the useful chemical reactions in the body.

A catalyst is a substance which increases the speed of a reaction, without being changed or used up in the reaction.

Enzyme action

Enzymes have special shapes so that they can catalyse reactions. Chemical reactions usually involve substances either being split apart or joined together. Every enzyme has a unique shape that fits onto the substance involved in a reaction. Enzymes are really picky — they usually only catalyse one reaction. This is because, for the enzyme to work, the substance has to fit its special shape — see Figure 1.

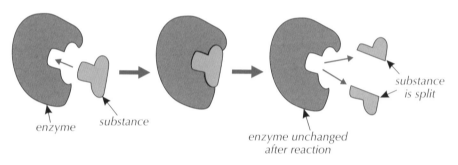

Figure 1: *Diagram to show how an enzyme works.*

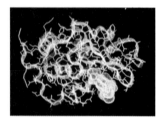

Figure 2: *Computer model of an enzyme bound to a substance (yellow) — they fit perfectly together.*

If the substance doesn't match the enzyme's shape, then the reaction won't be catalysed.

Optimum conditions for enzymes

Enzymes need the right conditions, such as the right temperature and pH, for them to work best — these are called **optimum conditions**.

Temperature

Changing the temperature changes the rate of an enzyme-catalysed reaction. Like with any reaction, a higher temperature increases the rate at first. But if it gets too hot, some of the bonds holding the enzyme together break. This destroys the enzyme's special shape and so it won't work any more. It's said to be denatured.

Therefore enzymes have a temperature at which they are most active — this is called the optimum temperature (see Figure 3). Enzymes in the human body normally work best at around 37 °C.

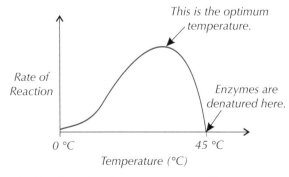

Figure 3: *Graph to show how temperature affects enzyme action.*

pH

Tip: A low pH means that an environment is acidic. A high pH means that it is alkaline.

The pH also affects enzymes. If it's too high or too low, the pH interferes with the bonds holding the enzyme together. This changes the shape and denatures the enzyme.

All enzymes have a pH that they work best at — this is called the optimum pH (see Figure 4).

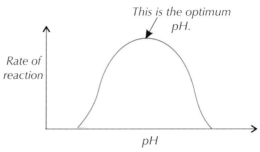

Figure 4: *Graph to show how pH affects enzyme action.*

The optimum pH is different for different enzymes depending on where they work.

> **Example**
>
> Pepsin is an enzyme used to break down proteins in the stomach (see page 161). It works best at pH 2, which means it's well-suited to the acidic conditions in the stomach.

Practice Questions — Fact Recall

Q1 a) What gives a protein its unique shape?

   b) Why does a protein need to have a unique shape?

Q2 Give three functions of proteins.

Q3 What is a catalyst?

Q4 True or false? All enzymes work best at pH 7.

Practice Question — Application

Tip: Respiration is the process of breaking down glucose, which releases energy. There's loads more about it on page 167.

Q1 Hexokinase is an enzyme found in the human body that's involved in respiration. It catalyses this reaction:

$$\text{glucose} \xrightarrow{\text{hexokinase}} \text{substance A}$$

Enzymes in the human body work best at 37 °C.

A scientist heats up hexokinase to 50 °C and adds it to some glucose. Suggest the effect this will have on the rate of the reaction compared to if the reaction was at 37 °C. Explain your answer.

2. Digestion

Digestion involves loads of reactions where large food molecules are broken down into smaller ones. Lots of enzymes are needed to catalyse all these reactions, so the body creates the ideal conditions for these enzymes to work in.

The digestive system

As you know from page 129, the digestive system is the organ system that breaks down food, so that nutrients can be absorbed into the body from the gut. (There's a reminder of what it looks like in Figure 1.)

Food is broken down in two ways:

- By mechanical digestion — this includes our teeth grinding down food and our stomach churning up food.

- By chemical digestion — where enzymes help to break down food.

You need to know all about how enzymes work in digestion.

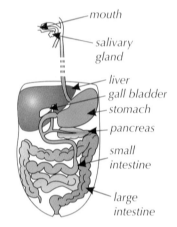

Figure 1: *The digestive system.*

Digestive enzymes

The enzymes involved in digestion work outside body cells. They're produced by specialised cells in glands and in the gut lining, and then released into the gut to mix with food molecules, such as starch, proteins and fats.

Starch, proteins and fats are big molecules. They're too big to pass through the walls of the digestive system. Sugars, amino acids, glycerol and fatty acids are much smaller molecules. They can pass easily through the walls of the digestive system. The digestive enzymes catalyse the breakdown of the big molecules into the smaller ones. Different digestive enzymes help to break down different types of food.

Amylase

Amylase is a digestive enzyme that catalyses the conversion of starch into sugars — see Figure 2.

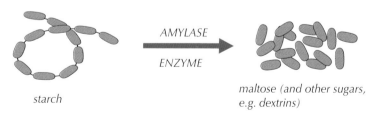

starch   AMYLASE ENZYME   *maltose (and other sugars, e.g. dextrins)*

Figure 2: *Diagram to show the breakdown of starch by amylase.*

Amylase is made in the salivary glands, the pancreas and the small intestine. It works in the mouth and the small intestine.

Learning Objectives:

- Know that digestive enzymes work outside body cells — they're made in glands and the gut lining, then released into the gut to work.

- Know that digestive enzymes help break down large food molecules into smaller ones.

- Understand what amylase does, where it is made and where it works.

- Understand what proteases do, where they are made and where they work.

- Understand what lipases do, where they are made and where they work.

- Understand how the stomach creates the ideal conditions for enzymes to work there.

- Know where bile is produced, stored and released.

- Understand how bile creates the ideal conditions for enzymes to work in the small intestine.

Specification Reference B2.5.2

Tip: Most absorption of food molecules happens in the small intestine (see page 129).

Tip: Enzymes produced by the salivary glands are released into the mouth. Enzymes produced by the pancreas are released into the small intestine.

Proteases

Protease enzymes are digestive enzymes that catalyse the conversion of proteins into amino acids — see Figure 3.

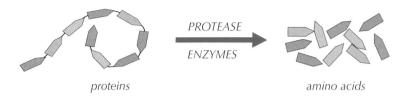

proteins   amino acids

Figure 3: *Diagram to show the breakdown of proteins by proteases.*

Proteases are made in the stomach, the pancreas and the small intestine. They work in the stomach and the small intestine.

Lipases

Tip: Lipids are fats and oils.

Lipase enzymes are digestive enzymes that catalyse the conversion of lipids into glycerol and fatty acids — see Figure 4.

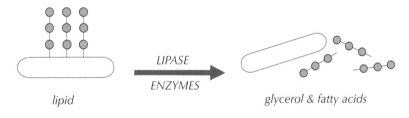

lipid   glycerol & fatty acids

Figure 4: *Diagram to show the breakdown of lipids by lipases.*

Tip: <u>Prote</u>ase enzymes break down <u>prote</u>ins. <u>Lip</u>ase enzymes break down <u>lip</u>ids.

Lipases are made in the pancreas and the small intestine. They work in the small intestine.

Summary of digestive enzymes

The table in Figure 5 summarises all the information you need to know about the digestive enzymes for your exam. Use Figure 5 to make sure you know exactly where each enzyme is made and where it works.

Exam Tip
Make sure you can locate where different enzymes are made and work on a diagram of the digestive system — look back at Figure 1 on the previous page.

Enzyme(s) →	Amylase	Proteases	Lipases
Help(s) to break down...	Starch	Proteins	Lipids
...into...	Sugars	Amino acids	Glycerol and fatty acids
Made in the...	Salivary glands, pancreas and small intestine	Stomach, pancreas and small intestine	Pancreas and small intestine
Work(s) in the...	Mouth and small intestine	Stomach and small intestine	Small intestine

Figure 5: *Table summarising the key facts about amylase, proteases and lipases.*

The stomach

The stomach is an organ in the digestive system. It pummels food with its muscular walls.

The stomach produces the protease enzyme, pepsin. It also produces **hydrochloric acid**. It produces hydrochloric acid for two reasons:

1. To kill bacteria.
2. To give the right pH for protease enzymes, such as pepsin, to work (pH 2 — acidic).

Bile

Bile is produced in the liver. It's stored in the gall bladder before it's released into the small intestine.

The hydrochloric acid in the stomach makes the pH too acidic for enzymes in the small intestine to work properly. Bile is alkaline — it neutralises the acid and makes conditions alkaline. The enzymes in the small intestine work best in these alkaline conditions.

Bile also emulsifies fats. In other words it breaks the fat into tiny droplets (see Figure 7). This gives a much bigger surface area of fat for the enzyme lipase to work on — which makes its digestion faster.

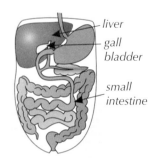

Figure 6: *Bile is produced in the liver, stored in the gall bladder and released into the small intestine.*

large fat droplet   tiny fat droplets

Figure 7: *Diagram to show the emulsification of fat by bile.*

Practice Questions — Fact Recall

Q1 In general, where are digestive enzymes produced?

Q2 True or false? Digestive enzymes build small molecules up into larger molecules.

Q3 Name the digestive enzyme produced in the salivary glands.

Q4 Where are protease enzymes involved in digestion produced?

Q5 Name the type of enzyme that catalyses the breakdown of lipids.

Q6 Describe how each of the following produce ideal conditions for enzymes to work in:

a) the stomach

b) bile

Q1 Here is a labelled diagram of the digestive system.

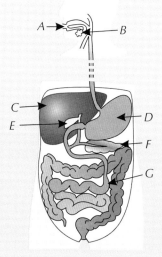

Complete this table using the appropriate letters from the diagram. (If there's more than one answer to the question, make sure you write down all the answers in the table.)

	Amylase	Proteases	Lipases	Bile
Made where?				
Work(s) where?				

Q2 An experiment was done to show how digestion in the stomach works. In the experiment, three equally sized pieces of meat were added to each of three test tubes. Then the test tubes were filled with equal volumes of the following substances:

> **Tip:** Meat is a source of protein.

Test tube 1 — hydrochloric acid (HCl acid)
Test tube 2 — pepsin
Test tube 3 — pepsin and hydrochloric acid (HCl acid)

The results are shown in the photograph:

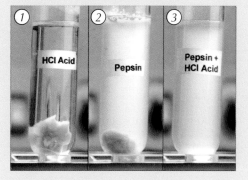

Describe and explain what the results show.

3. Enzymes in Home and Industry

Enzymes are really handy if you want to speed up chemical reactions. We humans have made good use of them in the home and in industry.

Mass production of enzymes

Some microorganisms produce enzymes which pass out of their cells and catalyse reactions outside them (e.g. to digest the microorganism's food). We can grow these microorganisms on a large scale and then harvest the enzymes they produce. The enzymes can then be used to catalyse useful reactions by adding them to products that we use at home or to industrial processes.

Uses of enzymes in the home

Detergents (e.g. washing powders) can be **biological** or **non-biological**. Non-biological detergents contain chemicals that break up stains on your clothes. Biological detergents contain the same chemicals as non-biological ones, but also contain a mixture of enzymes.

Biological detergents contain mainly protein-digesting enzymes (**proteases**) and fat-digesting enzymes (**lipases**). Because the enzymes break down animal and plant matter, they're ideal for removing stains like food or blood. Biological detergents are also more effective at working at low temperatures (e.g. 30 °C) than other types of detergents. Washing at lower temperatures is cheaper because less energy is used.

However, most biological detergents don't work well at high temperatures because the enzymes are denatured (see page 157). They might not work well in very acidic or alkaline tap water either — this is because the enzymes can be denatured at extremes of pH. Also, not everyone can use biological detergents because some of the enzymes can remain on clothes and can irritate sensitive skin.

Uses of enzymes in industry

Enzymes are used in industrial processes to make lots of different products, such as:

Baby foods

The proteins in some baby foods are '**pre-digested**' using protein-digesting enzymes (**proteases**). This means the proteins are partially broken down, so they're easier for the baby to digest.

Learning Objectives:

- Know that some microorganisms produce enzymes that catalyse reactions outside of their cells.
- Understand how these enzymes are used in the home in biological detergents.
- Know the advantages and disadvantages of using these enzymes in the home in biological detergents, including that they are more effective at low temperatures than non-biological detergents.
- Understand how these enzymes are used in industry to produce baby foods, sugar syrup and slimming foods.
- Know the advantages and disadvantages of using these enzymes in industry, including that they reduce the need for reactions to be carried out at high temperatures and pressures, but they can be denatured and may be expensive.

Specification Reference B2.5.2

Figure 1: *Biological washing powder is made up of granules, which contain enzymes that will break down stains.*

Sugar syrup

Carbohydrate-digesting enzymes (**carbohydrases**) can be used to turn starch syrup into sugar syrup (see Figure 2). Sugar syrup is used in lots of food products, such as sweets, jam and sports drinks.

starch syrup — **CARBOHYDRASE** → *sugar syrup*

Figure 2: The conversion of starch syrup to sugar syrup.

Slimming foods

Glucose syrup (a type of sugar syrup) can be turned into fructose syrup using an **isomerase** enzyme (see Figure 4). Fructose is sweeter than glucose, so you can use less of it — good for slimming foods and drinks.

glucose syrup — **ISOMERASE** → *fructose syrup*

Figure 4: The conversion of glucose syrup to fructose syrup.

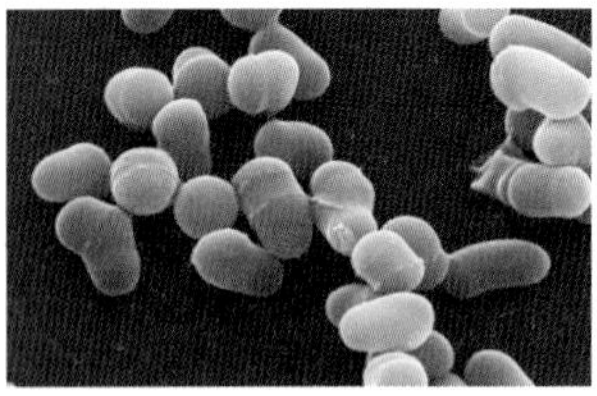

Figure 3: Microscope image of bacteria that produce the enzyme isomerase. By growing these bacteria we can get lots of isomerase, which we can use to make fructose syrup.

Evaluating the use of enzymes in industry

Enzymes are really useful in industry. They speed up reactions without the need for high temperatures and pressures. You need to know the advantages and disadvantages of using them, so here are a few to get you started:

Advantages

1. They're specific, so they only catalyse the reaction you want them to.

2. Using lower temperatures and pressures means a lower cost as it saves energy.

3. Enzymes work for a long time, so after the initial cost of buying them, you can continually re-use them.

4. They are biodegradable and therefore cause less environmental pollution.

Disadvantages

1. Enzymes can be denatured by even a small increase in temperature. They're also susceptible to poisons and changes in pH. This means the conditions in which they work must be tightly controlled.

2. Enzymes can be expensive to produce.

3. Contamination of the enzyme with other substances can affect the reaction.

Tip: Remember that catalysts increase the speed of a reaction, without being changed or used up. Enzymes are biological catalysts — they don't get used up in a reaction, so you can continually re-use them.

Tip: Even tiny little changes in pH or temperature will stop enzymes working at maximum efficiency (see pages 157-158). Enzymes only catalyse one reaction too, so you need to use a different one for each reaction.

Q1 a) Name the two main types of enzymes that biological washing powders contain.

b) State what type of molecules each of the enzymes you mentioned in a) help to break down.

Q2 Give one disadvantage of using biological washing powders instead of non-biological detergents.

Q3 Some baby foods contain proteins that have been 'pre-digested'. Explain what this means.

Q4 Name the type of enzyme used to convert starch into sugar syrup.

Q5 What reaction does the enzyme isomerase catalyse?

Practice Questions — Application

Q1 Sarah and John are in a supermarket. They're each trying to decide whether to buy biological or non-biological washing powder. Sarah, who is prone to eczema, needs to put some bedsheets on a hot wash. John just has a normal clothes wash to do and is trying to save money.

Tip: Eczema is a skin condition that can make the skin sensitive.

Suggest which type of washing powder Sarah and John should each buy. Explain your answers.

Q2 A soft drink manufacturer makes a popular lemonade product called Lem-Fizz using glucose syrup. The manufacturer wants to start making a 'diet' version of the product called Diet Lem-Fizz.

Tip: Products with less sugar in them will have fewer calories.

a) Suggest what type of sugar syrup the manufacturer should use in Diet Lem-Fizz. Explain your answer.

b) Suggest how the sugar syrup in your answer to a) could be made.

Section Checklist — Make sure you know...

Proteins and Enzymes

☐ That proteins are large molecules made up of long chains of amino acids and that these chains of amino acids fold up to give each protein a special shape.

☐ That a protein's special shape allows other molecules to fit into it, which allows the protein to do its job.

☐ That proteins can be structural components of tissues (such as muscles), hormones, antibodies and catalysts.

☐ That all enzymes are proteins.

☐ That enzymes are biological catalysts.

☐ That catalysts speed up chemical reactions without being changed or used up themselves.

cont...

☐ That an enzyme can only catalyse a reaction when a substance fits into its special shape.

☐ That high temperatures denature enzymes (cause enzymes to lose their specific shapes).

☐ That enzymes have different optimum pHs — the pH they work best at.

Digestion

☐ That digestive enzymes work outside body cells — they're produced by specialised cells in glands and in the lining of the gut, then released into the gut where they work.

☐ That digestive enzymes catalyse the breakdown of large food molecules (e.g. carbohydrates, proteins and fats) into smaller food molecules (e.g. sugars, fatty acids and glycerol, and amino acids).

☐ That amylase helps break down starch into sugars. It is made in the salivary glands, pancreas and small intestine, and works in the mouth and small intestine.

☐ That proteases help break down proteins into amino acids. They are made in the stomach, pancreas and small intestine, and work in the stomach and small intestine.

☐ That lipases help break down lipids (fats and oils) into fatty acids and glycerol. They are made in the pancreas and small intestine, and work in the small intestine.

☐ That the stomach produces hydrochloric acid, creating acidic conditions which are ideal for protease enzymes (e.g. pepsin) to work there.

☐ That bile is produced in the liver, stored in the gall bladder and released into the small intestine.

☐ That bile neutralises stomach acid, creating alkaline conditions in the small intestine that are ideal for the enzymes that work there.

Enzymes in Home and Industry

☐ That some microorganisms produce enzymes that catalyse reactions outside their cells.

☐ That biological detergents contain proteases and lipases, which break down proteins and lipids.

☐ The advantages of biological detergents (e.g. they work better at low temperatures than non-biological detergents) and their disadvantages (e.g. they denature at high temperatures and extremes of pH, and can cause skin irritation).

☐ That proteases are used to pre-digest proteins in baby food.

☐ That carbohydrase enzymes can be used to make sugar syrup from starch syrup.

☐ That an isomerase enzyme can be use to make fructose syrup from glucose syrup and why it is better to use fructose syrup in slimming foods.

☐ That the advantages of using enzymes in industry are that they're specific, they allow reactions to be carried out at lower temperatures and pressures (which reduces costs), they work for a long time and are biodegradable.

☐ That the disadvantages of using enzymes in industry are that they can become denatured easily, they can be expensive and contamination can affect the reaction.

1. Aerobic Respiration

We, and other organisms, need energy to do... well... everything really.
This energy comes from the reactions of respiration.

Respiration and enzymes

The chemical reactions that occur inside cells are controlled by enzymes.
All of the reactions involved in respiration are catalysed by enzymes. These
are really important reactions, as respiration releases the energy that the cell
needs to do just about everything.

Respiration is not breathing in and breathing out, as you might think.
Respiration is the process of releasing energy from the breakdown of glucose
— and it goes on in every cell in your body.

Respiration happens in plants too. All living things respire. It's how they
release energy from their food.

> Respiration is the process of releasing energy
> from glucose, which goes on in every cell.

What is aerobic respiration?

Aerobic respiration is respiration using oxygen. It's the most efficient way to
release energy from glucose. Aerobic respiration goes on all the time in plants
and animals.

Most of the reactions in aerobic respiration happen inside cell structures
called **mitochondria** (see page 120).

You need to learn the overall word equation for aerobic respiration:

> glucose + oxygen → carbon dioxide + water + ENERGY

Energy from respiration

Organisms use the energy released from respiration to fuel all sorts of
processes. You need to know about the following ways in which an organism
may use energy from respiration:

Learning Objectives:

- Know that the chemical reactions that occur inside cells (including those involved in respiration) are controlled by enzymes.
- Know that respiration using oxygen is called aerobic respiration.
- Know that aerobic respiration involves reactions that use glucose and oxygen to release energy.
- Know that aerobic respiration is happening all the time in all plants and animals.
- Know that the reactions of aerobic respiration happen mainly in mitochondria.
- Know the word equation for aerobic respiration.
- Know the ways in which energy released from respiration is used by organisms.

Specification Reference
B2.6.1

Tip: You can also have anaerobic respiration, which happens without oxygen, but that doesn't release nearly as much energy as aerobic respiration — see page 171.

Figure 1: *Animals, including humans, need energy from respiration to contract their muscles and move.*

1. Organisms use energy to build up larger molecules from smaller ones (like proteins from amino acids).

2. Animals use energy to allow their muscles to contract (which in turn allows them to move about).

3. Mammals and birds use energy to keep their body temperature steady (unlike other animals, mammals and birds keep their bodies constantly warm).

4. Plants use energy to build sugars, nitrates and other nutrients into amino acids, which are then built up into proteins.

Practice Questions — Fact Recall

Q1 What catalyses the reactions of respiration in a cell?

Q2 What is aerobic respiration?

Q3 Give three ways in which mammals use energy from respiration.

Q4 Plants use energy from respiration to make amino acids.
Name two types of molecule that are needed in order to make amino acids.

Practice Questions — Application

Q1 Here is a photograph of a cell structure under a microscope.

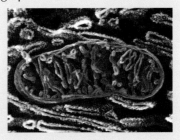

Most of the reactions of respiration take place in this cell structure. Suggest the name of the cell structure in this photograph.

Q2 This diagram shows the equation for aerobic respiration.

Glucose + $\boxed{A}$ → carbon dioxide + $\boxed{B}$ + $\boxed{C}$

a) What is A in the equation?

b) What is B in the equation?

c) What is C in the equation?

Exam Tip
Make sure you know the word equation for aerobic respiration off by heart, as it can get you easy marks in the exam.

2. Exercise

When we exercise we need to get more glucose and oxygen to our muscles for respiration. The body has some clever ways of doing this...

Energy for exercise

When we move we use our muscles. Muscles are made of muscle cells. These use oxygen to release energy from glucose (aerobic respiration — see page 167), which is used to contract the muscles.

When we do exercise we use our muscles more. An increase in muscle activity requires more glucose and oxygen to be supplied to the muscle cells. Extra carbon dioxide also needs to removed from the muscle cells (because it's toxic at a high concentration). For this to happen the blood has to flow at a faster rate. Therefore physical activity:

- increases your breathing rate and makes you breathe more deeply to meet the demand for extra oxygen.

- increases the speed at which the heart pumps to make your blood flow more quickly, delivering more oxygen and glucose to cells for respiration, and taking more carbon dioxide away.

Fitness

When you're not exercising your heart rate is said to be at its resting level. During exercise your heart rate increases. Then, when you stop exercising, your heart rate returns to its resting level. The time it takes for this to happen is called the recovery period. When you're exercising your heart rate can be monitored and recorded, and the data shown on a graph.

> **Example**
>
> This graph shows how a person's heart rate changes during exercise.
>
>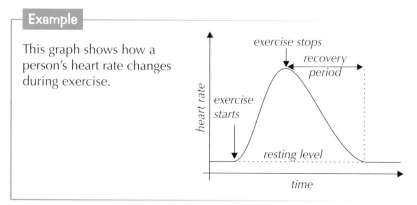

You need to know that the fitter you are:

- the lower your resting heart rate will be,
- the lower your increase in heart rate during exercise will be,
- and the shorter your recovery period will be.

Learning Objectives:

- Understand how and why heart rate, and breathing rate and depth change when a human exercises.
- Be able to interpret data on exercise.
- Know that, during exercise, glucose can be released from glycogen that's stored in muscles.

Specification Reference B2.6.1

Exam Tip
Your breathing rate can also be monitored and recorded during exercise. In the exam you might be given some data on heart rate or breathing rate during exercise and asked to say what is happening and why. So make sure you learn this page really well.

Figure 1: *A person having their breathing rate and heart rate recorded during exercise.*

Glycogen

Some glucose from food is stored as glycogen. Glycogen's mainly stored in the liver, but each muscle also has its own store.

During vigorous exercise muscles use glucose rapidly, so some of the stored glycogen is converted back to glucose to provide more energy — see Figure 2.

Figure 2: *Diagram to show the conversion of glycogen to glucose in a muscle cell during exercise.*

Practice Questions — Fact Recall

Q1 Describe what happens to your breathing during exercise.

Q2 a) Some glycogen is stored in the liver.
   Where else is glycogen stored?

   b) During vigorous exercise, describe and explain what happens to the glycogen at the place you answered in a).

Practice Questions — Application

Tip: Beats per minute (bpm) is a unit used for measuring heart rate.

Q1 Charlotte is working out on the cross trainer machine at the gym. She starts monitoring her heart rate whilst she is warming up and then as she's running. Her heart rate increases from 80 to 146 bpm. Explain why her heart rate has increased.

Q2 Samir is running in a race. His breathing rate is recorded at rest, at the end of the race and after the race. The results are shown in the table:

Time of record	Breathing rate (breaths per minute)
At rest, before race	16
At the end of the race	44
Eight minutes after the race	16

a) Describe the results shown in the table.

b) Explain the results shown in the table.

3. Anaerobic Respiration

When you're exercising hard, aerobic respiration isn't always enough to keep you going. Don't worry though, your body has another trick up its sleeve...

What is anaerobic respiration?

When you do vigorous exercise and your body can't supply enough oxygen to your muscles, they start doing anaerobic respiration instead of aerobic respiration.

Anaerobic respiration is the incomplete breakdown of glucose, which produces **lactic acid**. It takes place in the absence of oxygen. Here is the word equation for the process:

$$\text{glucose} \rightarrow \text{energy} + \text{lactic acid}$$

Comparison to aerobic respiration [Higher]

Unfortunately anaerobic respiration does not release nearly as much energy as aerobic respiration because glucose is not completely broken down. However, it's useful in emergencies — it means that you can keep on using your muscles for a while longer.

Lactic acid

Anaerobic respiration causes lactic acid to build up in the muscles, which gets painful. It also causes **muscle fatigue** — the muscles get tired and they stop contracting efficiently. After you've finished exercising the blood flowing through your muscles will remove the lactic acid.

Oxygen debt [Higher]

After resorting to anaerobic respiration, when you stop exercising you'll have an "oxygen debt". In other words you have to "repay" the oxygen that you didn't get to your muscles in time, because your lungs, heart and blood couldn't keep up with the demand earlier on.

This means you have to keep breathing hard for a while after you stop, to get more oxygen into your blood. Blood flows through your muscles to remove the lactic acid by oxidising it to carbon dioxide (CO_2) and water.

While high levels of CO_2 and lactic acid are detected in the blood (by the brain), the pulse and breathing rate stay high to try and rectify the situation.

Figure 1: *Immediately after a race an athlete will still be breathing hard and have a high heart rate in order to replace their oxygen debt.*

Q1   Explain when the body uses anaerobic respiration.

Q2   Describe what anaerobic respiration is.

Q3   a) What is muscle fatigue?

b) What can muscle fatigue be caused by?

Q4   What is an oxygen debt?

Section Checklist — Make sure you know...

Aerobic respiration

☐ That enzymes catalyse the reactions that occur inside cells (including respiration reactions).

☐ That aerobic respiration is respiration using oxygen and that it involves reactions that use glucose and oxygen to release energy.

☐ That aerobic respiration is happening all the time in animals and plants, and that most of the respiration reactions happen in the mitochondria.

☐ The word equation for aerobic respiration: glucose + oxygen → carbon dioxide + water + ENERGY.

☐ That the energy released from respiration is used by organisms to make larger molecules from smaller ones, for muscle contraction (animals), to maintain a constant body temperature (mammals and birds), and to make amino acids from sugars, nitrates and other molecules, which can then be made into proteins (plants).

Exercise

☐ That, during exercise, a person's breathing rate and depth will increase to get oxygen into the body.

☐ That, during exercise, a person's heart rate increases, so that blood flow to their muscles increases in order to supply them with more oxygen and glucose, and take away carbon dioxide (CO_2).

☐ How to interpret data on exercise.

☐ That glycogen is stored in muscles and that, during exercise, it can be converted back to glucose for energy.

Anaerobic respiration

☐ That muscles will start to respire anaerobically if they can't get enough oxygen to respire aerobically.

☐ That anaerobic respiration is the incomplete breakdown of glucose, which forms lactic acid. It takes place in the absence of oxygen.

☐ **H** That anaerobic respiration releases less energy than aerobic respiration because glucose is not fully broken down. It takes place in the absence of oxygen.

☐ That the build up of lactic acid can cause muscle fatigue (muscles become tired and don't contract efficiently), but it will eventually be removed from the muscles by blood flow.

☐ **H** That an oxygen debt occurs after anaerobic respiration — you have to 'repay' the oxygen you didn't manage to get to your muscles in time, in order to oxidise the lactic acid to CO_2 and water.

Exam-style Questions

1 Enzymes are needed for many processes in the body.

1 (a) (i) What type of biological molecule is an enzyme? Circle the correct answer.

a lipid   a hormone   a protein   an amino acid

(1 mark)

1 (a) (ii) What is the function of an enzyme?

(1 mark)

1 (b) *In this question you will be assessed on the quality of your English, the organisation of your ideas and your use of appropriate specialist vocabulary.*

One of the processes in the body that requires enzymes is digestion.
Describe the action, production and release of different types of enzymes in digestion.

(6 marks)

2 A food manufacturer is choosing an isomerase enzyme to catalyse the reaction of glucose syrup into fructose syrup at his factory.

The graph below shows the activity of two isomerase enzymes (A and B) at different temperatures.

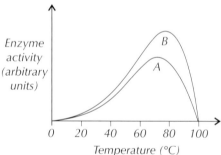

2 (a) (i) Which isomerase enzyme should the manufacturer use?   Explain your answer.

(1 mark)

2 (a) (ii) The manufacturer is also deciding on the right conditions for the reaction.
Explain why the reaction should not be carried out at temperatures above 80 °C.

(2 marks)

2 (b) The manufacturer makes slimming foods.
Explain why he uses fructose syrup instead of glucose syrup in his products.

(2 marks)

2 (c) Other types of enzymes are also used in the food industry, such as proteases that are used to make baby food. Give **three** advantages of using enzymes in industry.

(3 marks)

3 A student wants to find out how his heart rate changes during exercise. The exercise he chooses is to run on a running machine for five minutes. He records his heart rate before the run, immediately after he stops running and one minute after he has stopped. He repeats the exercise three times. His results are shown in this table:

Time of record	Heart rate (beats per minute)		
	1st go	2nd go	3rd go
At rest, before run	72	71	72
At the end of the run	151	163	154
One minute after the run	131	142	129

3 (a) (i) Calculate the student's mean heart rate at the end of his runs.

(2 marks)

3 (a) (ii) At one minute after each run, the student's heart rate still hadn't reached its resting level. Explain why the student's heart rate remained high one minute after each run.

(5 marks)

3 (b) Respiration gives the student energy to contract his muscles and run. Give **two** other ways the student's body will use energy from respiration.

(2 marks)

4 A scientist is investigating the reactions of aerobic and anaerobic respiration.

4 (a) (i) What is the word equation for aerobic respiration?

(2 marks)

4 (a) (ii) When do animals respire?

(1 mark)

4 (b) In a cell, energy is present in the form of a molecule called ATP. The scientist conducts an experiment to find out how much ATP each type of respiration releases per glucose molecule. His results are shown in this table:

Type of respiration	Number of ATP molecules released per glucose molecule
Aerobic	32
Anaerobic	2

Describe and explain the difference in release of energy between aerobic and anaerobic respiration shown in the table.

(2 marks)

1. DNA

DNA is a pretty important molecule because it's what makes us unique. This means that DNA tests can be used to identify people. Therefore it's really important that you learn all about it...

Chromosomes, DNA and genes

DNA stands for **deoxyribonucleic acid**. It contains all the instructions to put an organism together and make it work. It's found in the **nucleus** of animal and plant cells, in really long molecules called **chromosomes** (see Figure 1).

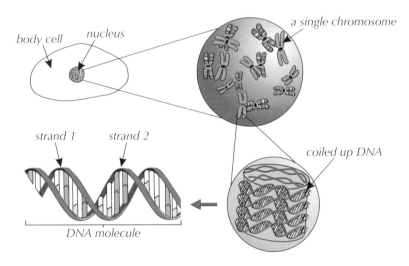

Figure 1: Diagram showing the structure of DNA and where it is found in a cell.

As you can see from Figure 1, DNA has a **double helix** structure. This means that it's made up of two separate strands that are coiled around each other to form a spiral.

A **gene** is a section of DNA. Genes are found on chromosomes.

Genes and proteins Higher

A gene contains the instructions needed to make a specific **protein**. Cells make proteins by stringing amino acids together in a particular order. Different proteins have a different number and order of amino acids. Only 20 amino acids are used, but they make up thousands of different proteins. Genes simply tells cells in what order to put the amino acids together (see Figure 2, on the next page).

Learning Objectives:

- Know that genetic information is found in chromosomes.
- Know that long molecules of DNA (deoxyribonucleic acid) form chromosomes and that DNA has a double helix structure.
- Know that genes are small sections of DNA.
- **H** Understand that genes tell cells which combination of amino acids to put together, which in turn determines the protein they produce.
- Know that everybody's DNA is unique (with the exception of identical twins).
- Understand that DNA fingerprinting is a technique used to identify a person based on their DNA.

Specification Reference
B2.7.1, B2.7.2

Tip: You might remember learning about genes and chromosomes in Biology 1 — however, there's a bit more you need to know now.

Tip: H Amino acids are the building blocks that make up proteins.

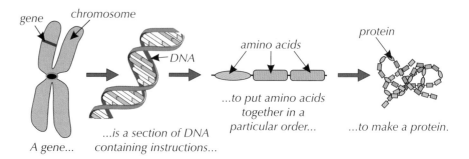

gene *chromosome*

DNA

amino acids

protein

...to put amino acids together in a particular order...

...to make a protein.

A gene... *...is a section of DNA containing instructions...*

Figure 2: H *Diagram showing how a gene codes for a protein.*

DNA also determines what proteins the cell produces, e.g. haemoglobin, keratin. That in turn determines what type of cell it is, e.g. red blood cell, skin cell.

Tip: H Another way of saying a gene contains the instructions for a protein is to say a gene 'codes for' a protein.

DNA fingerprinting

Tip: A clone is an exact (genetically identical) copy of an organism.

Almost everyone's DNA is unique. The only exceptions are **identical twins**, where the two people have identical DNA, and clones.

DNA fingerprinting (or genetic fingerprinting) is a way of cutting up a person's DNA into small sections and then separating them. This produces a DNA fingerprint — a pattern of bands on a gel (see Figure 3). Every person's genetic fingerprint has a unique pattern (unless they're identical twins or clones of course). This means you can tell people apart by comparing DNA samples.

Uses of DNA fingerprinting

DNA fingerprinting has some useful applications:

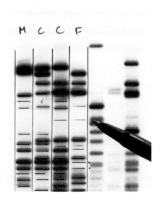

M C C F

Figure 3: *A DNA fingerprint.*

1. **Paternity testing** — to see if a man is the father of a particular child. The DNA fingerprint of the child is compared to the DNA fingerprint of the possible father. If lots of bands on the DNA fingerprints match, then that man is most probably the child's father.

Tip: Half of the child's DNA fingerprint will match the mother's DNA fingerprint and half will match the father's, as we inherit half our DNA from our mum and half from our dad (see p.180).

> **Example**
>
> This DNA fingerprint shows that Male 2 is most likely to be the father of this child, as more of his bands match the child's than male 1.
>
> Two bands from Male 1's DNA fingerprint match the child's (bands 17 and 20), whereas six bands from Male 2's DNA fingerprint match the child's (bands 21, 22, 23, 24, 27 and 29).
>
>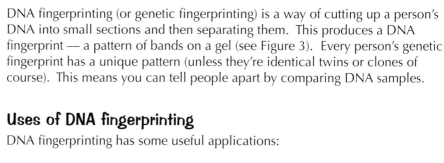
>
> *Child* *Male 1* *Male 2*

2. **Forensic science** — DNA (from hair, skin flakes, blood, semen, etc.) taken from a crime scene is compared with a DNA sample taken from a suspect. If the suspect's DNA fingerprint matches the DNA found at a crime scene then the suspect was probably at the crime scene.

Ethical issues involved in DNA fingerprinting

Some people would like there to be a national genetic database of everyone in the country. That way, DNA from a crime scene could be checked against everyone in the country to see whose it was. But others think this is a big invasion of privacy, and they worry about how safe the data would be and what else it might be used for.

There are also scientific problems — false positives can occur if errors are made in the procedure or if the data is misinterpreted.

Tip: If a suspect's DNA matches DNA found at a crime scene it doesn't necessarily mean that they committed the crime. It just provides evidence that they were probably at the crime scene.

Practice Questions — Fact Recall

Q1 What does DNA stand for?

Q2 What are chromosomes made up of?

Q3 Describe the structure of a DNA molecule.

Q4 How does a gene help a cell to make a specific protein?

Q5 Why can DNA fingerprinting be used to identify a person?

Practice Questions — Application

At a murder scene, a forensic science unit find some blood that isn't the victim's blood. They extract DNA from the blood and compare it to DNA samples from four suspects (A-D), on a DNA fingerprint:

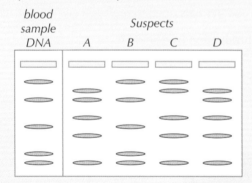

Exam Tip
If you need to compare two or more DNA fingerprints in the exam, use a ruler to see which bands line up exactly.

Q1 a) Looking at the DNA fingerprint, which suspect do you think is most likely to have committed the murder? Explain your answer.

b) Can you say for sure that it was them? Explain your answer.

Q2 Two of the suspects are identical twins.
Which two suspects are identical twins? Explain your answer.

- Know that body cells contain two sets of chromosomes and that these chromosomes are found in pairs.
- Know that body cells divide by mitosis.
- Know that mitosis allows organisms to grow or to replace damaged cells.
- Know that organisms that reproduce asexually use mitosis to produce genetically identical offspring.
- Know that during mitosis, body cells copy their genetic material, and then undergo a single division to form two genetically identical cells.

Specification Reference
B2.7.1

2. Cell Division — Mitosis

Our body cells are able to make copies of themselves so that we can grow or repair any damaged tissue. It's pretty clever stuff...

Body cells and chromosomes

Body cells normally have two copies of each chromosome — one from the organism's 'mother', and one from its 'father'. So, humans have two copies of chromosome 1, two copies of chromosome 2, etc.

Figure 1 shows the 23 pairs of chromosomes from a human cell. (The 23rd pair are a bit different — see page 186.)

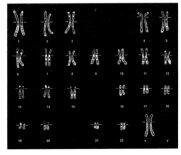

Figure 1: *The 23 pairs of chromosomes from a female human body cell.*

When a body cell divides to make a copy of itself, it needs to make new cells identical to the original cell — with the same number of chromosomes. This type of cell division is called **mitosis**:

> Mitosis is when a cell reproduces itself by splitting to form two identical offspring.

Uses of mitosis

Mitosis is used:

1. When plants and animals want to **grow**.

2. When plants and animals need to **replace cells** that have been damaged.

3. In **asexual reproduction** (see below).

Asexual reproduction

Some organisms reproduce by mitosis in a process called asexual reproduction.

Tip: Alleles are different versions of the same gene. New plants formed from asexual reproduction are genetically identical, so they will have the same versions of genes, i.e. the same alleles.

> **Example**
>
>
>
> **Figure 2:** *Strawberry plant with runners (red stems).*
>
> Strawberry plants form runners by mitosis (see Figure 2). These runners take root and become new plants. These new plants (the offspring) have exactly the same **alleles** as the parent — so there's no variation.

What happens during mitosis?

Here are the steps involved in mitosis:

1. In a cell that's not dividing, the DNA is all spread out in long strings.

2. If the cell gets a signal to divide, it needs to duplicate its DNA — so there's one copy for each new cell. The DNA is copied and forms X-shaped chromosomes. Each 'arm' of the chromosome is an exact duplicate of the other.

3. The chromosomes then line up at the centre of the cell and cell fibres pull them apart. The two arms of each chromosome go to opposite ends of the cell.

4. Membranes form around each of the sets of chromosomes. These become the nuclei of the two new cells.

5. Lastly, the cytoplasm divides. You now have two new cells containing exactly the same DNA — they're identical.

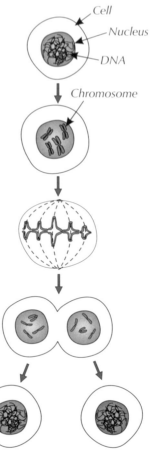

Figure 3: *Diagram showing the stages in mitosis.*

Tip: When a cell has copied its DNA, the left arm of an X-shaped chromosome has the same DNA as the right arm.

Tip: The key things to remember about mitosis are that when a body cell divides it copies its DNA first and then splits into two, to form two genetically identical daughter cells.

Practice Questions — Fact Recall

Q1   How many copies of each chromosome does a body cell have?

Q2   Give three uses of mitosis.

Q3   How many times does a body cell divide during mitosis?

Practice Questions — Application

This photograph shows the last stage in mitosis — two new daughter cells are forming.

Q1   Will these new cells be genetically identical or genetically different to the parent cell?

Q2   How many sets of chromosomes will these cells have?

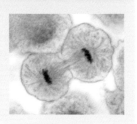

Learning Objectives:

- Know that there is one set of chromosomes in gametes (sex cells).
- Know that at fertilisation, two gametes join, forming a body cell which contains two sets of chromosomes.
- Understand how sexual reproduction results in variation.
- Know that gametes are formed by meiosis.
- Know that meiosis occurs in cells in the reproductive organs (the ovaries and testes in humans).
- Know that, when two gametes have joined at fertilisation, the fertilised egg grows by mitosis.
- **H** Know that during meiosis, a cell copies its genetic material and then divides twice to form four gametes. These gametes each contain one set of chromosomes.

Specification Reference
B2.7.1, B2.7.2

3. Cell Division — Meiosis

Another type of cell division. This one is different to mitosis though — it only happens in the cells of the reproductive organs and it produces sex cells.

Sexual reproduction and gametes

During sexual reproduction, two cells called gametes (sex cells) combine to form a new individual.

Gametes only have one copy of each chromosome. This is so that you can combine one sex cell from the 'mother' and one sex cell from the 'father' and still end up with the right number of chromosomes in body cells.

> ### Example
>
> Human body cells have 46 chromosomes. The gametes (sperm and egg cells) have 23 chromosomes each. This means that when an egg and sperm combine at **fertilisation** you get a single body cell with 46 chromosomes again (see Figure 1).
>
>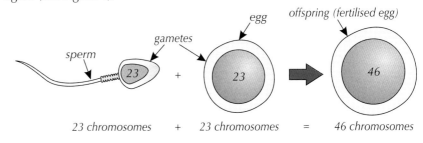
>
> **Figure 1:** *Diagram showing the change in number of chromosomes at fertilisation.*

The new individual will have a mixture of two sets of chromosomes — half from the mother and half from the father. This means he or she will have a mixture of two sets of genes (or two sets of alleles, see page 193).

The new individual will therefore inherit features from both parents, which is how sexual reproduction produces **variation**.

Meiosis

Tip: To remind you that meiosis produces gametes, remember that they both have the word 'me' in them — meiosis and gametes.

To make new cells which only have half the original number of chromosomes, cells divide by meiosis.

> Meiosis produces cells which have half the normal number of chromosomes.

In humans, it only happens in the **reproductive organs** (e.g. ovaries in females and testes in males) so these are where gametes are produced.

After two gametes join at fertilisation, the cell grows by repeatedly dividing by mitosis.

What happens during meiosis? `Higher`

Here are the steps involved in meiosis:

1. As with mitosis, (see p.178-179) before the cell starts to divide, it duplicates its DNA — one arm of each chromosome is an exact copy of the other arm.

2. In the **first division** in meiosis (there are two divisions) the chromosome pairs line up in the centre of the cell.

3. The pairs are then pulled apart, so each new cell only has one copy of each chromosome. Some of the father's chromosomes (shown in blue) and some of the mother's chromosomes (shown in red) go into each new cell.

4. In the **second division** the chromosomes line up again in the centre of the cell. It's a lot like mitosis. The arms of the chromosomes are pulled apart.

5. You get four gametes each with only a single set of chromosomes in it.

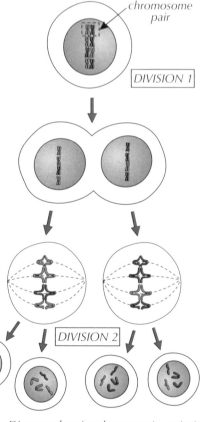

Figure 2: Diagram showing the stages in meiosis.

Figure 3: Microscope image showing pairs of chromosomes being pulled apart during the first division in meiosis.

Tip: H Meiosis explains why you may be similar to, but not the same as, your siblings — you'll have different mixtures of your mother's and father's chromosomes. (Identical twins are an exception to this though, as they result from the splitting of a fertilised egg, so they always have the same combination of chromosomes.)

Comparing mitosis and meiosis `Higher`

Make sure you learn the key differences between mitosis and meiosis, as summarised in this table:

Question	Mitosis	Meiosis
Where does it occur?	in body cells	in cells in the reproductive organs only
What type of cells are produced?	body cells	gametes
How many cell divisions take place?	one	two
How many new cells are produced?	two	four
How many sets of chromosomes do the new cells have?	two	one

Exam Tip H Questions asking about the differences between mitosis and meiosis often come up in the exam. Learning them now will make your life much easier.

Practice Questions — Fact Recall

Q1 How many sets of chromosomes do gametes contain?

Q2 Where are gametes produced?

Q3 Following fertilisation, how does the resulting cell grow?

Q4 How many cell divisions occur in meiosis?

Q5 How many new cells are produced when a cell divides by meiosis?

Q6 True or False? Gametes are all genetically identical.

Practice Questions — Application

Q1 As well as humans, there are other animals that reproduce by sexual reproduction. These animals have different numbers of chromosomes in their body cells and in their gametes, as shown in the table:

Type of animal cell	Number of chromosomes
Dog body cell	78
Cat egg cell	19
Horse sperm cell	32

Using your knowledge and the information provided in the table, suggest:

a) how many chromosomes there are in a dog sperm cell.

b) how many chromosomes there are in the body cell of a cat.

c) how many chromosomes there are in a horse egg cell.

Q2 Mary is learning about meiosis. She thinks that the gametes produced when a cell divides by meiosis will have half a set of chromosomes in them.

a) i) Why does this not happen when a cell divides by meiosis?

   ii) Two gametes combine during fertilisation. If Mary was right, what would be wrong with the fertilised egg?

b) Mary keeps getting mitosis and meiosis confused.
   Give three differences between these two types of cell division.

4. Stem Cells

All the cells in an organism originate from stem cells. Scientists are attempting to use these cells to do some pretty amazing things...

Cell Differentiation

Differentiation is the process by which a cell becomes specialised for its job (see page 128). In most animal cells, the ability to differentiate is lost at an early stage, but lots of plant cells don't ever lose this ability. In animal embryos, cells divide to produce new cell types, but in mature animals, cells divide mainly to replace damaged cells.

What are stem cells?

Some cells are undifferentiated. They can develop into different types of cell depending on what instructions they're given. These cells are called stem cells (see Figure 1).

undifferentiated
stem cell

Differentiation

differentiated
white blood cell

Figure 1: *Diagram showing stem cell differentiation.*

Stem cells are found in early human embryos. They're exciting to doctors and medical researchers because they have the potential to turn into any kind of cell at all. This makes sense if you think about it — all the different types of cell found in a human being have to come from those few cells in the early embryo.

Adults also have stem cells, but they're only found in certain places, like bone marrow. These aren't as versatile as embryonic stem cells — they can't turn into any cell type at all, only certain ones.

Learning Objectives:

- Know that most animal cells lose the ability to differentiate at an early stage but lots of plant cells never lose the ability to differentiate.

- Know that mature animals mainly use cell division to replace and repair cells.

- Know that human embryonic stem cells can differentiate into any type of human cell.

- Know that stem cells from adult bone marrow can be made to differentiate into different cell types.

- Know that it's possible to make stem cells from embryos differentiate into many different types of cell, e.g. nerve cells.

- Know that stem cells could be used to treat some medical conditions, e.g. paralysis.

- Be able to give informed opinions on the issues around using embryonic stem cells in medical research.

Specification Reference B2.7.1

Adult stem cells in medicine

Medicine already uses adult stem cells to cure disease.

> **Example**
>
> People with some blood diseases (e.g. sickle cell anaemia — a disease which affects the shape of the red blood cells) can be treated by bone marrow transplants. Bone marrow is the tissue found inside bone. It contains stem cells that can turn into new blood cells to replace the faulty old ones.

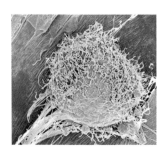

Figure 2: *Microscope image of a stem cell found in adult bone marrow.*

Embryonic stem cells in medicine

Scientists can also extract stem cells from very early human embryos and grow them. These embryonic stem cells could be used to replace faulty cells in sick people in the future (see Figure 4).

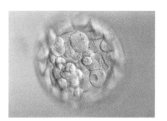

Figure 3: Microscope image of a four-day old human embryo. Stem cells can be taken from the embryo at this stage.

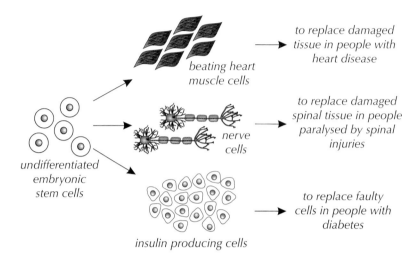

beating heart muscle cells

to replace damaged tissue in people with heart disease

undifferentiated embryonic stem cells

nerve cells

to replace damaged spinal tissue in people paralysed by spinal injuries

insulin producing cells

to replace faulty cells in people with diabetes

Figure 4: Diagram showing some potential uses of embryonic stem cells in medicine.

To get cultures of one specific type of cell, researchers try to control the differentiation of the stem cells by changing the environment they're growing in. So far, it's still a bit hit and miss — lots more research is needed.

Issues involved in stem cell research

Embryonic stem cell research has exciting possibilities, but it's also pretty controversial.

Some people are against it, because they feel that human embryos shouldn't be used for experiments since each one is a potential human life.

However, others think that curing patients who already exist and who are suffering is more important than the rights of embryos. One fairly convincing argument in favour of this point of view is that the embryos used in the research are usually unwanted ones from fertility clinics which, if they weren't used for research, would probably just be destroyed. But of course, campaigners for the rights of embryos usually want this banned too.

Campaigners for the rights of embryos feel that scientists should concentrate more on finding and developing other sources of stem cells, so people could be helped without having to use embryos. Some research has been done into getting stem cells from alternative sources. For example, some researchers think it might be possible to get cells from umbilical cords to behave like embryonic stem cells.

In some countries stem cell research is banned, but it's allowed in the UK as long as it follows strict guidelines.

Tip: Obtaining stem cells from an embryo destroys the embryo.

Exam Tip
Questions on the issues associated with the use of embryonic stem cells might crop up in the exam, so make sure you know arguments for and against the use of embryonic stem cells.

Q1 Describe the differences in the ability of plant and animal cells to differentiate.

Q2 What is a stem cell?

Q3 What type of cell can early embryonic stem cells turn in to?

Q4 Give one place where stem cells can be found in an adult human.

Practice Questions — Application

Q1 Alzheimer's disease is a condition which damages the neurones (nerve cells) in the brain. These neurones die, but are not replaced, leading to a decrease in the amount of neurones in the brain. Symptoms of Alzheimer's disease include memory loss, confusion and changes in personality.

a) Suggest a way in which embryonic stem cells could potentially be used to treat people with Alzheimer's disease.

b) Give another possible use of embryonic stem cells in medicine.

Q2 Embryonic stem cells used for medical research are mostly taken from embryos left over from fertility clinics, which would otherwise be destroyed. Suggest a reason why some people are happier with using these embryos for stem cell research, rather than creating embryos purely with the purpose of being used for research.

Q3 Embryos begin to develop a nervous system 14 days after fertilisation. Some people think that it's morally acceptable to use an embryo for stem cell research before this point, as the embryo has no senses, so cannot be considered a life yet. Suggest a reason why some people may not agree with this view.

Exam Tip
It's important that you can look at something from the point of view of someone with different opinions to you.

- Know that the genes
  which determine sex
  are carried on just
  one of the 23 pairs
  of chromosomes
  found in human
  body cells — the sex
  chromosomes.

- Know that females
  have two of the same
  sex chromosome
  (XX) whereas males
  have two different sex
  chromosomes (XY).

- Be able to interpret
  genetic diagrams
  showing sex
  inheritance.

- **H** Be able to
  construct genetic
  diagrams showing
  sex inheritance.

**Specification Reference
B2.7.2**

5. X and Y Chromosomes

*We all know that there are loads of differences between males and females.
It's all to do with two little chromosomes — X and Y.*

Sex chromosomes

There are 22 matched pairs of chromosomes in every human body cell
(see page 178). The 23rd pair are labelled XX or XY. They're the two
chromosomes that decide whether you turn out male or female.

All **men** have an **X** and a **Y** chromosome: **XY**
The Y chromosome causes male characteristics.

All **women** have **two X** chromosomes: **XX**
The XX combination allows female characteristics to develop.

When making sperm, the X and Y chromosomes from the original male
cell are drawn apart in the first division of meiosis (see page 181 for more
on meiosis). There's a 50% chance each sperm cell gets an X chromosome
and a 50% chance it gets a Y chromosome (see Figure 1).

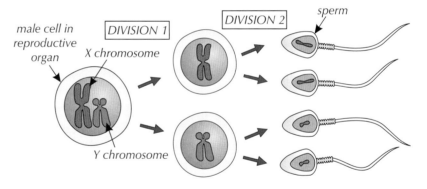

Figure 1: *Diagram showing sperm production by meiosis in males.*

A similar thing happens when making eggs. But the original cell has two
X chromosomes (as it's from a female), so all the eggs end up with one X
chromosome (see Figure 3).

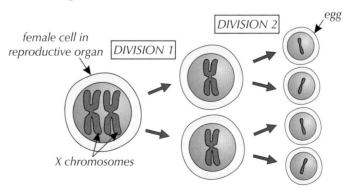

Figure 3: *Diagram showing egg production by meiosis in females.*

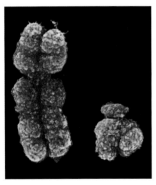

Figure 2: *Here's what
the sex chromosomes
actually look like. The Y
chromosome (shown in
blue) is smaller than the
(pink) X chromosome.*

Sex inheritance and genetic diagrams

At fertilisation, the sperm fertilises the egg, and the chromosomes from the gametes combine, forming a new individual with the correct number of chromosomes (see page 180). Whether the individual is male or female depends on the combination of sex chromosomes it receives — this is sex inheritance.

Genetic diagrams can be used to show sex inheritance.

Interpreting genetic diagrams

You need to be able to interpret genetic diagrams showing sex inheritance.

Examples

Figure 4 is a type of genetic diagram called a Punnett square, showing sex inheritance. The pairs of letters in the middle show the possible combinations of the gametes.

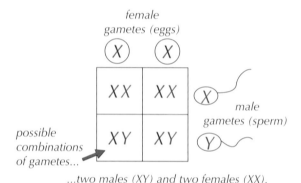

...two males (XY) and two females (XX).

Figure 4: *Punnet square showing sex inheritance.*

Figure 5 is another type of genetic diagram showing sex inheritance. The possible combinations of gametes are shown in the bottom circles.

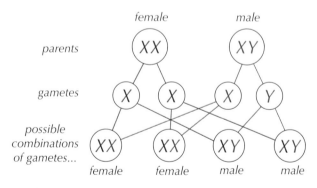

Figure 5: *Genetic diagram showing sex inheritance.*

You can use genetic diagrams to find the probability of getting a boy or a girl. Both Figure 4 and Figure 5 show two XX results and two XY results, so there's the same probability of getting a boy or a girl. This can also be written as a 50:50 ratio. Don't forget that this 50:50 ratio is only a probability at each pregnancy. If you had four kids they could all be boys.

Exam Tip
Most genetic diagrams you'll see in exams concentrate on a gene, instead of a chromosome. But the principle's the same. Don't worry — there are loads of other examples on pages 194-199.

Tip: Only one of these possible combinations would actually happen for any one offspring.

Figure 6: *Having lots of sons doesn't increase the chances of having a daughter in the next pregnancy. There's still a 50:50 chance of having a boy or a girl at each pregnancy.*

Constructing genetic diagrams Higher

You need to be able to construct genetic diagrams to show sex inheritance.

Example 1 — Higher

Drawing a Punnett square to show sex inheritance in humans.

1. First, draw a grid with four squares.

2. Put the possible gametes from one parent down the side, and those from the other parent along the top.

3. Then in each middle square you fill in the letters from the top and side that line up with that square — the pairs of letters in the middle show the possible combinations of the gametes.

Figure 7 shows these steps:

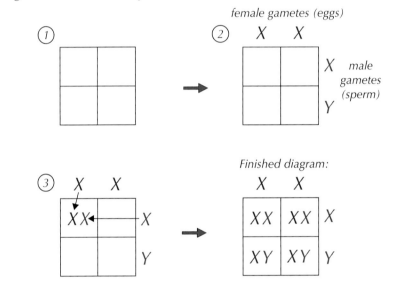

Figure 7: How to draw a Punnett square to show sex inheritance in humans.

Example 2 — Higher

Drawing a different type of genetic diagram to show sex inheritance in humans.

1. Draw two circles at the top of the diagram to represent the parents. Put the female sex chromosomes in one and the male sex chromosomes in the other.

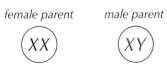

2. Draw two circles below each of the parent circles to represent the possible gametes. Put a single chromosome from each parent in each circle. Draw lines to show which chromosomes come from each parent.

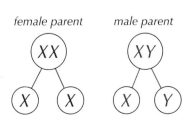

3. One gamete from the female combines with one gamete from the male during fertilisation, so draw criss-cross lines to show all the possible ways the X and Y chromosomes could combine.

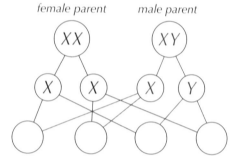

female parent   male parent

Tip: **H** Remember one gamete from the female combines with one gamete from the male during fertilisation. It's quite easy to get confused, so check you aren't drawing lines that put both the male's gametes or both the female's gametes into the same circle.

4. Then write the possible combinations of gametes in the bottom circles.

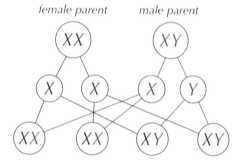

female parent   male parent

Practice Questions — Fact Recall

Q1 How many of the 23 pairs of human chromosomes determine sex?

Q2 True or False? All sperm cells carry the Y chromosome.

Q3 Who has the sex chromosome combination XX — males or females?

Practice Questions — Application

Rachael and her husband Henry are expecting their first child.

Q1 Complete this genetic diagram to show the possible combinations of sex chromosomes that the baby could have.

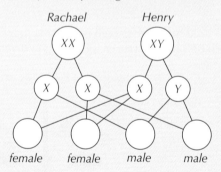

Rachael   Henry

female   female   male   male

Q2 What is the probability that their child will be a boy?

Q3 If Rachael gets pregnant again, do her chances of having a boy change? Explain your answer.

Q4 Draw a Punnet square to show the possible combinations of sex chromosomes that Rachael and Henry's baby could have.

Learning Objectives:

- Understand how Mendel's work led him to develop the idea of inherited factors.

- Know that Mendel's inherited factors are what we now know as genes.

- Understand why Mendel's work was not appreciated until after he had died.

Specification Reference B2.7

Figure 1: *Gregor Mendel.*

Tip: 'Crossed' just means 'bred together'.

Tip: Genetic diagrams of these crosses are shown on the next page.

6. The Work of Mendel

We haven't always known as much about genetics and inheritance as we do now. The work of a monk called Gregor Mendel helped us on our way...

Who was Gregor Mendel?

Gregor Mendel was an Austrian monk who trained in mathematics and natural history at the University of Vienna. On his garden plot at the monastery, Mendel noted how characteristics in plants were passed on from one generation to the next. The results of his research were published in 1866 and eventually became the foundation of modern genetics.

Mendel's work

Mendel did lots of experiments with pea plants. In one experiment he crossed two pea plants of different heights — a tall pea plant and a dwarf pea plant. The offspring produced were all tall pea plants (see Figure 2).

A tall pea plant and a dwarf pea plant are crossed...

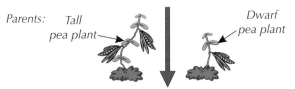

...resulting in all tall pea plants.

Figure 2: *Diagram of the first cross in Mendel's pea plant height experiment.*

He then bred two of these tall pea plants together. The resulting offspring consisted of three tall pea plants and one dwarf pea plant (see Figure 3).

Two pea plants from the 1st set of offspring are crossed...

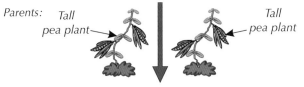

...resulting in three tall pea plants and one dwarf pea plant.

Figure 3: *Diagram of the second cross in Mendel's pea plant height experiment.*

Explaining Mendel's results

From his pea plant height experiment, Mendel had shown that the height characteristic in pea plants was determined by separately inherited "hereditary units" passed on from each parent.

Tip: "Hereditary units" can also be called "inherited factors".

This can be explained using genetic diagrams, where **T** represents the hereditary unit for tall plants and **t** represents the hereditary unit for dwarf plants.

First cross

As shown in Figure 4, in the first of Mendel's crosses, a tall and a dwarf pea plant are crossed together.

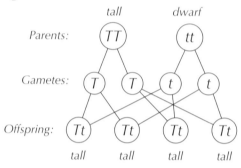

Figure 4: Genetic diagram of the first cross in Mendel's pea plant height experiment.

The resulting offspring are **Tt** — they are all tall plants, but they all carry the hereditary unit for dwarf plants.

Second cross

In the second cross, two tall pea plants from the first cross are crossed together (see Figure 5).

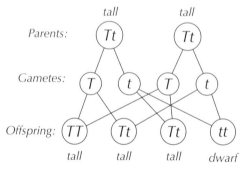

Figure 5: Genetic diagram of the second cross in Mendel's pea plant height experiment.

The resulting offspring are **TT**, **Tt**, **Tt** and **tt** — this gives three tall plants and one dwarf plant.

The ratios of tall and dwarf plants in the offspring show that the hereditary unit for tall plants, **T**, is **dominant** over the hereditary unit for dwarf plants, **t**, i.e. plants with hereditary units for both types of plant (**Tt**) will be tall plants.

Exam Tip
In Mendel's pea plant experiments he also investigated lots of other pea plant characteristics, such as flower colour:

So don't be put off if you have a question in the exam about one of Mendel's other experiments — just use what you've learnt here to answer the question.

Tip: Figure 5 shows that when two tall (Tt) pea plants are crossed, there's a 3:1 ratio of tall:dwarf pea plants in the offspring. Or a 25% chance of getting a dwarf plant from this cross. There's more about ratios and probabilities on p.194.

Mendel's conclusions

From all his experiments on pea plants, Mendel reached these three important conclusions about heredity in plants:

1. Characteristics in plants are determined by "hereditary units".

2. Hereditary units are passed on from both parents, one unit from each parent.

3. Hereditary units can be dominant or recessive — if an individual has both the dominant and the recessive unit for a characteristic, the dominant characteristic will be expressed.

We now know that the "hereditary units" are of course genes. But in Mendel's time nobody knew anything about genes or DNA, and so the significance of his work was not to be realised until after his death.

Practice Questions — Fact Recall

Q1 What three important conclusions did Mendel come to about hereditary units in plants?

Q2 What name do we now give to Mendel's hereditary units?

Q3 Why didn't Mendel get any credit for his work while he was alive?

Practice Question — Application

Q1 Mendel did experiments on pea plants with different seed colours. From these experiments he found that there is a hereditary unit in pea plants that gives them green seeds and one that gives them yellow seeds. The hereditary unit for yellow pea seeds is dominant.

Tick or cross the boxes in the table to show which hereditary units pea plants with the following seed colours could have. (You can tick more than one option for each seed colour.)

Seed colour of pea plant	Type of hereditary unit		
	Just green	Just yellow	Both green and yellow
Green			
Yellow			

7. Alleles and Genetic Diagrams

The next few pages are all about how our genes determine our characteristics...

What are alleles?

Alleles are different versions of the same gene (see Figure 1). Gametes only have one allele, but all the other cells in an organism have two — because we inherit half of our alleles from our mother and half from our father. In genetic diagrams letters are usually used to represent alleles.

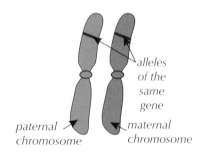

alleles of the same gene

paternal chromosome

maternal chromosome

Figure 1: *Diagram showing two alleles for the same gene.*

Some characteristics of an organism are determined by single genes. Organisms can have two alleles for a particular gene that are the same, or they can have two alleles for a particular gene that are different. If the two alleles are different, only one can determine what characteristic is present. The allele for the characteristic that's shown is called the **dominant** allele (use a capital letter for dominant alleles — e.g. 'C'). The other one is called **recessive** (and you show these with small letters — e.g. 'c').

For an organism to display a recessive characteristic, both its alleles must be recessive (e.g. cc). But to display a dominant characteristic the organism can be either CC or Cc, because the dominant allele overrules the recessive one if the plant/animal/other organism has two different alleles.

Genetic terminology `Higher`

If you're a higher tier student, then you need to know the fancy words used to describe things to do with genetics. Learn these definitions:

> - **Homozygous** — When an organism has two alleles for a particular gene that are the same, e.g. TT.
>
> - **Heterozygous** — When an organism has two alleles for a particular gene that are different, e.g Tt.
>
> - **Genotype** — What alleles you have, e.g. you could have the genotype Bb for hair colour.
>
> - **Phenotype** — The characteristics you have, e.g. brown eyes, blonde hair, etc.

Monohybrid inheritance

Characteristics that are determined by a single gene can be studied using monohybrid crosses. This is where you cross two parents to look at just one characteristic. In the exam they could ask you about the inheritance of any characteristic controlled by a single gene, as the principle's always the same.

Learning Objectives:
- Know that some characteristics of an organism are controlled by just one gene.
- Know that 'alleles' is the term given to different forms of the same gene.
- Know that if two alleles of the same gene are present, then the allele for the characteristic displayed by the organism is dominant, and the allele for the characteristic that isn't displayed is recessive.
- **H** Understand and be able to use the terms 'heterozygous' and 'homozygous'.
- **H** Understand and be able to use the terms 'genotype' and 'phenotype'.
- Be able to predict and explain the outcomes of genetic diagrams showing monohybrid inheritance, for all combinations of dominant and recessive alleles of a gene.
- **H** Be able to construct genetic diagrams for monohybrid crosses.

Specification Reference
B2.7.2

Genetic diagrams of monohybrid inheritance

Genetic diagrams allow you to see how certain characteristics are inherited. Remember Mendel's pea plant experiments? (If not, flick back to pages 190-192). Mendel also observed that pea plants produced peas that were either wrinkly or round. The inheritance of round or wrinkly peas is an example of monohybrid inheritance and can be shown using genetic diagrams.

Figure 2: The peas produced by pea plants can either be wrinkly (left) or round (right).

Tip: In this example, a plant producing wrinkly peas must have 'rr' alleles. However, a plant producing round peas could have two possible combinations of alleles — RR or Rr.

Example 1

The gene which causes wrinkly peas is recessive, so you can use a small 'r' to represent it. Round peas are due to a dominant gene, which you can represent with a capital 'R'. If you cross one pea plant which produces wrinkly peas (rr) and one that produces round peas (in this case RR), all of the offspring will produce round peas — but they'll have the alleles Rr.

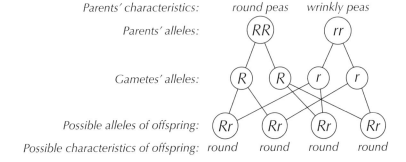

You need to be able to use genetic diagrams to predict and explain the outcomes of monohybrid crosses between individuals for lots of different combinations of alleles. The outcomes are given as ratios and can be used to work out the probability of having offspring with a certain characteristic.

A 3:1 ratio in the offspring

A cross could produce a 3:1 ratio of certain characteristics in the offspring.

Example 2

If two of the offspring from Example 1 are now crossed, this is what you'll get in the next generation:

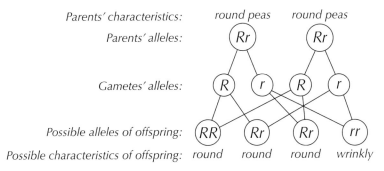

This gives a 3:1 ratio of plants producing round peas:plants producing wrinkly peas in this generation of offspring. This means there's a 1 in 4 or 25% chance of any new pea plant having wrinkly peas. Remember that "results" like this are only probabilities — they don't say definitely what'll happen.

Exam Tip
In the exam you might be given the results of a breeding experiment and asked to say whether a characteristic is dominant or recessive. To figure it out, look at the ratios of the characteristic in different generations. For example, in Example 2 here the 3:1 ratio of round to wrinkly peas shows that the round allele is dominant.

All the offspring are the same

More than one cross could result in all of the offspring showing the same characteristic. Here you have to do some detective work to find out what's gone on:

Example 3

Back to the pea plant example — if you cross a pea plant that produces round peas and has two dominant alleles (RR), with a pea plant that produces wrinkly peas (rr), all the offspring will produce round (Rr) peas:

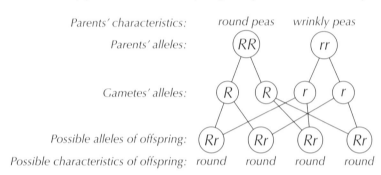

This means there's a 100% probability of any new pea plant having round peas.

But, if you crossed a pea plant that produces round peas, and has two dominant alleles (RR), with a pea plant that produces round peas, but has a dominant and a recessive allele (Rr), you would also only get offspring that produce round peas:

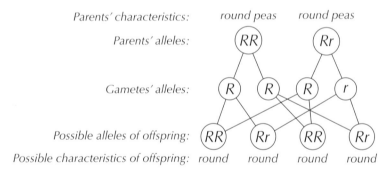

To find out which cross you'd done, you'd have to breed the offspring together and see what kind of ratio you got — then you'd have a good idea. If it was a 3:1 ratio of round to wrinkly in the offspring, it's likely that you originally had RR and rr plants (see Example 2 on the previous page).

> **Tip:** **H** The offspring of this cross are all heterozygous (Rr) — they have two different alleles for a particular gene.

A 1:1 ratio in the offspring

On the next page there's an example of when a cross produces a 1:1 ratio in the offspring — half the offspring are likely to show one characteristic and half are likely to show another characteristic. This time we're using cats with long and short hair. (Peas are a bit dull...).

A cat's long hair is caused by a dominant allele 'H'. Short hair is caused by a recessive allele 'h'. A cat with long hair (Hh) was bred with another cat with short hair (hh):

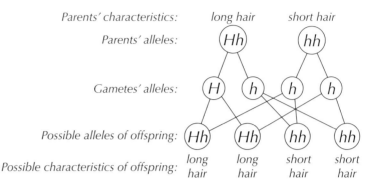

Tip: H Half the offspring of this cross are homozygous (hh) — they have two alleles the same for a particular gene.

The cats had 8 kittens — 4 with long hair and 4 with short hair. This is a 1:1 ratio, which gives a 50% probability of a new cat being born to these parents having long hair.

Constructing genetic diagrams [Higher]

You need to be able to construct genetic diagrams of monohybrid crosses.

Drawing a genetic diagram to show a cross between a pea plant with wrinkly peas (rr) and a pea plant with round peas (RR):

1. Draw two circles at the top of the diagram to represent the parents. Put the round pea genotype in one and the wrinkly pea genotype in the other.

2. Draw two circles below each of the parent circles to represent the possible gametes. Put a single allele from each parent in each circle.

3. One gamete from the female combines with one gamete from the male during fertilisation, so draw criss-cross lines to show all the possible ways the alleles could combine.

4. Then write the possible combinations of alleles in the offspring in the bottom circles.

Exam Tip H
If you're asked to construct a genetic diagram in the exam you could also draw a Punnett square (see page 188).

Tip: H Remember, an organism's genotype is the alleles it has. Its phenotype is the characteristics it shows.

These steps are illustrated here:

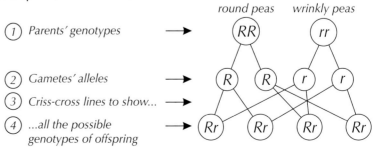

Practice Questions — Fact Recall

Q1 What are alleles?

Q2 What is a dominant allele?

Q3 What is meant by the term 'homozygous'?

Q4 What is meant by the term 'phenotype'?

Exam Tip H
Make sure you learn
what the terms
'genotype', 'phenotype',
'homozygous' and
'heterozygous' mean.
It'll help you pick up
easy marks in the exam.

Practice Questions — Application

Q1 Charlotte has some guinea pigs with rough coats and some
guinea pigs with smooth coats. The allele for a rough coat is
represented by 'R'. The allele for a smooth coat is represented by
'r'. She crosses a rough coated guinea pig (RR) with a smooth coated
guinea pig (rr). Here is a genetic diagram of the cross:

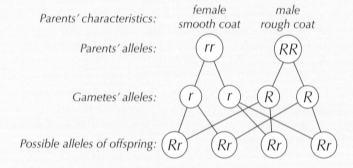

a) What type of coat will the offspring have?

b) i) Charlotte breeds two guinea pigs together that are both
heterozygous for a rough coat. Construct a genetic diagram to
show the possible genotypes their offspring could have.

ii) From the genetic diagram, what is the probability of the
offspring having a smooth coat?

Q2 A female cat has the genotype Ss. 'S' is the allele for spots and is
dominant. 's' is the allele for no spots and is recessive.

a) Is the cat homozygous or heterozygous for the spot allele?

b) What genotype would a cat without spots have?

c) What other possible genotype could a spotty cat have?

- Know that some disorders are genetic, and what this means.

- Know that cystic fibrosis is a genetic disorder affecting the cell membranes.

- Understand that people will only be sufferers of cystic fibrosis if both their parents have the faulty allele because it's a recessive disorder.

- Know what a carrier is in relation to cystic fibrosis.

- Know that polydactyly is a genetic disorder that results in a person having extra fingers or toes.

- Understand that people will suffer from polydactyly if only one parent has the allele because it is a dominant disorder.

- Be able to interpret family trees.

- Know that embryos can be screened for genetic disorders and understand issues associated with this.

Specification Reference
B2.7.3

8. Genetic Disorders

It's not just an organism's characteristics that can be passed on to its offspring. Some disorders can be inherited too. These are known as genetic disorders.

What are genetic disorders?

Genetic disorders are disorders that are caused by an abnormal gene or chromosome, which can be inherited by an individual's offspring. You need to know about two genetic disorders — **cystic fibrosis** and **polydactyly**.

Cystic fibrosis

Cystic fibrosis is a genetic disorder of the cell membranes. It results in the body producing a lot of thick sticky mucus in the air passages (which makes breathing difficult) and in the pancreas.

The allele which causes cystic fibrosis is a recessive allele, carried by about 1 person in 25. Because it's recessive, people with only one copy of the allele won't have the disorder — they're known as **carriers** (they carry the faulty allele, but don't have any symptoms).

For a child to have the disorder, both parents must be either carriers or sufferers. There's a 1 in 4 chance of a child having the disorder if both parents are carriers. This is shown in Figure 1, where '**f**' is used for the recessive cystic fibrosis allele.

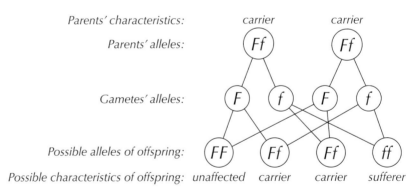

Parents' characteristics: carrier   carrier

Parents' alleles: Ff   Ff

Gametes' alleles: F   f   F   f

Possible alleles of offspring: FF   Ff   Ff   ff

Possible characteristics of offspring: unaffected   carrier   carrier   sufferer

Figure 1: *Genetic diagram to show the inheritance of cystic fibrosis from two carriers.*

Polydactyly

Polydactyly is a genetic disorder where a baby's born with extra fingers or toes (see Figure 2). It doesn't usually cause any other problems so isn't life-threatening.

Figure 2: *X ray of a hand with an extra finger. This person is suffering from polydactyly.*

The disorder is caused by a dominant allele and so can be inherited if just one parent carries the defective allele. The parent that has the defective allele will be a sufferer too since the allele is dominant.

There's a 50% chance of a child having the disorder if one parent has the polydactyly allele. This is shown in Figure 3, where '**D**' is used for the dominant polydactyly allele.

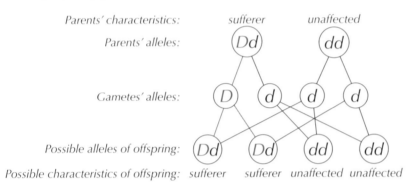

Parents' characteristics: sufferer / unaffected
Parents' alleles: Dd / dd
Gametes' alleles: D / d / d / d
Possible alleles of offspring: Dd / Dd / dd / dd
Possible characteristics of offspring: sufferer / sufferer / unaffected / unaffected

Figure 3: *Genetic diagram to show the inheritance of polydactyly from a sufferer and an unaffected individual.*

> **Tip:** Remember that there are no carriers for polydactyly. If you carry the faulty gene then you are a sufferer because the disorder is caused by a dominant allele, so you only need one copy to have the disorder.

Family trees

In genetics, a family tree is a diagram, which shows how a characteristic (or disorder) is inherited in a group of related people. In the exam you might be asked to interpret a family tree.

> **Exam Tip**
> In the exam you might get a family tree showing the inheritance of a dominant allele — in this case there won't be any carriers shown.

Example

Here is a family tree for cystic fibrosis:

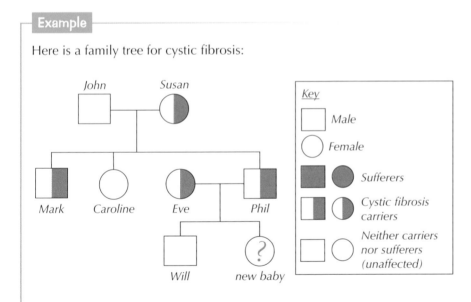

Key
☐ Male
○ Female
■ ● Sufferers
◧ ◐ Cystic fibrosis carriers
☐ ○ Neither carriers nor sufferers (unaffected)

From the family tree, you can tell that:

1. The allele for cystic fibrosis isn't dominant because plenty of the family carry the allele but aren't sufferers.

2. There is a 25% chance that Eve and Phil's new baby will be a sufferer and a 50% chance that it will be a carrier, as Eve and Phil are carriers but not sufferers. This is because the case of the new baby is just the same as in the genetic diagram on the previous page — so the baby could be unaffected (FF), a carrier (Ff) or a sufferer (ff).

> **Exam Tip** H
> A good way to work out a family tree is to write the genotype of each person onto it.

Figure 4: *A single cell being extracted from an embryo in order to be screened for genetic disorders.*

Embryonic screening

Embryonic screening is a way of detecting genetic disorders, such as cystic fibrosis, in embryos. There are different methods used to do this:

1. **Pre-implantation genetic diagnosis (PGD).** During IVF, embryos are fertilised in a laboratory, and then implanted into the mother's womb. Before being implanted, it's possible to remove a cell from each embryo and analyse its genes (see Figure 4) — this is called pre-implantation genetic diagnosis (PGD). Embryos with 'healthy' alleles would be implanted into the mother — the ones with 'faulty' alleles destroyed.

2. **Chorionic villus sampling (CVS).** CVS is usually carried out between 10 and 13 weeks of pregnancy. It involves taking a sample of cells from part of the placenta and analysing their genes. The part of the placenta that's taken and the embryo develop from the same original cell — so they have the same genes. If the embryo is found to have a genetic disorder, the parents can decide whether or not to terminate (end) the pregnancy.

Tip: The placenta is an organ that attaches the embryo to the lining of the womb. It provides the developing embryo with nutrients and takes away waste.

Issues surrounding embryonic screening

There is a huge debate raging about embryonic screening. Here's why:

Arguments for screening

- It helps to stop people suffering from certain genetic disorders.

- Treating disorders costs the Government (and the taxpayers) a lot of money, so screening embryos could reduce healthcare costs.

- During IVF, most of the embryos are destroyed anyway — PGD just ensures that the selected one is healthy.

- If a genetic disorder is diagnosed through CVS, parents don't have to have a termination — but it does give them the choice.

Arguments against screening

- There may come a point where everyone wants to screen their embryos so they can pick the most 'desirable' one, e.g. they want a blue-eyed, blond-haired, intelligent boy.

- It implies that people with genetic problems are 'undesirable' — this could increase prejudice.

- After PGD, the rejected embryos are destroyed — they could have developed into humans, so some people think destroying them is unethical.

- There's a risk that CVS could cause a miscarriage. And if a genetic disorder is diagnosed through CVS, it could lead to a termination (abortion).

Tip: There are laws to stop embryonic screening going too far. At the moment, parents can't even select their baby's sex (unless it's for health reasons).

Exam Tip
You could be given some data about screening for genetic disorders in the exam, and then asked questions about it. You'll just need to read the information given to you carefully, and apply what you know.

Many people think that screening isn't justified for genetic disorders that don't affect a person's health:

> **Example**
>
> Polydactyly causes a physical disfigurement but it isn't life-threatening, so lots of people don't agree with screening for it. In comparison, conditions such as cystic fibrosis are potentially life-threatening and so more people agree to screening for them.

Practice Questions — Fact Recall

Q1 Name the genetic disorder that affects a person's cell membranes.

Q2 Is cystic fibrosis caused by a dominant or recessive allele?

Q3 What do sufferers of the genetic disorder polydactyly have?

Q4 Why would an embryo be screened before it is inserted into the mother's uterus during IVF?

Practice Questions — Application

Q1 If 'f' represents the recessive allele for cystic fibrosis and 'F' represents the dominant allele:

a) give the alleles a carrier of cystic fibrosis would have.

b) give the alleles that a sufferer of cystic fibrosis would have.

Q2 The family tree below shows the inheritance of the genetic disorder polydactyly in a family.

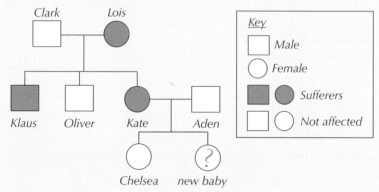

Using the family tree, answer the following questions:

a) From the diagram, how do you know that the allele for polydactyly is dominant?

b) If the new baby was a girl with polydactyly, what symbol would she have on the family tree?

For the following questions, use 'D' to represent the allele for polydactyly and 'd' to represent the allele for a non-sufferer.

c) Give the genotype of the following individuals:

  i) Clark   ii) Kate

d) Lois has the genotype Dd. Draw a Punnet square to show the inheritance of the polydactyly allele from parents Lois and Clark.

e) Kate and Aden are having a baby.

  i) Draw a genetic diagram to show the inheritance of polydactyly from Kate and Aden.

  ii) What is the probability the new baby will have polydactyly?

Section Checklist — Make sure you know...

DNA

☐ That our chromosomes are made up of long molecules of DNA (deoxyribonucleic acid) and so they contain our genetic information.

☐ That DNA has a double helix structure and that genes are small sections of DNA.

☐ ⬛ That our genes determine the proteins a cell produces by telling the cell what order to put amino acids together in.

☐ That (apart from identical twins), a person's DNA is unique and, as a result of this, a technique called DNA fingerprinting can be used to identify an individual based on their DNA.

Cell Division — Mitosis

☐ That body cells contain two sets of chromosomes and that these chromosomes are found in pairs.

☐ That body cells divide by mitosis, allowing organisms to grow and replace damaged cells.

☐ That some organisms (e.g. strawberry plants) reproduce asexually using mitosis and that the offspring have the same genes as the parent.

☐ That when a cell divides by mitosis it first copies its genetic material and then divides once, producing two cells which are genetically identical.

Cell Division — Meiosis

☐ That gametes only contain one set of chromosomes and that at fertilisation they combine to form a body cell containing two sets of chromosomes.

☐ How sexual reproduction results in variation — the offspring inherits alleles from both parents.

☐ That gametes are produced when cells divide by meiosis in the reproductive organs (testes or ovaries in humans).

☐ That once two gametes have joined at fertilisation, the fertilised egg grows by mitosis.

☐ ⬛ That when a cell divides by meiosis, it first copies its genetic information, and then divides twice to produce four gametes that are genetically different.

Stem Cells

☐ That most animal cells lose the ability to differentiate (become specialised for a particular job) early on, but lots of plants don't ever lose this ability. In mature animals, cell division is mainly used for growth and repair.

☐ That embryonic stem cells are found in early human embryos and can be made to differentiate into any type of cell. This means they could potentially be used to treat many medical conditions by replacing damaged or dead cells, such as nerve cells in people with paralysis.

☐ That adult stem cells can be taken from bone marrow and made to differentiate into certain types of cell. Adult stem cells already have some uses in medicine, e.g. in bone marrow transplants.

☐ How to give informed opinions on the use of embryos as a source of stem cells for medical research.

cont...

X and Y Chromosomes

☐ That on one of the 23 pairs of chromosomes in a human body cell are the genes that determine sex, and that these chromosomes are called sex chromosomes — females have two XX sex chromosomes and males have an X sex chromosome and a Y sex chromosome.

☐ How to predict the outcome of genetic diagrams showing sex inheritance.

☐ 🄷 How to construct genetic diagrams showing sex inheritance.

The Work of Mendel

☐ How Mendel's experiments with pea plants led him to develop the idea of hereditary units/inherited factors and what that meant — characteristics are determined by separate units, that organisms receive one unit from each parent and that these units can be dominant or recessive.

☐ That what Mendel called inherited factors are what we now know as genes.

☐ That Mendel's work was not appreciated until after his death because people were not aware of things like genes and DNA at the time.

Alleles and Genetic Diagrams

☐ That some characteristics of an organism are controlled by just one gene and that different forms of the same gene are called alleles.

☐ That if an individual has two different alleles for a characteristic, that the allele for the characteristic that is displayed is dominant, and the other allele is recessive.

☐ 🄷 That if an organism has two alleles for a gene that are the same, then it is homozygous. If the two alleles for the gene are different then it's heterozygous.

☐ 🄷 That 'genotype' means the alleles an organism has (e.g. Gg, bb) and that 'phenotype' means the characteristics an organism has (e.g. blue eyes, blonde hair).

☐ That a monohybrid cross is where you cross two parents to look at one characteristic inherited by a single gene. And how to predict and explain the outcomes of genetic diagrams for all combinations of dominant and recessive alleles in monohybrid crosses.

☐ 🄷 How to construct genetic diagrams of monohybrid inheritance.

Genetic Disorders

☐ That genetic disorders are inherited disorders.

☐ That cystic fibrosis is a genetic disorder of the cell membranes caused by a recessive allele. This means both of a sufferer's parents must have the faulty allele for the sufferer to inherit the condition. If a person inherits just one faulty allele for cystic fibrosis then they will be a carrier.

☐ That polydactyly is a genetic disorder where people have extra fingers and toes, and it's caused by a dominant allele. This means anyone who inherits a single polydactyly allele from one of their parents will have the condition.

☐ How to interpret family trees.

☐ What embryonic screening is and the issues surrounding it.

Exam-style Questions

1   DNA fingerprinting can be used to identify the father of a child.

DNA samples are taken from a child and from men who may be the father of the child (Males 1-4). A DNA fingerprint is produced from the samples, as shown here:

1 (a)   Which man is most likely to be the child's father? Explain your answer.

(2 marks)

1 (b)   Which of the bands in the child's DNA fingerprint would match the mother's DNA fingerprint? Explain your answer.

(3 marks)

2   Kaye and Mark are expecting a baby.

2 (a)   Kaye has dimples in her cheeks, but Mark does not.
The presence of dimples is thought to be caused by a dominant allele represented by the letter **D**. The recessive allele is represented by the letter **d**. Kaye is heterozygous for the dimples gene.

2 (a) (i)   Draw a genetic diagram to show the possible inheritance of the dimples gene by the baby.

(2 marks)

2 (a) (ii)   What is the probability that the baby will have dimples?

(1 mark)

Kaye and Mark have found out that they are expecting baby boy.

2 (b)   What combination of sex chromosomes will the baby have?

(1 mark)

2 (c)   Explain why the baby will be genetically different to both Kaye and Mark.

(3 marks)

3   Mitosis and meiosis are types of cell division.

3 (a)   Tick the boxes to say whether the following statements apply to mitosis or meiosis.

Statement	Mitosis	Meiosis
Only occurs in the reproductive organs.		
It produces gametes.		
It produces body cells.		

(3 marks)

3 (b)   A cell divides by mitosis once every half hour.

3 (b) (i) Starting with one cell, calculate how many cells there will be after 2 hours.

(2 marks)

3 (b) (ii) Will the offspring be genetically identical or genetically different to the original parent cell?

(1 mark)

4   Family trees can show the inheritance of characteristics, such as cystic fibrosis.

4 (a)   What is cystic fibrosis?

(2 marks)

This family tree shows the inheritance of the cystic fibrosis in a family.

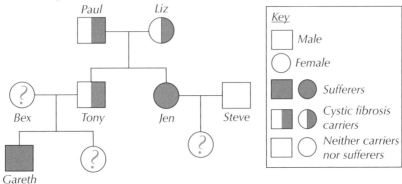

4 (b)   Is Gareth heterozygous or homozygous for the cystic fibrosis allele?
Explain your answer

(1 mark)

4 (c)   Looking at the family tree, could Jen and Steve have a child with cystic fibrosis?
Draw a genetic diagram to help you explain your answer.
In your genetic diagram use **f** to represent the allele for cystic fibrosis and
F to represent the healthy allele.

(4 marks)

4 (d)   Bex and Tony have a child with cystic fibrosis. However, Bex doesn't
suffer from cystic fibrosis. Therefore, what combination of alleles must Bex
have for the cystic fibrosis gene? Explain your answer.

(3 marks)

Learning Objectives:
- Know what fossils are.
- Know that fossils provide evidence for the existence of early organisms.
- Know that fossils show how life on Earth evolved.
- Understand the main ways in which fossils form.
- Understand why scientists have different views on how life on Earth began.
- Understand why there are so few fossils of early organisms.

Specification Reference B2.8.1

1. Fossils

Fossils might sound a bit dull, but they're actually dead interesting. Without them, we wouldn't know that dinosaurs ever existed.

What are fossils?

Fossils are the remains of organisms from many years ago, which are found in rocks. Fossils provide the evidence that organisms lived ages ago. They also show how life on Earth **evolved** — by comparing fossils with species that are alive today, we can see that many of today's species have developed from much simpler organisms over millions of years.

How do fossils form?

Fossils form in rocks in one of three ways:

1. From gradual replacement by minerals

Things like teeth, shells, bones, etc., which don't **decay** easily, can last a long time when buried. They're eventually replaced by minerals as they decay, forming a rock-like substance shaped like the original hard part (see Figures 1 and 2).

The surrounding sediments also turn to rock, but the fossil stays distinct inside the rock and eventually someone digs it up. Most fossils are made this way.

Tip: When organisms die, they usually get broken down (digested) by microorganisms such as bacteria and fungi. This process is known as decay. Decay can take place at different rates. Very occasionally, it doesn't happen at all (see next page).

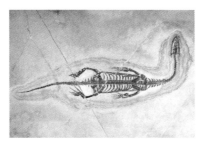

Figure 1: *Fossil of a reptile skeleton, dug out of the rock in China.*

Figure 2: *Fossils of ammonite shells. Ammonites were ancient marine organisms.*

Tip: The soft tissue of this reptile (Figure 1) and the soft bodies of the ammonites (Figure 2) decayed away quickly, so they haven't formed part of the fossils.

2. From casts and impressions

Sometimes, fossils are formed when an organism is buried in a soft material like clay. The clay later hardens around it and the organism decays, leaving a **cast** of itself. An animal's burrow (see Figure 3, next page) or a plant's roots can be preserved as casts. Things like footprints can also be pressed into soft materials, leaving an impression when the material hardens (see Figure 4, next page).

Figure 3: *Fossilised burrows made in the sea bed by small organisms millions of years ago.*

Figure 4: *The footprint of an early human-like primate, preserved in hardened volcanic ash.*

3. From preservation in places where no decay happens

The microbes involved in decay need the right conditions in order to break down material — that means plenty of oxygen (for aerobic respiration, see p.167), enough moisture, and the right temperature and pH for their enzymes to work properly (see pages 157-158). If the conditions aren't right, decay won't take place and the dead organism's remains will be preserved.

Tip: As it happens, the conditions needed for decay are usually right — so it's very rare for dead organisms to be preserved in this way.

> **Examples**
>
> - In amber (a clear yellow 'stone' made from fossilised tree sap) and tar pits there's no oxygen or moisture so decay microbes can't survive (see Figure 5).
>
> - In glaciers it's too cold for the decay microbes to work.
>
> - Peat bogs are too acidic for decay microbes. Whole human bodies have been preserved as fossils in peat bogs (see Figure 6).
>
>
>
> **Figure 5:** *Fossil of a midge, preserved in amber.*
>
>
>
> **Figure 6:** *Photo of the 'Tollund Man'. This well preserved fossil of a man was discovered in a bog.*

Tip: The 'Tollund Man' lived over 2000 years ago. He was so well preserved in the bog that scientists were able to tell what he ate for his last meal from the contents of his stomach (barley gruel, yum).

The origins of life on Earth

There are various **hypotheses** suggesting how life first came into being, but no one really knows the answer.

Maybe the first life forms came into existence in a primordial swamp (or under the sea) here on Earth. Maybe simple organic molecules were brought to Earth on comets — these could have then become more complex organic molecules, and eventually very simple life forms.

Tip: 'Primordial' means 'original' or 'first'. So primordial swamps were the first swamps.

Tip: Organic molecules are molecules containing carbon, e.g. amino acids.

Tip: Validity and reliability are explained on pages 2-3.

Tip: Tectonic plates are the large 'pieces' of rock that make up the Earth's crust.

These hypotheses can't be supported or disproved because there's a lack of **valid** and **reliable evidence**. There's a lack of evidence because:

- Scientists believe many early organisms were soft-bodied, and soft tissue tends to decay away completely, without forming fossils.

- Fossils that did form millions of years ago may have been destroyed by **geological activity**, e.g. the movement of tectonic plates may have crushed fossils already formed in the rock.

This means that the **fossil record** is incomplete — in other words, we don't have fossils of every organism or even every type of organism that has ever lived.

Practice Questions — Fact Recall

Q1   What is a fossil?

Q2   What do fossils provide evidence of?

Q3   Explain why there is a lack of valid and reliable evidence to support any hypothesis about how life on Earth began.

Practice Question — Application

Q1   Suggest how each of the following fossils was formed:

A

Fossilised animal burrows preserved in rock.

B

A fossilised snail shell.

C

A fossilised leaf imprint in rock.

D

A fossilised baby mammoth, found in frozen ground in Siberia.

2. Extinction and Speciation

Life on Earth is changing all the time — species die out and new ones emerge. It's all to do with extinction and speciation...

What is extinction?

The fossil record contains many species that don't exist any more — these species are said to be **extinct**. Dinosaurs and mammoths are extinct animals, with only fossils to tell us they existed at all.

Why do species become extinct?

Species become extinct for these reasons:

- The environment changes too quickly (e.g. destruction of habitat).

- A new predator kills them all (e.g. humans hunting them).

- A new disease kills them all.

- They can't compete with another (new) species for food.

- A catastrophic event happens that kills them all (e.g. a volcanic eruption or a collision with an asteroid).

- A new species develops (this is called speciation — see below).

Example

Dodos (a type of large, flightless bird) are now extinct. Humans not only hunted them, but introduced other animals which ate all their eggs, and also destroyed the forest where they lived — they really didn't stand a chance.

Speciation

A **species** is a group of similar organisms that can reproduce to give fertile offspring (offspring that are able to breed themselves). **Speciation** is the development of a new species.

Isolation

Isolation is where populations of a species are separated. This can happen due to a physical barrier. E.g. floods and earthquakes can cause barriers that geographically isolate some individuals from the main population. Isolation can eventually lead to speciation.

Example

The chimpanzee and bonobo are two separate species of ape that evolved from a common ancestor. It's thought that two populations of the ancestor became isolated from each other when the Congo River formed.

Learning Objectives:

- Know the six main causes of extinction.

- Know that the formation of new species is called speciation.

- Know that speciation starts with the isolation of populations.

- **H** Understand how genetic variation and natural selection lead to speciation — populations can no longer interbreed to produce fertile offspring.

Specification Reference B2.8.1

Tip: If an environment changes too rapidly, a species may not be able to evolve quickly enough to survive. If so, the species will eventually die out.

Tip: If lots of species die out at the same time (e.g. due to a catastrophic event), it's known as a mass extinction.

Figure 1: *An artist's impression of the dodo.*

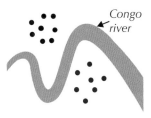

● = chimp ● = bonobo

Figure 2: *Diagram to show the isolation, and so speciation, of chimp and bonobo populations.*

The population to the north of the river became chimpanzees and the population to the south became bonobos (see Figure 2).

Natural selection `Higher`

When two populations are isolated due to a physical barrier, conditions on either side of the barrier will be slightly different, e.g. the climate may be different. Because the environment is different on each side, different characteristics will become more common in each population due to natural selection. Here's how:

1. Each population shows variation because they have a wide range of **alleles**.

2. In each population, individuals with characteristics that make them better adapted to their environment have a better chance of survival and so are more likely to breed successfully.

3. So the alleles that control the beneficial characteristics are more likely to be passed on to the next generation.

Eventually, individuals from the different populations will have changed so much that they won't be able to breed with one another to produce fertile offspring. This means the two groups have become separate species — in other words, speciation has occurred.

The whole process is shown in Figure 3.

Tip: H Alleles are different forms of a gene. See page 193 for more.

Tip: H Populations can sometimes split up into more than two groups — this could result in the formation of several new species.

Exam Tip H
In the exam, you could be asked to apply your knowledge of how speciation occurs to explain the formation of any new species. So make sure you know the main stages involved — isolation, then genetic variation and natural selection lead to speciation.

Key:
● = *individual organism*
● = *individual organism of new species*

Two populations of the same species.

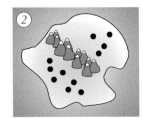

Physical barriers separate populations.

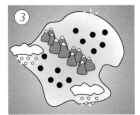

Populations adapt to new environments.

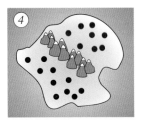

Development of a new species.

Figure 3: H *Diagram to show how speciation occurs.*

Q1 Give two ways in which a species may become extinct.

Q2 What is speciation?

Q3 Describe one way in which populations of a species may become isolated from one another.

Q4 Why do populations of the same species show variation?

Q5 How can you tell that speciation has taken place?

Section Checklist — Make sure you know...

Fossils

☐ That fossils are the remains of organisms from many years ago, which are found in rocks.

☐ That fossils provide evidence that organisms lived long ago and show how species evolved.

☐ That fossils can be made when hard body parts (that don't decay easily) are gradually replaced by minerals, from casts and impressions, and from preservation in places where no decay happens.

☐ That there are various hypotheses as to how life on Earth began, but that these can't be supported or disproved because there's not enough valid and reliable evidence.

☐ That there's a lack of valid and reliable evidence because there are so few fossils of early organisms — their soft bodies decayed easily and didn't form fossils, and geological activity has destroyed many fossils that did form.

Extinction and Speciation

☐ The reasons why species become extinct — the environment changes too quickly, a new predator or disease appears, they can't compete with other species, a catastrophic event happens (e.g. a volcanic eruption or an asteroid collision) which kills them or a new species develops.

☐ That speciation is the formation of a new species and that it can happen when populations become geographically isolated.

☐ **H** How, following isolation, genetic variation and natural selection can lead to speciation: each isolated population has different alleles; natural selection causes different characteristics, and therefore different alleles, to become more common in each population; eventually, the populations become so different they can no longer interbreed to produce fertile offspring.

Exam-style Questions

1   The photograph below shows part of the Grand Canyon in Arizona, USA.
The canyon is several kilometres wide and nearly two kilometres deep in places.

Two closely-related, but separate squirrel species live either side of the canyon.
They are thought to be descended from a single original squirrel species,
present in the area before the canyon formed.

1 (a)   Use your knowledge of speciation to explain how the two separate
squirrel species formed.

(5 marks)

1 (b)   A bird species is found on both sides of the canyon.

Suggest why the formation of the canyon did not cause the bird species to
form two separate species.

(2 marks)

1 (c)   Fossils of shelled organisms are often found in the Grand Canyon.

1 (c) (i)   Suggest how these fossils may have formed.

(2 marks)

1 (c) (ii)   Why didn't the soft bodies of these shelled organisms form part of the fossils?

(1 mark)

1 (c) (iii)   Give **one** way in which some fossils can be destroyed over time.

(1 mark)

1. Osmosis

Osmosis is an important process for life — it's how cells get the water they need to carry out chemical reactions.

What is osmosis?

> Osmosis is the movement of water molecules across a partially permeable membrane from a region of high water concentration to a region of low water concentration.

A **partially permeable membrane** is just one with very small holes in it. So small, in fact, only tiny molecules (like water) can pass through them, and bigger molecules (e.g. sucrose, a sugar) can't. This is shown in Figure 1.

The water molecules actually pass both ways through the membrane during osmosis. This happens because water molecules move about randomly all the time. But because there are more water molecules on one side than on the other, there's a steady net flow of water into the region with fewer water molecules, i.e. into the stronger sugar solution. This means the strong sugar solution gets more dilute. The water acts like it's trying to "even up" the concentration either side of the membrane.

Learning Objectives:
- Know the definition of osmosis.
- Understand how water moves into or out of a cell by osmosis.
- Understand why when the body loses water or ions, they need to be replaced.
- Know that soft drinks usually contain water, sugar and ions.
- Know why a sports drink contains water, sugar and ions.
- Be able to evaluate claims made about sports drinks.

Specification Reference
B3.1.1

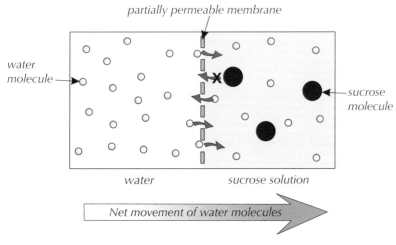

Figure 1: *Diagram to show how osmosis works.*

Osmosis is a type of **diffusion** — passive movement of water particles from an area of high water concentration to an area of low water concentration.

Tip: You might remember diffusion from Biology 2 — it's the spreading out of particles from an area of high concentration to an area of low concentration. It's passive, which means it doesn't need energy.

The movement of water in and out of cells

Tissue fluid surrounds the cells in the body — it's basically just water with oxygen, glucose and stuff dissolved in it. It's squeezed out of the blood capillaries to supply the cells with everything they need.

The tissue fluid will usually have a different concentration to the fluid inside a cell. This means that water will either move into the cell from the tissue fluid, or out of the cell, by osmosis.

Tip: Water moves in and out of all cells by osmosis, not just animal cells. So plant cells gain and lose water by osmosis too.

If a cell is short of water, the solution inside it will become quite concentrated (i.e. there'll be a low concentration of water molecules). This usually means the solution outside the cell is more dilute (there's a higher concentration of water molecules), and so water will move into the cell by osmosis. If a cell has lots of water, the solution inside it will be more dilute, and water will be drawn out of the cell and into the fluid outside by osmosis. This is summarised in Figure 2.

Tip: Cells that gain water by osmosis get a bit bigger (animal cells that gain too much water will eventually burst). Cells that lose water get a bit smaller.

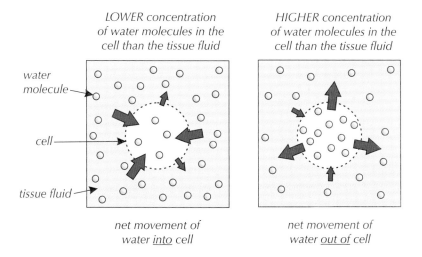

Figure 2: Diagram to show the movement of water molecules into and out of a cell.

Osmosis and sports drinks

When you exercise, you lose water and ions (e.g. sodium) in your sweat. It's important that these get replaced — if the balance between ions and water in the body is wrong, it could mean too much or too little water is drawn into cells by osmosis. Having the wrong amount of water can damage cells or mean they don't work as well as normal.

Most soft drinks, including sports drinks, contain water, sugar and ions. Sports drinks can be used to help your body keep things in order after exercise. The water and ions replace those lost in sweat, while the sugar can replace the sugar that's used up by muscles during exercise.

Evaluating claims made about sports drinks

Some sports drink manufacturers claim that their products will rehydrate you faster than plain water, or improve your endurance (how long you can keep exercising for). To judge whether you can believe claims like these or not, you need to watch out for all the same things as with other health claims — in other words:

- Is the report a scientific study, published in a reputable journal?

- Was it written by a qualified person (not connected with the people selling it)?

- Was the sample of people asked/tested large enough?

- Have there been other studies which found similar results?

Figure 3: Woman drinking a sports drink designed to replace the water, ions and sugar lost during exercise.

Practice Questions — Fact Recall

Q1 What is osmosis?

Q2 Explain how a cell that is short of water gains water from the surrounding tissue fluid.

Q3 Name three things usually present in sports drinks.

Practice Questions — Application

Q1 An experiment is carried out to investigate osmosis.

A potato is cut up into cylinders of the same known length and width.

Some of the potato cylinders are placed in a beaker of pure water. Others are placed in beakers with different concentrations of sugar solution. This is shown in the diagram.

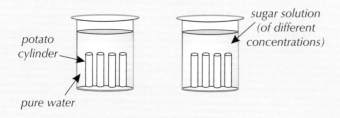

potato cylinder

pure water

sugar solution (of different concentrations)

The potato cylinders are left in the beakers for 24 hours. They are then removed and the length of each potato cylinder is recorded. The mean change in potato cylinder length for each beaker is then worked out.

Exam Tip
There are loads of similar experiments to this, which show osmosis at work, and you could get asked questions about one in the exam — so make sure you understand what's happening here.

The results of this experiment are shown in the table.

Tip: 'M' is a unit of concentration. The solution with a concentration of 0.00 M is pure water.

Concentration of solution (M)	Mean change in potato cylinder length (mm)
0.00	+ 3.1
0.25	+ 2.1
0.50	− 1.2
0.75	− 2.6
1.00	?

a) i) Describe what happened to the potato cylinders in the 0.00 M and 0.25 M solutions.

   ii) Explain the changes you described in part a) i) in terms of osmosis.

b) Predict the mean change in length for the potato cylinders in the 1.00 M solution.

c) What was:

Tip: There's more on variables on page 6.

   i) the dependent variable in this experiment?

   ii) the independent variable in this experiment?

d) Give two variables that had to be controlled in this experiment to make it a fair test.

Q2 Laura is running a marathon. As she goes round the course she is handed sports drinks by the organisers. Suggest why.

Q3 Sports drink manufacturers often claim that drinking sports drinks improves your sporting performance or helps you to recover quicker after exercise. In 2012, a report was published that looked at the quality of evidence behind some of these claims, and claims made about other sports products.

The team behind the report analysed 74 studies that were used as evidence to back up the manufacturers' claims. Many of the studies involved trials of sports drinks. The team found that:

- Excluding the two largest studies, the average number of participants per study was 16.

Tip: In a blind trial of a sports drink, the participants wouldn't know whether they were being given a sports drink or a control (e.g. an ordinary soft drink). This is done to help prevent bias (see page 3).

- Two thirds of the study participants were men.

- Most of the studies did not carry out any repeats.

- Most studies did not carry out a blind trial.

The scientists behind the report concluded that the evidence was not of a high enough quality to inform people about the pros and cons of sports products, such as sports drinks. Using the information given, suggest and explain two reasons why the scientists came to this conclusion.

2. Active Transport

Learning Objectives:
- Know the definition of active transport.
- Know that cells can absorb ions from very dilute solutions using active transport.

Specification Reference
B3.1.1

Molecules can move into and out of cells via a process called active transport. But it needs energy...

What is active transport?

Active transport is the movement of particles against a concentration gradient (i.e. from an area of low concentration to an area of high concentration) using energy released during respiration.

Tip: Active transport is the <u>opposite</u> of diffusion — it moves particles in the opposite direction (i.e. from a low to a high concentration) and it requires <u>energy</u> to make it work.

Example

Active transport is used in the digestive system when there is a low concentration of nutrients in the gut, but a high concentration of nutrients in the blood. Here's how it works:

When there's a higher concentration of nutrients in the gut they diffuse naturally into the blood. BUT — sometimes there's a lower concentration of nutrients in the gut than there is in the blood (see Figure 1).

This means that the concentration gradient is the wrong way. The nutrients should go the other way if they followed the rules of diffusion. This is where active transport comes in.

Active transport allows nutrients to be taken into the blood, despite the fact that the concentration gradient is the wrong way. This is essential to stop us starving. But active transport needs ENERGY from respiration to make it work.

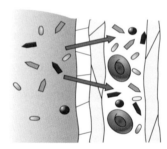

Inside the gut   *Inside the blood*

Figure 1: *Diagram to show active transport in the gut.*

Tip: Active transport is also used by plants — it's how they get minerals from the soil (where there's a lower mineral concentration) into their root hair cells (where there's a higher mineral concentration). See page 227.

Active transport, like diffusion and osmosis, can be used to move substances in and out of cells. It allows cells to absorb ions from very dilute solutions.

Practice Questions — Fact Recall

Q1 What is active transport?

Q2 True or false? Cells cannot absorb ions from very dilute solutions.

3. Gas and Solute Exchange

- Know how dissolved substances move from one area to another.

- Know how exchange surfaces are adapted for exchanging materials.

- Know that in bigger and more complex organisms, exchanging materials gets more difficult.

- Know that organ systems can be specialised for exchanging materials.

Specification Reference B3.1.1

Solutes are dissolved substances. Living organisms need to be able to exchange dissolved substances with their environment in order to survive.

Movement of substances

Life processes need gases or other dissolved substances (solutes) before they can happen. For example, for photosynthesis to happen, carbon dioxide and water have to get into plant cells. And for respiration to take place, glucose and oxygen both have to get inside cells. Waste substances also need to move out of the cells so that the organism can get rid of them.

Dissolved substances move to where they need to be by diffusion and active transport. Water moves by osmosis.

Exchange surfaces

In life processes, the gases and other dissolved substances have to move through some sort of **exchange surface**. The exchange surface structures have to allow enough of the necessary substances to pass through. For this reason, exchange surfaces are adapted to maximise effectiveness:

Tip: There's more on diffusion on pages 125-126, osmosis on pages 213-214 and active transport on the previous page.

- They are thin, so substances only have a short distance to diffuse. The posh way of saying this is that the substances have a 'short diffusion pathway'.

- They have a large surface area so lots of a substance can diffuse at once.

- Exchange surfaces in animals have lots of blood vessels, to get stuff into and out of the blood quickly.

Tip: Gas exchange in animals means taking in oxygen from the environment and releasing carbon dioxide.

- Gas exchange surfaces in animals (e.g. alveoli, page 220) are often ventilated too — air moves in and out.

In single-celled organisms, substances can be exchanged with the environment directly across their outer surface. But exchanging substances gets more difficult in bigger and more complex organisms, as the place where substances are needed (or waste is made) ends up being a long way from exchange surfaces. As a result, specialised organ systems are often needed for exchanging materials.

| Example |

Oxygen is able to diffuse from the air into a bacterial cell across the cell surface. A bacterium can get all the oxygen it needs for respiration this way.

Tip: 100 trillion is 10^{14} or 100 000 000 000 000. I wonder who counted.

But in the human body, there are around 100 trillion cells and they all need to get enough oxygen to respire. Oxygen can't just diffuse in through your skin — it would never reach the cells deep inside you.

So humans need a specialised gas exchange surface (the alveoli, see page 220) for the oxygen to diffuse across and a specialised breathing system to get it there. They also need a circulatory system (see page 232) to transport the oxygen to every cell.

Practice Questions — Fact Recall

Q1 a) Give three ways that substances can move into and out of a cell.

b) By which of these three ways can dissolved substances move into and out of a cell?

Q2 Give three ways in which exchange surfaces in animals may be adapted for effective exchange.

Practice Question — Application

Q1 These photographs show an earthworm and an elephant. They are both animals.

An earthworm exchanges gases through its skin. An elephant has a specialised breathing system and exchanges gases in its lungs.

a) Suggest and explain two features that an earthworm's skin may have to make it effective as a gas exchange surface.

b) Explain why elephants need a specialised organ system for gas exchange while earthworms do not.

- Know that alveoli increase the surface area of the lungs in humans.

- Know that villi increase the surface area of the small intestine in humans to aid the absorption of nutrients by active transport and diffusion.

- Know that villi also have a good blood supply to aid the absorption of nutrients.

Specification Reference
B3.1.1

4. Exchange in Humans

Amongst other things, humans exchange gases and nutrients with their environment. And you're about to learn how they do it...

Gas exchange

The job of the **lungs** is to transfer oxygen to the blood and to remove waste carbon dioxide from it. To do this the lungs contain millions of little air sacs called **alveoli** (see Figure 1) where gas exchange takes place.

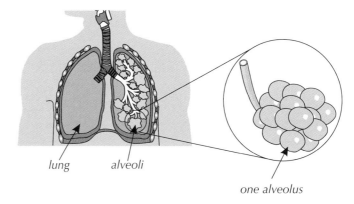

Figure 1: Diagram to show the location and structure of the alveoli.

Tip: It's one alveol<u>us</u> and two or more alveol<u>i</u>.

The alveoli are surrounded by a network of tiny blood vessels known as capillaries (see Figure 2). There is a higher concentration of oxygen in the air than in the blood, so oxygen diffuses out of the air in the alveoli and into the blood in the capillaries. Carbon dioxide (CO_2) diffuses in the opposite direction (see Figure 3). Air enters and leaves the alveoli via small tubes called bronchioles.

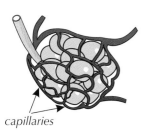

Figure 2: The alveoli are surrounded by a network of capillaries.

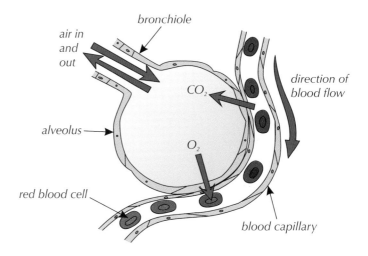

Figure 3: Diagram to show gas exchange across an alveolus.

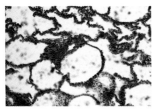

Figure 4: Alveoli and surrounding capillaries as seen under a light microscope.

Adaptations of the alveoli

The alveoli are specialised to maximise the diffusion of oxygen and CO_2. They have:

- An enormous surface area (about 75 m² in humans).
- A moist lining for dissolving gases.
- Very thin walls.
- A good blood supply.

Absorbing the products of digestion

Nutrients, e.g. glucose and amino acids, are absorbed into the bloodstream from the **small intestine** — either by diffusion or active transport (see page 217). To aid this absorption, the inside of the small intestine is covered in millions and millions of tiny little projections called **villi** (see Figure 5).

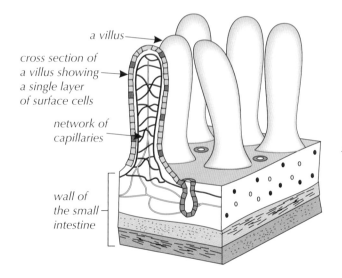

a villus

cross section of a villus showing a single layer of surface cells

network of capillaries

wall of the small intestine

Figure 5: *Diagram showing the structure of villi in the small intestine.*

Tip: It's one vill<u>us</u> and two or more vill<u>i</u>.

Figure 6: *A 3D view of villi in the small intestine, as seen under a microscope.*

Villi increase the surface area in a big way so that digested food is absorbed much more quickly into the blood. They also have:

- a single layer of surface cells.
- a very good blood supply to assist quick absorption.

Tip: Notice how many features the alveoli and the villi have in common — they both have a large surface area, very thin walls and a good blood supply. Lots of exchange surfaces have these features as they make diffusion more effective — see p.218.

Practice Questions — Fact Recall

Q1 Give one feature of the alveoli that helps them to maximise gas exchange in the lungs.

Q2 Explain how villi aid the absorption of nutrients in the small intestine.

5. The Breathing System

Exchanging substances is a complicated process for large, complex organisms (see page 218). That's why humans have a breathing system.

What is the breathing system?

You need to get oxygen from the air into your bloodstream so that it can get to your cells for respiration. You also need to get rid of the carbon dioxide in your blood. This all happens inside your **lungs**. The breathing system (and the action of breathing) is how air gets in and out of your lungs. The breathing system is made up of structures in the thorax.

The thorax

The lungs are in the **thorax** (see Figure 1). The thorax is the top part of your body. It's separated from the lower part of the body (the **abdomen**) by a muscle called the **diaphragm**. The lungs are like big pink sponges and are protected by the **ribcage**.

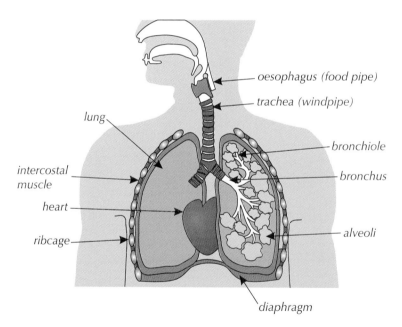

Figure 1: Diagram showing the main structures in the thorax.

The air that you breathe in goes through the trachea. This splits into two tubes called 'bronchi' (each one is 'a bronchus'), one going to each lung. The bronchi split into progressively smaller tubes called bronchioles.

The bronchioles finally end at small bags called **alveoli** where the gas exchange takes place by diffusion (see page 220).

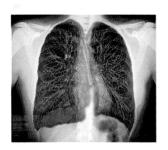

Figure 2: A 3D MRI scan of the thorax. The lungs appear black and the bronchioles orange.

Ventilation

To put it simply, ventilation is just breathing in and breathing out. The fancy way of saying it is:

Ventilation is the movement of air into and out of the lungs.

Exam Tip
Don't get ventilation and respiration mixed up in the exam. Respiration is the process of <u>releasing energy from glucose</u> and it takes place in every cell in the body. Ventilation is the <u>movement of air</u> into and out of the lungs.

Breathing in

To breathe in, the intercostal muscles contract, moving the ribcage up and out. The diaphragm also contracts, making it flatten. These two actions increase the volume of the thorax (i.e. the thorax gets bigger), which decreases the pressure in the thorax. This decrease in pressure draws air into the lungs. This is shown in Figure 3.

Tip: Remember, an <u>increase</u> in <u>volume</u> causes a <u>decrease</u> in <u>pressure</u>.

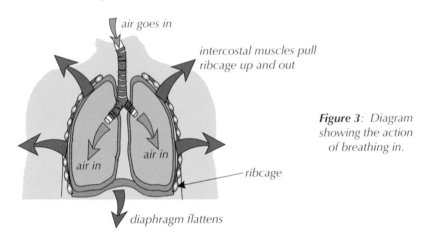

air goes in

intercostal muscles pull ribcage up and out

air in *air in*

ribcage

diaphragm flattens

Figure 3: Diagram showing the action of breathing in.

Breathing out

Breathing out is exactly the opposite to breathing in. To breathe out, the intercostal muscles relax, moving the ribcage down and in. The diaphragm also relaxes, making it bulge upwards. These two actions decrease the volume of the thorax (i.e. the thorax gets smaller), which increases the pressure in the thorax. This increase in pressure forces air out of the lungs. This is shown in Figure 4.

Tip: When the diaphragm contracts, it's flat. When it relaxes, it bulges upwards. Think of it like trying to hold your stomach muscles in — you contract your muscles to flatten your stomach and relax them to release it.

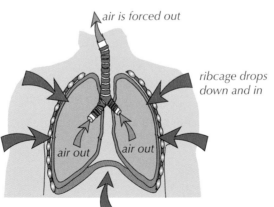

air is forced out

Figure 4: Diagram showing the action of breathing out.

ribcage drops down and in

air out *air out*

diaphragm moves up

Exam Tip
You need to be able to explain how the contraction and relaxation of muscles changes the pressure in the thorax in the exam.

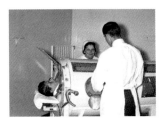

Figure 5: *Medical staff attending to a patient in an iron lung.*

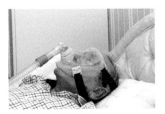

Figure 6: *A man attached to a modern ventilator.*

Artificial ventilators

Artificial ventilators are machines that move air (often with extra oxygen) into or out of the lungs. They help people who can't breathe by themselves, e.g. if they're under general anaesthetic, or have a lung injury or disease.

They used to be a giant case (an 'iron lung') from the neck to the abdomen, with only the patient's head poking out (see Figure 5). Air was pumped out of the case, causing the pressure in the case to drop. This allowed the lungs to expand, so air was drawn into the lungs. Air pumped into the case had the opposite effect, forcing air out of the lungs. However, iron lungs could interfere with blood flow to the lower body.

Nowadays, most ventilators work by pumping air into the lungs. This expands the ribcage — when they stop pumping, the ribcage relaxes and pushes air back out of the lungs. This doesn't interfere with blood flow, but it can occasionally cause damage (e.g. burst alveoli) if the lungs can't cope with the artificial air flow. A modern ventilator is shown in Figure 6.

Practice Questions — Fact Recall

Q1 a) What is the name given to the area of the human body in which the lungs are located?

b) What separates this area from the lower part of the human body?

Q2 Give one role of the ribcage.

Q3 What is 'ventilation'?

Q4 True or false? When you breathe in, the diaphragm relaxes, making it bulge upwards.

Q5 True or false? An increase in the volume of the thorax leads to a decrease in pressure in the thorax, which draws air into the lungs.

Q6 Give one advantage of a modern ventilator over an iron lung.

Practice Question — Application

Q1 A doctor asks a patient to breathe into a machine called a spirometer. The spirometer records changes in the patient's lung volume and produces this graph.

At which point on the graph (labelled A-D) is:

a) the patient likely to be taking a very deep breath in?

b) the patient likely to be taking a normal breath in?

c) the pressure in the lungs likely to be highest?

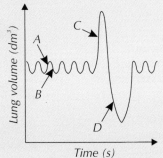

6. Exchange in Plants

Remember, like all living organisms, plants need to exchange materials with their environment in order to survive. That's what this topic is all about.

Leaf structure

Plants need **carbon dioxide** for photosynthesis. Carbon dioxide **diffuses** into the air spaces within the leaf, then it diffuses into the cells where photosynthesis happens. The leaf's structure is adapted so that this can happen easily.

The underneath of the leaf is an **exchange surface**. It's covered in little holes called **stomata** which the carbon dioxide diffuses in through. Oxygen (produced in photosynthesis) and water vapour also diffuse out through the stomata. This is shown in Figure 1.

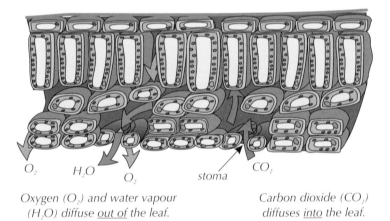

O_2 H_2O O_2 *stoma* CO_2

Oxygen (O_2) and water vapour (H_2O) diffuse out of the leaf.   *Carbon dioxide (CO_2) diffuses into the leaf.*

Figure 1: *Diagram to show movement of gases into and out of a leaf.*

The flattened shape of the leaf increases the area of this exchange surface so that it's more effective.

The walls of the cells inside the leaf form another exchange surface. The air spaces inside the leaf increase the area of this surface so there's more chance for carbon dioxide to get into the cells.

Water loss in plants

Water vapour is lost from all over the leaf surface, but most of it is lost through the stomata. If the plant is losing water faster through its leaves than it can be replaced by the roots (see page 227) the stomata can be closed by **guard cells**. Without these guard cells, the plant would soon lose so much water that it would **wilt** (droop).

Learning Objectives:
- Know how carbon dioxide enters plant leaves.
- Know the function of stomata.
- Know how the surface area of leaves is increased.
- Know how plants lose most of their water.
- Know the function of guard cells.
- Know how plants prevent wilting.
- Know the conditions under which evaporation is quickest.
- Be able to evaluate how environmental conditions affect water loss from plants.
- Know how the surface area of roots is increased.
- Know that water and mineral ions are absorbed by plant roots.

Specification Reference B3.1.3

Tip: 'Stomata' is the plural of 'stoma'. So you get one stoma, but two or more stomata.

Tip: Having a large surface area means that lots of a substance (e.g. CO_2) can diffuse across the exchange surface at once. See page 218 for more.

The role of guard cells

Two guard cells surround each stoma. Guard cells have a special kidney shape, with thin outer walls and thickened inner walls, to allow them to control the size of the stoma.

When the plant has lots of water, the guard cells fill with it and go turgid (plump). This makes the stomata open so gases can be exchanged for photosynthesis. When the plant is short of water, the guard cells lose water and become flaccid (limp), making the stomata close (see Figure 2).

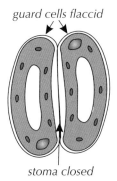

guard cells turgid   guard cells flaccid

stoma open   stoma closed

Figure 2: *Diagram showing how guard cells open and close a stoma.*

Guard cells are also sensitive to light and close at night to save water without losing out on photosynthesis.

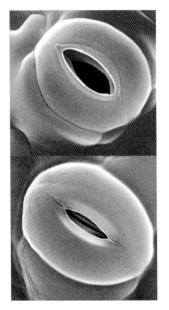

Figure 3: *An open stoma (top) and a closed stoma (bottom). The guard cells are shown in red.*

Factors affecting water loss in plants

Water vapour **evaporates** from the cells inside the leaf. Then it escapes by diffusion through the stomata because there's a lot of it inside the leaf and less of it in the air outside.

Evaporation and water loss are quickest in hot, dry, windy conditions. Here's why:

- Heat gives the water particles more energy to evaporate.

- Dry conditions mean there's a low concentration of water molecules in the air and a higher concentration of water molecules in the leaf. This means water molecules will diffuse out of the leaf into the air. The bigger the difference in concentration, the faster the rate of diffusion.

- Wind carries the water vapour away from the leaf, maintaining a low concentration of water molecules in the air surrounding the leaf. Again, this increases the rate of diffusion.

Tip: Wet clothes dry as water evaporates from the fabric. You wouldn't expect clothes hung out in the garden to dry very quickly on a cold, wet day — so don't expect evaporation from a plant to be quick under those conditions either.

Root hair cells

The cells on the surface of plant roots grow into long "hairs" which stick out into the soil. This gives the plant a big surface area for absorbing water and mineral ions from the soil (see Figure 4).

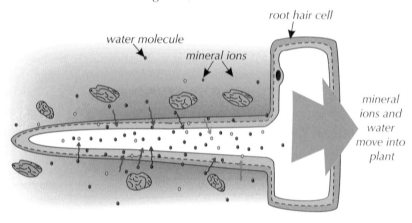

Figure 4: *Diagram to show the absorption of water and mineral ions by a root hair cell.*

Figure 5: *Root hair cells as seen under a microscope.*

Most of the water and mineral ions that get into a plant are absorbed by the root hair cells. Water moves into the cells by osmosis. Mineral ions move in by active transport, since the concentration of mineral ions in the root hair cells is usually higher than in the soil. There's more on active transport on page 217.

Practice Questions — Fact Recall

Q1 How and where does carbon dioxide enter a leaf?

Q2 How is the surface area of a leaf increased for gas exchange?

Q3 Name the cells that control the size of the stomata.

Q4 Why is it useful for a plant to be able to close its stomata?

Q5 How do water and mineral ions enter a plant?

Practice Question — Application

Q1 Ben is investigating water loss in plants. He weighs two of the same type of plant, then leaves both plants in a room for 24 hours.
One of the plants is placed next to a fan, the other one isn't.
All other variables are controlled. After 24 hours, Ben weighs the plants again.

a) Both plants have lost mass. Explain why.

b) Which plant do you think will have lost the most mass?
   Explain your answer.

c) Ben wants to find out how temperature affects water loss in plants.
   Suggest how he could alter his experiment to investigate this.

Section Checklist — Make sure you know...

Osmosis

☐ That osmosis is the movement of water molecules across a partially permeable membrane from a region of high concentration to a region of low concentration.

☐ How differences in the concentration of water molecules inside and outside of a cell will cause water molecules to move into or out of the cell by osmosis.

☐ That if the balance between the water and ion content of the body is wrong it could damage cells or mean they don't work as well, so water and ions must be replaced in the body.

☐ That a sports drink contains water and ions (to restore those lost in sweat) and sugar (to replace the sugar used up by the muscles during exercise).

☐ How to evaluate claims made about the effectiveness of sports drinks.

Active Transport

☐ That active transport is the movement of particles against a concentration gradient (i.e. from an area of low concentration to an area of high concentration) using energy released during respiration.

☐ That active transport allows cells to absorb ions from very dilute solutions.

Gas and Solute Exchange

☐ That dissolved substances move by diffusion and active transport, and that water moves by osmosis.

☐ How exchange surfaces are adapted for exchanging materials — they're thin (so substances only have a short distance to diffuse), they have a large surface area (so lots of a substance can diffuse at once), they have lots of blood vessels (in animals, to get stuff in and out of the blood quickly), they're often ventilated (for gas exchange in animals).

☐ That exchanging materials with the environment is more difficult in larger, more complex organisms than in simpler organisms — so complex organisms often need a specialised organ system for exchange.

Exchange in Humans

☐ That alveoli (tiny air sacs) increase the surface area of the lungs in humans, maximising the diffusion of oxygen into the blood and carbon dioxide out of the blood.

☐ That villi increase the surface area of the small intestine in humans, aiding the absorption of nutrients (by active transport and diffusion) into the blood.

☐ That villi also contain a network of capillaries to aid the absorption of nutrients (by active transport and diffusion) into the blood.

cont...

The Breathing System

☐ That the function of the breathing system is to get air into and out of the lungs for gas exchange.

☐ That the lungs are found in the thorax (the top part of your body), which is separated from the abdomen (the lower part of your body) by a muscle called the diaphragm.

☐ That the ribcage protects the lungs.

☐ That ventilation is the movement of air into and out of the lungs.

☐ That to breathe in, the intercostal muscles and diaphragm contract, causing the volume of the thorax to increase. This decreases the pressure in the thorax, drawing air into the lungs.

☐ That to breathe out, the intercostal muscles and diaphragm relax causing the volume of the thorax to decrease. This increases the pressure in the thorax, forcing air out of the lungs.

☐ How to evaluate the development and use of artificial ventilators, such as the 'iron lung' (which worked by pumping air in and out of a case into which the patient was sealed) and the more modern ventilator (which works by pumping air into a patient's lungs).

Exchange in Plants

☐ That carbon dioxide diffuses into a plant leaf from the air through the stomata (tiny holes on the underside of the leaf).

☐ That the flattened shape of the leaf and the internal air spaces between cells increase the surface area of the leaf for gas exchange.

☐ That plants lose most of their water through the stomata.

☐ That if a plant loses water from its leaves faster than it can be replaced by the roots, the stomata can be closed by the guard cells.

☐ That closing the stomata helps to stop a plant losing so much water that it wilts (droops).

☐ That guard cells surround stomata and control their size.

☐ That evaporation is quickest in hot, dry windy conditions.

☐ How to evaluate the environmental conditions that affect water loss in plants.

☐ That root hair cells on the surface of plant roots stick out into the soil and increase the surface area of the roots for the absorption of water and mineral ions.

Exam-style Questions

1   The diagram shows some of the main structures in the human breathing system.

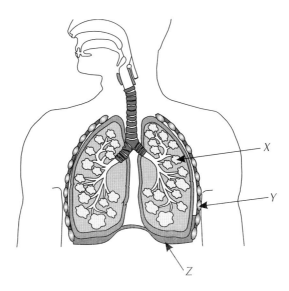

1 (a)   *In this question you will be assessed on the quality of your English,*
the organisation of your ideas and your use of appropriate specialist vocabulary.
Explain how structures **Y** and **Z** on the diagram cause ventilation.

(6 marks)

1 (b)   Structure **X** is an alveolus. The alveoli are the gas exchange surface of the lungs.
Ventilation is a way of maximising the effectiveness of this gas exchange surface.

Give **three** other ways in which the alveoli are adapted to be an effective
gas exchange surface.

(3 marks)

2   Desert plants are adapted for life in hot, dry conditions.
Like most plants, they exchange gases through their stomata.

2 (a)   What are stomata?

(1 mark)

2 (b)   Suggest and explain how the following adaptations help plants to survive in
desert conditions:

2 (b) (i)   Stomata are kept closed during the day, when it is hot and dry,
and only opened at night, when it is cool.

(3 marks)

(ii)   Stomata are located in sunken pits. The pits help to trap water vapour close to the
surface of the leaf.

(2 marks)

3   In humans, glucose is absorbed into the bloodstream in the small intestine.
This is often done using active transport, which requires respiration.

3 (a)   Explain why glucose may be absorbed using active transport,
and why this requires respiration.

(2 marks)

3 (b)   Coeliac disease can cause the villi in the small intestine to become inflamed if
left untreated. The inflammation flattens the villi.

Suggest how this would affect the absorption of glucose in the small intestine.
Explain your answer.

(2 marks)

3 (c)   Water from food is absorbed into the bloodstream in the large intestine.

State by what process water is absorbed in the large intestine and explain
how it works.

(2 marks)

4   Eleanor is investigating osmosis using potatoes.

She cuts small wells into two pieces of potato, and sets up two experiments (A and B).
She then leaves the potatoes for five hours.

The diagrams show how the appearance of each experiment changes after five hours.

Experiment A

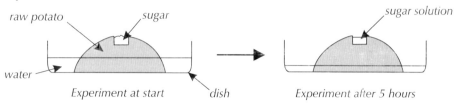

Experiment B

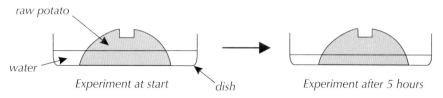

4 (a)   Explain the changes that Eleanor saw in experiment A.

(3 marks)

4 (b)   Suggest an explanation for why the water level in the dish in experiment B
didn't decrease as much as much as that in experiment A.

(3 marks)

1. Circulatory System — The Heart

Multicellular organisms need a way to transport materials between their cells. Humans (like many animals) have a transport system called the circulatory system to do just that, and the heart has a major role to play in it...

Function of the circulatory system

The circulatory system's main function is to get food and oxygen to every cell in the body. As well as being a delivery service, it's also a waste collection service — it carries waste products like carbon dioxide and urea to where they can be removed from the body. The circulatory system includes the heart, blood vessels and the blood.

A double circulatory system

Humans have a double circulatory system — two circuits joined together:

- The first circuit pumps deoxygenated blood (blood without oxygen) to the lungs to take in oxygen. The blood then returns to the heart (see Figure 1a).

- The second one pumps oxygenated blood around all the other organs of the body. The blood gives up its oxygen at the body cells and the deoxygenated blood returns to the heart to be pumped out to the lungs again (see Figure 1b).

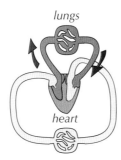

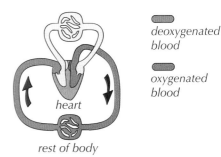

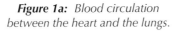

Figure 1a: *Blood circulation between the heart and the lungs.*

Figure 1b: *Blood circulation between the heart and the rest of the body.*

Structure of the heart

The heart is a pumping organ that keeps the blood flowing around the body. The walls of the heart are mostly made of **muscle tissue**, which contracts to pump the blood.

The heart has four chambers (the **right atrium**, **right ventricle**, **left atrium** and **left ventricle**) which it uses to pump blood around (see Figure 2). The main blood vessels leading into and out of these chambers are the **vena cava**, **pulmonary artery**, **aorta** and **pulmonary vein**.

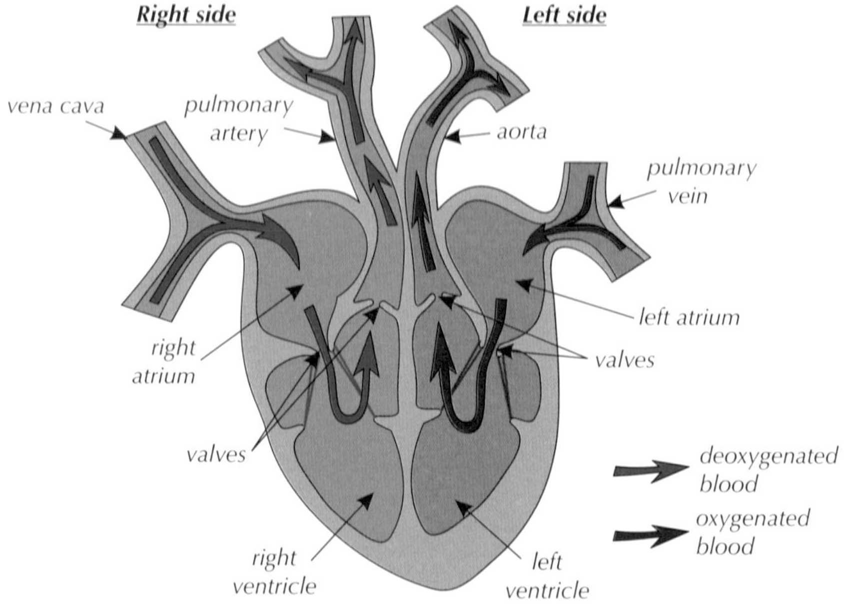

Exam Tip
You need to learn the names of these chambers and the main blood vessels leading into and out of the heart for your exam.

Right side   *Left side*

vena cava
pulmonary artery
aorta
pulmonary vein
left atrium
right atrium
valves
valves
right ventricle
left ventricle
deoxygenated blood
oxygenated blood

Tip: Don't be confused about the way the right and left side of the heart are labelled in this diagram — this is the right and left side of the person whose heart it is.

Figure 2: *Diagram showing the structure of the heart and the direction of blood flow through the heart.*

The heart has **valves** to make sure that blood goes in the right direction — they prevent it flowing backwards.

Blood flow through the heart

You need to know how the heart uses its four chambers to pump blood around the body. Here's what happens:

1. Blood flows into the two atria from the vena cava and the pulmonary vein (see Figure 3).

Tip: 'Atria' is the plural of 'atrium'. So you get one atrium, but two atria.

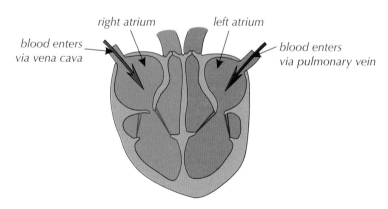

right atrium   left atrium
blood enters via vena cava
blood enters via pulmonary vein

Figure 3: *Diagram showing blood flowing into the heart.*

2. The atria contract, pushing the blood into the ventricles (see Figure 4).

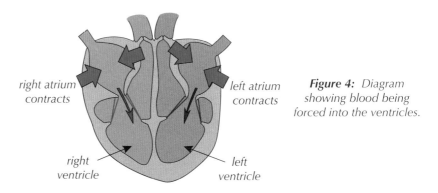

right atrium contracts

left atrium contracts

right ventricle

left ventricle

Figure 4: *Diagram showing blood being forced into the ventricles.*

3. The ventricles contract, forcing the blood into the pulmonary artery and the aorta, and out of the heart (see Figure 5).

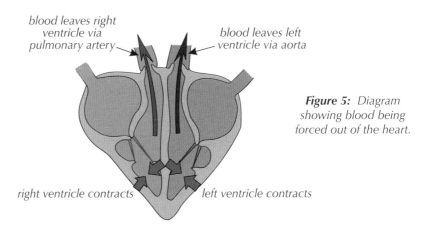

blood leaves right ventricle via pulmonary artery

blood leaves left ventricle via aorta

Figure 5: *Diagram showing blood being forced out of the heart.*

right ventricle contracts

left ventricle contracts

4. The blood then flows to the organs through arteries, and returns through veins (see pages 235-236).

5. The atria fill again and the whole cycle starts over.

Practice Questions — Fact Recall

Q1 What is the function of the circulatory system?

Q2 The human circulatory system is made up of two separate circuits. What is the function of each circuit?

Q3 What type of tissue makes up much of the walls of the heart?

Q4 Name the four chambers of the heart.

Q5 Name the two blood vessels which:

    a) carry blood into the heart,   b) carry blood out of the heart.

Q6 Explain how blood flows through the heart.

2. Circulatory System — The Blood Vessels

Learning Objectives:
- Know that arteries carry blood away from the heart, towards the organs.
- Know that artery walls are thick and contain muscle and elastic fibres.
- Know that capillaries carry blood very close to cells in the organs of the body.
- Know that substances are exchanged between body cells and the blood through the walls of the capillaries.
- Know that capillaries have very thin walls and are very narrow.
- Know that veins carry blood to the heart.
- Know that veins have thinner walls than arteries, and often have valves to keep blood flowing in the right direction.

Specification Reference B3.2.1

Our blood makes its way around our body in blood vessels. There are three different types of blood vessels you need to know about...

Arteries

Arteries are blood vessels which carry blood away from the heart, towards the organs. The heart pumps the blood out at high pressure, so the artery walls are strong and elastic. They contain thick layers of muscle to make them strong, and elastic fibres to allow them to stretch and spring back. The walls are thick compared to the size of the hole down the middle (the lumen) — see Figure 1.

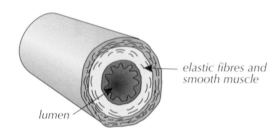

elastic fibres and smooth muscle

lumen

Figure 1: *Diagram to show the structure of an artery.*

Capillaries

Arteries branch into capillaries. Capillaries are involved in the exchange of materials at the tissues — they carry the blood really close to every cell in the body to exchange substances with them. They supply food and oxygen to the cells, and take away waste products like carbon dioxide.

Capillaries are really tiny — too small to see. They have permeable walls, so the substances being exchanged with the cells can diffuse in and out. Their walls are usually only one cell thick (see Figure 2). This increases the rate of diffusion by decreasing the distance over which it occurs. Capillaries are also very narrow. This gives them a large surface area compared to their volume, which also increases the rate of diffusion.

Tip: Diffusion is the process by which substances move from an area of high concentration to an area of low concentration.

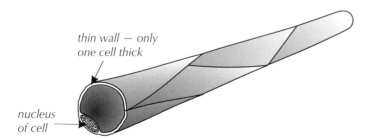

thin wall — only one cell thick

nucleus of cell

Figure 2: *Diagram to show the structure of a capillary.*

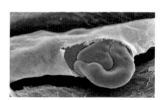

Figure 3: *A torn capillary with blood cells leaking out — you can see how thin the walls of the capillary are.*

Veins

Capillaries eventually join up to form veins. Veins carry blood to the heart.

The blood is at lower pressure in the veins, so the walls don't need to be as thick as artery walls. Veins have a bigger lumen than arteries to help the blood flow despite the lower pressure (see Figure 4). They also have valves to help keep the blood flowing in the right direction (see Figure 5).

Figure 4: Diagram to show the structure of a vein.

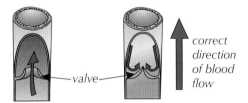

Figure 5: Diagram to show how valves prevent the back flow of blood.

Figure 6: A cross-section through an artery and a vein — the walls of the blood vessels are pink. The walls of the artery (left) are much thicker than the walls of the vein (right).

Practice Questions — Fact Recall

Q1 Describe the structure of an artery.

Q2 What type of blood vessel has walls that are only one cell thick?

Q3 Describe briefly how substances in the blood pass into body cells.

Q4 Give two differences between the structure of a vein and the structure of an artery.

Practice Questions — Application

Q1 Alan has a condition known as SVCS. This condition is very serious as it obstructs blood flow going into the heart. Which type of blood vessel (artery, capillary or vein) do you think SVCS affects? Give a reason for your answer.

Q2 The graph on the right shows the relative pressure inside two different blood vessels — one is a vein and one is an artery. Which blood vessel (A or B) would you expect to contain a higher proportion of muscle tissue in its walls? Explain your answer.

3. Circulatory System — The Blood

Blood is a vital part of the circulatory system — it's constantly being pumped out by the heart, travelling through blood vessels to other organs of the body and then returning to the heart. Time to find out just what it's made of...

What is blood?

Blood is a tissue — it's a group of similar cells which work together to perform a specific function (see page 128). The function of the blood is to transport substances around the body. It's made up of **red blood cells**, **white blood cells** and **platelets**, which are all suspended in a liquid called **plasma**.

Red blood cells

The job of red blood cells is to transport oxygen around the body. They have a biconcave shape (see Figure 1) to give them a large surface area for absorbing oxygen and they contain a red pigment called **haemoglobin**, which carries the oxygen.

Red blood cells are different from most types of animal cell because they don't have a nucleus — this allows more room for haemoglobin, which means they can carry more oxygen.

Figure 1: *A red blood cell has a biconcave shape — it looks like it's been squashed in the middle on both sides.*

Transporting oxygen

All body cells need oxygen for respiration — a process which releases energy. Oxygen enters the lungs when you breathe in, then red blood cells transport the oxygen from the lungs to all the cells in the body:

- In the lungs, oxygen diffuses into the blood. The oxygen combines with haemoglobin in red blood cells to become **oxyhaemoglobin** (see Figure 2).

- In body tissues, the reverse happens — oxyhaemoglobin splits up into haemoglobin and oxygen, to release oxygen to the cells.

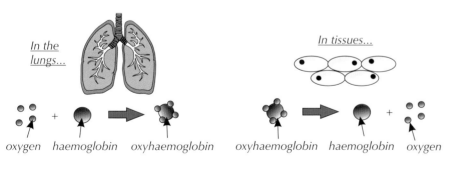

Figure 2: *Simplified diagram illustrating the formation and breakdown of oxyhaemoglobin.*

Learning Objectives:

- Know that blood is a tissue, which contains red blood cells, white blood cells and platelets suspended in plasma.

- Know that red blood cells contain a red pigment called haemoglobin, have no nucleus and transport oxygen from the lungs to the rest of the body cells.

- Know that haemoglobin combines with oxygen in the lungs to form oxyhaemoglobin, and that oxyhaemoglobin splits back into oxygen and haemoglobin at the body cells.

- Know that white blood cells help to protect the body from microorganisms and have a nucleus.

- Know that platelets are small parts of cells, which don't have a nucleus.

- Know that platelets are involved in blood clotting at a wound.

- Know where the soluble products of digestion, carbon dioxide and urea are transported to and from by the blood plasma.

Specification Reference B3.2.2

Tip: The more red blood cells you've got, the more oxygen can get to your cells. At high altitudes there's less oxygen in the air — so people who live there produce more red blood cells to compensate.

Tip: You've learnt about white blood cells before (see pages 25-26).

Figure 3: *A white blood cell.*

White blood cells

There are different types of white blood cell but they all have the same function — they defend against microorganisms that cause disease. They can do this in different ways:

- They can engulf and digest unwelcome microorganisms.

- They can produce antibodies to fight microorganisms.

- They can produce antitoxins to neutralise any toxins produced by the microorganisms.

Unlike red blood cells, white blood cells do have a nucleus.

Platelets

Platelets are small fragments (pieces) of cells. They have no nucleus. They help the blood to **clot** (clump together) at a wound — this seals the wound and stops you from losing too much blood (see Figure 4). It also stops microorganisms from getting in at the wound. A lack of platelets can cause excessive bleeding and bruising.

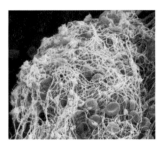

Figure 4: *A blood clot formed by the action of platelets.*

Figure 5: *A pouch of plasma, which has been extracted from donated blood.*

Tip: Urea is a waste product produced from the breakdown of amino acids in the liver.

Plasma

Plasma is a pale straw-coloured liquid which carries just about everything in blood. It carries:

- Red and white blood cells and platelets.

- Nutrients like glucose and amino acids. These are the soluble products of digestion, which are absorbed from the small intestine and taken to the cells of the body.

- Carbon dioxide from the organs to the lungs.

- Urea (see page 251) from the liver to the kidneys.

- Hormones.

- Antibodies and antitoxins produced by the white blood cells.

Practice Questions — Fact Recall

Q1 a) Name the red pigment found in red blood cells.

   b) Describe the role of this red pigment.

Q2 What is the function of white blood cells?

Q3 True or false? White blood cells don't have a nucleus.

Q4 What are platelets?

Q5 The table below lists three different substances which are transported in the blood plasma. Complete the table to show where each substance is transported from and to.

	Transported from:	Transported to:
Soluble products of digestion		
Carbon dioxide		
Urea		

Practice Questions — Application

Q1 Sufferers of Bernard-Soulier syndrome often bleed for a long time after an injury, even when they only have a very small wound. Suggest what component of the blood is abnormal in someone with Bernard-Soulier syndrome. Explain your answer.

Q2 Thalassaemia is a blood disorder in which the body does not make enough haemoglobin. Explain how this disorder can lead to organs not functioning properly because of a lack of oxygen.

Q3 Dr McKenna is looking at blood test results for two of her patients, Fay and Imogen. Their results, along with the normal range for each of the blood components tested, are shown in the following table:

	Red Blood Cells (10^{12}/l)	White Blood Cells (10^9/l)	Platelets (10^9/l)	Urea (mmol/l)	Blood Glucose (mmol/l)
Normal Range	3.9-5.6	4.0-11.0	150-400	3.0-7.0	3.3-5.6
Fay	4.2	3.2	250	3.2	3.6
Imogen	3.7	10.2	315	5.4	5.2

Tip: Don't worry about the unfamiliar units in this table. You don't need to know what they mean to answer the question.

Which patient, Fay or Imogen, do you think is the most at risk of getting an infection? Explain your answer.

Learning Objectives:

- Know what is meant by artificial hearts and heart valves, and be able to evaluate the use of these.

- Understand that stents are used to keep arteries open where there is restricted blood flow, and be able to evaluate their use.

- Be able to evaluate data on products which act as artificial blood.

Specification Reference
B3.2, B3.2.1

4. Circulation Aids

Sometimes things can go wrong with your circulatory system. Luckily, there's loads of things that can be done these days to aid your circulation...

Artificial hearts

Artificial hearts are mechanical devices that are put into a person to pump blood if their own heart fails (see Figure 1). They're usually used as a temporary fix, to keep a person alive until a donor heart (a replacement heart from another person) can be found. In some cases they're used as a permanent fix, which reduces the need for a donor heart.

> **Example**
>
> The SynCardia Total Artificial Heart is a modern artificial heart with a high success rate. The device kept one patient alive for 1374 days (which is nearly 4 years) before they were able to have a heart transplant.

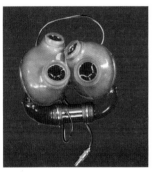

***Figure 1:** The first artificial heart to be inserted into a patient, in 1982.*

Advantages

The main advantage of artificial hearts is that they can extend the life of the patient. Another advantage is that they're less likely to be rejected by the body's immune system, which is a common problem with donor hearts and other donor organs (see page 257). They're less likely to be rejected because artificial hearts are made from metals or plastics, so the body doesn't recognise them as 'foreign' and attack in the same way as it does with living tissue.

Disadvantages

Surgery to fit an artificial heart can lead to bleeding and infection. Also, artificial hearts don't work as well as healthy natural ones — parts of the heart could wear out or the electrical motor could fail.

Blood doesn't flow through artificial hearts as smoothly as through natural hearts either, which can cause blood clots and lead to strokes (a problem caused when the blood supply to part of the brain is cut off). A patient receiving an artificial heart has to take drugs to thin their blood and make sure clots don't occur. This can cause problems with bleeding if they're hurt in an accident because their blood can't clot normally to heal the wounds.

Also, having an artificial heart in the body (and any battery and controller that might be inserted as well) may be uncomfortable for the patient.

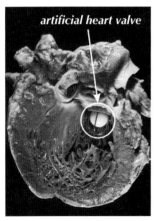

artificial heart valve

***Figure 2:** An artificial valve in a human heart (cut open).*

Artificial heart valves

If it's just the heart valves (p. 233) that are defective, they can be replaced with mechanical valves (see Figure 2). These devices make sure that blood only flows in the right direction through the heart, just like a normal heart valve would.

Replacing a valve is a much less drastic procedure than a whole heart transplant. But fitting artificial valves is still major surgery, which puts the patient at risk of infection, etc. and there can still be problems with blood clots.

Stents

Stents are wire mesh tubes that can be inserted inside arteries to widen them and keep them open (see Figure 3). They are particularly useful in people with coronary heart disease.

Figure 3: A stent that can be used to widen an artery.

Coronary heart disease and stents

Coronary heart disease is when the arteries that supply the blood to the heart muscle (the **coronary arteries**, see Figure 4) get blocked by fatty deposits. This causes the arteries to become narrow and blood flow is restricted — this can result in a heart attack.

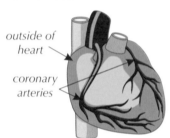

outside of heart

coronary arteries

Figure 4: The location of the coronary arteries.

Stents keep the coronary arteries open, making sure blood can pass through to the heart muscles (see Figure 6). This keeps the person's heart beating (and the person alive).

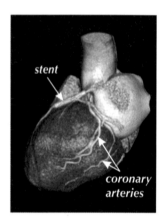

stent

coronary arteries

Figure 5: A CT scan of a human heart, which has had a stent inserted into one of its arteries.

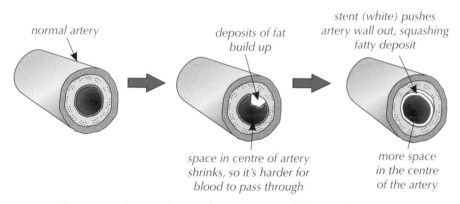

normal artery

deposits of fat build up

stent (white) pushes artery wall out, squashing fatty deposit

space in centre of artery shrinks, so it's harder for blood to pass through

more space in the centre of the artery

Figure 6: A diagram showing how a stent can help to widen an artery.

Pros and cons of stents

Stents are a way of lowering the risk of a heart attack in people with coronary heart disease. But over time, the artery can narrow again as stents can irritate the artery and make scar tissue grow. There's also a risk of blood clotting on the stent, so the patient has to take drugs to stop this from happening (which can cause problems with bleeding, see previous page).

> **Exam Tip**
> You might need to <u>evaluate</u> the use of a circulation aid (e.g. a stent) in your exam. Make sure you're aware of some of the advantages and disadvantages of each one.

Artificial blood products

Artificial blood is a blood substitute, which can be used to keep people alive in an emergency when they have lost a lot of blood. It has advantages over using donated blood (see below).

Donated blood

Many people in the UK donate blood. Donated blood is usually separated into its components, which can then be used in blood transfusions (when one person receives blood products that have come from another person).

Tip: A lack of oxygen in the blood can have very serious effects on the body. That's why the main aim for a person who has lost a lot of blood is to make sure that they have enough red blood cells or that the ones they have can circulate properly.

Example

Red blood cells can be given to people who have had major surgery, to replace the red blood cells lost in blood during the operation.

However most donated blood products can't be stored for very long, and only 4% of the population donate blood, so there's not always enough available when it's needed. There's also a risk of infection, and there can be problems with rejection (when the patient's immune system attacks the new cells).

Artificial blood product — volume expanders

When someone loses a lot of blood, their heart can still pump the remaining red blood cells around (to get oxygen to their organs), as long as the volume of their blood can be topped up.

Some artificial blood products (called volume expanders) can be used to replace the lost volume of blood.

Example

Normal saline is a solution which has a salt concentration close to that of normal blood. It's commonly used in hospitals when a patient has lost a lot of blood, such as following an accident or after an operation.

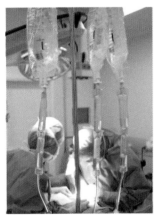

Figure 7: The clear liquid in the bags is normal saline. It's being put into the patient's veins during their operation.

Volume expanders are safe (if no air bubbles get into the blood) and can keep people alive even if they lose two thirds of their red blood cells. This may give the patient enough time to produce new blood cells. If not, the patient will need a blood transfusion.

Artificial blood product — oxygen-carrying substitutes

Ideally, an artificial blood product would replace the function of the red blood cells, so that there's no need for a blood transfusion. These are being developed but currently have problems with side-effects.

- Scientists are working on haemoglobin-based products — they want to just use the haemoglobin from red blood cells, which should mean there's less chance of rejection than from using the whole red blood cell.

- An artificial blood is being developed from plastic. It contains iron atoms which bind oxygen (just like haemoglobin). It would have an advantage over donated blood because it can be stored for longer.

Practice Questions — Fact Recall

Q1 What is an artificial heart?

Q2 a) What is a stent?

b) Describe how a stent can be used to treat people with coronary heart disease.

Practice Questions — Application

Q1 Perfluorocarbon emulsions are biologically inert liquids made from chemicals in a laboratory. Perfluorocarbon emulsions can carry oxygen, so scientists are developing these liquids as a blood substitute.

a) Explain why perfluorocarbon emulsions may be useful for people who have lost a lot of blood.

b) Explain why the use of perfluorocarbon emulsions to treat people with severe blood loss may be better than using donated blood products.

Tip: If something is 'biologically inert' it won't cause a reaction when put inside the body.

Q2 Dr Mustaf is a heart surgeon. He reads an article in a medical journal about artificial hearts. He makes notes about two of the artificial hearts he's read about:

Artificial heart one:

- Has been implanted in more than 1100 patients.
- Is connected to a battery pack outside the body with wires that pass through a small hole in the skin.

Artificial heart two:

- Has been implanted into 14 patients.
- Is powered by a battery which is inserted into the body and can be charged through the skin.

Dr Mustaf decides to recommend artificial heart two to a patient. Based on the information given, evaluate the decision to treat a patient with artificial heart two.

- Understand that flowering plants have two separate systems for transporting substances around.

- Know that dissolved sugars are transported from leaves to other areas of a plant (such as growing regions and storage organs) in phloem tubes.

- Know that water and mineral ions are transported up a plant in xylem tubes, from the roots to the leaves.

- Understand how water is moved through the plant in the transpiration stream.

Specification Reference
B3.2.3

Tip: A root tuber is an enlarged section of a root that is used to store energy for the plant. We eat the root tubers of some plants, e.g. sweet potatoes.

5. Transport of Substances in Plants

Just like animals, plants also have transport systems to move substances around...

Transport tissues in plants

Flowering plants have two separate types of tissue — phloem and xylem — for transporting substances around. Both types of tissue form 'tubes', which go to every part of the plant, but they are totally separate.

Phloem

Phloem tubes are made of columns of living cells with small holes in the ends to allow substances to flow through (see Figures 1 and 2).

Phloem tubes transport food substances (mainly dissolved sugars) made in the leaves to growing regions (e.g. new shoots) and storage organs (e.g. root tubers) of the plant. The transport goes in both directions — from the leaves down to the roots, and from the roots up to the leaves.

Figure 1: *Diagram showing the inside of a phloem tube.*

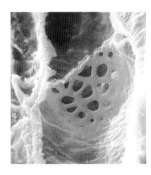

Figure 2: *Microscope image of the inside of a cut phloem tube — the small holes between the cells can be seen clearly.*

Xylem

Xylem tubes are made of dead cells joined end to end with no end walls between them and a hole down the middle (see Figures 3 and 4).

Xylem tubes carry water and mineral ions up the plant – from the roots to the stem and leaves. Substances are moved through the xylem in the **transpiration stream** (see next page).

Figure 3: *Diagram showing the inside of a xylem tube.*

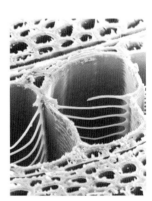

Figure 4: *Microscope image showing a cut xylem tube (dark green).*

The transpiration stream

Transpiration is the loss of water from a plant. The transpiration stream is the movement of water through a plant from the roots to the leaves.
It happens like this:

1. Water from inside a leaf evaporates and diffuses out of the leaf, mainly through the stomata (tiny holes found mainly on the lower surface of the leaf) — see Figure 5.

2. This creates a slight shortage of water in the leaf, and so more water is drawn up from the rest of the plant through the xylem vessels to replace it.

3. This in turn means more water is drawn up from the roots, and so there's a constant transpiration stream of water through the plant.

This is shown in Figure 6.

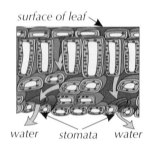

surface of leaf

water   stomata   water

Figure 5: *Cross-section of a leaf showing how water moves out during transpiration.*

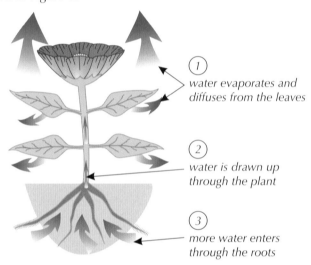

① water evaporates and diffuses from the leaves

② water is drawn up through the plant

③ more water enters through the roots

Figure 6: *Diagram showing how water moves through a plant in the transpiration stream.*

Tip: The rate of transpiration depends on the conditions in the plant's environment. Transpiration happens fastest in hot, dry, windy conditions because this is when evaporation happens fastest — see page 226 for more.

Transpiration is just a side-effect of the way leaves are adapted for photosynthesis. They have to have stomata in them so that gases (such as carbon dioxide) can be exchanged easily. When the stomata are open, water escapes through them because there's more water inside the plant than in the air outside.

Practice Questions — Fact Recall

Q1 a) What is transported in phloem tubes?

    b) Which area of a plant do the phloem tubes transport substances from?

    c) Give two examples of places in a plant which phloem tubes transport substances to.

Q2 Give two substances that are transported in xylem tubes.

Q3 Explain how water is transported from the roots of a plant to its leaves.

Q1 A potometer is a special piece of apparatus used to estimate transpiration rate. A group of students set up a potometer as shown here:

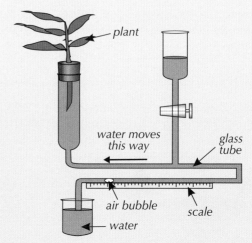

As water is lost from the plant's leaves, more water will be drawn through the glass tube and into the plant. As water gets drawn through the glass tube, the air bubble will move along the scale. The distance the air bubble moves in a set amount of time can be used as an estimate of the transpiration rate.

The students wanted to find out how temperature affected transpiration rate, so they measured how far the bubble moved in the potometer when they did the experiment at three different temperatures. Their results are shown in the table:

Temperature (°C)	Distance moved by the bubble in 20 minutes (mm)
10	26
15	31
20	37

a) Explain the trend shown in the students' results.

b) Suggest one way in which the students could have improved the validity of their investigation.

c) The students coated the underside of half of the plant's leaves with nail varnish, then did the experiment again at 10 °C.
Would you expect the bubble to have moved more or less than 26 mm in this experiment? Explain your answer.

Section Checklist — Make sure you know...

Circulatory System — The Heart

☐ That the circulatory system transports materials around the body.

☐ That humans have a double circulatory system — one circuit transports blood between the heart and the lungs, and the other transports blood between the heart and the rest of the body.

☐ That the heart is the organ which pumps blood around the body.

☐ That the walls of the heart are mainly made of muscle tissue.

☐ That the four chambers of the heart are called the right atrium, right ventricle, left atrium and left ventricle.

☐ That the vena cava, pulmonary artery, aorta and pulmonary vein are the four major blood vessels associated with the heart.

☐ That the heart has valves so blood doesn't flow in the wrong direction.

☐ That blood flows into the atria through veins (the vena cava and the pulmonary vein), and is then forced into the ventricles when the atria contract. It is then forced out of the heart through arteries (the pulmonary artery and the aorta) when the ventricles contract.

Circulatory System — The Blood Vessels

☐ That blood is carried away from the heart in arteries, which have thick walls containing muscle and elastic fibres.

☐ That blood is carried close to the cells of the body in capillaries and that substances are exchanged between the cells of the body and the blood by passing through the walls of these capillaries.

☐ That capillaries are very narrow and have thin, permeable walls.

☐ That blood returns to the heart in veins, which have thinner walls than arteries and often have valves to prevent blood from flowing in the wrong direction.

Circulatory System — The Blood

☐ That blood is a tissue and its main components are red and white blood cells, platelets and plasma.

☐ That red blood cells contain haemoglobin (a red pigment), don't have a nucleus and carry oxygen from the lungs to all the cells in the body.

☐ That oxyhaemoglobin is formed in the blood at the lungs when oxygen combines with haemoglobin, and that oxyhaemoglobin splits back into oxygen and haemoglobin at body cells.

☐ That white blood cells have a nucleus and help to defend the body against disease caused by microorganisms.

☐ That platelets are fragments of cells, don't have a nucleus and help blood to clot at a wound.

☐ That plasma carries just about everything in the blood including the soluble products of digestion (from the gut to the cells of the body), carbon dioxide (from the organs to the lungs), and urea (from the liver to the kidneys).

cont...

Circulation Aids

- ☐ That artificial hearts and heart valves are mechanical devices that can be used to treat someone with heart failure or whose valves don't work properly.

- ☐ Some of the advantages and disadvantages of artificial hearts and heart valves, so you can evaluate their use.

- ☐ That stents are mesh tubes that are inserted into narrowed arteries (often coronary arteries) to widen them and keep them open.

- ☐ Some of the pros and cons of stents, so you can evaluate their use.

- ☐ How to evaluate data on the production and use of artificial blood products.

Transport of Substances in Plants

- ☐ That flowering plants have two separate transport systems (made of phloem tissue and xylem tissue).

- ☐ That phloem tubes transport dissolved sugars from the leaves to other parts of the plant, such as growing regions and storage organs.

- ☐ That xylem tubes transport water and mineral ions from the roots of a plant to the stem and leaves.

- ☐ That in the transpiration stream, water is moved from a plant's roots, up the xylem and out of the leaves.

Exam-style Questions

1   Sharon is a scientist who studies plants. She is interested in the transport of substances around different types of flowering plants. Use words in the box to complete the following sentences.

mineral ions   roots   flowers   xylem   leaves   phloem   dissolved sugars

Xylem vessels transport water and .... around a plant.

Phloem vessels transport substances from the ....
to other areas of the plant.

The transpiration stream is the movement of water from a plant's

.... through the .... vessels.   *(4 marks)*

2   After a heart attack, many patients have a stent fitted into the affected coronary artery. This could be a bare-metal stent or a drug-eluting stent, which gradually releases a drug to prevent new cells from growing over the stent.

In a trial, patients needing a stent were randomly given either a bare-metal stent or a drug-eluting stent. Following their surgery, the patients were monitored and any health problems recorded. The results for 154 patients who received the drug-eluting stent and 153 patients who received the bare-metal stent are shown in the table:

	Number of patients who died following treatment	Number of patients who had another heart attack	% of patients whose artery renarrowed
Drug-eluting stent	3	3	9
Bare-metal stent	7	3	21

2 (a)   Calculate the percentage of patients that died after receiving the drug-eluting stent.

(1 mark)

2 (b)   Explain why stents are often used in people who have had a heart attack.

(3 marks)

2 (c)   Based on the information given, some doctors may conclude that drug-eluting stents are more beneficial than bare-metal stents. Do you think this is a valid conclusion? Explain your answer.

(3 marks)

3   The diagram below represents the heart.

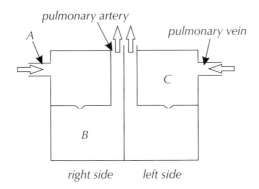

3 (a)   Name each of the structures labelled A-C on the diagram.

(3 marks)

Cross-sections through the pulmonary artery and the pulmonary vein are shown here.

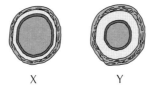

3 (b)   Which diagram (X or Y) shows the pulmonary vein? Explain your answer.

(1 mark)

3 (c)   A person with heart valve disease can have an artificial heart valve fitted
to treat the disease.

3 (c) (i)   Describe the function of heart valves.

(1 mark)

3 (c) (ii)   Give **two** problems that may arise from being fitted with an artificial heart valve.

(2 marks)

4   In the circulatory system of a fish, blood is pumped from the heart, across the gills
(to pick up oxygen), to the body tissues and then back to the heart in a single circuit.

4 (a)   Give **one** similarity and **one** difference between the circulatory system of a fish and
that of a human.

(2 marks)

4 (b)   *In this question you will be assessed on the quality of your English,
the organisation of your ideas and your use of appropriate specialist vocabulary.*

Blood is an essential part of the circulatory system.
Name and describe the functions of the main components of the blood.

(6 marks)

1. What is Homeostasis?

You might remember homeostasis from page 45. It's all to do with keeping conditions in the body constant. Here's a bit of a recap...

Maintaining a constant internal environment

The maintenance of a constant internal environment is called **homeostasis**. Homeostasis is really important — if conditions in the body aren't controlled properly, cells can become seriously damaged. There are a number of conditions in the body that need to be controlled within very narrow ranges:

Examples

- Water and ion content — when we eat and drink, water and ions enter the body. If the water or ion content of the body gets too high or low, too much water could move into or out of cells and damage them.

- Body temperature.

- Blood glucose level.

Removing waste products

Waste products are constantly being produced in the body. If you don't get rid of them they could build up to dangerous levels, which can be damaging to the body. You need to know about two waste products:

1. Carbon dioxide

Carbon dioxide is produced by body cells as a waste product of respiration. It's toxic in high quantities so it's got to be removed. It's carried in the blood to the lungs, where it leaves the body when you breathe out (see page 222).

2. Urea

Proteins can't be stored by the body — so any excess amino acids are broken down and used to make fats and carbohydrates, which can then be stored. This process occurs in the liver. **Urea** is produced as a waste product from the reactions.

Urea is poisonous. It's released into the bloodstream by the liver. The kidneys then filter it out of the blood. It's temporarily stored in the bladder in urine and then excreted (removed) from the body.

Practice Questions — Fact Recall

Q1 How is carbon dioxide removed from the body?

Q2 Where is urine stored before it leaves the body?

Learning Objectives:

- Know how water and ions enter the body, and why the body's cells can get damaged if water or ion content is not controlled properly.

- Know that carbon dioxide and urea are waste products, which need to be removed from the body.

- Know how the carbon dioxide produced through respiration is removed from the body.

- Know how urea is produced and how it is removed from the body.

Specification Reference B3.3.1

Tip: All of the examples are covered in more detail later in this section.

Tip: Respiration is the process of releasing energy from glucose using oxygen. It goes on in every cell and produces carbon dioxide and water as waste products.

Tip: There's more about urea and how the kidneys help to remove it from the body on pages 252-254.

Learning Objectives:

- Know that the body loses more water when it is hot, and so more water needs to be taken in via food and drink in order to balance this loss.

- Know that the first stage in urine production is the filtering of the blood by the kidneys.

- Know that the kidneys then reabsorb all the sugar, as well as the amount of dissolved ions and water needed by the body.

- Know that urea, and excess ions and water are lost from the body in the urine.

Specification Reference B3.3.1, B3.3.2

2. The Kidneys and Homeostasis

The kidneys are organs that help to regulate the level of a number of substances in the body. This means that they play a pretty big role in homeostasis...

The role of the kidneys

The kidneys (see Figure 1) produce **urine**. In doing so, they perform three important roles:

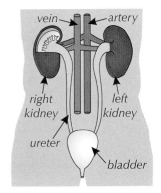

1. The removal of urea

As you saw on page 251, urea is poisonous. It is filtered out of the blood by the kidneys and removed from the body in the urine.

2. Adjustment of ion content

Ions are taken into the body in food, and then absorbed into the blood. Excess ions are removed by the kidneys and lost from the body in urine.

Figure 1: Diagram showing the location of the kidneys and associated structures.

Example

A salty meal will contain far too much sodium and so the kidneys will remove the excess sodium ions from the blood.

Some ions are also lost in sweat (which tastes salty, you may have noticed). But the important thing to remember is that the balance of ions is always maintained by the kidneys.

3. Adjustment of water content

Water is taken into the body as food and drink and is lost from the body in three main ways — in the urine, in the sweat, and in the air that we breathe out.

The body has to constantly balance the water coming in against the water going out. Our bodies can't control how much we lose in our breath, but we do control the other factors. This means the water balance is between:

- liquids consumed

- amount sweated out

- amount excreted by the kidneys in the urine.

Examples

On a cold day, if you don't sweat, you'll produce more urine which will be pale and dilute.

On a hot day, you sweat a lot, and you'll produce less urine which will be dark-coloured and concentrated. The water lost when it is hot has to be replaced with water from food and drink to restore the balance.

Urine production

Nephrons (see Figure 2) are the 'filtration units' of the kidneys — they're tiny structures within the kidney that filter the blood. There are thousands of nephrons in each kidney. Urine is produced by the nephrons.

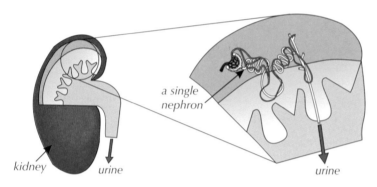

Figure 2: *Diagram showing the location of a single nephron within the kidney.*

Urine production involves three main steps — **ultrafiltration**, **reabsorption** and the **release of waste products**. These steps take place in different places along the nephron, as shown in Figure 3.

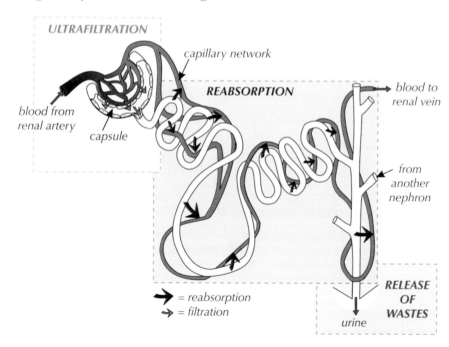

Exam Tip
You don't need to learn the structure of the nephron for your exam — as long as you know what's going on along it.

Figure 3: *Diagram showing where ultrafiltration, reabsorption and the release of waste products happen along a single nephron.*

You need to know what happens in each of these steps:

1. Ultrafiltration

Blood from the renal artery enters the kidney. A high pressure is built up in the blood vessels, which squeezes water, urea, ions and sugar out of the blood and into an area called the capsule at the start of the nephron.

The membranes between the blood vessels and the capsule act like filters, so big molecules like proteins and blood cells are not squeezed out. They stay in the blood (see Figure 4).

Tip: In certain types of kidney disease the start of the nephron can become damaged. This means that some large molecules (e.g. proteins) can pass through the membranes between the blood vessels and the capsule, into the fluid in the nephron, and end up in the urine. These diseases can be detected by a urine test.

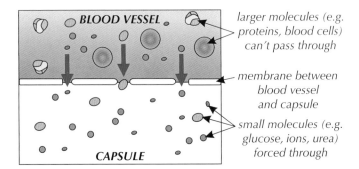

Figure 4: Diagram showing which molecules pass into the capsule during ultrafiltration of the blood in the nephron.

2. Reabsorption

As the liquid flows along the nephron, useful substances are reabsorbed back into the blood:

Tip: You might remember active transport from page 217. It's the movement of particles against a concentration gradient (i.e. from an area of low concentration to an area of high concentration) using energy released during respiration.

- All the sugar (glucose) is reabsorbed. This involves the process of **active transport**, since the concentration of sugar is lower in the fluid in the nephron than in the surrounding blood vessels.

- Sufficient ions (i.e. the amount of ions required by the body) are reabsorbed, again via active transport. Excess ions are not reabsorbed.

- Sufficient water is reabsorbed. Excess water is not.

3. Release of waste products

The remaining substances (urea, excess ions and water) continue out of the nephron, into the ureter and down to the bladder as urine.

Tip: The ureter is a tube which connects the kidney to the bladder.

Practice Questions — Fact Recall

Q1 True or False? The hotter your body gets, the less water you need to take in.

Q2 Describe the first stage in the production of urine by the kidney.

Q3 Name two substances that the kidney reabsorbs.

Q4 Name three substances that should be present in the urine of a healthy person.

Practice Questions — Application

Q1 This table shows the average rate of filtration and reabsorption of various substances found in the blood, in a person with healthy kidneys.

Substance	Filtration rate	Reabsorption rate
Water	180 litres per day	178.2 litres per day
Glucose	800 millimoles per day	?
Potassium ions	720 millimoles per day	500 millimoles per day

a) i) What percentage of the filtered water is reabsorbed?

ii) What do you think would happen to this percentage if the person went for a run on a hot day and didn't consume any extra liquid? Explain your answer.

iii) What effect do you think this would have on the urine produced by the person?

b) How many millimoles of glucose will be reabsorbed per day? Explain your answer.

c) Calculate the average amount of potassium ions found in the urine of this person per day.

Q2 On a hot summer's day, Katherine has been running on the beach and hasn't drunk anything. Cate has drunk one small glass of orange juice whilst reading a book in the shade. Julia has been sat in her air conditioned office and has drunk four cups of tea.

Put one tick in each column to complete the table.

Person	Largest volume of urine	Smallest volume of urine	Most concentrated urine	Most dilute urine
Katherine				
Cate				
Julia				

Exam Tip
In the exam you could be given some figures to do with the kidneys and asked to do some calculations using them. Just make sure you read the information carefully, so that you're using the correct figures. And the good news is that you can take a calculator into the exam with you. Hooray.

Tip: Remember, glucose is just a type of sugar.

- Know that kidney dialysis or a kidney transplant are treatments for kidney failure.

- Know that kidney dialysis has to be carried out regularly, and that it aims to return the concentration of dissolved substances in the blood to normal.

- Know how a dialysis machine works.

- Know what a kidney transplant is.

- Understand why donor kidneys are sometimes rejected and what can be done to prevent this.

- Be able to evaluate kidney dialysis and kidney transplants as treatment options for people with kidney failure.

Specification Reference
B3.3.1

3. Kidney Failure

As you've seen, the kidneys are a really important pair of organs. If they stop working properly it can cause big problems in the body...

The effects of kidney failure

The kidneys play a number of important roles in the body (see page 252). If the kidneys don't work properly, waste substances build up in the blood and you lose your ability to control the levels of ions and water in your body. This can cause problems in the heart, bones, nervous system, stomach, mouth, etc. If left untreated, kidney failure will eventually result in death.

Fortunately there are treatment options available. People with kidney failure can be kept alive by:

1. Having **dialysis** treatment — where machines do the job of the kidneys.

2. Having a **kidney transplant** — where the diseased kidney is replaced by a healthy one.

Kidney dialysis

Dialysis machines take over the role of failing kidneys and filter the blood. Dialysis has to be done regularly to keep the concentrations of dissolved substances (e.g. glucose, ions, etc.) in the blood at normal levels, and to remove waste substances.

How does a dialysis machine work?

In a dialysis machine the person's blood flows alongside a partially permeable membrane, surrounded by dialysis fluid (see Figure 2).

Figure 1: *A dialysis machine.*

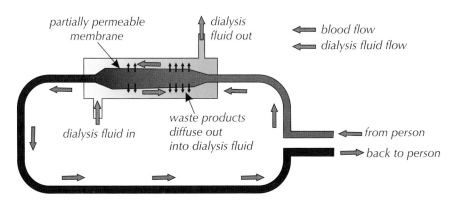

Figure 2: *Diagram showing how a dialysis machine works.*

Tip: Substances diffuse from an area of high concentration to an area of low concentration. This means that if there's a higher concentration of a substance in the blood, it will diffuse across the partially permeable membrane into the dialysis fluid.

The partially permeable membrane allows things like ions and waste substances through, but not big molecules like proteins (just like the membranes in the kidney). The dialysis fluid has the same concentration of dissolved ions and glucose as healthy blood. This means that useful dissolved ions and glucose won't be lost from the blood during dialysis. Only waste substances (such as urea) and excess ions and water diffuse across the membrane.

Problems with dialysis

Although kidney dialysis can keep a person alive until they can get a kidney transplant (see below), it has a number of disadvantages:

- Dialysis is not a pleasant experience and many patients with kidney failure have to have a dialysis session three times a week. Each session takes 3-4 hours — not much fun.

- Dialysis can lead to infections and can cause blood clots.

- Dialysis patients have to be careful about what they eat to avoid too much of a particular ion building up between dialysis sessions.

- Patients have to limit the amount of fluid they take in, as the kidneys play an important role in maintaining the water content of the body. When the kidneys aren't functioning properly, fluid can build up in the body, which can be dangerous — for example, it can cause the volume of blood to increase, leading to high blood pressure.

- Kidney dialysis machines are expensive things for the NHS to run.

Tip: Dialysis isn't a cure for kidney failure. It's a treatment which can keep people alive while they are on the waiting list for a donor kidney. It is also used for people who may be unable to have a kidney transplant — people can stay alive on dialysis for many years.

Kidney transplants

At the moment, the only cure for kidney disease is to have a kidney transplant. Healthy kidneys are usually transplanted from people who have died suddenly, say in a car accident, and who are on the organ donor register or carry a donor card (provided their relatives give the go-ahead). But kidneys can also be transplanted from people who are still alive (as we all have two kidneys, but can survive with just one).

Figure 3: An NHS donor card. People carry this card to let medical staff know that they wish to donate their organs after they have died.

Rejection

A problem of kidney transplants is that the donor kidney can be rejected by the recipient's immune system — this happens when **antigens** on the donor kidney aren't recognised as being part of the body by the recipient's white blood cells. The white blood cells produce **antibodies** to attack the donor cells as a result (see Figure 4).

Tip: The recipient is the person who receives the kidney.

Tip: Antigens are unique proteins found on a cell's surface. Antibodies are proteins produced by white blood cells in response to the presence of a foreign antigen. See p.25.

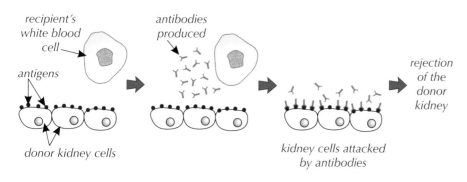

Figure 4: Diagram showing the possible reaction of a recipient's immune system in response to a donor kidney.

Preventing rejection

To help prevent rejection of the donor organ, precautions are taken:

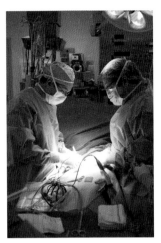

Figure 5: Surgeons performing a kidney transplant.

- A donor with a **tissue-type** that closely matches the patient's is chosen. Tissue-type is based on a cell's antigens. The more similar the tissue-types of the donor and the patient, the more similar the antigens. This reduces the chance of the patient's white blood cells identifying the donor antigens as 'foreign' and producing antibodies to attack the donor organ.

- The recipient is treated with drugs that suppress the immune system. These drugs reduce the production and release of antibodies by the white blood cells, so that the immune system won't attack the transplanted kidney.

Other problems with kidney transplants

There are problems other than rejection associated with kidney transplants:

- There are long waiting lists for kidneys.

- Even if a kidney with a matching tissue-type is found, there's still the possibility that it'll be rejected.

- Taking drugs that suppress the immune system means the person is vulnerable to other illnesses and infections.

- A kidney transplant is a major operation, so it can be risky.

Despite these problems, kidney transplants can put an end to the hours spent on dialysis, allowing recipients to lead a relatively normal life. Transplants are also cheaper than long-term dialysis treatment.

> **Exam Tip**
> In the exam you might be asked to compare the treatment options available for someone with kidney failure. Make sure you know both the positive and negative aspects of being on dialysis or having a kidney transplant.

Practice Questions — Fact Recall

Q1 True or False? People with kidney failure only need dialysis once.

Q2 Give an example of a substance that can't pass through the partially permeable membrane used to filter the blood in a dialysis machine.

Q3 Explain what happens when a donor kidney is rejected by the recipient's immune system.

Q4 Give two ways of reducing the chances of a donor organ being rejected in a kidney transplant.

Q5 True or False? Everyone needing a kidney transplant gets a new kidney straight away.

Q1 The level of dissolved sodium found in dialysis fluid before a dialysis session is similar to the typical level of dissolved sodium found in the blood plasma.

a) Why is the level of dissolved sodium in the dialysis fluid similar to the level in the blood plasma?

Blood plasma contains urea. Dialysis fluid does not.

b) i) Why does the blood plasma contain urea?

ii) Explain why it's important that the dialysis fluid doesn't contain urea.

Blood plasma also contains glucose.

c) Suggest how the amount of glucose in the dialysis fluid would compare to the amount of glucose in the blood plasma. Explain your answer.

Q2 Nomia has kidney failure. She is currently having dialysis and she is hoping to have a kidney transplant in the future. Her doctor is explaining what a kidney transplant will involve.

a) Suggest three problems associated with having a kidney transplant that the doctor might tell Nomia about.

b) Suggest two reasons why having a kidney transplant may be a better option for Nomia than being on dialysis.

Tip: Plasma is the liquid part of the blood (see page 238). It carries lots of different substances.

Tip: Dissolved sodium is an ion.

Tip: A dialysis machine is like an artificial kidney. If you're struggling with Q1, think about the role of a healthy kidney in the body — it regulates the water and ion content of the blood and removes waste products.

Learning Objectives:

- Know that the thermoregulatory centre in the brain monitors and controls body temperature.

- Know that the thermoregulatory centre has receptors which detect the temperature of the blood in the brain, and know how it receives information about skin temperature from receptors in the skin.

- Know that sweating helps to reduce body temperature.

- Know that when we are too hot, blood flow to the skin increases, which may make the skin appear red.

- **H** Understand the response of the sweat glands and the blood vessels supplying the skin capillaries when core body temperature is too high.

- **H** Understand the response of the muscles and the blood vessels supplying the skin capillaries when core body temperature is too low.

Specification Reference B3.3.2

Figure 2: *Exercise can increase body temperature. This can make the skin appear red, as blood flow to the skin increases in an attempt to cool the body.*

4. Controlling Body Temperature

Ever wondered why you get all sweaty when you're too hot, and shivery when you're too cold? It's just your body acting to control your temperature...

Monitoring body temperature

Body temperature needs to be kept at around 37 °C (because this is the temperature at which enzymes in the human body work best — see page 45). In order to do this, body temperature must be carefully monitored and controlled.

This is where a part of the brain called the **thermoregulatory centre** comes in. It acts as your own personal thermostat. To do this, it receives information about body temperature from receptors — groups of cells which are sensitive to stimuli (see page 39). These include:

1. Receptors in the thermoregulatory centre that are sensitive to the temperature of the blood flowing through the brain.

2. Receptors in the skin that send information about skin temperature via nervous impulses.

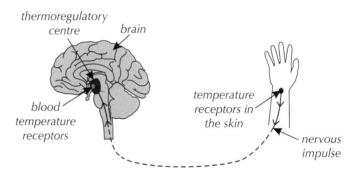

Figure 1: *Diagram showing how the thermoregulatory centre monitors temperature.*

How is body temperature controlled?

If you're getting too hot or too cold, your body can respond to try and cool you down or warm you up.

Examples

If you're too hot...

- You sweat more, which cools the body down.

- Blood flow to the skin increases, so heat is lost from the skin more easily. The increased blood flow may make the skin look red.

Responding to high core body temperature Higher

When your core body temperature gets too high, your body responds in the following ways:

1. Hairs on the skin lie flat. This means less air is trapped near the surface of the skin, so there isn't a layer of insulating air surrounding the skin. This allows heat to be lost more easily.

2. Sweat is produced by sweat glands. When sweat evaporates from the skin, it removes heat, helping to reduce body temperature.

3. The blood vessels supplying the skin capillaries **dilate** (get wider) so more blood flows close to the surface of the skin. This makes it easier for heat to be transferred from the blood to the environment.

Tip: H Core body temperature refers to the temperature deep inside the body, rather than the temperature at the skin or in the limbs.

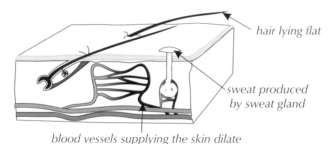

hair lying flat

sweat produced by sweat gland

blood vessels supplying the skin dilate

Figure 3: H *Diagram showing some of the body's responses to a high core body temperature.*

Responding to low core body temperature Higher

When your core body temperature drops too low, your body responds in the following ways:

1. Hairs on the skin stand up. This traps an insulating layer of air next to the skin, reducing heat loss.

2. No sweat is produced.

3. Blood vessels supplying skin capillaries **constrict** (get narrower) to reduce the skin's blood supply. This means less blood flows close to the surface of the skin and less heat is transferred from the skin to the environment.

4. When you're cold you **shiver** (your muscles contract automatically). This needs respiration, which releases some energy to warm the body.

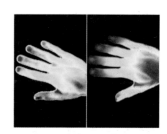

Figure 5: H *A thermogram showing a hand before (left) and after (right) constriction of the blood vessels supplying the skin capillaries in the fingers. The colours show the variation in temperature in different parts of the hand — red is warmest, blue is coldest. After constriction of the blood vessels, the fingers are much cooler.*

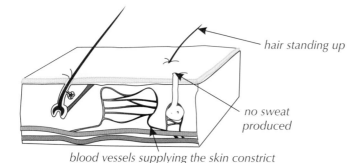

hair standing up

no sweat produced

blood vessels supplying the skin constrict

Figure 4: H *Diagram showing some of the body's responses to a low core body temperature.*

Practice Questions — Fact Recall

Q1   The thermoregulatory centre regulates body temperature.

   a) Where in the body is the thermoregulatory centre located?

   b) Where does the thermoregulatory centre receive inputs about body temperature from?

Q2   Explain why a person's skin may appear red when they're too hot.

Q3   a) What happens to the blood vessels supplying the skin capillaries when you get too hot?

   b) Explain how the response you gave in part a) helps to reduce body temperature.

Practice Question — Application

Q1   Gena is out walking and has forgotten her coat.
The weather has changed and the temperature has begun to fall.

   a) Describe the way Gena's body will respond in order to help her try and maintain her body temperature.

   b) Explain how the responses you gave in part a) help Gena to maintain her body temperature.

5. Controlling Blood Glucose Level

Learning Objectives:
- Know that the pancreas monitors and controls blood glucose level.
- Know that the pancreas produces insulin and understand how this hormone affects blood glucose level.
- **H** Know that the pancreas produces glucagon and understand how this hormone affects blood glucose level.
- Know what type 1 diabetes is and understand why it can result in the blood glucose level being too high.
- Know how type 1 diabetes can be controlled.
- Be able to evaluate modern methods in the treatment of type 1 diabetes.

Specification Reference B3.3.3

Your blood glucose level needs to carefully regulated. This is done with the help of hormones produced by the pancreas. However, if things don't work quite as they should, it can result in a condition called diabetes...

Glucose concentration of the blood

Glucose is a type of sugar. Throughout the day the blood glucose level varies:

Examples

- Eating foods containing carbohydrate puts glucose into the blood from the digestive system.
- The normal metabolism of cells removes glucose from the blood.
- Vigorous exercise removes much more glucose from the blood.

Hormonal control of blood glucose

The level of glucose in the blood must be kept steady. Changes in the blood glucose level are monitored by the **pancreas**. The pancreas produces hormones which help to control the blood glucose level.

Insulin

Insulin is a hormone produced by the pancreas. It decreases the blood glucose level when it gets too high. Here's what happens:

1. After a meal containing carbohydrate, a person's blood glucose level rises. This rise is detected by the pancreas.

2. The pancreas responds by producing insulin, which is secreted into the blood.

3. Insulin causes body cells to take up more glucose from the blood. Cells in the liver and muscles can take up glucose and convert it into a storage molecule called **glycogen**.

4. This causes the blood glucose level to fall.

This process is shown in Figure 1.

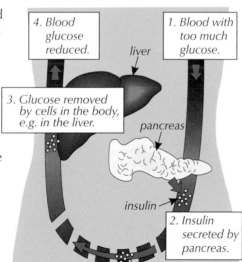

4. Blood glucose reduced.

liver

1. Blood with too much glucose.

3. Glucose removed by cells in the body, e.g. in the liver.

pancreas

insulin

2. Insulin secreted by pancreas.

Figure 1: *Diagram showing the role of insulin in the control of blood glucose.*

Glucagon Higher

Glucagon is another hormone produced by the pancreas. It increases the blood glucose level when it gets too low. Here's what happens:

Exam Tip H

The words 'glucagon' and 'glycogen' look and sound very similar. You need to make sure you get the spelling of these words spot on in the exam. E.g. if you write 'glycogon' the examiner won't know whether you mean glucagon or glycogen so you won't get the marks.

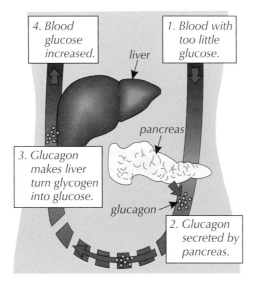

4. Blood glucose increased.

liver

1. Blood with too little glucose.

pancreas

3. Glucagon makes liver turn glycogen into glucose.

glucagon

2. Glucagon secreted by pancreas.

Figure 2: H *Diagram showing the role of glucagon in the control of blood glucose.*

1. If a person's blood glucose level decreases, the fall is detected by the pancreas.

2. The pancreas responds by producing glucagon, which is secreted into the blood.

3. Glucose can be stored in the muscles and liver as glycogen (see previous page). Glucagon causes the glycogen to be converted back into glucose, which enters the blood.

4. This causes the blood glucose level to rise.

Type 1 diabetes

Type 1 diabetes is a condition where the pancreas produces little or no insulin. The result is that a person's blood glucose can rise to a level that can kill them.

Tip: Remember, insulin <u>reduces</u> blood glucose level.

Controlling type 1 diabetes

Type 1 diabetes needs to be controlled in the following ways:

1. **Limit the intake of foods rich in simple carbohydrates**, i.e. sugars (which cause the blood glucose level to rise rapidly). People with type 1 diabetes are also advised to spread their intake of starchy carbohydrates (e.g. pasta, rice, bread, etc.) throughout the day and to pick varieties of these foods that are absorbed more slowly (so they don't cause such a sharp rise in the blood glucose level).

2. **Regular exercise** — this helps to lower the blood glucose level.

3. **Insulin therapy** — this usually involves injecting insulin into the blood. People with type 1 diabetes usually have several injections of insulin throughout the day, which are likely to be at mealtimes. Insulin injections make sure glucose is removed from the blood quickly once the food has been digested. This stops the level of glucose in the blood from getting too high and is a very effective treatment.

The amount of insulin that needs to be injected depends on the person's diet and how active they are, since these things will affect their blood glucose level.

Figure 3: *A person injecting insulin.*

Insulin used to be extracted from the pancreases of pigs or cows, but now human insulin is made by genetic engineering. This human insulin doesn't cause adverse reactions in patients, like animal insulin did.

Insulin injections help to control a person's blood glucose level, but it can't be controlled as accurately as having a normal working pancreas, so they may still have long-term health problems.

Tip: Insulin can't be taken in a pill or tablet — the enzymes in the stomach completely destroy it before it reaches the bloodstream. That's why it's normally injected.

Modern treatment options

There are some new treatment options available, and some currently being researched, for people with type 1 diabetes:

1. Diabetics can have a **pancreas transplant**. A successful operation means they won't have to inject themselves with insulin again. But as with any organ transplant, your body can reject the tissue (see page 257). If this happens you have to take costly immunosuppressive drugs (drugs that suppress the immune system), which often have serious side-effects.

2. Modern research into **artificial pancreases** and **stem cell research** may mean the elimination of organ rejection, but there's a way to go yet.

Tip: You covered stem cells on pages 183-184. They have the ability to turn into a range of different cell types. It's possible that stem cells could be made into pancreatic cells and used to replace the faulty insulin-producing cells in type 1 diabetics.

Practice Questions — Fact Recall

Q1 Where in the body is the hormone insulin produced?

Q2 What effect does insulin have on the body's cells?

Q3 Where in the body is the hormone glucagon produced?

Q4 What is type 1 diabetes?

Practice Question — Application

Q1 In a study, a hormone was injected into a subject while their blood glucose level was monitored. The results are shown in the graph.

a) What hormone do you think was injected? Explain your answer.

b) i) Name the other main hormone that affects the blood glucose level.

ii) What do you think would happen to the blood glucose level if this hormone had been injected instead? Explain your answer.

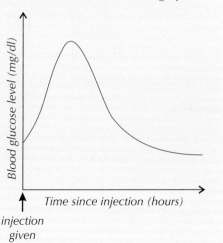

What is Homeostasis?

☐ That water and ions enter the body via food and drink, and that if the water and ion content of the body is not carefully controlled then too much water could move into or out of cells and damage them.

☐ That the carbon dioxide produced as a waste product of respiration is removed from the body via the lungs when you breathe out.

☐ That urea is a waste product produced when amino acids are broken down in the liver, and that it is removed via the kidneys in the urine. The urine is stored in the bladder before it leaves the body.

The Kidneys and Homeostasis

☐ That the body loses more water when it is hot, and that this needs to be replaced via food or drink in order to balance the water content of the body.

☐ That to produce urine, the kidneys filter the blood and then reabsorb all of the sugar and the required amounts of ions and water. The remaining urea, excess ions and water are lost as urine.

Kidney Failure

☐ That treatments for kidney failure include kidney dialysis or having a kidney transplant.

☐ That patients with kidney failure must have regular dialysis sessions in order to try to maintain normal levels of dissolved substances in the blood.

☐ That dialysis fluid contains the same concentration of dissolved ions and glucose as healthy blood, so that when the patient's blood flows alongside partially permeable membranes in a kidney dialysis machine, glucose and useful ions are not lost.

☐ That urea leaves the blood during dialysis, preventing it from accumulating in the body.

☐ That a kidney transplant involves replacing a damaged kidney with a healthy donor kidney.

☐ That without precautions, donor kidneys can be rejected — and that this happens when white blood cells do not recognise the antigens (unique proteins on a cell's surface) on the donor kidney cells. As a result, they produce antibodies to attack the donor cells.

☐ That precautions to prevent the rejection of donor organs include using a donor organ that matches the recipient's tissue-type, and the recipient taking drugs which suppress their immune system.

☐ How to evaluate the use of kidney dialysis and kidney transplants as treatments for kidney failure.

Controlling Body Temperature

☐ That an area of the brain called the thermoregulatory centre monitors and controls body temperature.

☐ That receptors in the thermoregulatory centre detect the temperature of the blood in the brain, and that the thermoregulatory centre receives information about skin temperature from receptors in the skin, sent via nervous impulses.

☐ That sweating helps to decrease body temperature.

cont...

☐ That blood flow to the skin increases when you're too hot. This may make the skin appear red.

☐ **H** That when core body temperature is too high, dilation of the blood vessels supplying the skin capillaries causes increased blood flow to the skin, increasing heat loss to the environment. The sweat glands also produce more sweat, which has a cooling effect on the body as it evaporates.

☐ **H** That when core body temperature is too low, constriction of the blood vessels supplying the skin capillaries causes decreased blood flow to the skin, decreasing heat loss to the environment. The muscles also shiver (they contract automatically), which requires respiration and so releases some energy, helping to raise body temperature.

Controlling Blood Glucose Level

☐ That the pancreas is responsible for monitoring and controlling a person's blood glucose level.

☐ That the hormone insulin is produced and secreted by the pancreas in response to an increase in blood glucose level, and that insulin causes the body's cells to take up more glucose from the blood.

☐ **H** That the hormone glucagon is produced and secreted by the pancreas in response to a decrease in blood glucose level, and that glucagon causes the body's cells to convert glycogen back into glucose.

☐ That type 1 diabetes is a condition where the pancreas produces little or no insulin, which means blood glucose can rise to a dangerous level.

☐ That type 1 diabetes must be controlled by carefully controlling diet, taking regular exercise and insulin therapy.

☐ How to evaluate modern methods for the treatment of type 1 diabetes.

Exam-style Questions

1   Urea is a waste product produced in the liver, which the body needs to get rid of.

1 (a) (i)   How is urea produced by the body?

(1 mark)

1 (a) (ii)   Urea enters the bloodstream from the liver and travels to the kidneys where it is removed from the body in the urine.
Describe how urine is formed in a healthy kidney.

(4 marks)

1 (b)   As well as removing waste products from the body, the kidneys also regulate the ion content of the blood.
This table shows average values for the way a healthy kidney handles sodium ions.

Ion	Amount filtered (g per day)	% reabsorbed
Sodium	575 g	99.5

1 (b)   Calculate the amount of sodium ions found in the urine per day.

(2 marks)

2   Chi has kidney failure. She is having dialysis while she waits for a donor kidney to become available.
Chi has been on the waiting list for a long time, as some of the donor kidneys that became available were unsuitable for her.

2 (a) (i)   What is the purpose of kidney dialysis?

(2 marks)

2 (a) (ii)   Give **three** disadvantages of treating kidney failure with dialysis.

(3 marks)

2 (b) (i)   Suggest why some of the donor kidneys may have been unsuitable for Chi.
Explain your answer.

(3 marks)

2 (b) (ii)   A suitable donor kidney has become available for Chi.
Before the kidney transplant, the doctor tells Chi that she will have to take some drugs to suppress her immune system. Explain why she will need to take these drugs.

(1 mark)

3   Richard has been for a run on a hot day. His body temperature has increased.

3 (a)   Describe how Richard's brain detects this increase in body temperature.

(3 marks)

3 (b)   Describe and explain how Richard's body will respond to the increase in body temperature.

(4 marks)

4   Kaye has recently been diagnosed with type 1 diabetes. Her doctor has prescribed her insulin injections to help her control her blood glucose level.

4 (a) (i)   Explain why people with type 1 diabetes need to inject insulin.

(3 marks)

4 (a) (ii)   Apart from insulin injections, give **two** things that Kaye should do to control her diabetes. Explain your recommendations.

(4 marks)

4 (b)   Kaye has been reading about current treatments of type 1 diabetes.
She finds the following article on the internet.

A pancreas transplant is a procedure in which a healthy donor pancreas is transplanted into a person with type 1 diabetes. The aim of the surgery is that the donor pancreas will take over the role of the patient's pancreas.

Many sufferers of type 1 diabetes successfully control their condition by injecting insulin at mealtimes. Pancreas transplants are often reserved for those who have poor control over their diabetes. If the patient's doctor thinks that they are a suitable candidate for the procedure then they will be put on the waiting list for an organ as there is a shortage of donor organs available.

The transplantation procedure is a major operation. There is a risk of infection and some pain following the operation. The pancreas recipient must also take immunosuppressants (drugs which suppress the immune system) for the rest of their lives.

Pancreas transplants can be very successful, with some data reporting 50-60% of recipients no longer requiring insulin injections five years after the surgery.

In this question you will be assessed on the quality of your English, the organisation of your ideas and your use of appropriate specialist vocabulary.

Use the information from the article and your own knowledge to evaluate the use of pancreas transplants as an alternative treatment option to insulin injections for people with type 1 diabetes.

(6 marks)

1. Human Impact on the Environment

How humans impact the environment makes it onto the news a lot nowadays — everything we do has an effect, and it's not usually good...

The increasing human population

There are currently over seven billion people in the world — the population is rising very quickly, and it's not slowing down (see Figure 1).

This is mostly due to modern medicine and farming methods, which have reduced the number of people dying from disease and hunger. This is great for all of us humans, but it means we're having a bigger effect on the environment we live in.

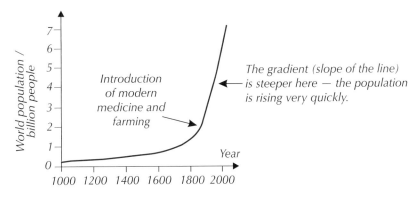

Figure 1: *Graph showing the increasing population of the world.*

Demands on the environment

When the Earth's population was much smaller, the effects of human activity were usually small and local. Nowadays though, our actions can have a far more widespread effect. Our increasing population puts pressure on the environment, as we take the resources we need to survive.

People around the world are also demanding a higher **standard of living** (and so demand luxuries to make life more comfortable — cars, computers, etc.). So we use more raw materials (e.g. oil to make plastics), but we also use more energy for the manufacturing processes. This all means we're taking more and more resources from the environment more and more quickly.

Unfortunately, many raw materials are being used up quicker than they're being replaced. So if we carry on like we are, one day we're going to run out.

Tip: Recycling means we can re-use existing materials rather than using up new resources.

Waste

As we make more and more things we produce more and more waste. And unless this waste is properly handled, more harmful pollution will be caused. This affects water, land and air.

Water

Sewage and toxic chemicals from industry can pollute lakes, rivers and oceans, affecting the plants and animals that rely on them for survival (including humans). And the chemicals used on land to help grow crops (e.g. fertilisers, pesticides and herbicides) can be washed into water.

> **Example**
>
> If too much fertiliser is added to a field and it rains, then the excess fertiliser can get washed into nearby rivers and lakes. The nutrients in the fertiliser allow lots of algae to grow, causing an algal bloom (see Figure 2). The bloom blocks out the light, so plants in the water can't photosynthesise and die. Microorganisms feeding on the dead plants use up the oxygen in the water, which can eventually lead to the death of fish and other animals.

Land

We use toxic chemicals for farming (e.g. pesticides and herbicides). We also bury nuclear waste underground, and we dump a lot of household waste in landfill sites, where it doesn't break down so easily (and some doesn't break down at all).

Air

Smoke and gases released into the atmosphere can pollute the air.

> **Examples**
>
> - Burning some fossil fuels releases sulfur dioxide. When sulfur dioxide mixes with clouds it forms dilute sulfuric acid, which falls as acid rain. Acid rain can damage buildings and kill plants.
>
> - Carbon dioxide (CO_2) is also released when fossil fuels are burnt. The increasing level of CO_2 is contributing to global warming and climate change (see pages 277-278).

Land use

Humans also reduce the amount of land and resources available to other animals and plants. The four main human activities that do this are:

- Building

- Farming

- Dumping waste

- Quarrying for metal ores (digging into the Earth to extract rocks that contain metal)

Tip: Fertilisers are chemicals added to soil to provide nutrients for crop growth. Pesticides are chemicals that kill pests (like insects) that eat and damage the crops. Herbicides kill weeds that compete with the crops for nutrients, water, etc.

Figure 2: *Algal bloom in a pond. The algae is the thick yellow-green material that you can see covering the surface of the water.*

Exam Tip
You need to learn the sulfur dioxide example.

Tip: Fossil fuels are fuels formed from the remains of organisms that died a very, very long time ago.
The three main types of fossil fuel are oil, gas and coal.

Tip: Finding land to dump and bury waste (landfill sites) will become more of a problem as the population grows and we produce more waste.

Environmental data

In the exam, you might be asked to analyse or interpret some data related to environmental issues — such as pollution or energy use.

Example

The graph in Figure 3 shows how the GDP and energy consumption of a country has increased over time.

GDP stands for gross domestic product and it can be used as an indicator of a country's standard of living — a higher GDP usually means a higher standard of living.

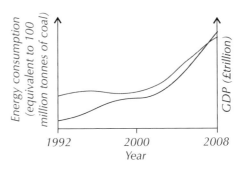

Figure 3: *Graph to show changes in GDP and energy consumption in a country from 1992 to 2008.*

You could be asked to describe any general trends shown by the data...
As the GDP (and so the standard of living) of the country increased, so did its energy usage. You could say there's a positive correlation between GDP (or standard of living) and energy usage.

You could be asked to give an explanation for any trends shown by the data...
A higher standard of living usually means more access to both services (such as health care and transport) and products (like cars, computers and TVs). These things require energy to run or to make (and sometimes both). So as the standard of living increases, so too does energy consumption.

You could be asked to suggest what this might mean for the environment...
An increase in energy use can mean more pollution — energy often comes from power stations, which burn fossil fuels or produce nuclear waste. Burning fossil fuels releases sulfur dioxide (which causes acid rain, see p. 271) and carbon dioxide (which is contributing to global warming, see p. 278).

If people own and use more products, it also means more resources will be used to make these products and more waste will be created when they're thrown away.

Tip: A positive correlation just means that as one thing increases, so does another (see p. 13).

Exam Tip
You could be asked to evaluate the methods used to collect environmental data too — see page 281.

Q1 True or false? The population of the world is decreasing, but people's standard of living is increasing.

Q2 How can the chemicals used to grow crops cause water pollution?

Q3 How do humans cause land pollution?

Q4 Name a gas which causes acid rain.

Practice Question — Application

Q1 The graph below shows the amount of waste recycled and the amount sent to landfill in one city for three separate years.

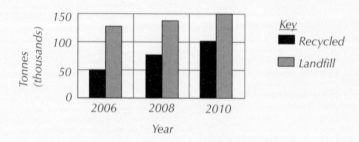

Figure 4: Landfill sites take up room, pollute the land around them and are ugly (they cause visual pollution).

a) Describe the trends shown by the graph.

b) What percentage of the total waste shown in the graph for 2010 was recycled?

c) Landfill reduces the amount of space available for other animals. Give two other human activities that reduce the space available for other animals and plants.

d) Suggest why the amount of space taken up by landfill sites around the world is increasing.

e) Suggest one reason why it is important to recycle products such as metal cans.

- Know the reasons why deforestation is carried out.

- Understand the problems that deforestation can cause — an increase in the amount of methane in the atmosphere, reductions in biodiversity, the release of carbon dioxide into the atmosphere and a reduction in the amount of carbon dioxide that can be stored in forests.

- Understand that destroying peat bogs increases the amount of carbon dioxide in the atmosphere.

- Know why it's important to use peat-free compost.

Specification Reference
B3.4.2

2. Deforestation and the Destruction of Peat Bogs

Forests and areas with peat bogs don't just look nice, they're important habitats for many animals and plants, and they're natural stores of carbon dioxide. So destroying them has important implications for humans and the environment.

Deforestation

Deforestation is the cutting down of forests. This causes big problems when it's done on a large-scale, such as cutting down rainforests. It's done for various reasons:

- To provide timber to use as a building material.

- To clear more land for farming, which is important to provide more food, e.g. from more rice fields or farming more cattle. It's also important for growing crops from which **biofuels** based on ethanol (see page 283) can be produced.

- To produce paper from wood.

Problems caused by deforestation

Deforestation leads to four main problems:

1. More methane in the atmosphere

Methane is a greenhouse gas (see p. 277). An increasing level of methane in the atmosphere is contributing to global warming (the increase in the average global temperature, see p. 278). Clearing forests to grow rice or rear cattle eventually means more methane in the atmosphere. Here's why:

Tip: Decomposers are microorganisms like bacteria and fungi that break down dead or decaying materials.

- Rice is grown in warm, waterlogged conditions — ideal for decomposers. These microorganisms produce methane. So the more rice grown, the more methane that is produced and released into the atmosphere.

- Cattle also produce methane and so rearing more cattle means that more methane is released.

Figure 1: The bacteria in a cow's digestive system produce methane as they help to break down the food the cow eats. The cow then releases the methane when it breaks wind.

2. Less biodiversity

Biodiversity is the variety of different species in a habitat — the more species, the greater the biodiversity. Habitats like tropical rainforests can contain a huge number of different species, so when they are destroyed there is a danger of many species becoming extinct — reducing biodiversity.

Extinction causes a number of lost opportunities, e.g. there are probably loads of useful products that we will never know about because the organisms that produced them have become extinct. Newly discovered plants and animals are a great source of new foods, new fibres for clothing and new medicines.

3. More carbon dioxide released into the atmosphere

Carbon dioxide (CO_2) is another greenhouse gas. An increasing level of carbon dioxide in the atmosphere is contributing to global warming (see p. 278). Deforestation increases the amount of carbon dioxide released into the atmosphere, as carbon dioxide is released when trees are burnt to clear land — see Figure 2. Microorganisms feeding on bits of dead wood also release carbon dioxide as a waste product of respiration.

4. Less carbon dioxide taken in

Green plants and trees take in carbon dioxide from the atmosphere during photosynthesis. They then store it as carbon compounds in their tissues (e.g. wood). Cutting down loads of trees means that the amount of carbon dioxide removed from the atmosphere during photosynthesis is reduced — see Figure 2.

Tip: There's more on natural stores of carbon dioxide on page 277.

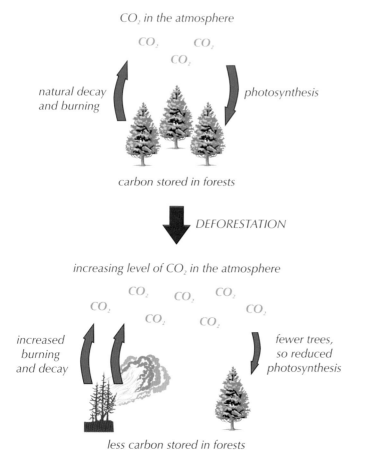

Tip: The destruction of peat bogs also leads to the release of more CO_2 (see next page).

Figure 2: *The amount of carbon dioxide in the atmosphere should stay fairly constant (top cycle). But deforestation leads to an increase in the atmospheric carbon dioxide level (bottom cycle).*

The destruction of peat bogs

Figure 3: Some peat.

Bogs are areas of land that are acidic and waterlogged. Plants that live in bogs don't fully decay when they die, because there's not enough oxygen. The partly-rotted plants gradually build up to form **peat** (a brown, soil-like material, see Figure 3). So the carbon in the plants is stored in the peat instead of being released into the atmosphere.

However, peat bogs are often drained so that the area can be used as farmland, or the peat is cut up and dried to use as fuel (Figure 4). Peat is also sold to gardeners as compost. Peat starts to decompose when the bogs are drained, so carbon dioxide is released. If we continue to destroy peat bogs, more carbon dioxide will be released, which will contribute to global warming (see page 278). When peat is burned as fuel it also releases carbon dioxide.

Figure 4: A peat bog that's had some peat harvested from it. The brown trench is where peat blocks have been dug up and taken away.

So one way people can do their bit is by buying peat-free compost for their gardens (e.g. manure, leaf mould or bark chippings) to reduce the demand for peat.

Practice Questions — Application

Tip: The bar chart in Q1 is a composite bar chart — it's just like a normal one except the bars are placed on top of each other instead of side by side. Here's the information for 2011 shown in composite form (left) and normal form (right):

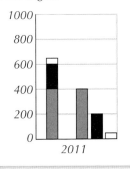

Q1 The graph shows how much forest was cleared each year in one region of a rainforest and the use of the area after clearance.

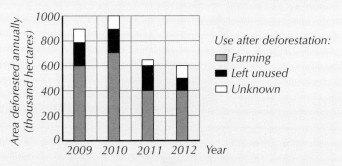

Use after deforestation:
- Farming
- Left unused
- Unknown

a) How much forest was cleared in this region in 2009?

b) i) How much land was used for farming after clearance in 2012?

   ii) What kind of farming might be taking place on the cleared land?

c) Some of the land has been left unused. Suggest one reason why it might have been cleared.

d) Deforestation causes an increase in the atmospheric carbon dioxide level. Explain why.

Q2 Dave needs some compost for his vegetable plot. A peat-free variety is being advertised as an environmentally-friendly option. Explain why the manufacturers are making this claim.

3. Carbon Dioxide and the Greenhouse Effect

Now we've hit the jackpot, the pollutant that everyone is talking about — carbon dioxide and why it's problematic.

Learning Objectives:

- Know that carbon dioxide is sequestered (stored) in lakes, oceans, and ponds.
- Understand why carbon dioxide stores are important.
- Know that atmospheric levels of methane and carbon dioxide are increasing.
- Understand that increasing levels of atmospheric carbon dioxide and methane are contributing to global warming.

Specification Reference B3.4.3

Natural stores of carbon dioxide

Many processes lead to carbon dioxide (CO_2) being released into the atmosphere, e.g. burning fossil fuels (see page 271), deforestation (see pages 274-275) and the destruction of peat bogs (see page 276). Too much carbon dioxide in the atmosphere causes global warming (see next page).

Luckily, the CO_2 can be **sequestered** ('locked up') in natural stores, including:

- Oceans, lakes and ponds.

- Green plants (including trees), where it's stored as carbon compounds. Green plants remove CO_2 from the atmosphere during photosynthesis.

- Peat bogs (see previous page).

Storing CO_2 in these ways is really important because it means CO_2 is removed from the atmosphere.

The greenhouse effect

The temperature of the Earth is a balance between the heat it gets from the Sun and the heat it radiates back out into space. Gases in the atmosphere naturally act like an insulating layer. They absorb most of the heat that would normally be radiated out into space, and re-radiate it in all directions, including back towards the Earth. This is the **greenhouse effect** (see Figure 1) and the gases involved are called greenhouse gases. The greenhouse effect helps to keep the Earth warm.

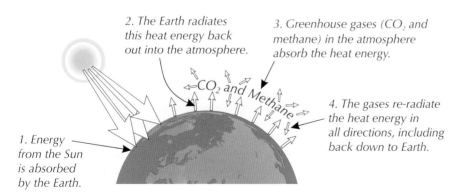

2. The Earth radiates this heat energy back out into the atmosphere.

3. Greenhouse gases (CO_2 and methane) in the atmosphere absorb the heat energy.

CO_2 and Methane

4. The gases re-radiate the heat energy in all directions, including back down to Earth.

1. Energy from the Sun is absorbed by the Earth.

Tip: This is what happens in a greenhouse. The sun shines in, and the glass helps keep some of the heat in.

Figure 1: *Diagram illustrating the greenhouse effect.*

If the greenhouse effect didn't happen, then at night there'd be nothing to keep any heat in, and we'd quickly get very cold indeed. But recently we've started to worry that this effect is getting a bit out of hand...

Global warming

Tip: Scientists now agree that human activities are causing global warming — our activities are causing more greenhouse gases to be released.
E.g. deforestation is causing more CO_2 and methane to be released (see pages 274-275). Burning fossil fuels is also causing more CO_2 to be released.

The main greenhouse gases we worry about are carbon dioxide and methane — because the levels of these two gases are rising quite sharply. These rises are causing a gradual increase in the average global temperature. This is known as **global warming**.

Global warming is a type of **climate change** and it causes other types of climate change, e.g. changing rainfall patterns. Global warming could have many consequences for our planet — see pages 279-280 for more.

Figure 2: *A flow chart summarising the causes and effects of an increasing greenhouse effect.*

Practice Questions — Fact Recall

Q1 List three places where CO_2 is naturally stored.

Q2 Describe how gases in the atmosphere help to keep the Earth warm.

Q3 The levels of some greenhouse gases in the atmosphere are increasing. Name two of these gases.

Q4 Briefly summarise the connection between gases in the atmosphere and global warming.

Practice Question — Application

Q1 Scientists are currently investigating the possibility of storing CO_2 in spaces in the Earth under the North Sea. Suggest why scientists are interested in finding new places to store CO_2.

Exam Tip
Remember — application questions might seem hard at first, but they're not too bad. They're all about applying what you already know about a subject (like CO_2 stores) to an unfamiliar situation (like underground stores in the North Sea).

4. Climate Change

What we've been working towards for most of this section so far — the most worrying consequence of all our polluting ways — climate change (which includes global warming).

Learning Objectives:
- Know what the five main consequences of global warming could be.
- Be able to analyse and evaluate the methods used to collect data on environmental issues and climate change, by looking at the data's validity and reliability.

Specification Reference
B3.4, B3.4.3

The consequences of global warming

You already know that global warming is the gradual increase in the average global temperature. An increase of even a few degrees could have serious consequences for our planet. You need to learn these five:

1. Other types of climate change

Global warming is a type of climate change. Global warming can cause the Earth's climate to change in other ways too.

Examples

- It's thought that many regions will suffer more extreme weather, e.g. longer, hotter droughts.

- Hurricanes form over water that's warmer than 27 °C — so with more warm water, you'd expect more hurricanes.

However, the climate is a very complicated system. It's hard to predict exactly what will happen, but lots of people are working on it, and it's not looking too good.

2. Rising sea level

As the sea gets warmer, it expands, causing sea level to rise. Sea level has risen a little bit over the last 100 years. If it keeps rising it'll be bad news for people living in low-lying places like the Netherlands, East Anglia and the Maldives — they'd be flooded.

Higher temperatures also make ice melt. Water that's currently 'trapped' on land (as ice in glaciers and at the poles) runs into the sea, causing sea level to rise even more.

Examples

- The coastline of Louisiana (a southern state of the USA) has seen a sea level rise of at least 8 inches in the last 50 years.

- The Helheim glacier (a thick mass of ice in Greenland) has retreated (melted) by 4 km in four years. We know this because of satellite images like the ones in Figure 1. The glacier had stayed in roughly the same position up until 2001.

Figure 1: *Satellite images of the Helheim glacier in 2001 (top), 2003 (middle) and 2005 (bottom).*

3. Changes in the distribution of organisms

The distribution of organisms is just where they're usually found within a certain area. E.g. in the UK, red squirrels are found in the north of England and in Scotland. Wild plants and animals are found in places where they can survive — where it's the right temperature and they have access to the right resources like water, food and shelter. As the average global temperature goes up and other changes to the weather occur, the distribution of many wild animal and plant species may change.

Some species may become more widely distributed, e.g. species that need warmer temperatures may spread further as the conditions they thrive in exist over a wider area. Other species may become less widely distributed, e.g. species that need cooler temperatures may have smaller ranges as the conditions they thrive in exist over a smaller area.

Examples

- The Comma is a species of butterfly that was until recently only found in England and Wales. Its distribution is extending further north though, into Scotland, and this is thought to be due to global warming.

- An increasing number of warm-water striped dolphins are being spotted in the waters around England. At the same time there's been a decline in spottings of the cold-water white-beaked dolphins. This could be because the sea around England is getting warmer.

Figure 2: A Comma butterfly.

4. Changes to migration patterns

Lots of birds and other animals migrate — they move to different areas at different times of the year. For example, swallows come to the UK in summer but they spend their winters in hotter countries. Global warming could lead to changes in migration patterns. This includes changes to where organisms migrate (e.g. some birds may migrate further north, as more northern areas are getting warmer), when they migrate, and possibly if they migrate at all.

Example

Studies have shown that some birds living in Africa over winter have started to migrate back to their European summer breeding grounds earlier than ever before. This could be directly due to temperature change, or because the temperature is causing the birds' food sources to appear at earlier times.

5. Less biodiversity

Biodiversity (see page 274) could be reduced — if some species are unable to adapt to a change in the climate, then they won't survive and the species will become extinct. For example, if it's too hot for them where they usually live but they can't survive in other habitats because there isn't the right food source, then they might die out.

Evaluating evidence

To find out how our climate is changing, scientists are busy collecting data about the environment.

Figure 3: Automatic weather stations (some like this, others more fancy) are found all over the world now. They automatically collect data on things like temperature, wind speed and direction, and rainfall.

Examples

- We use satellites to monitor snow and ice cover, and to measure the temperature of the sea surface.

- We're recording the temperature and speed of the ocean currents, to try and detect any changes.

- Automatic weather stations (like the one in Figure 3) are constantly recording atmospheric temperatures.

In the exam, you could be asked to evaluate some data on environmental issues such as global warming. You need to look carefully at the methods that have been used to collect the data and consider if the evidence provided is valid and reliable. Here are some things to think about:

Does the data cover a wide enough area to give valid results?

Generally, observations of a very small area aren't much use. Noticing that your local glacier seems to be melting does not mean that ice everywhere is melting, and it's certainly not a valid way to show that global temperature is changing. (That would be like going to Wales, seeing a stripy cow and concluding that all the cows in Wales are turning into zebras.) Looking at the area of ice cover over a whole continent, like Antarctica, would be better.

Tip: There's more on what makes evidence valid in the How Science Works section (page 3).

Does the data cover a wide enough time scale to give valid results?

The same thing goes for time. It's no good going to the Arctic, seeing four polar bears one week but only two the next week and concluding that polar bears are dying out because the ice is disappearing. You need to do your observations again and again, year after year.

Has the data been reproduced by anyone else?

Scientists can make mistakes — so don't take one person's word for something, even if they've got a PhD. But if lots of scientists get the same result, it's probably right. That's why most governments around the world are starting to take climate change seriously.

Could the people collecting or presenting the results be biased?

For example, research that's been funded by or carried out on behalf of an oil company might be more likely to downplay the link between human activities and global warming (because burning oil releases CO_2). Whereas research carried out by environmental campaigners might be more likely to overemphasise it. Results from an independent study are less likely to be biased.

Tip: Independent people have nothing to gain from the results of the study, no matter what the outcome. People who are biased might gain or lose depending on what the data says, and so might try to influence the results.

Q1 How does global warming cause other types of climate change?

Q2 Explain how global warming can lead to changes in the distribution of organisms.

Q3 Besides causing other types of climate change and causing changes to the distribution of organisms, give three other possible consequences of global warming.

Practice Questions — Application

Q1 Since the 1950s, a species of bird has started to become more common in a small island country. Since it started appearing more regularly, the average global temperature has risen. Farming practices across the country have also changed quite a lot in this time. A newspaper runs the following headline: "Bird increase caused by global warming".

Tip: Don't panic if you don't know anything specifically about birds. Use your knowledge about the consequences of global warming and apply that to birds.

a) Is there enough evidence given here to support the newspaper's headline? Give reasons for your answer.

b) Besides causing distribution changes, suggest one other way in which global warming might affect birds found in the country.

Q2 The graph shows how the global mean sea level changed between 1940 and 2000. The data was gathered from several separate studies, all published in peer-reviewed journals. The raw data was collected from numerous sites around the globe.

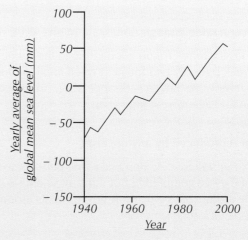

a) Calculate the change in global mean sea level between 1940 and 2000.

b) Do you think this data is reliable? Give reasons for your answer.

c) Explain the link between global warming and a rising sea level.

5. Biofuels

Burning fossil fuels produces carbon dioxide and other air pollutants. Burning biofuels releases carbon dioxide too, but the plant materials biofuels are made from took in carbon dioxide when they were growing. This makes biofuels 'carbon neutral', which means they don't contribute to global warming.

Learning Objectives:
- Know that biofuels are fuels made by fermenting natural materials.
- Know that biogas is a biofuel.
- Know that biogas is mainly made from methane.
- Know how biogas is made — by the anaerobic fermentation of plant matter or waste material.

Specification Reference B3.4.3

Making biofuels

Biofuels are fuels made by the **fermentation** of natural products (including waste products). Fermentation is when bacteria or yeast break down sugars (glucose, etc.) by **anaerobic respiration**. Anaerobic respiration is respiration that takes place when there's no oxygen.

Ethanol

Ethanol is a fuel produced when yeast break down glucose by anaerobic fermentation. This word equation shows what happens:

$$\text{glucose} \rightarrow \text{ethanol} + \text{carbon dioxide} + \text{energy}$$

Sugar cane juices can be used as a source of glucose, or glucose can be derived (made) from maize starch by the action of carbohydrase (an enzyme). The ethanol is distilled to separate it from the yeast and remaining glucose before it's used.

In some countries, e.g. Brazil, cars are adapted to run on a mixture of ethanol and petrol — this is known as 'gasohol'.

Biogas

Biogas is another type of biofuel (so it's also made by anaerobic respiration). It's usually made of about 70% methane and 30% carbon dioxide. Lots of different microorganisms are used to produce biogas. The microorganisms ferment plant material and animal waste (e.g. faeces) containing carbohydrates. Sludge waste from, e.g. sewage works or sugar factories, is used to make biogas on a large scale.

Biogas is made in a simple fermenter called a digester or generator. Biogas generators need to be kept at a constant temperature to keep the microorganisms respiring away. There are two types of biogas generators — batch generators and continuous generators. These are explained on p. 286.

Biogas can't be stored as a liquid (it needs too high a pressure), so it has to be used straight away — for heating, cooking, lighting, or to power a turbine to generate electricity.

Figure 1: Biogas can also be collected from landfill sites. The waste (buried under the grey bit) releases gases as it ferments.

Practice Questions — Fact Recall

Q1   What are biofuels?

Q2   What is fermentation?

Q3   True or false? Anaerobic respiration is respiration that requires oxygen.

Q4   Biogas is made from carbon dioxide and what other gas?

Q5   How is biogas made?

Practice Questions — Application

Tip: For Q1, think about the conditions required to make biofuel.

Q1   Biogas can be collected from landfill sites where the waste is buried underground. Suggest why it is important that the waste is buried.

Q2   Radioactive waste is produced in nuclear power stations.
It is normally made up of things like oil-based plastics, metals, etc.
It doesn't contain any carbohydrates.

Could this waste be used to produce biogas?
Explain your answer.

6. Using Biogas Generators

Learning Objectives:
- Be able to evaluate the use of biogas generators on both a small and a large scale.
- Understand how temperature can affect biogas production.

Specification Reference B3.4

Biogas is usually made in a generator, but not all biogas generators are born equal — some are big, some are small, some keep working round the clock...

The standard generator

Whether a generator is big or small, or for batch or continuous use (see next page), it needs to have the following:

- an inlet for waste material to be put in,

- an outlet for the digested material to be removed through,

- an outlet so that the biogas can be piped to where it is needed (see Figure 1).

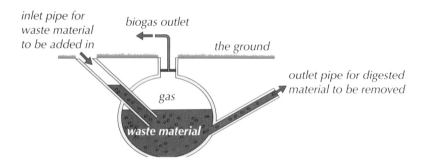

Figure 1: *A diagram showing a simple biogas generator.*

Figure 2: *A large-scale biogas production plant. The gas is stored in the white round part and the digestion takes place in the large containers at the back.*

The scale of fuel production

Biogas production can happen on a large or small scale.

- Large-scale biogas generators are now being set up in a number of countries. Suitable waste (food scraps, etc.) are collected separately or can be separated from general household rubbish and sent to special biogas plants (see Figure 2).

- Small biogas generators are used in some countries to make enough gas for a village or a family to use in their cooking stoves and for heating and lighting (see Figure 3).

Whatever the size of generator, all types of waste can be used to produce the biofuel — human waste, waste from keeping pigs, and food waste (e.g. kitchen scraps) can be digested by bacteria to produce biogas. Any by-products can also be used to fertilise crops and gardens.

Figure 3: *A small-scale biogas generator being used in India. Animal manure is fed into the generator to be fermented.*

Types of generators

There are two main types of biogas generator — batch generators and continuous generators. **Batch generators** make biogas in small batches and are the simplest and so cheapest generator to make. They're manually loaded up with waste, which is left to digest, and the by-products are cleared away at the end of each session. They don't have to be filled up as often as continuous generators, but they don't produce biogas at a steady rate.

Continuous generators make biogas all the time. Waste is continuously fed in, and biogas is produced at a steady rate. Continuous generators are more suited to large-scale biogas projects.

Designing generators

When biogas generators are being designed, the following four factors need to be considered:

1. Cost

Continuous generators are more expensive than batch ones, because waste has to be mechanically pumped in and digested material mechanically removed all the time.

2. Convenience

Batch generators are less convenient because they have to be continually loaded, emptied and cleaned.

3. Efficiency

Tip: Gas is most quickly produced at 35 °C because this is the temperature at which the enzymes in the microorganisms work best.

The generator shouldn't have any leaks or gas will be lost. Also, gas is produced most quickly at about 35 °C. If the temperature falls below this, then gas production will be slower. Generators in cooler areas may need to be heated or insulated (to keep in the heat).

> **Example**
>
> In the UK, the walls of the generators will be thick or made from insulating material. The heat created during fermentation will then help keep the generator at the right temperature. In some places, solar heaters can also be used to help keep generators warm.

Tip: As the microorganisms in the generators respire, they produce heat. The same is true in a compost bin or landfill site — if you dug into the compost bin, you'd feel the heat coming off it.

If the temperature goes above 35 °C, production will also be slower. So in countries where it gets hot the generators might need to be cooled.

> **Example**
>
> In India, the generators might be buried underground where it's cooler.

4. Position

The waste will smell during delivery, so generators should be sited away from homes. The generator is also best located fairly close to the waste source.

The benefits of using biogas

There are lots of benefits to using biogas generators and biofuels in general — some are economic and social benefits, and others are environmental.

Social and economic benefits

- The raw material needed to produce biogas is cheap and readily available.

- The digested material is a better fertiliser than undigested dung — so people can use it to grow more crops.

- In some developing rural communities women have to spend hours each day collecting wood for fuel. Biogas saves them this drudgery.

- Biogas generators act as a waste disposal system, getting rid of human and animal waste that'd otherwise lie around, causing disease and polluting water supplies.

Environmental benefits

- Methane is a greenhouse gas and is one of those responsible for global warming. It's given off from untreated waste, which may be kept in farmyards or spread on agricultural land as fertiliser. Burning it as biogas means it's not released into the atmosphere.

- The use of biogas doesn't produce significant amounts of sulfur dioxide or nitrogen oxides, which cause acid rain.

- The waste material used to produce biogas could otherwise end up in landfill sites, where it takes up space and causes land and air pollution.

- Biofuels and biogas are a 'greener' alternative to fossil fuels. The carbon dioxide released into the atmosphere when they're burnt was taken in by plants which lived recently, so they're 'carbon neutral' — the carbon they take in is equal to the carbon they give out (see Figure 4).

Tip: Burning most fuels releases carbon dioxide into the atmosphere.

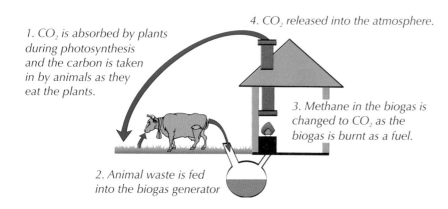

4. CO_2 released into the atmosphere.

1. CO_2 is absorbed by plants during photosynthesis and the carbon is taken in by animals as they eat the plants.

3. Methane in the biogas is changed to CO_2 as the biogas is burnt as a fuel.

2. Animal waste is fed into the biogas generator

Figure 4: Diagram to illustrate how biogas is carbon neutral — animal waste is used in a simple biogas generator to produce fuel for the home.

Practice Questions — Fact Recall

Q1 Describe the main parts of a simple biogas generator.

Q2 What's the difference between a batch generator and a continuous generator?

Q3 What four things need to be taken into account when designing a biogas generator?

Q4 Why is it important that biogas generators are kept at a temperature of about 35 °C?

Q5 Suggest two social or economic benefits of using a biogas generator.

Q6 Explain what is meant when biogas is described as 'carbon neutral'.

Q7 Other than being carbon neutral, give one other environmental benefit of using biogas.

Practice Questions — Application

Q1 A town is rapidly growing in size, so it is producing more waste and requires more energy production. The town council is looking at two options for energy production — a large-scale biogas generator or a coal-fuelled power station. Some information on both ways of generating energy are given below.

Information	Biogas generator	Coal-fuelled power station
Fuel type	Waste material	Coal
Cost of fuel	Free / cheap	Expensive
Cost to build	Same	Same
Pollution	Carbon dioxide and some sulfur dioxide	Carbon dioxide and sulfur dioxide

Which option would you suggest they build?
Give reasons for your answer.

Q2 Lydia's family own a small farm in a rural tropical location where the average daily temperature in summer can hit 40 °C. In summer, the fields around their farm are used to graze animals. In winter, the fields are left to recover. They usually buy wood to burn as fuel at home. The family are thinking of building a biogas generator.

Describe and explain the features of the generator you think they should build.

7. Managing Food Production

Learning Objectives:
- Know that the amount of energy and biomass at each stage in a food chain reduces as you go along the chain.
- Know that it is more efficient to produce food from plants than from animals.
- Understand that if you reduce the number of stages in a food chain used for food production, then the efficiency of food production is increased.
- Understand how and why controlling the conditions food animals are kept in can increase the efficiency of food production.
- Know that fish stocks are declining and that quotas and restrictions in net sizes can help to conserve species (which is an example of sustainable food production).

Specification Reference B3.4.4

As you saw way back at the start of this section, the human population is increasing. This means we need to grow more food and find more water. Part of this means producing more grub, more efficiently.

Improving the efficiency of food production

Humans rely on plants for food because plants are at the start of all food chains. Plants use the energy from sunlight to convert carbon dioxide and water into compounds (such as carbohydrates). Humans and other animals then eat, digest and absorb the compounds, which they use for energy and to grow.

We grow plants to feed ourselves and to feed animals (which we then eat). The more that plants and animals grow, the more energy we can get from them. Improving food efficiency is all about making sure that more of the energy plants and animals take in is used to grow and provide us with food.

There are two main ways to increase the efficiency of food production that you need to know about:

1. Reducing the number of stages in a food chain

There's less energy and less **biomass** (living material) every time you move up a stage in a food chain. This is because at every stage some energy is lost, e.g. in waste, respiration and movement. So for a given area of land, you can produce a lot more food (for humans) by growing crops rather than by having grazing animals. This is because you are reducing the number of stages in the food chain, so reducing the amount of energy lost. For example, only 10% of what beef cattle eat becomes useful meat for people to eat. The loss of energy in a food chain is shown in Figure 1.

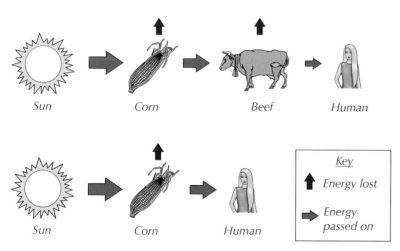

Sun   Corn   Beef   Human

Sun   Corn   Human

Key

↑ *Energy lost*

→ *Energy passed on*

Figure 1: *Diagram to show that energy (originally from the Sun) is lost at each stage of the food chain — and so by reducing the number of stages in a food chain, you reduce the amount of energy lost.*

Tip: There's more on food chains, energy and biomass on pages 83-87.

Tip: Typically, only 10% of the energy at each stage of a food chain is passed on to the next stage. 90% of the energy is lost.

Tip: Some food products take longer to grow or produce than others. For example, it takes longer (and so requires more energy) to raise a cow than it does a chicken. So 'growing time' affects efficiency of food production too.

Figure 2: *Chickens being farmed in barns. The temperature can be controlled, so less energy is wasted by the chickens.*

Tip: Fish stocks are the numbers of fish of different species we think are left in seas and oceans around the world.

However, people do need to eat a varied diet to stay healthy, and there's still a lot of demand for meat products. Also, some land is unsuitable for growing crops, e.g. moorland or hillsides. In these places, animals like sheep and deer might be the best way to get food from the land.

2. Reducing the energy lost at each stage of a food chain

In countries like the UK, animals such as pigs and chickens are often **intensively farmed**. Intensively farmed animals (sometimes known as **factory farmed** animals) are kept close together indoors in small pens, so that they're warm and can't move about. This saves them wasting energy on:

- movement,
- keeping warm.

This makes the transfer of energy from the animal feed to the animal more efficient — so the animals will grow faster on less food. This allows us to produce more food, more quickly. It also makes things cheaper for the farmer, and for us, when the animals finally turn up on supermarket shelves.

Preventing overfishing

Fish stocks are declining because we're overfishing (fishing too much). This means there's less fish for us to eat, the ocean's food chains are affected and some species of fish may disappear altogether in some areas. To tackle this problem, we need to maintain fish stocks at a level where the fish continue to breed. This is **sustainable food production** — having enough food without using resources faster than they renew. Fish stocks can be maintained (conserved) in these ways:

1. Using fishing quotas

These are limits on the number and size of fish that can be caught in certain areas. This prevents certain species from being overfished.

2. Controlling net size

There are different limits to the mesh size of the fish net, depending on what's being fished. This is to reduce the number of 'unwanted' and discarded fish — the ones that are accidently caught, e.g. shrimp caught along with cod. Using a bigger mesh size will let the 'unwanted' species escape. It also means that younger fish will slip through the net, allowing them to reach breeding age.

Practice Questions — Fact Recall

Q1 True or false? Energy is lost at each stage in a food chain.

Q2 Explain why more food can be produced on the same area of land by growing crops instead of grazing animals.

Q3 Why is it more efficient to intensively farm animals for food rather than letting them roam free?

Q4 Describe two methods of conserving fish stocks.

8. Modern Food Production and Distribution

How to keep everyone fed and watered is a large problem. It requires us to think up new ways to produce food and produce food more efficiently (which can lead to other problems and concerns).

New food sources — mycoprotein

As the population of the world increases, it'll be important to find new food sources to add to those that currently exist. A fairly modern food source that is becoming increasingly popular is mycoprotein.

Mycoprotein means protein from fungi. It's used to make meat substitutes for vegetarian meals, e.g. Quorn™. A fungus called **Fusarium** is the main source of mycoprotein. The fungus is grown in fermenters (big containers full of liquid culture medium) using glucose syrup as food. The glucose syrup is obtained by digesting maize starch with enzymes.

The fungus respires aerobically, so oxygen is supplied, together with nitrogen (as ammonia) and other minerals. The mixture is also kept at the right temperature and pH. It's important to prevent other microorganisms growing in the fermenter, so the fermenter is initially sterilised using steam. The incoming nutrients are also heat sterilised and the air supply is filtered. Once ready, the mycoprotein is harvested, purified and dried. It's then processed further by adding flavourings and other ingredients.

The benefits of producing mycoprotein

Food made from microorganisms mightn't sound very appetising, but there are definitely advantages to it. In some developing countries it's difficult to find enough protein. Meat is a big source of protein, but animals need lots of space to graze, plenty of nice grass, etc. Mycoprotein grown in a fermenter is an efficient way of producing protein to feed people. The microorganisms grow very quickly, and don't need much space. And they can even feed on waste material that would be no good for feeding animals.

The positives and negatives of intensive farming

Intensive farming (see previous page) helps us improve the efficiency of food production. This is useful — it means cheaper food for us and generally better standards of living for farmers. It also helps to feed an increasing human population. But it also has disadvantages:

- Some people think that forcing animals to live in unnatural and uncomfortable conditions is cruel. There's a growing demand for farmed products produced with animal welfare taken into account.

Learning Objectives:

- Know that the fungus *Fusarium* is used to make mycoprotein and know the conditions required to produce it.
- Be able to evaluate the different methods used to provide food to an increasing population.
- Be able to suggest some advantages and disadvantages of intensive farming.
- Understand that the methods chosen to produce food often have to be a compromise.
- Be able to evaluate the pros and cons of managing the production of food.
- Understand what food miles are and what they mean.
- Be able to evaluate the pros and cons of managing the distribution of food.
- Be able to evaluate the different methods used to provide water to an increasing population.

Specification Reference B3.4, B3.4.4

Figure 1: *A selection of food products made from mycoprotein.*

Figure 2: Free range chickens.

Example

Food labelled as 'free range' lets consumers know that the animals used to produce it were free to roam around outdoors. Organic meat production also has high animal welfare standards and the animals aren't given growth hormones. Organic and free range farming is less efficient than intensive farming, so organic and free range foods cost more than if they were produced using intensive farming methods. But some people are willing to pay this extra cost.

- The crowded conditions on factory farms create a favourable environment for the spread of diseases, like avian flu and foot-and-mouth disease.

- To try to prevent disease, animals are given antibiotics. When the animals are eaten these can enter humans. This allows microbes that infect humans to develop resistance to those antibiotics — so the antibiotics become less effective as human medicines.

- The animals need to be kept warm to reduce the energy they lose as heat. This often means using power from fossil fuels — which we wouldn't be using if the animals were grazing in their natural environment.

- Fish stocks are getting low. Yet a lot of fish is used to feed animals that are intensively farmed (they wouldn't usually eat this source of food).

Choosing what methods to use for farming can involve conflict and has to involve compromise if we are going to keep feeding the increasing population.

Problems with food distribution

All the food you buy in a shop has been transported a number of miles from where it was grown and produced to where it will be sold. The distance food travels before it reaches the consumer is known as **food miles**. Food that's imported from other countries has lots of food miles, e.g. some green beans you buy in the UK have come from Kenya. Food that's been grown locally will have fewer food miles.

Moving food a long way can be expensive and it's also bad for the environment. Planes, ships and trucks all burn scarce fossil fuels and release carbon dioxide into the atmosphere, contributing to global warming. Some shops and producers now put food miles on the labels of their products. This helps consumers make an informed choice about whether they want to buy a product that's travelled that far.

Figure 3: This label shows the beans were flown in by air and that they were grown in Kenya. So the consumer will know they'll have racked up quite a few food miles.

Water supplies

Humans need water to survive, as well as food, so an increasing population means increased pressure on sources of fresh water. This means countries need to spend more time and money on improving water supplies (so less water is lost, e.g. by leaky pipes) and on finding new sources.

Global warming is likely to cause worse droughts too, putting even more pressure on water supplies. As well as costing money, any changes made to water supplies can have other far-reaching and long-lasting effects.

Examples

- The warmer areas of some countries often suffer from droughts in the summer, whilst other areas may get plenty of rain. This means more reservoirs may need to be built in the rainy areas to supply water to the hotter regions. This could cause resentment as land is used in some areas to cater for the needs of people far away.

- Some rivers flow through many different countries on their journey from mountain to sea. If a country near the source (start) of the river blocks it to produce a reservoir, then this can cause social and economic problems for the other countries the river runs through. Situations like this can also cause tension between countries.

> **Tip:** Water conflict is the term given to disagreements over water supplies. Some people are predicting these will start to become more common, especially in places like the Middle East where water is already quite scarce.

Practice Questions — Fact Recall

Q1   What is mycoprotein?

Q2   Describe how mycoprotein is produced.

Q3   True or false? There are no benefits to intensive farming.

Q4   Give one example of a compromise involved in feeding an increasing human population.

Q5   Some foods have lots of 'food miles'. What does this mean?

Practice Questions — Application

Q1   A large river flows through two different states in a country. The state nearest the source of the river uses river water to stock a few different reservoirs and it intends to start taking more water from the river to irrigate new areas of farmland.

> **Tip:** 'Irrigate' just means artificially providing the farmland with water.

Suggest one problem this could cause for the state further down the river.

Q2   In a shop, a box of 6 eggs from chickens that were free to roam outside (free range eggs) costs £1.80 and a box of 6 intensively farmed ones costs £1.

a) Why do the free range eggs cost more to buy?

b) Why might someone still choose to buy the free range eggs instead of the intensively farmed ones?

Human Impact on the Environment

☐ That the human population of the world is rising and that standard of living is also increasing.

☐ That as these things increase, we will produce more waste — which could lead to more pollution if it's not properly handled.

☐ That waste can pollute water (e.g. sewage and chemicals used in industry and farming can enter water), land (e.g. toxic chemicals can be used in farming) and air (e.g. smoke and gases, including sulfur dioxide can be released by industry).

☐ That sulfur dioxide can cause acid rain.

☐ That humans use land for building, quarrying, farming and dumping waste, and that this leaves less room for other animals and plants.

Deforestation and the Destruction of Peat Bogs

☐ That deforestation (the cutting down of forests) is done to provide timber and produce paper.

☐ That deforestation is also done to clear land for farming. This is important to provide more food (e.g. from rice fields and cattle) and to grow crops to produce biofuels based on ethanol.

☐ How deforestation to grow rice or farm cattle can lead to an increase in the amount of methane in the atmosphere.

☐ How deforestation reduces biodiversity, increases the amount of carbon dioxide released into the atmosphere and reduces the amount of carbon dioxide locked up in wood.

☐ That carbon dioxide is released into the atmosphere when peat bogs are destroyed and that buying peat-free compost can help to reduce the destruction of peat bogs.

Carbon Dioxide and the Greenhouse Effect

☐ That carbon dioxide is sequestered (stored) in lakes, seas and oceans, removing it from the atmosphere.

☐ That atmospheric levels of the greenhouse gases carbon dioxide and methane are rising, and that this is contributing to global warming and climate change.

Climate Change

☐ That global warming is a type of climate change and can lead to other types of climate change.

☐ That global warming is causing sea water to expand and ice to melt, causing the sea level to rise.

☐ That global warming can affect the distribution of organisms, as well as the migration patterns of animals such as birds.

☐ That if organisms can't survive and adapt to changes caused by global warming they could die out, reducing the biodiversity of the Earth.

☐ How to analyse and evaluate environmental data and the methods used to collect it.

cont...

Biofuels

☐ That biofuels are fuels made from the fermentation of natural products by microorganisms.

☐ That biogas is a type of biofuel that's mainly made up of methane.

☐ That biogas is made from the anaerobic fermentation of plant material and animal waste containing carbohydrates.

Using Biogas Generators

☐ How to evaluate the use of biogas generators on both a small and a large scale — including taking into account factors such as cost, convenience, efficiency and position.

☐ How climatic conditions (i.e. temperature) can affect biogas production.

☐ Know what some of the benefits of using biogas generators and biofuels might be.

Managing Food Production

☐ That there's less energy and less biomass every time you move up a stage in a food chain.

☐ That for the same sized plot of land, more food can be produced growing crops than grazing animals because there are fewer stages in the food chain.

☐ That reducing the number of stages in a food chain means that less energy is lost overall, and that this idea can be used in food production to help produce food more efficiently.

☐ That intensively farmed animals (also known as factory farmed animals) are kept inside in enclosed and often small houses, so that they lose less energy moving about and keeping warm. This means the efficiency of food production is increased as they'll grow bigger on less food.

☐ That declining fish stocks can be conserved by using fish quotas and limiting net sizes — this is an example of sustainable food production.

Modern Food Production and Distribution

☐ That the fungus *Fusarium* can be grown in aerobic fermenters using glucose syrup as its food source. The mycoprotein can then be harvested, purified, and used as a protein-rich food source, which is suitable for vegetarians.

☐ How to evaluate the different methods of providing food to an increasing human population.

☐ The pros and cons of intensive (factory) farming — it helps to feed an increasing human population relatively cheaply, but there are costs to animal welfare and the environment.

☐ That because the world population is rising, we have to produce more food and this means we have to compromise when choosing what methods to use to provide food.

☐ How to evaluate the pros and cons of managing the production of food.

☐ What food miles are and the implications of food miles.

☐ How to evaluate the pros and cons of managing food distribution.

☐ How to evaluate different methods of providing water to the increasing human population.

1   The graph shows the number of biogas generators found in a developing country between 1994 and 2000. In 1997 the government of the country announced a scheme to help pay for the building of small biogas generators in villages across the countryside.

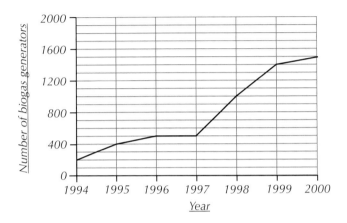

1 (a)   Explain fully what 'biogas' is.

(3 marks)

1 (b) (i)   By how much did the number of biogas generators in the country increase from 1994 to 2000?

(1 mark)

1 (b) (ii)   What effect did the government scheme have on the number of generators? Use data from the graph to support your answer.

(4 marks)

Biogas is a type of biofuel. In some countries large areas of rainforest have been cut down to provide land to grow crops to make biofuels.

1 (c)   Explain the effect clearing rainforests has on biodiversity.

(2 marks)

2   The human population is rising and standard of living is also generally increasing. This is leading to increased levels of water, land and air pollution.

In this question you will be assessed on the quality of your English, the organisation of your ideas and your use of appropriate specialist vocabulary.

Explain how human activities can cause water, land and air pollution.

(6 marks)

3   A charity is trying to encourage people to adopt a vegetarian diet for just one day each week to help the environment.

The table shows the amount the charity think this could save of various resources.

Resource	Amount saved per person per week (by not eating meat for one day)
Water	5500 L
Grain	1.5 kg
Land	12 m²
Fossil Fuel	1.6 L

3 (a) (i)   How many litres (L) of fossil fuel may be saved by one person eating vegetarian food one day a week for a whole year?

(1 mark)

3 (a) (ii)   Burning fossil fuels releases carbon dioxide into the atmosphere.
This is contributing to global warming.
Give **three** possible consequences of global warming.

(3 marks)

3 (b)   Using land to produce vegetables is more efficient than using land to grow animals.
Complete the following sentences.

Energy is .... at every stage in a food chain. So growing crops for food is

more efficient than raising animals because there are .... stages in the

food chain.

(2 marks)

3 (c)   Eating less meat could save 1.5 kg of grain per week.
Suggest why eating less meat saves grain.

(2 marks)

Some people choose to be vegetarians because they don't agree with the intensive farming of animals for food.

3 (d) (i)   Suggest **two** reasons why people might object to intensive farming practices.

(2 marks)

3 (d) (ii)   Explain the benefits of intensive farming.

(3 marks)

1. Controlled Assessment Structure

To get your GCSE, you'll need to do a controlled assessment as well as all your exams. This section tells you all about the controlled assessment and what you'll have to do.

Tip: There's loads of information in the How Science Works section that'll help you with your controlled assessment so have a look at pages 1-15 before you get started.

What is the controlled assessment?

The controlled assessment is a type of test that you'll sit during your Biology lessons at school. The assessment is known as an **investigative skills assessment (ISA)** and it'll involve doing some research and some practical work, as well as answering some questions on an exam paper. The controlled assessment is designed to test your How Science Works skills, not your knowledge and understanding of specific topics. So it's a good chance for you to show that you're really good at science and not just good at memorising facts.

What you'll have to do

There are five things that you'll need to do as part of the controlled assessment:

- First of all, you'll be given the outline of an investigation and you'll have to go away, come up with a hypothesis and plan an experiment.

- Next you'll have to sit an exam paper which will ask you questions about the research that you've done and the method you've chosen.

- Then you'll actually get to carry out the experiment that you've planned (or a similar one) and record some results.

- Once you've done the experiment you'll be given some time to process the data that you've got — you'll get to calculate some averages and draw some pretty graphs.

- Finally, you'll do another exam paper which will ask you questions about your experiment, your results and your conclusions, and ask you to compare your method and results to other people's and to case studies that you'll see.

Figure 1: *A student conducting an experiment.*

What is the controlled assessment worth?

Tip: The controlled assessment might feel more informal, but you should take it just as seriously as all your other exams.

The controlled assessment is worth 25% of the total marks for your GCSE. It is just as important as the other exams you'll do, even though you're doing some (or all) of it in class and not in an exam hall. Don't worry though, there's loads of stuff over the next few pages to help you prepare.

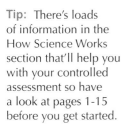

2. Planning and Research

The first step of the controlled assessment is to do some research and plan your experiment. Here's what you need to know...

What you'll be told

At the very beginning of your controlled assessment, your teacher will give you the context of an investigation. This context will usually be a problem that a scientist might come across out in the real world.

> **Example**
>
> The context for your investigation could be something like:
>
> **"A drug company is developing a new antacid (a drug used to treat indigestion). The company wants to know how pH affects the rate of protein digestion catalysed by the enzyme pepsin. This could help them to create an antacid that is effective at treating indigestion, but that doesn't affect the digestion of proteins in the stomach too much."**

What you need to do

Once you've been told the context of your investigation, you'll need to do some research, then come up with a hypothesis and two possible methods for an experiment to solve the problem that's been outlined. You should also research the context of the experiment a bit, so you understand why your investigation will be useful.

> **Tip:** You need to research two methods that you could use to investigate the problem, but you only need to look into one in detail.

> **Example**
>
> If you were given the context in the example above, you'd need to do a bit of research to find out the following:
>
> - How you would expect pH to affect the digestion of protein catalysed by pepsin — this'll let you come up with a suitable hypothesis.
>
> - What experiments you could do to investigate the effect of pH on the digestion of protein catalysed by pepsin — this'll involve finding a suitable reaction to use and finding a way of measuring the rate of protein digestion catalysed by pepsin.
>
> You also need to make sure you fully understand why it's useful to know how pH affects the digestion of protein catalysed by the enzyme pepsin.

> **Tip:** Although your teacher will give you a context for the experiment, you'll have to do all the research on your own.

When you're researching your method you need to think about what **hazards** might be associated with the experiment and what you need to do to make sure your experiment is a **fair test** (there's more on this on page 304). You should also think about what equipment you'll need and what recordings you'll need to make.

> **Tip:** You might be given time to do your planning research in a lesson or you might be given it to do for homework.

Where to find information

There are lots of places where you can find information. Textbooks are an excellent place to start. Your teacher might be able to provide these or you could get some from the library. The internet can also be an excellent source of information.

Exam Tip
As you're doing your research, think about why you've found a particular source useful. Was the explanation really clear? Or was there a helpful diagram? You could get asked about this in the exam.

When you're doing your research, make sure you look at a variety of resources — not just one book or website. Also, make sure you jot down exactly where you've found your information. You will be asked about the research you've done in your first ISA test and just saying you used 'a textbook' or 'the internet' won't be good enough — you'll need to give the names of any textbooks and their authors, and the names of any websites that you used.

How to write a good hypothesis

Tip: See page 1 for lots more on hypotheses.

Writing a really good hypothesis is important at this stage in the controlled assessment. A hypothesis is a specific statement about the things that you'll be testing and the result you're expecting to get.

Examples

These are all hypotheses:

- There is a link between the environmental carbon dioxide concentration and the rate of photosynthesis in a plant.

- Drinking a sports drink following a period of prolonged exercise will rehydrate you faster than just drinking water.

- The higher the wind speed, the faster the transpiration rate in a plant.

Tip: The independent variable is the factor you'll change, the dependent variable is the factor that you'll measure.

To get good marks for your hypothesis you need to make sure it's clear and that it includes an independent and a dependent variable.

Example

If the context of your investigation was finding out how pH affects the rate of protein digestion catalysed by pepsin (see previous page), your hypothesis could be:

"If pH increases, the rate of protein digestion catalysed by the enzyme pepsin will decrease."

This hypothesis is clear and the key variables (pH and the rate of protein digestion catalysed by pepsin) have been identified.

Your hypothesis should be based on the information that you have researched.

If you research antacids, you will find that they increase the pH of the stomach. If you research pepsin and protein digestion, you should find that pepsin works best in quite acidic conditions (around pH 2). This is good justification for the hypothesis that if pH increases, the rate of protein digestion catalysed by the enzyme pepsin will decrease.

Taking notes

As you're doing your research, you need to make some notes. You'll be given a sheet of A4 paper on which to make your notes and you'll be able to take these notes into your ISA tests with you — so it's in your interest to make them top notch. This example shows you what your notes sheet might look like and highlights the kind of notes you might make.

Hypothesis: If pH increases, the rate of protein digestion catalysed by the enzyme pepsin will decrease.
Research Sources: The Science of Digestion by M. Hungary. Published by RVN (no diagram, but control variables listed).   www.biofactopedia.com/enzymes (good diagram)
Method(s):   Add egg white suspension to solutions of different pHs (measure the pH using a pH meter). Add pepsin solution and start the stopwatch.   Time how long it takes for the cloudy solution to go clear. Do 2 repeats.   Fair test: use the same volumes of pepsin solution and egg white suspension in each test tube. Carry out each test at the same temperature.
Equipment: Test tubes   Measuring cylinders   Egg white suspension   Stopwatch   pH meter   1% pepsin solution   Pipettes   1 M hydrochloric acid (pH 0)   Acidic buffer (pH 2)   Acidic buffer (pH 6)   Acidic buffer (pH 4)   Alkaline buffer (pH 8)   Water bath
Risk Assessment Issues: Hydrochloric acid can burn if it touches the skin. Buffers and enzymes may irritate the skin. Wear gloves and goggles.
Relating the investigation to the context: If increasing the pH does decrease the rate of protein digestion catalysed by pepsin, then the drug company should try to adjust the antacids to produce a pH which relieves indigestion, but that doesn't affect protein digestion in the stomach too much.

Tip: You shouldn't write a really detailed method at this stage — in fact, your notes will be checked before you go into the ISA tests to make sure you've not gone into too much detail. Just jot down the main points of the method(s) you could use to help jog your memory.

Tip: You will need to explain how you are making your experiment a fair test in the first ISA test, so you should have researched the variables that will need to be controlled and the ways you will control them — making a <u>brief</u> note of them here.

3. Section 1 of the ISA Test

After you've done your planning, you'll do Section 1 of the ISA test. This asks you questions about the research that you've done and the method you'll use.

Hypotheses and variables

Exam Tip
You're allowed to take one A4 page of your research notes into the ISA test with you.

In Section 1 of the ISA test you'll be asked to give your hypothesis and explain how you'll test it. Your hypothesis should include an independent variable and a dependent variable. You could be asked to identify these.

> **Example**
>
> In my investigation, the independent variable is the pH of the test solution and the dependent variable is the time it takes for the test solution to go clear (i.e. for the egg white protein to be digested).

Have a look at page 6 to help you work out what the different variables in your experiment are.

You could also be asked to explain why you made this hypothesis. If so, you need to give reasons that are backed up by facts from your research.

How to write a good method

In this part of the assessment you'll almost certainly be asked to write down a description of the method you're going to use to test your hypothesis. You need to give a clear and detailed description of how you would carry out your experiment. You must remember to include things like:

1. A list of all the equipment you're going to need.

2. A logical, step-by-step guide as to what you're going to do, including an explanation of what you're going to measure and how you're going to measure it.

Exam Tip
You need to make sure you use correct spelling, punctuation and grammar too, otherwise you won't get full marks.

3. What control variables you're going to regulate and how you're going to regulate them.

4. What hazards there are and how you're going to make sure the experiment is safe.

1. The equipment list

Your method should start with a list of the equipment that you'll need.

> **Example**
>
> To do the experiment into the effect of pH on the rate of protein digestion catalysed by pepsin, you'd need the following equipment:
>
> - Some 1 M hydrochloric acid, acidic buffer (pH 2), acidic buffer (pH 4), acidic buffer (pH 6) and alkaline buffer (pH 8) for changing the pH of the test solution.

- Measuring cylinders for measuring out the above solutions.
- 15 test tubes.
- Some egg white suspension (substrate) and 1% pepsin solution (enzyme).
- Pipettes to measure out the pepsin solution and the egg white suspension.
- A water bath to control the temperature.
- A pH meter to measure the pHs of the test solutions.
- A stopwatch to measure the time it takes for the test mixture to go clear.

Tip: You can include a labelled diagram of the apparatus you're going to use if you want to, but you don't have to.

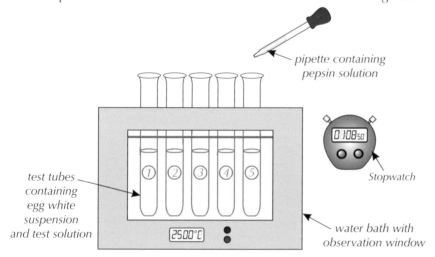

pipette containing pepsin solution

Stopwatch

test tubes containing egg white suspension and test solution

water bath with observation window

Figure 1: *Diagram of some of the equipment needed for this investigation.*

2. Describing the method

Once you've written your equipment list, you should then write down exactly what you're going to do, listing the steps in the order that you're going to do them. Here's an example of a method.

Tip: It's OK to give your method as a numbered list — this is an easy way to make sure you cover all the points in the right order.

Example

1. Use measuring cylinders to measure out 5 ml each of 1 M hydrochloric acid, acidic buffer (pH 2), acidic buffer (pH 4), acidic buffer (pH 6) and alkaline buffer (pH 8), and place each solution into a separate test tube.

2. Label each test tube accordingly, then put them in a water bath set to 25 °C.

3. Use a pipette to add 5 ml of egg white suspension to each test tube.

4. Measure (and then record) the pH of each test tube using the pH meter.

5. Then, use the pipette to add 10 ml of pepsin solution to the first test tube and simultaneously start the stopwatch.

6. Time how long it takes for the solution in the test tube to go clear.

7. Repeat steps 5 and 6 for each test tube.

8. Record the results in a table.

9. Repeat the whole experiment twice more and average the results.

Tip: Never just say you're going to do something. Always say how you're going to do it. E.g. don't just say you're going to measure the pH — say you're going to measure the pH using a pH meter.

Tip: Don't forget to repeat your experiment. This will allow you to spot anomalous results more easily and let you calculate means, which will make your results more accurate and reduce the impact of errors.

3. Controlling the variables

To make your experiment a **fair test**, you need to make sure you control all of the variables. In your method, you'll probably be asked how you're going to do this.

Tip: There's more on fair tests and controlling variables on pages 6-7.

Example

In my experiment, the control variables are the temperature the experiment is carried out at, the volume of pepsin solution used and the volume of the egg white suspension. I will control the temperature using a water bath and keep the volumes of pepsin solution and egg white suspension the same for each test.

Things that you might need to watch out for in other experiments include things like keeping the concentrations of the reactants the same and allowing reactions to continue for the same length of time.

4. Hazards

There will always be hazards associated with any experiment. In your plan you should identify these hazards and say how you're going to reduce any risk.

Example

In my experiment, the main hazard is the use of hydrochloric acid, which is corrosive and can burn the skin. Also the buffers and pepsin solution are irritants, so when doing this experiment safety goggles and gloves should be worn to protect the eyes and skin.

There are lots of other hazards that you might need to watch out for. See page 8 for more.

Figure 1: *Students wearing safety goggles.*

Method selection

During your research you will have investigated at least two methods that you could use. You may be asked to explain why you chose the method you did. Think about things like equipment choices, whether it is practical to do in class, how long it'll take to do and anything else that made you choose it.

Preliminary investigations

In this part of the test, you could be asked how a preliminary investigation (or a trial run) could have been useful. Trial runs are useful for working out what range of values would be best to use and the intervals between the values.

Tip: See pages 7-8 for lots more information on trial runs and why they are useful.

Example

In this experiment, a trial run could have been useful to:

- Work out the amount of pepsin solution and egg white suspension to use, in order to make sure the reaction happens quickly enough. This would involve testing a range of volumes to see which ones give a good reaction speed — you don't want to be waiting around forever.

- Work out how long to watch the reaction for — e.g. if it looks likely that the test solution isn't going to go clear at all, a sensible amount of time to wait for must be decided.

Table of results

In this part of the test, you will also need to draw a table for your results that you can fill in when you do the experiment. There are a few things to remember when drawing tables of results:

- Make sure you include enough rows and columns to record all of the data you need to. You might also need to include a column for processing your data (e.g. working out an average).

- Make sure you give each column a heading so you know what's going to be recorded where.

- Make sure you include units for all your measurements.

Here's an example of a jolly good table for results.

Tip: You don't have to draw your table of results by hand — you can use a computer instead.

Example

Test tube	Test solution	Repeat	pH	Time taken for test solution to go clear (mins)	Mean time taken for test solution to go clear (mins)
1	Hydrochloric acid (pH 0)	1			
		2			
		3			
2	Acidic buffer (pH 2)	1			
		2			
		3			
3	Acidic buffer (pH 4)	1			
		2			
		3			
4	Acidic buffer (pH 6)	1			
		2			
		3			
5	Alkaline buffer (pH 8)	1			
		2			
		3			

Tip: Your table for results won't look exactly like this one. For example, you might need more or fewer rows and columns depending on what kind of data you're collecting.

4. Doing the Experiment

If your plan isn't too outrageous, you'll then get to actually do the experiment you've planned. So grab your safety goggles and your lab coat...

Tip: If you're given an alternative method it doesn't necessarily mean your method was bad — it could be that your teacher thinks there are too many different methods in the class or that your school doesn't have the right equipment for you.

Good laboratory practice

When it comes to actually doing the investigation, you might be allowed to do the one you planned, or you might be given another method to use by your teacher. When you're doing your experiment it's important that you use good laboratory practice. This means working safely and accurately.
To ensure you get good results, make sure you do the following:

- Measure all your quantities carefully — the more accurately you measure things the more accurate your results will be.

- Try to be consistent — for example, if you need to stir something, stir every sample for the same length of time.

- Don't let yourself get distracted by other people — if you're distracted by what other people are doing you're more likely to make a mistake or miss a reading.

As you're going along, make sure you remember to fill in your table of results — it's no good doing a perfect experiment if you forget to record the data.

Figure 1: *A student working in a laboratory.*

Tip: See pages 11-13 for more on processing your results and calculating averages.

Tip: Your graph will be marked along with your exam papers so make sure it's nice and neat and all your axes are properly labelled.

Processing your results

Once you've got your data you might need to process it. This could involve calculating the mean (by adding all your data together and dividing by the number of values) or working out a change in something (by subtracting the start reading from the end reading).

Then you'll need to plot your data on a graph. It's up to you what type of graph you use. See pages 12-13 for more information on how to draw a good graph.

Things to think about

As you're doing the experiment there are some things you need to think about:

- Is the equipment you're using good enough?
- Is there anything you would do differently if you could do the experiment again?
- Have you got any anomalous results (see page 10) and, if so, can you think what might have gone wrong?
- Do the results you've got support your initial hypothesis?

These are all things that you could get asked about in the second part of your ISA, so it's a good idea to think about them while the experiment is still fresh in your mind.

5. Section 2 of the ISA Test

Once you've done your experiment and processed the results it's time for the final part of your controlled assessment — Section 2 of the ISA test.

Making conclusions

In Section 2 of the ISA test you will be asked to draw conclusions about your data. You could be asked what your data shows, or whether it supports your initial hypothesis. When drawing conclusions it's important to back them up with data from your results. You should describe the general trend(s) in the data, but also quote specific numerical values.

Tip: Remember, there's loads of information on processing data and making conclusions in the How Science Works section. Make sure you are really familiar with pages 11-15 before you go into your ISA tests.

Example

"Do your results support your initial hypothesis?"

Yes, because the general pattern of results was that as pH increased, the time it took for the test solution to go clear also increased. For example, when using acidic buffer (pH 2), the average time it took for the test solution to go clear was 6.50 minutes, whereas when using alkaline buffer (pH 8), the test solution still hadn't gone clear after 20 minutes. So overall, increasing the pH decreased the rate of protein digestion catalysed by the enzyme pepsin.

Tip: It doesn't matter if the answer to this question is yes or no — the important thing is that your results support your conclusion.

Comparing results

In Section 2 of the test you will probably be asked to compare your results with the results of other people in your class. This lets you see what similarities or differences there are between sets of results, and allows you to determine if your results are reproducible. If everyone in the class did the same experiment and got similar results to you, then your experiment is reproducible. If everyone got different results to you, your results aren't reproducible. It's OK to say your results aren't reproducible, though you should try to suggest why they weren't. And as always, back up anything you say by quoting some data.

Tip: Sharing results with the rest of your class gives you more data to calculate means from, which will make them more accurate.

Improving your method

In this part of the assessment, you might be given the opportunity to evaluate the experiment — in other words, to say how you would improve the experiment if you did it again.

Tip: When suggesting an improvement to the method, it's really important that you explain how the improvement would give you better data next time.

Example

- You could say that it would be better to use equipment with a higher resolution, so you could detect smaller changes and get more precise results.

- You could say that you'd carry out more repeats to check the repeatability and increase the accuracy of the results.

- You could say that you'd use a better technique (e.g. using a mechanical stirrer to ensure that the water in the water bath was at the same temperature throughout) to help make your experiment a fair test.

Tip: See page 9 for more on resolution.

Anomalous results

Tip: See page 10 for more information on anomalous results.

You could be asked whether or not there are any anomalous results in your data. Anomalous results are results that don't seem to fit with the rest of the data. If you're asked about anomalous results make sure you quote the result and explain why you think it is anomalous.

> **Example**
>
> I think the time it took for the test solution to go clear for acidic buffer (pH 4) at repeat 2 (4.5 minutes) was an anomalous result because it doesn't seem to fit with the rest of the data (it's too fast).

If you don't have any anomalous results, that's fine — just make sure you explain why you're sure none of your results are anomalous.

Tip: You could also be asked to suggest a reason for an anomalous result, e.g. in this case too little egg white suspension could have been added by mistake.

> **Example**
>
> I don't think there were any anomalous results in my data. An anomalous result is one that doesn't seem to fit with the rest of the data and all of my data points were very close to the line of best fit when plotted on a graph.

Analysing other data sources

In this final part of the controlled assessment you won't only get asked about your own data. You'll also be given some case studies to look at and be asked to analyse that data as well. You could be asked to compare this data to your own data and point out similarities and differences. Or you could be asked whether this data supports or contradicts your hypothesis.

Exam Tip
The important thing when analysing other data sources is to read the question carefully and make sure you answer it — don't just describe the data without referring back to the original question.

As with making conclusions about your own data, when you're answering questions about these secondary sources it's crucial that you quote specific pieces of data from the source. You shouldn't blindly trust the data in these sources either — you should think as critically about this data as you did about your own data. Don't assume that it's better than yours and be on the look out for mistakes.

Applying your results to a context

Another thing you could be asked to do is explain how your results can be applied to a particular context. This means thinking of a practical application of what you've found out. You should have done some research on this in the planning part of the controlled assessment. You can use the notes you made then to help you answer questions like this.

> **Example**
>
> We found out that, overall, increasing the pH decreased the rate of protein digestion catalysed by the enzyme pepsin. Applying this to the context of antacids — if an antacid causes the pH of the stomach to rise too high, it could affect the digestion of proteins in the stomach. A drug company could use this information to produce an antacid that creates a pH of around 3-4. This would increase the pH of the stomach, which would help relieve indigestion, but wouldn't decrease the rate of protein digestion too much.

1. The Exams

Unfortunately, to get your GCSE you'll need to sit some exams. And that's what this page is about — what to expect in your exams.

Assessment for GCSE Biology

To get your GCSE in Biology you'll have to do some exams that test your knowledge of biology and How Science Works. All the content that you need to know is in this book — there's even a dedicated How Science Works section on pages 1-15.

You'll also have to do a Controlled Assessment (also known as an 'ISA'). There's more about this on pages 298-308.

The exams

You'll sit three separate exams — remember that you could be asked questions on How Science Works in any of them. You're allowed to use a calculator in all of your GCSE Biology exams, so make sure you've got one.

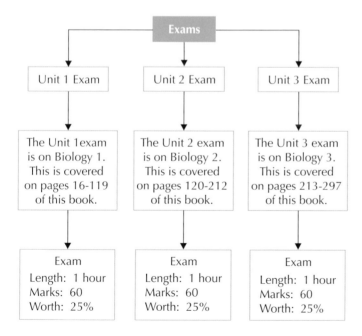

> **Exam Tip**
> Make sure you have a good read through these pages. It might not seem all that important now but you don't want to get any surprises just before an exam.

> **Exam Tip**
> If you're taking GCSE Science A, GCSE Additional Science or GCSE Further Additional Science, there's more information about what your exams will cover on the next page.

> **Exam Tip**
> As well as the exams, you'll have to do some research and carry out a practical investigation for your controlled assessment. There's more about this coming up on the next page.

Other GCSE Science qualifications

GCSE Science A

If you're taking GCSE Science A, your exams will cover everything in Biology 1 (as well as Chemistry 1 and Physics 1). All of the biology that you'll need to study for GCSE Science A is covered in the Biology 1 sections of this book (see pages 16-119).

(see pages 16-119)

GCSE Additional Science

If you're taking GCSE Additional Science, your exams will cover everything in Biology 2 (as well as Chemistry 2 and Physics 2). All of the biology that you'll need to study for GCSE Additional Science is covered in the Biology 2 sections of this book (see pages 120-212).

(see pages 120-212)

GCSE Further Additional Science

If you're taking GCSE Further Additional Science, your exams will cover everything in Biology 3 (as well as Chemistry 3 and Physics 3). All of the biology that you'll need to study for GCSE Further Additional Science is covered in the Biology 3 sections of this book (see pages 213-297).

(see pages 213-297)

Exam Tip
Remember, whichever science GCSEs you're taking, any exam could include questions on How Science Works.

Controlled assessment (ISA)

As well as your exams, you'll have to do a controlled assessment. The controlled assessment involves a test made up of two sections, which will be based on a practical investigation that you've researched, planned and carried out.

Exam Tip
It doesn't matter which exams you're taking — everyone has to do a controlled assessment.

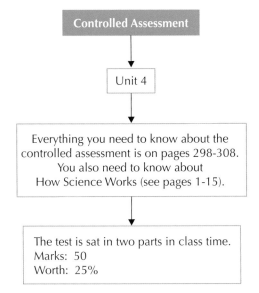

Controlled Assessment

Unit 4

Everything you need to know about the controlled assessment is on pages 298-308. You also need to know about How Science Works (see pages 1-15).

The test is sat in two parts in class time.
Marks: 50
Worth: 25%

Exam Tip
As well as the test, you'll have to do some research and carry out a practical investigation for your controlled assessment.

2. Exam Technique

Knowing the science is vitally important when it comes to passing your exams. But having good exam technique will also help. So here are some handy hints on how to squeeze every mark you possibly can out of those examiners.

Time management

Good time management is one of the most important exam skills to have — you need to think about how much time to spend on each question. Check out the length of your exams (you'll find them on page 309 and on the front of your exam papers). These timings give you about 1 minute per mark. Try to stick to this to give yourself the best chance to get as many marks as possible.

Don't spend ages struggling with a question if you're finding it hard to answer — move on. You can come back to it later when you've bagged loads of other marks elsewhere. Also, you might find that some questions need a lot of work for only a few marks, while others are much quicker — so if you're short of time, answer the quick and easy questions first.

Exam Tip
If a question is only worth 1 mark, don't waste time writing more than you need to.

Example

The questions below are both worth the same number of marks but require different amounts of work.

1 **(a)** What name is given to the tissue that covers the leaf?

(1 mark)

2 **(a)** By reading the information above and looking at the diagram, suggest **one** way in which the structure of a motor neurone cell helps it to carry out its function.

(1 mark)

Question 1 (a) only asks you to write down the name of a tissue — if you can remember it this shouldn't take you too long.

Question 2 (a) asks you to make a suggestion about something you don't already know the answer to. Since you need to interpret some information and a diagram, and then apply your existing scientific knowledge to work out your answer, it may take you a bit longer than just writing down a name.

So, if you're running out of time it makes sense to do questions like 1 (a) first and come back to 2 (a) if you've got time at the end.

Exam Tip
Don't forget to go back and do any questions that you left the first time round — you don't want to miss out on marks because you forgot to do the question.

Making educated guesses

Make sure you answer all the questions that you can — don't leave any blank if you can avoid it. If a question asks you to tick a box, circle a word or draw lines between boxes, you should never, ever leave it blank, even if you're short on time. It only takes a second or two to answer these questions, and even if you're not absolutely sure what the answer is you can have a good guess.

Exam Tip
If you're asked, for example, to tick two boxes, make sure you only tick two. If you tick more than two, you won't get the marks even if some of your answers are correct.

Example

Look at the question below.

1 (a) Which of the following are illegal drugs? Tick **two** boxes.

Cannabis ☐ Statins ☐

Nicotine ☐ Heroin ☐

(2 marks)

Say you knew that heroin was illegal, and that nicotine was in cigarettes, but weren't sure about the other two drugs.

You can tick heroin — you know it's illegal. If nicotine is in cigarettes then it must be legal, so leave that box blank. That leaves you with cannabis and statins. If you're not absolutely sure which is legal and which isn't, just have a guess. You won't lose any marks if you get it wrong and there's a 50% chance that you'll get it right.

Command words

Command words are just the bits of a question that tell you what to do. You'll find answering exam questions much easier if you understand exactly what they mean, so here's a brief summary of the most common ones:

Exam Tip
When you're reading an exam question, you might find it helpful to underline the command words. It can help you work out what type of answer to give.

Command word:	What to do:
Give / Name / State / Write down	Give a brief one or two word answer, or a short sentence.
Complete	Write your answer in the space given. This could be a gap in a sentence or table, or you might have to finish a diagram.
Describe	Write about what something's like, e.g. describe the trend in a set of results.
Explain	Make something clear, or give the reasons why something happens. The points in your answer need to be linked together, so you should include words like because, so, therefore, due to, etc.
Calculate	Use the numbers in the question to work out an answer.
Suggest	Use your scientific knowledge to work out what the answer might be.
Compare	Give the similarities and differences between two things.
Evaluate	Give the arguments both for and against an issue, or the advantages and disadvantages of something. You may also need to give an overall judgement.

Exam Tip
It's easy to get describe and explain mixed up, but they're quite different. For example, if you're asked to describe some data, just state the overall pattern or trend. If you're asked to explain data, you'll need to give reasons for the trend.

Some questions will also ask you to answer 'using the information provided' (e.g. a graph, table or passage of text) — if so, you must refer to the information you've been given or you won't get the marks.

3. Question Types

If all questions were the same, exams would be mightily boring. So really, it's quite handy that there are lots of different question types. Here are just a few...

Quality of written communication (QWC)

All of the exams you take for your GCSE will have at least one 6 mark question that assesses your quality of written communication — this just means that the examiner will assess your ability to write properly. This may seem like a bit of a drag, but you will lose marks if you don't do it. Here are some tips on how to get all the marks you can...

- Make sure your scribble (sorry, writing) is legible.

- Be careful with your spelling, punctuation and grammar — they need to be accurate.

- Make sure your writing style is appropriate for an exam. You need to write in full sentences and use fairly formal language. For example, the sentence "the build up of lactic acid causes muscle fatigue" is an appropriate style. "Loads of lactic acid makes your muscles dead tired" isn't — it's too informal.

- Organise your answer clearly. The points you make need to be in a logical order.

- Use specialist scientific vocabulary whenever you can. For example, if you're describing a reflex you'd need to use scientific terms like sensory neurone and motor neurone. You also need to use these terms correctly — it's no good knowing the words if you don't know what they mean.

You'll be told which questions will be used to assess the quality of your written communication. On the front of your exam paper it will say something like 'Question 2 should be answered in continuous prose' — and that's the question where your writing will be assessed. There'll also be a reminder when you get to the question itself. It'll say something like:

In this question you will be assessed on the quality of your English, the organisation of your ideas and your use of appropriate specialist vocabulary.

Evaluating information

In the exam, you may be given some information to read and then be asked to evaluate it.

Example

Drug X and drug Y are both weight-loss drugs. You may be given some information on how drug X and drug Y work, how effective they are and what side effects they have. You could then be asked to evaluate the use of drug X and drug Y in aiding weight loss.

Exam Tip
You'll need to use black ink or a black ball-point pen to write your answers, so make sure that you've got a couple ready for the exam.

Exam Tip
Make sure you write enough to get all the marks that are available. QWC questions are worth six marks, so a one sentence answer won't be enough — you'll need to write at least a paragraph or two.

Exam Tip
You should really be doing these things all the way through your exam — they're just particularly important on the QWC questions, so it's worth taking special care with them there.

In the previous example, you're basically being asked to compare the use of the two types of drug — including the advantages and disadvantages of each. This means you need to do more than just pick out relevant information from the question and repeat it in your answer — you need to make clear comparisons between the two.

> **Example**
>
> If the information tells you that people taking drug X lose 1 kilogram per week on average and that people taking drug Y lose 1.5 kilograms per week on average, you need to say in your answer that "people taking drug Y lose **more** weight per week on average than people taking drug X". It's even better to say that "people taking drug Y lose **0.5 kilograms more** weight per week on average than people taking drug X".

The question may ask you to write a conclusion too, e.g. make an overall judgement about which drug is best. If so, you must include a conclusion in your answer and you must back it up with evidence from the question.

Calculations

Questions that involve a calculation can seem a bit scary. But they're really not that bad. Here are some tips to help you out...

Figure 1: *A calculator. Under the pressure of an exam it's easy to make mistakes in calculations, even if they're really simple ones. So don't be afraid to put every calculation into the calculator.*

- Show your working — this is the most important thing to remember. It only takes a few seconds more to write down what's in your head and it might stop you from making silly errors and losing out on easy marks. You won't get a mark for a wrong answer, but you could get marks for the method you used to work out the answer.

- Check your answer — a good way to do this is to work backwards through your calculation. You should also think about whether your answer seems sensible — if it's a much bigger or smaller number than you were expecting, you might have gone wrong somewhere.

> **Example**
>
> A potato chip weighs 10.2 g at the start of the experiment. At the end of the experiment it weighs 11.6 g. To calculate the change in mass, you'd subtract 10.2 g from 11.6 g — which works out as 1.4 g. You'd expect the answer to be around 1 g, so this seems sensible. To check it though, just add 1.4 to 10.2 — you should end up with 11.6.

- Sometimes you'll be asked to pick some numbers out of a table or read values off a graph to use in your calculation. If so, always read the question carefully so you know exactly what figures you need to use. Make sure you read the headings in the table carefully too (or the axes on the graph) to make sure you understand what's being shown.

Exam Tip
These aren't the only calculations you could be asked to do in an exam — they're just examples of the sort of thing that's likely to come up.

In the exam, you should be prepared to do things like estimate a value, calculate a percentage or a mean, and put numbers into equations that you've been given. Higher students should also be able to rearrange these equations.

Answers

Biology 1

Biology 1.1 Keeping Healthy

1. Diet and Metabolic Rate
Page 18 — Fact Recall Questions
Q1 To release energy.
Q2 To keep your skin, bones, blood and everything else generally healthy.
Q3 Metabolic rate is the speed at which the chemical reactions in your body occur.
Q4 false
There are slight variations in the resting metabolic rate of different people.
Q5 The more active you are, the more energy you use.

Page 18 — Application Questions
Q1 Because the body needs protein for growth, cell repair and cell replacement.
Q2 a) Joe because he does a lot more exercise than Paula, so he's likely to have a lot more muscle / he's a man and Paula's a woman, so he's likely to have a lot more muscle.
   b) Joe because he is more active than Paula.
Q3 a) E.g. because he is more active than the man in the research station, so he will use more energy.
   b) E.g. carbohydrates and fats because they both release energy (and because fats help to keep you warm).

2. Factors Affecting Health
Page 20 — Fact Recall Questions
Q1 That their diet is badly out of balance.
Q2 Excess fat or carbohydrate in the diet can lead to obesity.
Q3 E.g. arthritis / type 2 diabetes / high blood pressure / heart disease.
Q4 true
Q5 Exercise increases the amount of energy used by the body and decreases the amount stored as fat. It also builds muscle so it helps to boost metabolic rate. Therefore people who exercise are less likely to suffer from health problems such as obesity.
Q6 E.g. some people may inherit factors that affect their metabolic rate. Some people may inherit factors that affect their blood cholesterol level.

3. Evaluating Food, Lifestyle and Diet
Page 23 — Application Questions
Q1 a) i) Food A
      ii) Too much high energy food in the diet could lead to obesity.
   b) $1.44 \div 6 \times 100 = \mathbf{24\%}$
   c) Food B because it is lower in fat, saturated fat, salt and calories / because it has more green and orange labels than Food A and no red labels.
Q2 No because, any two from: e.g. the trial was carried out by the manufacturers. / Not enough people were tested in the trial/the sample size wasn't big enough. / Only women were tested in the trial — the milkshake may not be as effective for men. / The manufacturers are relying on the women saying they've lost weight rather than actually measuring their weight loss. / No controls were used, so there was no comparison made between people drinking the slimming milkshake and people trying to lose weight using diet and exercise alone. / The results haven't been reproduced.

4. Fighting Disease
Page 26 — Fact Recall Questions
Q1 E.g. bacteria — cell damage, producing toxins. Viruses — cell damage.
Q2 By engulfing and digesting foreign cells/pathogens. By producing antitoxins. By producing antibodies to lock onto and kill invading cells.
Q3 That if they are infected with that particular pathogen again, their white blood cells will rapidly produce the antibodies to kill it and they won't get ill.

Page 26 — Application Questions
Q1 a) John should now be immune to measles. If he is infected with the measles virus again, his white blood cells should rapidly produce the antibodies against it — meaning he won't get ill.
   b) Antibodies are specific to a particular type of antigen. John has never had German measles before, so he won't have made antibodies against the antigens on the German measles virus. This means it will take his white blood cells time to produce antibodies against the virus, during which he could get ill.
Q2 a) E.g. by releasing toxins. Through cell damage.
   Clostridium tetani actually releases a powerful toxin that causes severe muscle spasms — but you don't need to know that to answer the question. You just need to be able to apply what you already know about how bacteria make you feel ill.
   b) E.g. it uses platelets to help blood clot quickly and seal wounds before *Clostridium tetani* can enter.

5. Fighting Disease — Vaccination
Page 28 — Application Question
Q1 a) A big outbreak of whooping cough.
  b) E.g. the vaccination will involve injecting a small amount of the dead or inactive whooping cough pathogen. The pathogen will carry antigens, which will trigger the white blood cells to produce antibodies to attack the pathogen. If the vaccinated person is infected with the whooping cough pathogen at a later date, their white blood cells should be able to rapidly mass produce antibodies to kill off the pathogen.
  c) If a large percentage of the population are vaccinated it means that the people who aren't vaccinated (i.e. very young babies) are less likely to catch the disease because there are fewer people to pass it on.

6. Fighting Disease — Drugs
Page 30 — Fact Recall Questions
Q1 false
Q2 A drug used to kill or prevent the growth of bacteria. E.g. penicillin / methicillin.
Q3 Different antibiotics kill different types of bacteria, so it's important to be treated with the right one.
Q4 Viruses reproduce using your own body cells, so it's difficult to develop drugs that destroy the virus without killing the body's cells.
Q5 a) E.g. MRSA/methicillin-resistant *Staphylococcus aureus*
    You could get asked about MRSA in your exam, so make sure you know what it is.
  b) natural selection
Q6 It helps to prevent antibiotic resistance from spreading.

Page 30 — Application Questions
Q1 a) Because antibiotics don't destroy viruses.
  b) E.g. because it won't tackle the underlying cause of Chloe's flu (it will only help to relieve her symptoms).
Q2 E.g. because it's important for doctors to avoid over-prescribing antibiotics in order to slow down the development of antibiotic resistance. James' infection is only mild.
Q3 E.g. people with a *Streptococcus pneumoniae* infection may have been treated with penicillin. A mutation may have caused some of these bacteria to be resistant to the penicillin, meaning that only the non-resistant bacteria would have been killed. The individual resistant bacteria would have survived and reproduced, increasing the population of penicillin-resistant *Streptococcus pneumoniae* bacteria.

7. Fighting Disease — Investigating Antibiotic Action
Page 32 — Application Question
Q1 a) i) E.g. by passing it through a flame.
     ii) To avoid contaminating his culture with unwanted microorganisms.
  b) i) 1, 2, 3 and 5. The bacteria were able to grow around these discs.
     ii) Disc 4. This had the largest clear zone around it, so it must have killed the most bacteria.
     iii) E.g. the size of the paper discs. / The concentration of the antibiotics.
  c) To prevent unwanted microorganisms from the air getting into the culture and contaminating it.
  d) Because harmful pathogens aren't likely to grow at this temperature.

8. Fighting Disease — Past & Future
Page 34 — Fact Recall Questions
Q1 That if doctors washed their hands in an antiseptic solution, it cut the death rate of women from puerperal fever in his hospital.
Q2 They have decreased them dramatically.
Q3 They're trying to develop new antibiotics that will be effective against antibiotic-resistant strains of bacteria.

Page 34 — Application Question
Q1 E.g. we'd never encountered the mutated version of the H1N1 virus before, so no one was immune to it. There were also no effective vaccinations/antiviral drugs against it. It may have also been hard to stop it spreading between countries as so many people now travel by plane.

Pages 37-38 — Biology 1.1
Exam-style Questions
1 a) i) $64 \div (1.56^2) = $ **26.3 *(1 mark)***
      ii) overweight *(1 mark)*
   If you got Kate's BMI wrong and this meant you ended up getting her weight description wrong too, don't panic. Providing the weight description you wrote down matches the BMI you gave for part a) i), you can still get the mark here.
   b) releasing energy *(1 mark)*
   c) To lose weight, you need to take in less energy than you use up *(1 mark)*. Exercise helps you to lose weight because it increases the amount of energy you use up *(1 mark)*.
2 a) by damaging your cells *(1 mark)*
   b) i) Robin will be injected with a small amount of dead or inactive hepatitis A virus *(1 mark)*. The virus will carry antigens, which will cause Robin's white blood cells *(1 mark)* to produce antibodies to attack the virus *(1 mark)*. If Robin is infected with the live hepatitis A virus at a later date, his white blood cells should be able to rapidly mass produce antibodies to kill off the virus *(1 mark)*.

ii) Antibodies are specific to a particular type of pathogen *(1 mark)*. This means that the hepatitis A vaccination will not cause Robin to produce antibodies that will be effective against the hepatitis B virus *(1 mark)*.

c) As a virus, hepatitis A will reproduce using the body cells of the person it infects *(1 mark)*. This makes it difficult to develop a drug against the virus without killing the body cells *(1 mark)*.

3 a) A microorganism that causes disease *(1 mark)*.

b) In 1980, there were just over 4 million reported measles cases *(1 mark)*. Between 1980 and 2010 the number of reported measles cases dropped to around 0.4 million (after rising to a peak of 4.5 million in around 1982) *(1 mark)*. The estimated vaccine coverage was around 12% of the population in 1980 *(1 mark)*. Between 1980 and 2010 it increased to around 85% *(1 mark)*.

The question asks you to use data from the graph to support your answer — so you must include some figures to get the marks. The graph has three different axes, which can make things a bit tricky. Take your time and work out what each one shows before answering the question.

c) E.g. the data suggests that as the estimated percentage vaccination coverage increased, the number of reported measles cases decreased — this supports the case for vaccinating people against measles *(1 mark)*. However it doesn't prove that the increase in vaccination coverage definitely caused the decrease in measles cases, since other factors may have been at work *(1 mark)*. It also doesn't tell us anything about the side effects of the vaccine *(1 mark)*.

4 a) Any two from, e.g. heat/sterilise the agar jelly *(1 mark)* / sterilise the inoculating loop before using it, e.g. by passing it through a flame *(1 mark)* / sterilise the Petri dish before using it *(1 mark)*.

b) Antibiotic 5 because this disc has the biggest clear zone around it *(1 mark)*. This means that more bacteria were killed/unable to grow around antibiotic 5 than around any of the other antibiotics / the bacteria were least resistant to antibiotic 5 *(1 mark)*.

It stands to reason that the best antibiotic for getting rid of the infection is the one that kills the most bacteria.

c) E.g. people infected with this bacteria may have been treated with these antibiotics *(1 mark)*. Mutations may have caused some of these bacteria to be resistant to these antibiotics *(1 mark)*, meaning that only the non-resistant bacteria were killed *(1 mark)*. The individual resistant bacteria would have survived and reproduced *(1 mark)*, increasing the population of the resistant strain *(1 mark)*.

Biology 1.2 Nerves and Hormones

1. The Nervous System
Page 41 — Fact Recall Questions
Q1 A change in your environment that you might need to respond to.

Q2 receptors

Q3 the nucleus

Q4 nose and tongue

Q5 glands

Q6 E.g. motor neurones, relay neurones

Page 41 — Application Questions
Q1 a) i) The sound of the cat moving.
    ii) Receptors in the dog's ears that are sensitive to sound.
    iii) sensory neurone
   b) i) motor neurone
    ii) They will contract.

Q2 A loud bang — ears — receptors sensitive to sound
A moving object — eyes — receptors sensitive to light
Walking on a slanted floor — ears — receptors sensitive to changes in position
Touching a hot object — skin — receptors sensitive to changes in temperature
An unpleasant smell — nose — receptors sensitive to chemical stimuli
Standing on a pin — skin — receptors sensitive to pain

2. Synapses and Reflexes
Page 44 — Fact Recall Questions
Q1 a) a synapse
   b) Chemicals diffuse across the gap between the two neurones, which sets off an electrical impulse in the next neurone.

Q2 A reflex is a fast, automatic response to a stimulus.

Q3 No
Reflexes are automatic — you don't have to think about them, so they don't pass through conscious parts of the brain.

Q4 a relay neurone

Q5 The secretion of a hormone from the gland.

Page 44 — Application Question
Q1 a) pain
   b) A muscle in the leg. It contracts, moving the foot away from the source of the pain (the pin).
   c) Stimulus → Receptor → Sensory neurone → Relay neurone → Motor neurone → Effector → Response

3. Homeostasis

Page 46 — Fact Recall Questions
Q1 The maintenance of a constant internal environment.
Q2 To keep it the temperature at which the enzymes in the body work best.
Q3 Through the skin as sweat. Via the kidneys as urine.
Q4 Any three from, e.g. through the skin as sweat / via the lungs in the breath / via the kidneys as urine / via faeces.
Q5 E.g. insulin
Q6 To ensure that the cells get a constant supply of energy.

4. Hormones

Page 48 — Fact Recall Questions
Q1 by the blood (plasma)
Q2 false
    They only affect particular cells, called target cells, in particular places.
Q3 E.g. FSH/follicle stimulating hormone / LH/luteinising hormone
Q4 E.g. oestrogen
Q5 nerves

5. The Menstrual Cycle

Page 51 — Fact Recall Questions
Q1 Causing an egg to mature in one of the ovaries and stimulating the ovaries to produce oestrogen
Q2 oestrogen
Q3 It stimulates the release of an egg at around the middle (day 14) of the menstrual cycle.
Q4 the pituitary gland and the ovaries

Page 51 — Application Question
Q1 a) LH (luteinising hormone). LH is the hormone responsible for stimulating the release of an egg. The concentration of the hormone on the graph increases just before the middle of the cycle (day 14) — the time at which an egg is normally released.
    b) the pituitary gland
    c) LH is needed to stimulate the release of an egg. This woman's LH level peaks at a much lower level than the other woman's, suggesting that she may not be releasing an egg during her menstrual cycle. This could be the reason why she's struggling to have children.

6. Controlling Fertility

Page 54 — Fact Recall Questions
Q1 It inhibits FSH production, which prevents egg maturation and therefore release.
Q2 progesterone
Q3 Large doses of oestrogen were thought to cause a lot more side effects.
Q4 E.g. they don't always work so they may have to used many times, which can be expensive. / They can result in unexpected multiple pregnancies.
Q5 The eggs are fertilised in the lab using the male's sperm.
Q6 When they are tiny balls of cells.

Page 54 — Application Question
Q1 a) FSH stimulates egg maturation in the ovaries. Jenny's low FSH level may mean that her eggs are not maturing (and therefore not being released), decreasing her fertility and chances of getting pregnant.
    b) $(6695 \div 16652) \times 100 = \mathbf{40.2\%}$
    c) IVF often involves the transfer of more than one embryo into the uterus, which results in an increased chance of multiple pregnancies, and therefore more multiple pregnancies in those undergoing IVF.

7. Plant Hormones

Page 58 — Fact Recall Questions
Q1 The growth response of a plant to gravity.
Q2 Auxin inhibits cell elongation in a root.
Q3 An uneven amount of water either side of a root produces more auxin on the side with more water. This inhibits growth on that side, causing the root to bend in that direction.

Page 58 — Application Questions
Q1 a) In Petri dish A, there will be an even distribution of auxin across the shoot of each cress seedling. In Petri dish B, auxin will accumulate on the shaded side of the cress seedling shoots.
    This causes the cress seedlings in Petri dish A to grow straight up and the cress seedlings in Petri dish B to bend towards the light.
    b) i) To make sure that any difference in growth between shoots in Petri dish A and those in Petri dish B was due to the difference in light position only and not due to any other variables.
       ii) Any two from, e.g. the number of cress seeds planted in each Petri dish / the temperature the Petri dishes were kept at / the type of cress seed used / the amount of water available in each dish /the light intensity.

Q2 a) For this type of plant, rooting powder B is the best type of rooting powder to use for the first three weeks of growth. This is because it's more effective at increasing root length each week for the first three weeks after planting, than rooting powder A.

It's important to remember that the results only apply to this particular type of plant. You also can't say what will happen after the three week period Dan recorded his results for.

b) It was a control. / To show that the results were likely to be due to the presence of the rooting powder and nothing else.

Pages 61-62 — Biology 1.2
Exam-style Questions

1 a) i)   the muscle in the upper arm *(1 mark)*
       ii) sensory neurone *(1 mark)*
   b) It would get faster *(1 mark)*. The presence of the drug increases the amount of chemical released at the synapses, so it would take less time for an impulse to be triggered in the next neurone *(1 mark)*.
   c) E.g. reflexes are fast *(1 mark)*, so we quickly respond to danger, decreasing our chances of injury *(1 mark)*. Reflexes are automatic *(1 mark)*, so we don't have to waste time thinking about our response, which reduces our chance of injury *(1 mark)*.

2 a) i)   C, because the plant is growing towards it *(1 mark)*.
       ii) Sample X because it has been taken from the side that has grown more/the side in the shade *(1 mark)*. Auxin makes the cells in plant shoots elongate faster *(1 mark)*, so that must be the sample containing the most auxin *(1 mark)*.
   b) Rooting powders contain plant hormones (such as auxin) *(1 mark)*. These promote root development, helping the new plant to grow *(1 mark)*.

3 How to grade your answer:
   0 marks:
   There is no relevant information.
   1-2 marks:
   A comparison is made between the two types of pill.
   3-4 marks:
   Two clear comparisons are made between the two types of pill. The answer has a logical structure and spelling, punctuation and grammar are mostly correct.
   5-6 marks:
   At least three clear, detailed comparisons are made between the two types of pill. The answer has a logical structure and uses correct spelling, grammar and punctuation.
   Here are some points your answer may include:
   The combined oral contraceptive pill has a lower failure rate than the progesterone-only pill, so it is a more effective form of contraception.
   Both pills should be taken at the same time everyday, but the combined oral contraceptive pill is still effective if taken up to 12 hours late, whereas the progesterone-only pill may only be taken up to 3 hours late.

This means that the combined pill offers more flexibility over when it is taken.
Women taking the combined oral contraceptive pill have a higher risk of blood clots than those taking the progesterone-only pill (which can be taken by some women who have a history of blood clots).
The progesterone-only pill is useful for women who are breast feeding, whereas the combined oral contraceptive pill cannot be taken by these women.
This question asked you to evaluate the use of the two types of oral contraceptive pill written about in the passage. In this case, 'evaluate' basically means compare, so it's not enough to just pick bits of information out of the text and say whether it's a good or bad point about that particular type of pill — you need to make clear comparisons between the two types to get the marks. E.g. 'The combined oral pill has a lower failure rate than the progesterone only pill, so it is a more effective form of contraception.' You could also get a mark here for making a sensible conclusion about which type of pill is best.

Biology 1.3 The Use and Abuse of Drugs

1. Drugs and Drug Claims
Page 65 — Fact Recall Questions
Q1 Because some of the chemical changes caused by drugs can lead to the body becoming dependent on the drug.
Q2 Any two from: e.g. heroin / cocaine / nicotine / caffeine.
   You need to know that heroin and cocaine are examples of addictive drugs for the exam — make sure you learn them.
Q3 a) E.g. stimulants / anabolic steroids
   b) E.g. stimulants increase heart rate. / Anabolic steroids increase muscle size.
Q4 Lower the risk of heart and/or circulatory diseases.

Page 65 — Application Question
Q1 a) i)   performance-enhancing drugs / stimulants.
       ii) Amphetamines increase heart rate, so glucose and oxygen will be transported to Beth's muscles faster (giving her more energy).
   b) E.g. because the use of performance-enhancing drugs in sport is banned by all sporting bodies.
   c) E.g. it's unfair if people gain an advantage by taking drugs, not just through training.
   d) E.g. drug-free sport isn't really fair anyway — different athletes have access to different training facilities, coaches, equipment, etc. / It would mean that athletes who take a banned substance without knowing are not penalised (punished).

2. Testing Medicinal Drugs
Page 68 — Fact Recall Questions
Q1 laboratory testing

Q2 human cells, tissues and animals

Q3 Any two from: e.g. to find out whether the drug works. / To find out about the drug's toxicity. / To find out the best dosage of the drug.

Q4 a) healthy volunteers
   b) It is very low.

Q5 A placebo is a substance that's like the drug being tested but doesn't do anything.

Q6 A double-blind trial is a clinical trial where neither the doctor nor the patients know who has been given the drug and who has been given the placebo, until the results of the trial have been gathered.

It's helpful to remember that 'double' means 'two' — so in a double-blind trial, there are two groups of people (doctors and patients) who don't know who receives the drug or who receives the placebo.

Page 68 — Application Questions
Q1 a) E.g. a capsule without paracetamol
   b) E.g. an inhaler without steroids
   c) E.g. an injection without cortisone

Q2 a) i) No, because it was a double-blind trial.
      ii) E.g. a pill without any weight-loss drug.
   b) E.g. Group 2 was included in the trial to make sure that the new drug, Drug X, worked as well as/ better than other, similar weight-loss drugs already available on the market (like Drug Y). / To see how Drug X compared to Drug Y.
   c) That, on average, people taking Drug X in this trial lost 4 lbs more than those taking the placebo, but 3 lbs less than those taking Drug Y.

3. Recreational Drugs
Page 70 — Fact Recall Questions
Q1 Illegal drugs, any two from: e.g. heroin / ecstasy / cannabis.
   Legal drugs, e.g. nicotine and alcohol.

Q2 Any two from: e.g. cannabis is a "stepping stone" — the effects of cannabis create a desire to try harder drugs. / Cannabis is a "gateway drug" — cannabis use brings people into contact with drug dealers. / It's all down to genetics — certain people are more likely to take drugs generally, so cannabis users will also try other drugs.

Q3 Legal drugs because so many people take them.

Pages 72-73 — Biology 1.3
Exam-style Questions
1 a) Cannabis *(1 mark)*, Ecstasy *(1 mark)*
  b) i) These are withdrawal symptoms *(1 mark)*. They occur when a drug addict stops taking a drug *(1 mark)*.
     ii) E.g. it may cost the NHS a lot of money to treat these diseases *(1 mark)*. / These diseases can cause a lot of sorrow/anguish to the people affected by them *(1 mark)*. / There may be a cost to economy in lost working days due to illness *(1 mark)*.

2 a) A sleeping pill *(1 mark)*.
  b) i) When thalidomide was given to pregnant women it caused abnormal limb development in many babies *(1 mark)*. This happened because the drug had not been tested as a drug for morning sickness *(1 mark)*.
     ii) Thalidomide was banned *(1 mark)*. Drug testing became much more thorough from then on *(1 mark)*.

3 How to grade your answer:
0 marks:
No relevant information is given.
1-2 marks:
There is a brief description of drug testing in either the laboratory or in a clinical trial.
3-4 marks:
There is a description of drug testing in both the laboratory and in a clinical trial. The answer mentions the need to discover the drug's effectiveness, toxicity or dosage. The answer has a logical structure and spelling, grammar and punctuation are mostly correct.
5-6 marks:
There is a detailed description of drug testing in both the laboratory and in clinical trials. The answer clearly explains the need to discover the drug's effectiveness, toxicity and dosage. The answer has a logical structure and uses correct spelling, grammar and punctuation.
Here are some points your answer may include:
The drug will usually be tested first on human cells and tissues in the laboratory.
The drug will then tested on live animals to see if it works and to find out about toxicity and dosage.
If the drug passes animal trials, it will then be tested on human volunteers in a clinical trial.
In a clinical trial, the drug will be given to healthy volunteers first in low doses. This is to make sure it has no harmful side effects.
If the results from healthy volunteers are good, the drug will be tested on sick volunteers. This is to find the optimum dose of the drug.

4 a) i) Tablets without any aspirin in them *(1 mark)*.
     ii) To make sure that the aspirin was the only thing responsible for any results obtained *(1 mark)*.

b) Up to around 6 years after joining the study, there was little difference in the proportion of participants diagnosed with colorectal cancer in the control group and in the treatment group *(1 mark)*. But between 6-10 years after joining the study, the proportion diagnosed in the control group increased compared to the treatment group *(1 mark)*. After 10 years, the proportion diagnosed with colorectal cancer was much higher in the control group than in the treatment group — 0.6 compared to 0.1 at 11 years *(1 mark)*.

c) Any three from, e.g. the study only looked at colorectal cancer, not all cancers *(1 mark)*. / The study only used participants who already had an increased risk of developing colorectal cancer due to genetic factors *(1 mark)*. / The results only show that taking aspirin for 2 years or more reduced the risk by around a half (0.14 for placebo and 0.06 for aspirin) *(1 mark)*. / The participants took 600 mg a day, and there's no indication of what 'an aspirin' contains *(1 mark)*.

Biology 1.4 Adaptations and the Environment

1. Adaptations and Competition
Page 77 — Fact Recall Questions
Q1 A characteristic which increases an organism's chance of survival in the environment in which it lives.
Q2 It enables the plant to store water for use during very dry periods.
Q3 Any two from: e.g. having thorns/sharp spines / the ability to produce poison / warning colours.
Q4 a) An organism that is adapted to survive in extreme conditions.
    b) Any two from: e.g. very hot conditions / very salty conditions / high pressure conditions.
Q5 light, space, water and minerals/nutrients
Q6 space/territory, food, water and mates

Page 77 — Application Question
Q1 *Equus assinus* lives in desert conditions. This is because its long ears help to give it a large surface area compared to its volume. This helps it to lose more body heat, which stops it from overheating in the hot desert. It has short fur so it has little insulation, which is good for losing body heat. It is a grey or brown colour which helps it to be camouflaged in its desert environment. This could help it to avoid predators or sneak up on prey. *Alopex lagopus* lives in arctic conditions. This is because its short ears and muzzle help to reduce its surface area compared to its volume, which reduces heat loss. Its thick coat gives it good insulation, which helps to keep it warm. Its white coat gives it camouflage in its snowy environment, which helps it to avoid predators or sneak up on prey.

2. Environmental Change
Page 79 — Fact Recall Questions
Q1 Any three from: e.g. a change in the occurrence of infectious diseases / a change in the number of predators / a change in the number of prey/the availability of food sources / a change in the number or types of competitors.
Q2 Any three from: e.g. a change in average temperature / a change in average rainfall / a change in the level of air pollution / a change in the level of water pollution.

Page 79 — Application Questions
Q1 a) i) It decreased.
        ii) a non-living factor
    Here the environmental change of acid rain was caused by a non-living factor.
    b) The population size of the frogs is likely to have decreased because there were fewer mayfly to eat.
    Here the environmental change was caused by a living factor — the mayfly.
Q2 a)
    $$\frac{12.2 - 13}{13} \times 100 = -6.2\%$$
    b) E.g. a rise in global temperature, which is a non-living factor.
    c) E.g. it has caused a decrease in the polar bear population size.

3. Measuring Environmental Change
Page 81 — Fact Recall Questions
Q1 An organism that is very sensitive to changes in its environment and so can be used to study environmental change.
Q2 sulfur dioxide
Q3 invertebrate animals
Q4 Any three from: e.g. temperature of the sea surface / amount of snow/ice cover / temperature of the atmosphere / amount of rainfall / dissolved oxygen concentration of water.

Page 81 — Application Questions
Q1 56 km, because at this distance there is the least percentage cover of lichen. Lichen are sensitive to the amount of sulfur dioxide in the atmosphere, so there will be fewer of them around sources of sulfur dioxide, such as power stations.
Q2 a) Polluted water has a low concentration of dissolved oxygen, so stonefly larvae can't tolerate polluted water. This means that area A is the cleanest as this is the only area of the river where there are lots of stonefly larvae.
    Remember, clean water will have a higher concentration of dissolved oxygen than polluted water.
    b) Areas B and C must be polluted because there are no stonefly larvae there. There is only a moderate level of water louse in Area C, whereas there is a high level of sludgeworms in both Area B and C. This suggests that sludgeworms are most well adapted to survive in polluted water.

Biology 1.5 Energy and Biomass in Food Chains

1. Pyramids of Biomass
Page 85 — Fact Recall Questions
Q1 Biomass is the mass of living material.
Q2 Each bar of a pyramid of biomass represents the biomass of one trophic level. Biomass nearly always decreases as you move up a food chain, so the bars of the pyramid will get smaller nearer the top.

Page 85 — Application Questions
Q1

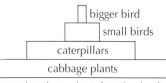

bigger bird
small birds
caterpillars
cabbage plants

Remember the producer (e.g. the plant) always goes at the bottom of the pyramid.
Q2 a) phytoplankton
 b) bass
 c) Because biomass has been lost between the krill trophic level and the herring trophic level in the food chain.

2. Energy Transfer in Food Chains
Page 87 — Fact Recall Questions
Q1 light energy
Q2 chemical energy
Q3 Green plants and algae absorb light energy from the Sun and use it to convert carbon dioxide and water to chemical energy during photosynthesis. The energy's stored in the cells of the plants and algae and then it gets passed along the food chain when animals eat the plants or algae.
Q4 False.
 Energy is lost at every stage of a food chain.

Page 87 — Application Question
Q1 This is because the ducks respire and energy is released from respiration. Some of this energy is used to fuel life processes, such as movement, but much of the energy is lost to the environment as heat. Energy is also lost in the ducks' waste materials, as well as in ducks that die before the fox can eat them (these ducks are broken down by microorganisms and the energy is passed to them).

Biology 1.6 Waste Materials and The Carbon Cycle

1. Decay
Page 89 — Fact Recall Questions
Q1 To use them for growth and other life processes.
Q2 a) The material in dead organisms is broken down/ digested/decayed by microorganisms. This process releases the elements back into the soil.
 Don't write that microorganisms 'eat' the dead material — you won't get a mark for that in the exam.
 b) In waste products.
Q3 Warm, moist and oxygenated.
 'Oxygenated' or 'aerated' means plenty of oxygen is present.
Q4 A stable community is one in which the materials taken out of the soil are balanced by those that are put back in — there's a constant cycle happening.
Q5 It recycles elements/nutrients back into the soil which plants can use for growth.

Page 89 — Application Question
Q1 To let oxygen in — microorganisms which break down waste material need oxygen for respiration.
Q2 Sunny areas of the garden will have higher temperatures. Microorganisms work best in warm conditions, so compost is made faster.
Q3 The presence of water vapour would increase the moisture inside the compost bin and, as microorganisms work best in moist conditions, it would help compost to be made more quickly.
 To answer these questions you just need to remember the conditions that microorganisms need to work best and apply that knowledge to the question.

2. The Carbon Cycle
Page 91 — Fact Recall Questions
Q1 photosynthesis
 If you're asked to name a process in the carbon cycle, make sure you give the actual name of the process, don't just describe it. For example, put 'feeding/eating' and not 'food'.
Q2 To make carbon compounds / carbohydrates, fats and proteins.
Q3 It becomes part of the fats and proteins in the animals.
Q4 They release carbon dioxide when they respire.
Q5 It is released as carbon dioxide when the fossil fuels are burnt/combusted.

Exam-style Questions

1 How to grade your answer:

0 marks:
No relevant information is given.

1-2 marks:
There is a brief description of one or two steps in the carbon cycle, but no names of any processes are given.

3-4 marks:
There is a description of three or four steps in the carbon cycle, but not all of the processes are named. The answer has a logical structure and spelling, grammar and punctuation are mostly correct.

5-6 marks:
There is a detailed description of five or six steps in the carbon cycle with named processes. The answer has a logical structure and uses correct spelling, grammar and punctuation.

Here are some points your answer may include:
The grass absorbs carbon dioxide from the air in photosynthesis.
The grass uses this carbon to make carbon compounds.
This carbon is passed onto the cows when the cows eat the grass, and onto humans when the humans eat the cows, so it moves through the food chain.
Dead organisms/waste materials are broken down/ decayed by detritus feeders/microorganisms.
All the organisms/the grass/cows/humans/ microorganisms respire and release carbon dioxide into the atmosphere.
Burning fossil fuels/wood also releases carbon dioxide into the air.

2 a) It provides the light energy *(1 mark)* needed for producers/green plants and algae to photosynthesise *(1 mark)* and produce chemical energy *(1 mark)*, which is passed on throughout the food chain by organisms eating each other *(1 mark)*.
   b) C, because algae are at the start of the food chain/ are producers *(1 mark)*.
   c) i) Width of bar A = 12 squares.
          Width of bar B = 30 squares.
          So ratio of bar B to bar A = 30:12 = **2.5:1**
          (2 marks for correct answer, otherwise 1 mark for correctly finding the widths of bar A and bar B).
      ii) Biomass is lost in waste products/faeces/urine *(1 mark)*, in the parts of organisms which are inedible *(1 mark)* and in organisms that die before they're eaten *(1 mark)*.
   This question is about how biomass is lost between trophic levels of a food chain, so be careful not to waste time writing about how energy is lost as well.

3 a) i) A characteristic that helps an organism to survive in its environment *(1 mark)*.

      ii) It has a thick bushy tail to help it keep warm at night when temperatures drop very low *(1 mark)*. It has a long, pointed muzzle so it can catch prey through the narrow entrance of a burrow *(1 mark)*. It has thick pads on the bottom of its feet to protect them as it's moving over rocky ground *(1 mark)*.
   You might not have come across any of these adaptations before, but just use the information you're given about the rocky mountains and think sensibly about how the features would help the wolf survive there.
   b) i) It is decreasing *(1 mark)*.
      ii) The outbreak of rabies is responsible for the trend *(1 mark)*. In the years when there were rabies outbreaks the population size fell *(1 mark)*. For example, the numbers fell from 401 to 327 in 2008 / 341 to 265 in 2011 when there was also a rabies outbreak *(1 mark)*.
   There's a lot of data to look at in the table so think carefully about what you're looking for. The numbers of prey don't really change much throughout the study so that's unlikely to have caused the change in the number of wolves, so it's sensible to look at the outbreaks of rabies.
      iii) It has made the wolf population move to higher ground *(1 mark)* from an average height of 3.4 km above sea level in 2007 to an average height of 4 km above sea level in 2012 *(1 mark)*.

Biology 1.7 Genetic Variation and its Control

1. Variation
Page 95 — Application Questions
Q1 E.g. how often you train / how hard you train / how well you are coached / how good the facilities you train at are / how good your diet is.
   You're not expected to know the answer to this question, just to make sensible suggestions.
Q2 The results from Study 1 suggest that genes must influence IQ because identical twins have the same genes and non-identical twins have different genes. The results from Study 2 suggest that environment also influences IQ. This is because identical twins have exactly the same genes, which means that differences in their IQs must be down to differences in their environment/the way they were brought up.

2. Genes, Chromosomes and DNA
Page 97 — Fact Recall Questions
Q1 in the nucleus
Q2 a) short sections of DNA/a chromosome (that control our characteristics)
    b) controlling the development of different characteristics

Page 97 — Application Questions
Q1 a) X
   b) Z
   c) Y
Q2 Because genes are too small.

3. Reproduction
Page 99 — Application Question
Q1 a) Asexual reproduction. There is only a single parent cell and no fusion of gametes. The offspring are genetically identical/clones.
   b) Sexual reproduction. There are two parents, gametes have fused together and offspring show genetic variation.
   Remember, sexual reproduction doesn't always involve sexual intercourse — it's the fusion of gametes that's important. Both animals and plants can reproduce sexually.
   c) Sexual reproduction. There are two parents and the offspring has characteristics of both parents, suggesting that it has a mixture of genes from both parents.
   d) Asexual reproduction. There is only one parent and no fusion of gametes. The offspring are genetically identical to the mother snake.

4. Cloning
Page 103 — Fact Recall Questions
Q1 a) Any two from: e.g. they can be produced quickly. / They can be produced cheaply. / Lots of ideal offspring/offspring with known characteristics can be produced.
   b) tissue culture
Q2 Embryo transplant. Adult cell cloning.

Page 103 — Application Questions
Q1 By giving it an electric shock.
Q2 No. The egg cell from the domestic cat will have had its nucleus/genetic material removed before the black-footed cat nucleus was inserted. So the embryo will only contain genetic material from the black-footed cat.
Q3 a) E.g. there are more domestic cats around than black-footed cats, so using domestic cats to carry the embryos may mean more black footed kittens can be produced.
   b) E.g. using skin cells from adults that have died as well as those that are still alive may increase the number of possible 'parents', so more black-footed cats can be produced.
   The idea behind using adult cell cloning to help save endangered species is that it's a way of producing lots of offspring relatively rapidly — you need to apply this idea to the question to make sensible suggestions here.
Q4 E.g. the cloned animals may also not be as healthy as normal ones. Cloning could also give the animals a reduced gene pool, meaning that if a new disease appears, they could all be wiped out.

5. Genetic Engineering
Page 106 — Fact Recall Questions
Q1 So that the animal or plant develops useful characteristics.
Q2 a) genetically modified
   b) E.g. insects, herbicides

Page 106 — Application Questions
Q1 Enzymes would be used to cut out the *Bt* crystal protein gene from the *B. thuringiensis* chromosome. Enzymes would then be used to cut a chromosome from the cotton plant and then to insert the crystal protein gene.
Q2 E.g. if insects ate the crop, they'd be poisoned by the protein. If less of the crop was eaten by insects, this could improve crop yield.
Q3 E.g. it could affect the number of weeds/flowers/insects that live in and around the crop. / People might develop allergies to the crop. / The gene for the *Bt* protein might get into the natural environment affecting, e.g., weeds.

Pages 108-109 Biology 1.7
Exam-style Questions
1 a) chromosomes, characteristics, gametes, variation *(1 mark for each correct answer)*
   b) i) genes *(1 mark)*
      ii) It is caused by differences in their environment *(1 mark)*. / A named environmental factor, e.g. diet *(1 mark)*.
   c) Sexual reproduction is the fusion of male and female gametes *(1 mark)* from two parents *(1 mark)*, which results in the offspring having a mixture of their parents' genes *(1 mark)*, so they are genetically different to their parents *(1 mark)*.
   Even though these twins are genetically identical to each other (i.e. clones), they are not clones of their parents because they have been produced by sexual reproduction.
2 a) i) The embryo will be split (many times) *(1 mark)* before any cells become specialised *(1 mark)*. The cloned embryos will then be implanted into host mothers to continue developing *(1 mark)*.
      ii) Asexual reproduction because: any two from, e.g. there was only one parent *(1 mark)*. / There was no fusion of gametes *(1 mark)*. / There was no mixing of genes *(1 mark)*.
   b) Because gametes were taken from the male and female pig and then fused *(1 mark)*. This will have created an embryo with a mixture of genes from both parents *(1 mark)*.

c) How to grade your answer:

0 marks:

No relevant information is given.

1-2 marks:

There is a brief description of one possible benefit and one possible concern of cloning pigs.

3-4 marks:

There is a description of at least two possible benefits and two possible concerns of cloning pigs. The answer has a logical structure and spelling, grammar and punctuation are mostly correct.

5-6 marks:

There is a detailed description of at least three possible benefits and three possible concerns of cloning pigs. The answer has a logical structure and uses correct spelling, grammar and punctuation.

Here are some points your answer may include:

Cloning could produce lots of 'ideal' pigs quickly, which could benefit farmers (who want to quickly increase the size of their herds/quality of their stock).

Studying cloned pigs could help scientists to understand the development of the embryo/ageing/age-related disorders.

Cloning pigs could help to save rare/endangered types/breeds of pig.

Cloning pigs will result in a reduced gene pool.

If a new disease appears, the cloned pigs could all be wiped out.

It's possible that cloned pigs may not be as healthy as normal pigs.

Cloning pigs could lead to the cloning of humans.

Biology 1.8 Evolution

1. Evolution and Natural Selection

Page 111 — Fact Recall Questions

Q1 over 3 billion years ago

Q2 They evolved from simple organisms.

Q3 a) The process by which species evolve.

b) (Charles) Darwin

Q4 a) A change in an organism's DNA.

b) A mutation in a gene can result in a useful characteristic. This characteristic may give the organism a better chance of surviving and reproducing and therefore passing on the mutation to future generations by natural selection. Over time the beneficial mutation will accumulate in the population, which may lead to changes in the species.

Page 112 — Application Questions

Q1 E.g. the original rats showed variation — some were resistant to warfarin, others weren't / a mutation appeared which made some rats resistant to warfarin. The warfarin-resistant rats were better adapted to the environment (because they weren't killed by the warfarin), so they were more likely to survive and breed successfully. This meant that the gene for warfarin-resistance was more likely to be passed on to the next generation.

You could get asked to explain the selection of pretty much any characteristic in the exam — make sure you can apply the key points of Darwin's theory to any context.

Q2 a) By around 3.5 – 2.1 = **1.4 cm** (accept any answer between 1.3 and 1.5 cm).

b) E.g. the reindeer population in 1810 would have shown variation — some would have had shorter fur and some longer fur. The reindeer with shorter fur would have been better adapted to the new, warmer environment they found themselves in (as they would have been less likely to overheat), so they would have been more likely to survive and breed successfully. This meant that the gene for short fur was more likely to be passed on to the next generation. This gene became more common in the population, eventually reducing the average fur length.

2. Ideas About Evolution

Page 114 — Application Questions

Q1 E.g. because of the different work they do/their different backgrounds / because Kyra is a geneticist and Neil is a psychologist.

Q2 It shows that the acquired characteristic of clipped flight feathers is not passed on from the parent birds to their offspring.

Q3 a) E.g. Lamarck may have argued that if an anteater used its tongue a lot to reach into ant nests, then its tongue would get longer. This acquired characteristic would then be passed on to the next generation and the anteater's offspring would have been born with long tongues.

b) E.g. tongue lengths in anteaters used to vary — some were long and some were short / a mutation occasionally caused some anteaters to be born with a long tongue. Long-tongued anteaters were better adapted to their environment/could get more food with their long tongues, so were more likely to survive and reproduce. So the gene(s) for a long tongue were more likely to be passed on to the next generation and eventually all anteaters were born with long tongues.

3. Classification

Page 117 — Fact Recall Questions
Q1 By studying their similarities and differences.
Q2 E.g. that they are in competition with each other.

Page 117 — Application Questions
Q1 An animal because it is able to move about (which plants can't do) and because it is unable to make its own food (which plants can do).
Q2 a) i) the lion
ii) the snow leopard
b) the jaguar
c) yes
The lion and the snow leopard are two of the most distantly related organisms on this tree, but they still share a common ancestor:

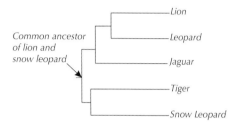

Page 119 — Biology 1.8
Exam-style Questions
1 a) crocodiles and birds *(1 mark)*
b) turtles *(1 mark)*
c) The original milk snake population showed variation — some had similar colouring to the coral snake, others didn't / A mutation appeared which caused some milk snakes to have similar colouring to the coral snake *(1 mark)*. Milk snakes that looked like the coral snake were less likely to be eaten *(1 mark)* and so more likely to reproduce and pass on the gene(s) for coral snake colouring to the next generation *(1 mark)*.
d) It went against common religious beliefs at the time *(1 mark)*. Darwin couldn't explain how useful characteristics appeared or were passed on (as he didn't know about genes) *(1 mark)*. There wasn't enough evidence to convince many scientists *(1 mark)*.

Biology 2.1 Cells and Simple Cell Transport

1. Cell Structure
Page 121 — Fact Recall Questions
Q1 the nucleus
Q2 In the cytoplasm.
Q3 respiration
Q4 A cell wall, a permanent vacuole and chloroplasts.
Q5 A yeast cell has a nucleus, cytoplasm, and a cell membrane surrounded by a cell wall.
Q6 E.g. in a yeast cell the genetic material is contained within a nucleus, whereas in a bacterial cell the genetic material floats in the cytoplasm. / A yeast cell has a nucleus and a bacterial cell doesn't.

2. Specialised Cells
Pages 123-124 — Application Questions
Q1 E.g. you'd expect to find a lot of ribosomes because they make proteins.
The function of a gastric chief cell is to secrete proteins — and ribosomes are where proteins are made in the cell. So it makes sense that you'd find a lot of ribosomes in a gastric chief cell.
Q2 a) C is most likely to be the correct structure of a root hair cell because this cell has a thin cell wall (unlike cell A), which should make it easier for water and mineral ions to be absorbed from the soil. Also cell C doesn't have any chloroplasts (unlike cell B), which are not needed because the root hair cells are in the soil and so can't photosynthesise/absorb light.
b) The cell's long extension gives it a bigger surface area for absorbing water and nutrients.
Q3 E.g. the folds in the cell membrane give the cells a large surface area for absorbing food molecules efficiently. Lots of mitochondria provide the energy from respiration needed to absorb food molecules.
This question is pretty tricky — you need to think about the unusual shape of the cell and look at the things it contains. Cells that need to absorb things tend to have a large surface area (e.g. like red blood cells and palisade leaf cells), so look for anything about the cell that increases its surface area. You also know that the cell needs energy — so look for mitochondria, which are the site of respiration (a process which releases energy).

3. Diffusion

Page 127 — Application Questions

Q1 Inside respiring cells. The carbon dioxide molecules must be diffusing from an area of higher concentration (inside respiring cells) to an area of lower concentration (the bloodstream).

Q2 a) The smoke particles diffuse from where there is a high concentration (near the stage), to where there is a low concentration (at the opposite end of the hall).

b) There are already some smoke particles in the air the second time the smoke machine is set off, whereas there weren't the first time. This means there is a smaller difference in the concentration of the smoke particles at each end of the hall, so the rate of diffusion is slower the second time.

Biology 2.2 Tissues, Organs and Organ Systems

1. Cell Organisation

Pages 130-131 — Fact Recall Questions

Q1 a) differentiation
b) true

Q2 a) A group of similar cells that work together to carry out a particular function.
b) To make and secrete substances such as enzymes and hormones.
c) e.g. muscular tissue and epithelial tissue

Q3 A group of different tissues that work together to perform a certain function.

Q4 organ system

Q5 A is the salivary glands, which produce digestive juices. B is the liver, which produces bile. C is the stomach, where food is digested. D is the pancreas, which produces digestive juices. E is the small intestine, where food is digested and soluble food molecules are absorbed. F is the large intestine, which absorbs water from undigested food, leaving faeces.

Page 131 — Application Questions

Q1 Glandular tissue, because this sort of tissue secretes hormones.
The hypophysis is actually just another name for the pituitary gland. You didn't need to know that to answer the question though.

Q2 A tissue, because it consists of a group of similar cells that work together to perform a particular function.

Q3 a) It contracts, to move the fertilised egg cell along the fallopian tube to the uterus.
b) An organ, because it consists of a group of different tissues that work together to perform a certain function.
c) egg cell, muscular tissue, uterus, reproductive system

2. Plant Tissues and Organs

Page 133 — Fact Recall Questions

Q1 e.g. stems, roots, leaves

Q2 mesophyll tissue

Q3 To transport things like water, mineral ions and sucrose around the plant.

Q4 epidermal tissue
Remember, 'epidermal tissue' is found in plants and 'epithelial tissue' is found in animals — they're very similar words, so be careful you don't get them mixed up in the exam.

Pages 134-135 — Biology 2.1-2.2 Exam-style Questions

1 a) A — cell wall *(1 mark)*. B — nucleus *(1 mark)*. C — cytoplasm *(1 mark)*. D — cell membrane *(1 mark)*.
b) A yeast, because it has a nucleus / its genetic material is not floating free in the cytoplasm *(1 mark)*.

2 a) i) small intestine *(1 mark)*
ii) A is the salivary glands *(1 mark)*. B is the pancreas *(1 mark)*. The role of both of these organs is to produce digestive juices *(1 mark)*.
b) Any two from: e.g. muscular tissue *(1 mark)*, which moves the stomach wall to churn up food *(1 mark)*. / Glandular tissue *(1 mark)*, which makes digestive juices to digest food *(1 mark)*. / Epithelial tissue *(1 mark)*, which covers the outside and inside of the stomach *(1 mark)*.

3 a) A cell which carries out a particular function *(1 mark)*.
b) A tissue *(1 mark)* because it shows several similar cells that work together to carry out a particular function *(1 mark)*.
c) E.g. it has long extensions so it can carry electrical signals further in the body. / It has branched ends so it can carry electrical signals to several different body cells at once *(1 mark)*.

4 a) epidermal tissue *(1 mark)*
b) Mesophyll tissue *(1 mark)*. Having lots of chloroplasts suggests that the cells are adapted for photosynthesis *(1 mark)* and it is in the mesophyll tissue that most photosynthesis takes place *(1 mark)*.
c) i) There must be a higher concentration of carbon dioxide outside the cell than inside *(1 mark)*. This is because when particles diffuse, they move from an area of high concentration to an area of low concentration *(1 mark)*.
ii) A decrease in the concentration of carbon dioxide in the air spaces outside the leaf cells would reduce the rate of diffusion of carbon dioxide into the cells *(1 mark)*. This is because the difference between the concentration of carbon dioxide inside the cells and outside the cells would be smaller *(1 mark)*.

Biology 2.3 Photosynthesis

1. The Basics of Photosynthesis

Page 137 — Fact Recall Questions
Q1 glucose
Q2 a) chloroplasts
   b) It absorbs light energy.
Q3

carbon dioxide + water $\xrightarrow{\text{light energy}}$ glucose + oxygen

Q4 carbon dioxide
Q5 oxygen

Page 137 — Application Questions
Q1 Plant C. It received the most hours of sunlight, so it will have photosynthesised for longer. As photosynthesis produces glucose, it will have produced the most glucose.
Q2 3, because this type of plant cell contains the most chloroplasts. Chloroplasts contain chlorophyll, which is needed for plants to photosynthesise.

2. The Rate of Photosynthesis

Page 141 — Fact Recall Question
Q1 a) A factor which stops photosynthesis from happening any faster.
   b) e.g. light intensity, carbon dioxide level, temperature

Page 141 — Application Questions
Q1

Environmental conditions	Most likely limiting factor
Outside on a cold winter's day.	temperature
In an unlit garden at 1:30 am, in the UK, in summer.	light
On a windowsill on a warm, bright day.	carbon dioxide concentration

Q2 a) oxygen
   b) Any two from: e.g. he kept the flasks at the same temperature. / He put flasks the same distance from the light source. / He used the same amount of pondweed in both flasks. / He took the pondweed from the same plant.

   Different plants may photosynthesise at different rates, so taking the pondweed from the same plant helps to make the experiment a fair test.
   c) Because before point X, increasing the light intensity increases the rate of photosynthesis.

d) Because carbon dioxide concentration is limiting the rate of photosynthesis in Flask A. Flask A has a lower carbon dioxide concentration than Flask B but all the other variables that could affect the rate of photosynthesis are the same for both flasks. Therefore the reason why the rate of photosynthesis levels off at a lower level in Flask A, is most likely to be because of the lower carbon dioxide concentration in this flask.

3. Artificially Controlling Plant Growth

Page 144 — Fact Recall Questions
Q1 E.g. so that they can create the ideal conditions for photosynthesis. This means that their plants photosynthesise faster, so a decent crop can be harvested much more often.
Q2 e.g. carbon dioxide concentration

Page 144 — Application Questions
Q1 a) $30 \div 8 =$ **3.75 cm per week**.
   b) $17.5 \div 8 =$ **2.19 cm per week**.
   Graphs like this with two y-axes can be tricky — just take your time and make sure you're reading the value off the correct axis.
Q2 Carbon dioxide concentration. Light, temperature and carbon dioxide concentration can all affect the rate of photosynthesis, which affects growth rate. The graph shows that there was very little difference in the temperature of each greenhouse throughout the experiment, and both greenhouses were exposed to the same amount of light. Therefore it's most likely to be the extra carbon dioxide produced by the paraffin heater in Greenhouse A which caused the higher average growth rate of plants in this greenhouse.
Q3 E.g. the cost of running the heaters.

4. How Plants and Algae Use Glucose

Page 146 — Fact Recall Questions
Q1 respiration
Q2 making strong cell walls
Q3 nitrate ions
Q4 as lipids/fats and oils
Q5 Starch is insoluble, so it doesn't draw in water and cause the cells to swell up.

Biology 2.4 Organisms and Their Environment

1. Distribution of Organisms

Page 148 — Fact Recall Questions

Q1 Where organisms are found in a particular area.

Q2 E.g. temperature / availability of water / availability of oxygen / availability of carbon dioxide / availability of nutrients / availability of light.

2. Studying Distribution

Page 152 — Fact Recall Questions

Q1 E.g. you would place the quadrat on the ground at a random position in the first sample area and count the number of the organisms within the quadrat. You would then repeat this many times. Next you would repeat this whole process in the second sample area. Finally you would work out an average number of organisms per quadrat or the population size in each sample area and compare the results.

Q2 Add all the values in the data set together and divide the total by the number of values you have.

Q3 The value which occurs most often.

Q4 The middle value when the data is in order of size.

Q5 A line can be marked out across the area you want to study and all of the organisms that touch the line can be counted. / Data can be collected using quadrats placed along the line.

Q6 E.g. by using a large sample size.

Page 153 — Application Question

Q1 a) i) $1 + 5 + 5 + 20 + 43 + 37 = 111$
       $111 \div 6 = \mathbf{18.5}$
    ii) 5
    iii) $5 + 20 = 25$
       $25 \div 2 = \mathbf{12.5}$

Remember the mean is the average you get by adding together all the values in the data and dividing it by the number of values that you have, the mode is the most common value, and the median is the middle value when the data is in order of size.

   b) End B, as the amount of bulrushes is lower here and you would expect there to be fewer bulrushes further away from the pond as they prefer moist soil or shallow water.

   c) It decreases the validity of her study. If she didn't control the other variables that could affect the distribution of bulrushes in her garden, it means she can't conclude that moist soil and shallow water cause bulrushes to grow best.

   d) E.g. there will be fewer bulrushes in the area closer to the pond because the pond is decreasing in size.

Pages 154-155 — Biology 2.3-2.4 Exam-style Questions

1 a) i) $55 + 41 + 57 = 153$
       $153 \div 3 = \mathbf{51}$
       (2 marks for correct answer, otherwise 1 mark for correct working)
    ii) The number of limpets increases as you move away from the water's edge, and then begins to decrease after the position of quadrat 3 ***(1 mark)***. The low number of limpets in quadrats closest to the water's edge could be due to competition for space from other organisms ***(1 mark)***. The decrease in the number of limpets after quadrat 3 could be due to there being less water available further from the water's edge, which increases the limpets' chance of drying out ***(1 mark)***.
    iii) This would increase their sample size ***(1 mark)*** which would make their samples more representative of the population at each distance ***(1 mark)***.
   b) i) To increase the validity of their results ***(1 mark)***.
    ii) Any two from: e.g. a difference in temperature / a difference in the availability of water / a difference in the availability of oxygen / a difference in the availability of nutrients ***(1 mark for each correct answer)***.

2 a) i) in the chloroplasts ***(1 mark)***
    ii)
                           light energy
       carbon dioxide + water → glucose + oxygen
       (1 mark for each correct answer)
   b) i) B. It took the shortest time for all of the discs to be floating ***(1 mark)*** suggesting that photosynthesis was happening the fastest in this condition ***(1 mark)***.
    ii) Increasing the light intensity will increase the rate of photosynthesis up to a point ***(1 mark)***. However, past this point increasing the light intensity will have no further effect on the rate of photosynthesis ***(1 mark)*** as other limiting factors may come into play, such as carbon dioxide concentration ***(1 mark)*** and temperature ***(1 mark)***.
    iii) It should take less than 18 minutes because the rate of photosynthesis should be faster ***(1 mark)***, as there is more carbon dioxide available in the solution for photosynthesis ***(1 mark)***.

How to grade your answer:
0 marks:
No relevant information is given.
1-2 marks:
One or two uses of glucose by a plant are described.
3-4 marks:
Three or four uses of glucose by a plant are described. The answer has a logical structure and spelling, grammar and punctuation are mostly correct.
5-6 marks:
At least five uses of glucose by a plant are described. The answer has a logical structure and uses correct spelling, grammar and punctuation.
Here are some points your answer may include:
Some of the glucose is used for respiration.
Some glucose is converted into cellulose which is used to make strong cell walls.
Some glucose is combined with nitrate ions from the soil to make proteins.
Some glucose is converted into starch for storage.
Some glucose is converted into lipids (fats and oils) for storage.

Biology 2.5 Proteins — Their Functions and Uses

1. Proteins and Enzymes
Page 158 — Fact Recall Questions
Q1 a) The folding up of the long chains of amino acids that make up the protein.
   b) So that other molecules can fit into the protein and the protein can carry out its function.
Q2 Any three from: e.g. structural components of tissues/ muscles / hormones / antibodies / catalysts/enzymes.
Q3 A catalyst is a substance which increases the speed of a reaction, without being changed or used up in the reaction.
Q4 False
   Different enzymes work best at different pHs.

Page 158 — Application Question
Q1 It should slow down the rate of reaction. This is because heating hexokinase up to a high temperature/50 °C will probably cause the bonds in hexokinase to break and the enzyme to lose its shape. This would mean that glucose will no longer be able to fit into hexokinase and the reaction won't be catalysed.
   For questions like this you just need to apply your own knowledge — e.g. that enzymes lose their shape at high temperatures and that enzymes need their unique shape to work — to the specific enzyme named in the question.

2. Digestion
Page 161 — Fact Recall Questions
Q1 By specialised cells in the glands and in the gut lining.
Q2 False
   Digestive enzymes catalyse the breakdown of big molecules into smaller molecules, e.g. protease enzymes catalyse the breakdown of proteins into amino acids.
Q3 amylase
Q4 In the stomach, the pancreas and the small intestine.
Q5 lipases
Q6 a) The stomach produces hydrochloric acid, which creates acidic conditions for pepsin/enzymes in the stomach to work in.
   b) Bile is released into the small intestine. There, it neutralises the stomach acid and creates the ideal alkaline conditions for enzymes in the small intestine to work in.

Page 162 — Application Questions
Q1

	Amylase	Proteases	Lipases	Bile
Made where?	B, F, G	D, F, G	F, G	C
Work(s) where?	A, G	D, G	G	G

Make sure you learn where digestive enzymes and bile are produced and where they work — you can pick up easy marks with this information in the exam. However, it's easy to get things mixed up, so watch out. E.g. bile is made in the liver but stored in the gall bladder — make sure you don't get those two organs mixed up.

Q2 The photograph shows that in the test tubes with hydrochloric acid only and pepsin only (test tubes 1 and 2), the meat hasn't been fully digested. However, in the test tube with both pepsin and hydrochloric acid (test tube 3) the meat sample has been completely digested. This has happened because to digest meat, which contains protein, pepsin (a protease enzyme) is needed. Also, pepsin in the stomach works best under acidic conditions, which are provided by hydrochloric acid released by the stomach. Therefore the meat was only broken down in the test tube that had both the pepsin and the acidic conditions.

3. Enzymes in Home and Industry
Page 165 — Fact Recall Questions
Q1 a) proteases and lipases
　　b) Proteases help break down proteins.
　　　Lipases help break down fats/lipids.
Q2 E.g. they don't work well at high temperatures. / They might not work very well in very acidic or alkaline tap water. / They can irritate sensitive skin.
　　Enzymes are the 'biological' bit of biological detergents. So, biological detergents usually don't work well at high temperatures or extremes of pH because the enzymes are denatured and so won't work anymore.
Q3 It means that the baby foods contain proteins that have already been partially broken down by enzymes, so that they are easier for babies to digest.
Q4 carbohydrase
Q5 E.g. the reaction that turns glucose syrup into fructose syrup.

Page 165 — Application Questions
Q1 Sarah should buy non-biological washing powder because the enzymes in biological washing powders usually denature at high temperatures, so they may not work as well on a hot wash. Also, biological washing powder may irritate sensitive skin like Sarah's.
　　John should buy biological washing powder because it's more effective at lower temperatures than non-biological washing powders. This means he can save energy and money by putting his washing machine on a lower temperature cycle.
Q2 a) The manufacturer should use fructose syrup in Diet Lem-Fizz because it is sweeter than glucose syrup, so a smaller amount is needed.
　　b) Fructose syrup can be made from glucose syrup using an isomerase enzyme.

Biology 2.6 Aerobic and Anaerobic Respiration

1. Aerobic Respiration
Page 168 — Fact Recall Questions
Q1 enzymes
Q2 Respiration using oxygen. / The process of releasing energy from glucose using oxygen.
Q3 E.g. mammals use energy to build larger molecules from smaller ones, to contract muscles and to keep their body temperature steady.
Q4 E.g. sugars and nitrates.
　　Plants use energy from respiration to make sugars, nitrates and other nutrients into amino acids. They then use amino acids to make proteins.

Page 168 — Application Questions
Q1 mitochondrion/mitochondria
　　'Mitochondrion' is the singular of mitochondria.
Q2 a) oxygen
　　b) water / energy
　　c) energy / water

2. Exercise
Page 170 — Fact Recall Questions
Q1 During exercise, your breathing rate and depth both increase.
Q2 a) muscles
　　b) During exercise, glycogen in the muscles is converted back to glucose to provide more energy.
　　Energy is released from glucose via respiration.

Page 170 — Application Questions
Q1 Charlotte's heart rate has increased to increase blood flow to the muscles. This means that the muscles receive more oxygen and glucose for respiration, and can get rid of more carbon dioxide.
Q2 a) Samir's breathing rate increases from 16 breaths per minute at rest, to 44 breaths per minute by the end of the race. By eight minutes after the race Samir's breathing rate has decreased back to 16 breaths per minute.
　　b) During the race, Samir's breathing rate increases to provide more oxygen for respiration, so that more energy is released to keep his muscles contracting. By eight minutes after the race his breathing rate has decreased back to its resting level. This is because his muscle activity has decreased and his body doesn't need as much energy from respiration, so he doesn't need to take in as much oxygen.

3. Anaerobic Respiration
Page 172 — Fact Recall Questions
Q1 The body uses anaerobic respiration during vigorous exercise when it can't get enough oxygen to the muscles for aerobic respiration.
　　We're not respiring by anaerobic respiration all the time — just when increased muscle activity means we can't get oxygen to our muscles fast enough for them to respire aerobically.
Q2 Anaerobic respiration is the incomplete breakdown of glucose which produces lactic acid. (It takes place in the absence of oxygen.)
Q3 a) It's when muscles get tired and stop contracting efficiently.
　　b) E.g. build up of lactic acid.
Q4 Oxygen debt is when, after vigorous exercise, a person has to "repay" the oxygen that they didn't get to their muscles in time, because their lungs, heart and blood couldn't keep up with the demand earlier on.

1   a) i)   a protein *(1 mark)*
         ii) To act as a biological catalyst. / To speed up the
              rate of a reaction (in a living organism) without
              being changed or used up itself *(1 mark)*.
     b) How to grade your answer:
         0 marks:
         No relevant information is given.
         1-2 marks:
         There is a brief description of the function of at
         least one type of digestive enzyme, but where it's
         made or where it works may not be covered.
         3-4 marks:
         There is a description of the function of at least
         two types of digestive enzyme, with mention of
         where they are made or where they work. The
         answer has a logical structure and spelling,
         grammar and punctuation are mostly correct.
         5-6 marks:
         There is a detailed description of the function
         of three types of digestive enzyme, including
         where each of them is made and where each of
         them works in the digestive system. The answer
         has a logical structure and uses correct spelling,
         grammar and punctuation.
         Here are some points your answer may include:
         Amylase is a digestive enzyme that catalyses the
         conversion of starch into sugars. Amylase is made
         in the salivary glands, the pancreas and the small
         intestine. It works in the mouth and the small
         intestine.
         Protease enzymes are digestive enzymes that
         catalyse the conversion of proteins into amino
         acids. Proteases are made in the stomach, the
         pancreas and the small intestine. They work in the
         stomach and the small intestine.
         Lipase enzymes are digestive enzymes that
         catalyse the conversion of lipids into glycerol
         and fatty acids. Lipases are made in the pancreas
         and the small intestine. They work in the small
         intestine.
2   a) i)   B, because it has a higher peak enzyme activity
              (1 mark).
         ii) Above 80 °C the enzyme activity of each
              enzyme decreases *(1 mark)*. This is because
              the high temperatures cause the enzymes to
              become denatured / the enzymes' shapes to
              change so that they can't catalyse the reaction
              (1 mark).
     b) Fructose syrup is sweeter than glucose syrup
         (1 mark), so it can be used in smaller amounts,
         which is good for slimming foods *(1 mark)*.

     c) Any three from: e.g. they're specific, so they only
         catalyse the reaction you want them to. / They
         allow reactions to happen at lower temperatures
         and pressures and so at a lower cost as it saves
         energy. / Enzymes work for a long time, so after
         the initial cost of buying them, you can continually
         use them. / They are biodegradable and therefore
         cause less environmental pollution. *(1 mark for
         each correct answer)*
3   a) i)   (151 + 163 + 154) / 3 = **156 beats per minute**
              *(1 mark for correct working, 1 mark for
              correct answer)*
         *Make sure that you always include units in your answer —
         in this case, the units are beats per minute.*
         ii) Because the student was respiring
              anaerobically *(1 mark)* so will have had an
              oxygen debt *(1 mark)*. This means his heart
              rate had to remain high to keep blood flowing
              through the muscles *(1 mark)* to deliver oxygen
              to them *(1 mark)*, in order to get rid of lactic
              acid by oxidising it to carbon dioxide and
              water *(1 mark)*.
     b) E.g. making larger molecules from smaller
         ones *(1 mark)*. Keeping the body at a steady
         temperature *(1 mark)*
4   a) i)   glucose + oxygen → carbon dioxide + water
              + energy
              *(1 mark for glucose and oxygen on the left-
              hand side of the equation, 1 mark for carbon
              dioxide and water on the right)*
         ii) constantly/all the time *(1 mark)*
     b) Anaerobic respiration releases less ATP than
         aerobic respiration, which shows that it releases
         less energy *(1 mark)*. This is because glucose
         is not completely broken down in anaerobic
         respiration *(1 mark)*.

Biology 2.7 Cell Division and Inheritance

1. DNA

Page 177 — Fact Recall Questions
Q1 Deoxyribonucleic acid
Q2 (long molecules of) DNA
Q3 It has a double helix structure.
Q4 By telling the cell what order to put amino acids in.
Q5 Because everyone's DNA fingerprint is unique (except
    identical twins).

Page 177 — Application Questions
Q1 a) Suspect B because their DNA exactly matches the
        DNA of the blood found at the crime scene.
    b) No. The DNA match only provides evidence that
        suspect B was probably at the crime scene, not
        that they committed the crime.
Q2 Suspects A and D as their DNA fingerprints are
    identical.

2. Cell Division — Mitosis
Page 179 — Fact Recall Questions
Q1 two
Q2 For growth, to replace damaged cells and for asexual reproduction.
Q3 one

Page 179 — Application Questions
Q1 genetically identical
Mitosis produces cells that are genetically identical to the parent cells.
Q2 two
If a cell has two sets of chromosomes it means that it will have two copies of each chromosome.

3. Cell Division — Meiosis
Page 182 — Fact Recall Questions
Q1 one
Q2 In the reproductive organs/the testes and the ovaries in humans.
Q3 By repeatedly dividing by mitosis.
Q4 two
Q5 four
Q6 False
Gametes are all genetically different.

Page 182 — Application Questions
Q1 a) 39
   b) 38
   c) 32
Q2 a) i) Before the first division, the cell duplicates its DNA.
This creates X-shaped chromosomes, where each 'arm' of the chromosome has the same DNA.
      ii) It would only have one set of chromosomes. (It should have two sets of chromosomes.)
   b) Any three from: e.g. mitosis occurs in body cells, meiosis occurs in cells of the reproductive organs only. / Mitosis produces body cells, meiosis produces gametes. / Mitosis is used for growth, cell replacement or asexual reproduction, meiosis is used for gamete production. / Mitosis involves one cell division, meiosis involves two. / Two new cells are produced when a cell divides by mitosis, four new cells are produced when a cell divides by meiosis. / Mitosis produces cells which have two sets of chromosomes in them, meiosis produces cells that only contain one set of chromosomes.

4. Stem Cells
Page 185 — Fact Recall Questions
Q1 In most animal cells, the ability to differentiate is lost at an early stage, whereas lots of plant cells don't ever lose this ability.
Q2 An undifferentiated cell that has the potential to differentiate into different types of cell.
Q3 any type of cell
Q4 E.g. in the bone marrow.

Page 185 — Application Questions
Q1) a) Stem cells could be made to differentiate into neurones, which could replace the damaged/dead neurones.
    b) E.g. producing nerve cells to replace damaged tissue in people with paralysis. / Producing beating heart muscle cells for people with heart disease. / Producing insulin-producing cells for people with diabetes.
Q2 Because the embryos leftover from fertility clinics will be destroyed anyway.
Q3 E.g. because the embryo still has the potential to develop life before this point.

5. X and Y Chromosomes
Page 189 — Fact Recall Questions
Q1 one
Q2 False
Half carry X chromosomes, and half carry Y chromosomes.
Q3 females

Page 189 — Application Questions
Q1

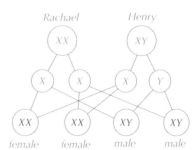

Q2 50% or 50:50 or ½.
Q3 No. There is always a 50% chance of having a boy and a 50% chance of having a girl at each pregnancy.
Q4

Rachael's gametes

	X	X	
X X	X X		X
X Y	X Y		Y

Henry's gametes

6. The Work of Mendel
Page 192 — Fact Recall Questions
Q1 Characteristics in plants are determined by "hereditary units". Hereditary units are passed on from both parents, one unit from each parent. Hereditary units can either be dominant or recessive — if an individual has both the dominant and the recessive unit for a characteristic, the dominant characteristic will be expressed.
Q2 genes

Q3 No one knew about genes or DNA when Mendel was still alive, so the significance of his work wasn't realised until after he had died.

These days people recognise Mendel as one of the founding fathers of genetics. He was just a bit ahead of his time. Poor Mendel.

Page 192 — Application Question
Q1

Seed colour of pea plant	Type of hereditary unit		
	Just green	Just yellow	Both green and yellow
Green	✓	✗	✗
Yellow	✗	✓	✓

The yellow hereditary unit is dominant, so if the pea plant has both yellow and green hereditary units its seeds will be yellow. If the plant just has yellow hereditary units its seeds will also be yellow. For its seeds to be green, the plant has to have two of the green hereditary units.

7. Alleles and Genetic Diagrams
Page 197 — Fact Recall Questions
Q1 Different versions of the same gene.
Q2 The allele for the characteristic that's shown if two different alleles for the same gene are present.
Q3 When an organism has two alleles for a particular gene that are the same, e.g. TT.
Q4 The characteristics you have.

Page 197 — Application Questions
Q1 a) a rough coat
You need to have worked out from the letters that the rough coat allele (R) is dominant over the smooth coat allele (r).
b) i) E.g.

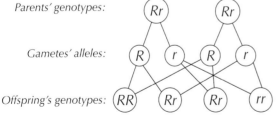

Parents' phenotypes: female rough coat   male rough coat
Parents' genotypes: Rr   Rr
Gametes' alleles: R r   R r
Offspring's genotypes: RR Rr Rr rr

You could have drawn a Punnet square here too.
ii) 1 in 4 or 25%
Q2 a) heterozygous
b) ss
c) SS

8. Genetic Disorders
Page 201 — Fact Recall Questions
Q1 cystic fibrosis
Q2 recessive
You need to have two recessive alleles for cystic fibrosis to be a sufferer of the disease.
Q3 extra fingers or toes
Q4 E.g. to see if the embryo carries a genetic disorder.

Page 201 — Application Questions
Q1 a) Ff
b) ff
Q2 a) Because there are no carriers of the disease, just sufferers.
b) a purple circle
c) i) dd
ii) Dd
You know from the diagram that Kate is a sufferer of polydactyly, so she must have at least one copy of the dominant allele 'D'. You also know that she doesn't have two copies of the dominant allele, as her father Clark is not a sufferer, so she couldn't have inherited a second 'D' allele from him. Therefore her genotype must be Dd.
d)

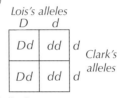

Lois's alleles
D   d

| Dd | dd | d |
| Dd | dd | d |

Clark's alleles

e) i) E.g

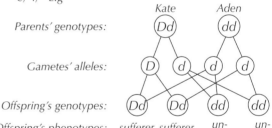

Parents' genotypes: Kate (Dd)   Aden (dd)
Gametes' alleles: D d   d d
Offspring's genotypes: Dd Dd dd dd
Offspring's phenotypes: sufferer sufferer un-affected un-affected

ii) The probability of the new baby having polydactyly is 50%/1 in 2.

Pages 204-205 — Biology 2.7
Exam-style Questions
1 a) Male 1 because bands 7, 11 and 12 match bands 1, 5 and 6 in the child's DNA sample *(1 mark)* whereas none of Male 2, Male 3 or Male 4's bands match those in the child's DNA sample *(1 mark)*.
b) Bands 2, 3 and 4 *(1 mark)*. You get half of your DNA from your father and half from your mother *(1 mark)*, so you'd expect the mother to share the remaining bands on the DNA fingerprint *(1 mark)*.

2 a) i) E.g.

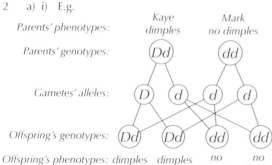

Parents' phenotypes: Kaye dimples   Mark no dimples

Parents' genotypes:

Gametes' alleles:

Offspring's genotypes:

Offspring's phenotypes: dimples dimples no dimples no dimples

(1 mark for correctly identifying Mark's genotype, 1 mark for correctly identifying possible genotypes of the offspring.)

You could have drawn a Punnett square to answer this question instead.

    ii) The baby has a 50%/1 in 2 chance of having dimples *(1 mark)*.

b) XY *(1 mark)*

Males have the XY chromosome combination, females have the XX chromosome combination.

c) Because the baby has been produced via sexual reproduction *(1 mark)*, where two gametes fuse *(1 mark)* bringing together two different sets of chromosomes (one from the mother and one from the father) to form the new individual *(1 mark)*.

3 a)

Statement	Mitosis	Meiosis
Only occurs in the reproductive organs.		✓
It produces gametes.		✓
It produces body cells.	✓	

(1 mark for each correct answer)

b) i) 2 ÷ 0.5 = 4 divisions

       2^4 (or $2 \times 2 \times 2 \times 2$) = 16 cells

       (1 mark for correctly calculating that 4 divisions will take place in 2 hours, 1 mark for 16 cells.)

There will be 4 divisions in two hours, so 1 cell will become 2 cells in the first division, 2 cells will become 4 cells in the second division, 4 cells will then become 8, and 8 cells will become 16.

    ii) genetically identical *(1 mark)*

Q4 a) Cystic fibrosis is a genetic disorder *(1 mark)*, which affects the cell membranes *(1 mark)*.

    b) Homozygous, because he is a sufferer of a recessive disorder *(1 mark)*.

---

c) E.g.

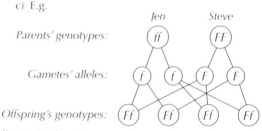

Parents' genotypes: Jen   Steve

Gametes' alleles:

Offspring's genotypes:

Offspring's phenotypes: carrier carrier carrier carrier

(1 mark for correctly identifying the parents' genotypes, 1 mark for correctly identifying possible genotypes of the offspring.)

No, because to suffer from cystic fibrosis you need to have the genotype ff *(1 mark)*. Jen and Steve's offspring will only have the genotype Ff, so they could only be carriers, not sufferers *(1 mark)*.

You could have drawn a Punnett square to answer this question instead.

d) Ff *(1 mark)*. For a child to have cystic fibrosis, both parents must carry the cystic fibrosis allele *(1 mark)*, as it is a recessive disorder *(1 mark)*.

Tony is a carrier so his alleles must be Ff. As their child has cystic fibrosis (ff) it must have inherited a cystic fibrosis allele from both Tony and Bex, as it's a recessive disorder. Bex doesn't suffer from cystic fibrosis, then she must be a carrier (Ff).

Biology 2.8 Fossils and Speciation

1. Fossils

Page 208 — Fact Recall Questions

Q1 The remains of an organism from many years ago that are found in a rock.

Q2 That organisms lived ages ago and how today's species have evolved over time.

Q3 Early organisms were soft-bodied and soft tissue tends to decay away completely, without forming fossils. Plus fossils that did form millions of years ago may have been destroyed by geological activity, e.g. the movement of tectonic plates. So the fossil record is incomplete.

Page 208 — Application Question

Q1 A E.g. an organism (or organisms) burrowed into soft material. The material later hardened around the burrows to form casts in the rock.

     B E.g. the hard shell of the snail decayed away slowly. It was gradually replaced by minerals as it decayed, forming a rock-like substance shaped like the shell.

     C E.g. a leaf became buried in a soft material. The material later hardened around the leaf, which decayed, leaving a cast of itself in the rock.

     D E.g. the mammoth died and it's body became trapped in frozen ground. It was too cold for decay microbes to work, so the mammoth's body was preserved.

2. Extinction and Speciation

Page 211 — Fact Recall Questions

Q1 Any two from: e.g. the environment changes too quickly. / A new predator kills them all. / A new disease kills them all. / They can't compete with another (new) species for food. / A catastrophic event happens that kills them all. / A new species develops.

Q2 The development of a new species.

Q3 E.g. due to the formation of a physical barrier.

Q4 Because they have a wide range of alleles.

Q5 When individuals from different populations have changed so much that they can no longer interbreed to produced fertile offspring.

Page 212 — Biology 2.8
Exam-style Questions

1 a) Populations of the original squirrel species became separated/isolated by the formation of the canyon *(1 mark)*. Each population showed variation because they had a wide range of alleles *(1 mark)*. In each population, individuals with characteristics that made them better adapted to their environment were more likely to survive and breed successfully *(1 mark)*. So the alleles that controlled beneficial characteristics were more likely to be passed onto the next generation *(1 mark)*. Eventually individuals from the different populations changed so much that they were unable to interbreed to produce fertile offspring *(1 mark)*.

Remember, the main steps leading to speciation are: isolation, genetic variation in the isolated populations, natural selection causing different characteristics and therefore different alleles to become more common in each population, populations change and are unable to interbreed.

  b) Individuals from bird species X were able to fly across the canyon *(1 mark)*, so there were no isolated populations *(1 mark)*.

Something that's a physical barrier for one species won't necessarily be a barrier for another. It depends on things like the size of the organisms involved, how they move around, how many of them there are, etc.

  c) i) The hard shells won't have decayed easily so they will have lasted a long time when buried *(1 mark)*. As the shells did decay, they will have been gradually replaced by minerals, forming a rock-like substance shaped like the original shells *(1 mark)*.

   ii) Soft tissue tends to decay away completely without forming fossils *(1 mark)*.

   iii) E.g. by geological activity / they may have been crushed by the movements of tectonic plates *(1 mark)*.

Biology 3.1 Movement of Molecules Into and Out of Cells

1. Osmosis
Page 215 — Fact Recall Questions

Q1 The movement of water molecules across a partially permeable membrane from a region of high water concentration to a region of low water concentration.

Q2 If a cell is short of water, the surrounding tissue fluid will usually have a higher concentration of water molecules/be more dilute than the solution inside the cell. This means water molecules will move by osmosis from the tissue fluid into the cell.

Q3 E.g. water, sugar, ions

Pages 215-216 — Application Questions

Q1 a) i) They got longer/increased in length (by an average of 3.1 mm in the 0.00 M solution and an average of 2.1 mm in the 0.25 M solution).

   ii) The solutions contained a higher concentration of water molecules/were more dilute than the fluid inside the potato cells. So water molecules moved into the potato cells by osmosis and the potato cylinders increased in size.

Cells that take on water by osmosis will also increase in mass. So you could vary this experiment slightly by measuring the change in mass of the potato cylinders.

  b) Accept any answer between – 3 mm and – 4 mm.

  c) i) the length of the potato cylinders

The dependent variable is the variable you measure — in this case potato cylinder length.

   ii) the concentration of the sugar solution

The independent variable is the variable you change.

  d) Any two from, e.g. the volume of each solution / the temperature each solution was kept at / the time the cylinders were left for / the type of sugar used.

Q2 Because as Laura runs, she will lose water and ions in her sweat. It is important to replace these because if the balance between ions and water in her body is wrong, it could damage her cells/mean that her cells don't work as well as normal. Sports drinks contain water and ions, so drinking them can replace those lost in sweat. Laura's muscles will also use up sugar as she runs — the sugar in the sports drink will replace the sugar she uses up.

Q3 Any two from, e.g. the sample size of the majority of the studies was too small. / Most of the study participants were men, so the results may not be relevant to women. / Most of the studies didn't repeat their trial and evidence is only reliable if it can be repeated. / Most of the studies didn't carry out any sort of blind trial. If the participants knew whether they were getting the sports drink or a control, this may have influenced the results.

2. Active Transport
Page 217 — Fact Recall Questions
Q1 The movement of particles against a concentration gradient (i.e. from an area of low concentration to an area of high concentration) using energy released during respiration.
Q2 False
Cells can absorb ions from very dilute solutions using active transport.

3. Gas and Solute Exchange
Page 219 — Fact Recall Questions
Q1 a) diffusion, active transport and osmosis
b) diffusion and active transport
Q2 Any three from: e.g. they may be thin. / They may have a large surface area. / They may have lots of blood vessels. / They may be ventilated.

Page 219 — Application Question
Q1 a) Any two from, e.g. it may be thin, so oxygen and carbon dioxide have a short distance to diffuse/a short diffusion pathway. / It may have a large surface area so lots of oxygen/carbon dioxide can diffuse at once. / It may have lots of blood vessels to get gases into and out of the blood quickly.
b) Because elephants are larger and more complex organisms than earthworms. This means that most of their cells are a long way from their gas exchange surface, which makes gas exchange more difficult.

4. Exchange in Humans
Page 221 — Fact Recall Questions
Q1 E.g. they have a large surface area. / They have a moist lining for dissolving gases. / They're thin. / They have a good blood supply.
Q2 They increase the surface area of the small intestine so that nutrients can be absorbed more quickly.

5. The Breathing System
Page 224 — Fact Recall Questions
Q1 a) the thorax
b) the diaphragm
Q2 To protect the lungs.
Q3 The movement of air into and out of the lungs. / Breathing in and breathing out.
Q4 false
When you breathe in, the diaphragm contracts and flattens (this increases the volume of the thorax, leading to a drop in pressure in the thorax, which draws air into the lungs).
Q5 true
Q6 E.g. it doesn't interfere with blood flow (which an iron lung does).

Page 224 — Application Question
Q1 a) C
Taking a very deep breath in will dramatically increase lung volume.
b) A
c) D
The pressure in the lungs will be highest when the lung volume is at its lowest.

6. Exchange in Plants
Page 227 — Fact Recall Questions
Q1 By diffusion through the stomata.
Q2 It has a flattened shape and there are air spaces inside the leaf.
Q3 guard cells
Q4 Because a plant loses most of its water through the stomata and if the plant loses more water than can be replaced by the roots, it will wilt. Closing the stomata helps to prevent this from happening.
Q5 By absorption through the root hair cells.
Water is absorbed by osmosis and mineral ions are absorbed by active transport.

Page 227 — Application Question
Q1 a) They have lost water by evaporation and diffusion (through their stomata).
b) The plant next to the fan. Diffusion is quicker in windy conditions, which the movement of the fan will recreate.
c) E.g. instead of using a fan he could leave one plant in a warmer/colder place than the other plant, e.g. in an airing cupboard/refrigerator.

Pages 230-231 — Biology 3.1
Exam-style Questions
1 a) How to grade your answer:
0 marks:
There is no relevant information.
1-2 marks:
There is a brief explanation of how ventilation occurs with little or no reference to structures Y and Z.
3-4 marks:
There is some explanation of how ventilation occurs with some reference to structures Y and Z. The answer has a logical structure and spelling, punctuation and grammar are mostly correct.
5-6 marks:
There is a detailed explanation of how ventilation occurs with full reference to structures Y and Z. The answer has a logical structure and uses correct spelling, grammar and punctuation.
Here are some points your answer may include:
To breathe in, the intercostal muscles contract, moving the ribcage (labelled Y on the diagram) up and out.
The diaphragm (labelled Z on the diagram) also contracts, making it flatten.

This increases the volume of the thorax, which decreases the pressure in the thorax, drawing air into the lungs.

To breathe out, the intercostal muscles relax so the ribcage moves in and down.

The diaphragm also relaxes, making it bulge upwards.

This decreases the volume of the thorax, decreasing the pressure in the thorax, forcing air out of the lungs.

b) Any three from: e.g. they have thin walls. / They have a large surface area. / They have lots of blood vessels/a good blood supply. / They have a moist lining *(1 mark for each correct answer)*.

2   a) small holes in the surface of a leaf *(1 mark)*

    b) i) A plant loses water through its stomata *(1 mark)*. Evaporation/water loss is quickest in hot, dry conditions *(1 mark)*. So closing the stomata when it is hot and dry and only opening them when it is cooler, will reduce water loss from the plant *(1 mark)*.

      ii) Trapping water vapour close to the surface of the leaf will reduce the difference in the concentration of water molecules between the inside and outside of the leaf *(1 mark)*. This will slow down evaporation/water loss from the plant *(1 mark)*.

Plants in dry conditions want to conserve as much water as possible because there's so little available in the environment.

3   a) Glucose may be absorbed by active transport when the concentration of glucose molecules in the small intestine is lower than the concentration of glucose molecules in the blood *(1 mark)*. Respiration is needed to provide energy for this process *(1 mark)*.

    b) The flattening of the villi would decrease the surface area of the small intestine *(1 mark)*, meaning less glucose would be absorbed *(1 mark)*.

    c) Osmosis *(1 mark)*. The water moves from an area of high concentration (in the large intestine) to an area of relatively low concentration (in the bloodstream) *(1 mark)*.

4   a) Water moves by osmosis from a region of high water concentration to region of a low water concentration *(1 mark)*. The potato has a lower water concentration than the water in the dish, so water moves from the dish into the potato cells *(1 mark)*. The potato has a higher water concentration than the sugar/well, so water moves from the potato into the well and dissolves the sugar/creates a sugar solution *(1 mark)*.

    b) There's no sugar in the well in the potato in experiment B, so no water is drawn out of the potato into the well at the top *(1 mark)*. This means the difference in the concentration of the solution in the potato cells and in the dish is smaller *(1 mark)*, so the movement of water molecules by osmosis is reduced *(1 mark)*.

Biology 3.2 Transport Systems in Animals and Plants

1. Circulatory System — The Heart
Page 234 — Fact Recall Questions
Q1 To transport food and oxygen to every cell in the body and to carry waste products such as carbon dioxide and urea to where they can be removed from the body.

Q2 One circuit pumps deoxygenated blood from the heart to the lungs, and then oxygenated blood from the lungs back to the heart. The other circuit pumps oxygenated blood from the heart to the rest of the body, and then deoxygenated blood from the rest of the body back to the heart.

Q3 muscle tissue

Q4 right atrium, right ventricle, left atrium, left ventricle

Q5 a) vena cava and pulmonary vein
     b) pulmonary artery and aorta

Q6 Blood flows through the pulmonary vein and the vena cava into the atria. The atria contract, pushing blood into the ventricles. The ventricles then contract, forcing the blood into the pulmonary artery and aorta, and out of the heart.

2. Circulatory System — The Blood Vessels
Page 236 — Fact Recall Questions
Q1 An artery has thick walls compared to its lumen. The walls have thick layers of muscle and elastic fibres.

Q2 a capillary

Q3 Capillaries carry blood very close to the body cells. The substances needed by the body cells diffuse out of the blood, through the walls of capillaries, and into the body cells.

Q4 Any two from: e.g. a vein has thinner walls than an artery. / A vein has a bigger lumen than an artery. / A vein would have valves whereas an artery wouldn't.

Page 236 — Application Questions
Q1 A vein, because veins carry blood into the heart.

Q2 A. Arteries carry blood at a higher pressure than veins and their walls are more muscular as a result. Blood vessel A carries blood at a higher pressure than blood vessel B, and so is more likely to be an artery and have more muscle in its walls.

3. Circulatory System — The Blood

Pages 238-239 — Fact Recall Questions

Q1 a) haemoglobin
   b) It carries oxygen.
Q2 To defend against microorganisms that cause disease.
Q3 False
   White blood cells do have a nucleus. Red blood cells don't (so they have more room for haemoglobin).
Q4 Small fragments/pieces of cells.
Q5

	Transported from:	Transported to:
Soluble products of digestion	small intestine	cells of the body
Carbon dioxide	organs	lungs
Urea	liver	kidneys

Page 239 — Application Questions

Q1 Platelets, because platelets help the blood to clot at the site of a wound.
Q2 Haemoglobin is needed to carry oxygen around the body in red blood cells, so without enough haemoglobin, organs won't get enough oxygen.
Q3 Fay, because the number of white blood cells in her blood is below the normal range / lower than the number of white blood cells in Imogen's blood. White blood cells help to defend the body against microorganisms, so with fewer white blood cells in her blood, Fay is more likely to get an infection.

4. Circulation Aids

Page 243 — Fact Recall Questions

Q1 A mechanical device that is put into a person to pump blood if their own heart fails.
Q2 a) A wire mesh tube that can be inserted inside arteries to keep them open.
   b) A stent can be put into a coronary artery that has a build up of fatty deposits, in order to widen the artery and allow blood to flow to the heart muscle.

Page 243 — Application Questions

Q1 a) When a person has lost a lot of blood, they will have lost a lot of red blood cells, which carry oxygen. This means less oxygen will be able to get to respiring cells. Perfluorocarbon emulsions could be used to transport the necessary oxygen to the cells.
   b) E.g. perfluorocarbon emulsions are biologically inert so there isn't a risk of an immune reaction being triggered, which there is with donated blood products. Also, as perfluorocarbon emulsions are made in a laboratory, it's possible that lots of the blood substitute can be ready for use at any given time — unlike donated blood products, the availability of which depends on the number of people who decide to give blood.

Q2 E.g. artificial heart two may be more convenient for the patient, as they will be able to move around more freely than if they had to carry a battery pack around with them. Also, artificial heart two doesn't need to have wires coming out of the patient's body, unlike artificial heart one. This may reduce the risk of infection compared to artificial heart one, as there are no openings in the skin where microorganisms could enter the body.
However, artificial heart two has only been implanted into 14 patients, whereas artificial heart one has been implanted into 1100 patients. So there's a greater chance that there may be problems with the use of artificial heart two, which have not yet been identified due to the small number of patients it has been used for. Overall, artificial heart two may be more convenient for the patient and have a lower risk of infection than artificial heart one, but there's a greater risk of unexpected problems occurring.
Remember, if you're asked to evaluate the use of something in the exam, you should give arguments for and against its use and use any relevant facts you're given to support the points you make. It's a good idea to sum up your evaluation at the end too.

5. Transport of Substances in Plants

Page 245 — Fact Recall Questions

Q1 a) food substances/dissolved sugars
   b) the leaves
   c) e.g. growing regions/new shoots, storage organs/ root tubers
Q2 water and mineral ions
Q3 Water is transported up a plant in the transpiration stream. Water escapes from the leaves by evaporation and diffusion. This creates a slight shortage of water in the leaves, which causes more water to be drawn up the xylem and into the leaves. This in turn causes more water to be drawn up the xylem from the roots.
Remember, the transpiration stream only goes on in the xylem — it doesn't involve the phloem.

Page 246 — Application Question

Q1 a) As temperature increases, the distance moved by the bubble in 20 minutes/the transpiration rate also increases. This is because at higher temperatures, water evaporates from the leaves more quickly. This means that water is drawn into the xylem from the glass tube more quickly, so the bubble moves further along the tube in a given time.
   b) E.g. they could have tested the transpiration rate at more temperatures/a wider range of temperatures.
   A valid experiment is one which answers the original question, in this case: how does temperature affect transpiration rate? Testing the transpiration rate at more temperatures gives them a better idea of this.

c) You would expect the bubble to have moved less than 26 mm in 20 minutes. Coating the underside of some of the leaves with nail varnish would have blocked some of the plant's stomata and reduced the amount of water that was able to escape from the leaves. Therefore the rate of transpiration would have been slower, so the bubble would have moved a shorter distance in 20 minutes.

Pages 249-250 — Biology 3.2
Exam-style Questions

1   mineral ions *(1 mark)*, leaves *(1 mark)*, roots *(1 mark)*, xylem *(1 mark)*.
2   a) (3 ÷ 154) × 100 = **1.9%** *(1 mark)*
    b) Stents can be inserted into narrowed arteries/ arteries with restricted blood flow *(1 mark)* to help keep them open/allow blood to flow more freely *(1 mark)*. People who have had a heart attack are likely to have narrowed coronary arteries, so putting stents in these arteries can prevent another heart attack *(1 mark)*.
    c) E.g. yes, because the results show that patients are less likely to die after having a drug-eluting stent inserted compared to a bare-metal stent *(1 mark)*. Also renarrowing of the artery is much less likely in patients treated with a drug-eluting stent (9%) compared to those treated with a bare-metal stent (21%) *(1 mark)*. The trial was fairly large (307 patients) which means the results are more likely to be representative of the whole population *(1 mark)*.
3   a) A — vena cava *(1 mark)*, B — right ventricle *(1 mark)*, C — left atrium *(1 mark)*.
    b) X, because veins have thinner walls than arteries *(1 mark)*.
    c) i)   They prevent the back flow of blood in the heart / prevent blood from flowing backwards in the heart *(1 mark)*.
       ii) Any two from: e.g. there is a risk of infection. / There is a risk of blood clots. / There is a risk of having a stroke *(2 marks for two correct answers)*.
4   a) Similarity:
       E.g. both circulatory systems involve the blood going to an organ to pick up oxygen. / Both systems involve a heart pumping blood around the body *(1 mark)*.
       Difference:
       E.g. The circulatory system of a fish is just one circuit, whereas that of a human is two separate circuits. / The circulatory system of a fish picks up oxygen at the gills, whereas that of a human picks up oxygen at the lungs *(1 mark)*.

b) How to grade your answer:
   0 marks:
   There is no relevant information.
   1-2 marks:
   One component of blood is given and its function briefly described, or at least two components of blood are given but their functions not correctly described.
   3-4 marks:
   At least two components of blood are given and the function of one or both components is described correctly. The answer has a logical structure and spelling, punctuation and grammar are mostly correct.
   5-6 marks:
   At least three components of blood are given, and their functions are described correctly and in detail. The answer has a logical structure and uses correct spelling, grammar and punctuation.
   Here are some points your answer may include:
   Red blood cells transport oxygen from the lungs to all the cells of the body. They contain a red pigment called haemoglobin, which carries the oxygen.
   White blood cells help to defend the body against disease/microorganisms.
   Platelets help blood to clot at a wound.
   Plasma carries just about everything in the blood including the soluble products of digestion (from the gut to the cells of the body), carbon dioxide (from the organs to the lungs) and urea (from the liver to the kidneys).

Biology 3.3 Homeostasis

1. What is Homeostasis?
Page 251 — Fact Recall Questions
Q1 Via the lungs when we breathe out.
Q2 In the bladder.

2. The Kidneys and Homeostasis
Page 254 — Fact Recall Questions
Q1 False
    The body loses more water as sweat when you are hot, so more water needs to be taken into the body to balance this loss.
Q2 Blood from the renal artery enters the kidney. A high pressure is built up in the blood vessels, which squeezes water, urea, ions and sugar out of the blood and into an area called the capsule at the start of the nephron. The membranes between the blood vessels and the capsule act like filters, meaning that big molecules like proteins and blood cells are not squeezed out.
Q3 Any two from: e.g. sugar / water / ions.
    All of the sugar is reabsorbed, but only the amount of water and ions actually needed by the body is reabsorbed.
Q4 E.g. urea / water / (excess) ions.

Page 255 — Application Questions

Q1 a) i) (volume of water reabsorbed ÷ volume of water filtered) × 100
= (178.2 ÷ 180) × 100 = **99%**

ii) It would increase. The person would lose more water in sweat, so the kidney would reabsorb more water in order to balance this loss.

iii) A small amount of concentrated urine would be produced.

b) 800 millimoles. All of the glucose filtered by the kidney should be reabsorbed in a person with healthy kidneys.

c) 720 – 500 = **220 millimoles per day**.
If a greater amount of a substance is filtered by the kidneys than is reabsorbed, then the remainder will end up in the urine.

Q2

Person	Largest volume of urine	Smallest volume of urine	Most concentrated urine	Most dilute urine
Katherine		✓	✓	
Cate				
Julia	✓			✓

3. Kidney Failure
Page 258 — Fact Recall Questions

Q1 False
People with kidney failure need to have dialysis regularly to keep the concentrations of dissolved substances in the blood at normal levels.

Q2 E.g. proteins.

Q3 The recipient's white bloods cells do not recognise the antigens on the donor kidney cells. As a result, they make antibodies to attack the donor cells.

Q4 E.g. using a donor with a tissue-type that closely matches the patient. / Using drugs that suppress the immune system.

Q5 False
There are waiting lists for organs such as kidneys. People needing a kidney transplant may have to wait a long time for a suitable donor organ to become available. They'll need to have dialysis while they are waiting.

Page 259 — Application Questions

Q1 a) So that useful sodium ions won't be lost from the blood during dialysis, as they won't diffuse across the barrier into the dialysis fluid.

b) i) Urea is a waste product which is carried to the kidneys in the blood.

ii) As there is some urea in the plasma there needs to be less in the dialysis fluid for urea to be removed from the blood. If there is no urea in the dialysis fluid at the start of the dialysis session, then there will be a concentration gradient between the blood and the dialysis fluid, allowing urea to leave the blood via diffusion.

c) E.g. there would be a similar amount. Glucose isn't a waste product — it's a substance that the body needs. If there are similar amounts in both the blood and the dialysis fluid then glucose won't be lost from the blood during dialysis.

Q2 a) Any three from: e.g. there are long waiting lists for donor kidneys. / There is a risk of rejection even if a kidney with a matching tissue-type is found. / The patient has to take drugs which suppress the immune system, which makes them vulnerable to other illnesses and infections. / A kidney transplant is a major operation, so it can be risky.

b) Any two from: e.g. she won't have to have dialysis. / She will no longer be at risk of infections that can be picked up during dialysis. / She won't be at risk of blood clots from dialysis. / She won't have to be as careful about what she eats. / She won't have to limit her fluid intake.

4. Controlling Body Temperature
Page 262 — Fact Recall Questions

Q1 a) the brain

b) Receptors in the thermoregulatory centre that are sensitive to the temperature of the blood flowing through the brain and receptors in the skin that are sensitive to skin temperature.

Q2 Because blood flow to the skin increases.

Q3 a) They dilate.

b) More blood flows close to the surface of the skin, which makes it easier for heat to be transferred from the blood to the environment.

Page 262 — Application Question

Q1 a) E.g. hairs on her skin will stand up. / The amount of sweat she produces will decrease. / The blood vessels supplying her skin capillaries will constrict/ get narrower. / She will shiver/her muscles will contract automatically.

b) E.g. her hairs standing up traps an insulating layer of air, reducing heat loss. / Her lack of sweat decreases the amount of cooling that occurs from sweat evaporating from her skin. / The constriction of blood vessels supplying the skin capillaries reduces the skin's blood supply, meaning that less heat is transferred from the skin to the environment. / Her shivering/the automatic contraction of her muscles helps to raise body temperature as it increases the rate of respiration, which releases some energy to warm the body.

5. Controlling Blood Glucose Level

Page 265 — Fact Recall Questions

Q1 the pancreas

Q2 Insulin makes body cells take up more glucose from the blood.

Q3 the pancreas

Q4 A condition where the pancreas produces little or no insulin, which means blood glucose can rise to a dangerous level.

Page 265 — Application Question

Q1 a) Glucagon, because the subject's blood glucose level rises following the injection. Glucagon causes glycogen to be converted back into glucose, which enters the blood, causing the blood glucose level to rise.

b) i) insulin

ii) The blood glucose level would fall following the injection, as insulin causes body cells to take up more glucose from the blood, causing the blood glucose level to fall.

Pages 268-269 — Biology 3.3

Exam-style Questions

1 a) i) Via the breakdown of amino acids *(1 mark)*.

ii) The kidney firstly filters the blood *(1 mark)*. All the sugar is reabsorbed *(1 mark)* and sufficient amounts of water and ions are reabsorbed *(1 mark)*. The remaining urea, excess water and ions make up the urine *(1 mark)*.

b) 100 – 99.5 = 0.5%

(575 ÷ 100) × 0.5 = **2.88 g per day**.

(2 marks for correct answer, otherwise 1 mark for correct working)

2 a) i) Kidney dialysis filters the blood to remove waste products such as urea, *(1 mark)* and to keep the concentration of dissolved substances in the blood at normal levels in patients with kidney failure *(1 mark)*.

ii) Any three from: e.g. having dialysis takes up a lot of time. / Dialysis can lead to infections. / Dialysis can cause blood clots. / Dialysis patients have to be careful about what they eat to avoid too much of a particular ion building up between dialysis sessions. / Patients have to limit the amount of fluid they take in, as fluid can build up in the body to a dangerous level/ cause problems such as high blood pressure. / Kidney dialysis machines are expensive for the NHS to run *(1 mark for each correct answer up to a maximum of 3 marks)*.

b) i) E.g. they may not have matched Chi's tissue-type *(1 mark)*. If the donor's tissue-type is not a close enough match to Chi's tissue-type, then the antigens on the cells of the donor kidney will not be a close enough match to the antigens on Chi's cells *(1 mark)*. As a result, Chi's white blood cells won't recognise the antigens and may produce antibodies to attack the donor kidney cells *(1 mark)*.

ii) E.g. to reduce the chance that her immune system/antibodies will attack the donor kidney and reject it *(1 mark)*.

3 a) The thermoregulatory centre *(1 mark)* in the brain contains receptors that are sensitive to the temperature of the blood flowing through the brain *(1 mark)*. The thermoregulatory centre also receives inputs about skin temperature from receptors in the skin (via nervous impulses) *(1 mark)*.

b) E.g. more sweat will be produced by his sweat glands *(1 mark)*. Sweat removes heat from the skin as it evaporates, helping to reduce body temperature *(1 mark)*. The blood vessels supplying his skin capillaries will dilate *(1 mark)* so more blood will flow close to the surface of the skin, making it easier for heat to be transferred from the blood to the environment *(1 mark)*.

4 a) i) People with type 1 diabetes produce little or no insulin *(1 mark)*. Injecting insulin stops their blood glucose level from rising to a dangerous level *(1 mark)* as insulin causes the body's cells to take up glucose from the blood *(1 mark)*.

ii) E.g. she should limit her intake of foods rich in simple carbohydrates *(1 mark)*, as these foods cause the blood glucose level to rise rapidly *(1 mark)*. / She should try to do regular exercise *(1 mark)* as this will help to lower her blood glucose level *(1 mark)*.

b) How to grade your answer:

0 marks:

There is no relevant information.

1-2 marks:

A comparison is made between the use of a pancreas transplant and the use of insulin injections to treat type 1 diabetes.

3-4 marks:

Two clear comparisons are made between the use of a pancreas transplant and the use of insulin injections to treat type 1 diabetes. The answer has a logical structure and spelling, punctuation and grammar are mostly correct.

5-6 marks:

At least three clear, detailed comparisons are made between the use of a pancreas transplant and the use of insulin injections to treat type 1 diabetes. The answer has a logical structure and uses correct spelling, grammar and punctuation.

Here are some points your answer may include:

If successful, pancreas transplants can result in the patient no longer having to inject insulin, whereas those using insulin injections as a treatment for type 1 diabetes usually inject themselves several times a day.

There is a risk of rejection with organ transplants, so recipients must take immunosuppressants for the rest of their lives. People using insulin injections to control their diabetes don't need to do this, although they do usually have to inject themselves with insulin several times a day.

Insulin injections are readily available, whereas there are waiting lists for donor pancreases, which are in short supply.

Most type 1 diabetics can use insulin, but pancreas transplants are usually reserved for those who have poor control over their diabetes.

Pancreas transplants require major surgery which is risky and can result in pain and, in some cases, infection. Injecting insulin has a much lower risk to health.

Biology 3.4 Humans and their Environment

1. Human Impact on the Environment

Page 273 — Fact Recall Questions

Q1 false
 Both the population of the world and the general standard of living are increasing.

Q2 They can be washed from the land into water.

Q3 By using toxic chemicals for farming (e.g. pesticides and herbicides), by burying nuclear waste and by creating landfill sites for other waste.

Q4 E.g. sulfur dioxide

Page 273 — Application Question

Q1 a) Both the amount of waste recycled and the amount sent to landfill has increased each year. But the amount recycled each year has increased by more than the amount sent to landfill (an extra 50 000 tonnes of waste was recycled in 2010 compared to 2006, but only 20 000 tonnes more was sent to landfill).

b) (100 000 ÷ 250 000) × 100 = **40%**
 To find the total amount of waste in 2010, you need to add together the amount recycled (100 000) and the amount sent to landfill (150 000), which equals 250 000. You can then work out the percentage of this figure that was recycled.

c) Any two from: e.g. building / farming / quarrying for metal ores.

d) The population of the world is increasing and so we are producing more waste, some of which ends up in landfill sites. Also, as the standard of living around the world increases we create even more waste. So the amount of space taken up by landfill sites, where waste is dumped, increases.

e) E.g. as the human population and standard of living increase, we use more raw materials (e.g. metal). It's important to recycle products, so that we don't run out of raw materials/so that we don't need to dig as many quarries to obtain raw materials. / As the human population and standard of living increase, we produce more waste. It's important to recycle products as it reduces the amount of waste sent to landfill and therefore the amount of space taken up by landfill sites.

2. Deforestation and the Destruction of Peat Bogs

Page 276 — Application Questions

Q1 a) 900 thousand hectares
 To find the total amount of forest cleared, you need to read off the value for the full height of the bar. Don't forget to include the units in your answer either.

b) i) 400 thousand hectares

ii) E.g. cattle farming, growing rice crops or growing crops to create biofuels.

c) E.g. to provide timber for use as a building material. / To produce paper.
 If the land wasn't wanted for anything, this suggests that the trees themselves were.

d) Carbon dioxide is released into the atmosphere when trees are burnt to clear land. Deforestation also means there are fewer trees to take in carbon dioxide from the atmosphere during photosynthesis. So deforestation leads to an increase in the atmospheric carbon dioxide level.

Q2 Peat bogs store carbon instead of releasing it into the atmosphere as carbon dioxide. If peat bogs are destroyed (e.g. to use the peat in compost), this carbon dioxide will be released, contributing to global warming. So peat-free compost helps to prevent the destruction of peat bogs, and so could be considered an environmentally-friendly option.

3. Carbon Dioxide and the Greenhouse Effect

Page 278 — Fact Recall Questions

Q1 Any three from: e.g. oceans / lakes / ponds / trees and plants / peat bogs.

Q2 The Earth absorbs heat energy from the Sun and radiates this heat back into the atmosphere. Gases in the atmosphere (greenhouse gases) absorb this heat energy and re-radiate it back out in all directions, including back down to the Earth, helping to keep it warm.

Q3 E.g. carbon dioxide and methane.

Q4 Increasing levels of gases such as methane and carbon dioxide in the atmosphere are causing an increase in the greenhouse effect. This has led to global warming.

Page 278 — Application Question

Q1 An increasing level of carbon dioxide (CO_2) in the atmosphere is contributing to global warming and climate change. Finding places to store CO_2 means it will be removed from the atmosphere, so it won't contribute to global warming.

4. Climate Change
Page 282 — Fact Recall Questions
Q1 The increase in temperature caused by global warming can cause changes to the weather and weather patterns. For example, some places might become hotter and so experience more droughts. As the oceans warm up, more hurricanes might form.

Q2 Organisms are found in places where they can survive. If the average global temperature increases the distribution of organisms may change. E.g. animals that require cooler temperatures may only exist in a smaller area and animals that require warmer temperatures may become more widely distributed.

Q3 E.g. rising sea level, changes to migration patterns, less biodiversity.

Page 282 — Application Questions
Q1 a) No. E.g. the bird species started to become more common at the same time the average global temperature was going up, but that's not enough to say that global warming has caused the bird species to become more common. This could be just coincidence and something else could have caused more birds to appear. For example, farming practices have changed a lot in the same time period, which might have affected bird numbers. Also, the average global temperature went up at that time, but there is nothing given here to suggest what happened to the temperature in that country (it may not have changed at all).

   b) E.g. global warming could cause a change in birds' migration patterns, so birds that come to the country for only part of the year could be around for a shorter/longer period of time or it might cause birds to arrive and leave at slightly different times of the year. / If some bird species fail to adapt to the changes in their environment caused by global warming, then they might die out. / Birds that live, feed or breed near the coast might have problems if the sea level rises because of global warming.

Q2 a) 120 mm
   In 1940 it was −70 mm and in 2000 it was 50 mm, so that's 70 + 50 = 120 mm. Make sure you read the question and axes correctly.

   b) E.g. yes. The data covers a large time span. It has been published in peer-reviewed journals. The data was collected from numerous sites around the world, so the sample size seems a good size. Several studies have been used to compile the data, so the data is reproducible.

   c) As the global temperature increases, sea water heats up and expands, causing the sea level to rise. Water that's trapped on land will also melt, adding more water to the sea and raising its level.

5. Biofuels
Page 284 — Fact Recall Questions
Q1 Fuels made from the fermentation of natural products.
Q2 When bacteria or yeast break down sugars by anaerobic respiration.
Q3 false
   Anaerobic respiration takes place in the absence of oxygen.
Q4 methane
Q5 Microorganisms are used to ferment plant material and animal waste containing carbohydrates.

Page 284 — Application Questions
Q1 Biogas is made from the fermentation of plant and animal material by microorganisms using anaerobic respiration (which takes place where there is no oxygen). Burying the waste underground prevents oxygen from reaching it, which means anaerobic respiration occurs and biogas is produced.

Q2 No. Biogas is made from the fermentation of animal waste and plant material containing carbohydrates. This waste contains no carbohydrates, so there's nothing for the microorganisms to ferment and produce biogas from.

6. Using Biogas Generators
Page 288 — Fact Recall Questions
Q1 It has an inlet for waste material to be added, an outlet for the digested material to be removed, and another outlet for biogas to be extracted.

Q2 Batch generators make biogas in small batches, whereas continuous generators are always working and producing biogas.
   When you're asked to talk about differences or make comparisons, make sure you use words like 'whereas', 'however', 'on the other hand'...

Q3 Cost, convenience, efficiency and position.
Q4 Because gas is produced most quickly at this temperature (as the enzymes in the microorganisms work best at this temperature).

Q5 Any two from: e.g. the raw material is cheap. / The digested material can be used as a fertiliser. / It might stop people having to walk a long way to get fuel. / It helps to get rid of waste products that can cause disease and pollution.

Q6 The carbon taken in by the materials used to make the fuel when they were growing is equal to that released when the biogas is burnt.

Q7 E.g. it stops methane, which contributes to global warming, being given off by the unused waste. / It doesn't produce significant amounts of sulfur dioxide, which can cause acid rain. / The waste material might otherwise end up in a landfill, causing pollution.

Page 288 — Application Questions

Q1 E.g. the biogas generator, because this will help to deal with the need for more energy and deal with some of the extra waste that is being generated (so less goes to landfill). It is also better for the environment than burning coal as biogas does produce carbon dioxide when burnt, but is carbon neutral. Burning biogas also doesn't release as much sulfur dioxide as burning coal, and sulfur dioxide can cause acid rain. The raw material is also cheap and more readily available, whereas coal would have to be bought in and is expensive.

Q2 E.g. a small-scale, batch generator because these generators are the simplest and cheapest type to build. Also, the family only have animals grazing at the farm during summer, so they might not produce enough waste to run a continuous or large-scale generator. The generator will have to be kept cool somehow to keep biogas production most efficient, e.g. by burying it underground, as the temperature in summer can be quite high (40 °C). It should be built close to where the animals are kept to make transporting the waste easier, but far enough away from any homes that the smell doesn't cause a problem.

7. Managing Food Production
Page 290 — Fact Recall Questions
Q1 true

Q2 If you use the land to grow crops rather than grazing animals, then you cut one stage out of the food chain. Energy is lost at every stage in a food chain, so by cutting out one stage, less energy is lost and more food can be produced.

Q3 Animals lose energy trying to keep warm and moving around. By intensively farming them you can reduce their movement and keep them warm, so they lose less energy. This means they have more energy to put into growing, and so grow faster on less food.

Q4 E.g. by using fishing quotas. These limit the number and size of fish that can be caught in certain areas, preventing certain species from being overfished. By controlling mesh size of the fish nets. Using a bigger mesh size will reduce the number of 'unwanted' and discarded fish, by allowing unwanted species to escape.

8. Modern Food Production and Distribution
Page 293 — Fact Recall Questions
Q1 Protein produced by fungi.

Q2 The fungus *Fusarium* is grown in fermenters, using glucose syrup (obtained by digesting maize starch with enzymes). Oxygen, together with nitrogen and other minerals are also supplied so the fungus can grow, and the whole mixture is kept at the right pH and temperature. When the fungi has grown, the mycoprotein is harvested, purified and dried and flavourings and other ingredients might be added.

Q3 false
Benefits include increased efficiency of food production, cheaper food, better standards of living for farmers and helping to feed an increasing human population.

Q4 E.g. intensive farming is one way of helping to feed an increasing human population and it also means cheaper food, but there are several disadvantages to farming this way (e.g. reduced animal welfare, etc.).

Q5 That the foods have been transported a long way from where they're produced to where they're sold.

Page 293 — Application Questions
Q1 Any one from: e.g. the state may not be able to provide its population with enough water to drink. / The state might have problems providing enough water for farmers to water their crops, so crops could fail. / Long-term, the river might dry up if the other state takes too much water.

Q2 a) Because the chickens are free to roam about, they will lose more energy than the intensively farmed chickens. This makes free range farming a less efficient method of farming, so the eggs cost more to produce and more to buy.

b) E.g. some people think it's cruel to force animals to live in intensive farming conditions. Free range animals live in more natural environments and have room to move around.

Pages 296-297 — Biology 3.4
Exam-style Questions
1 a) A type of biofuel made from the anaerobic fermentation *(1 mark)* of plant material and animal waste containing carbohydrates *(1 mark)*. It's mainly made of methane with some carbon dioxide in it *(1 mark)*.

b) i) $1500 - 200 = $ **1300** *(1 mark)*

ii) E.g. in the first two years after the scheme was introduced, there was a rapid increase in the number of biogas generators *(1 mark)*. In 1997 there were 500 generators in the country and two years later there were 1400 *(1 mark)*. But in the third year, the increase in generators tailed off *(1 mark)* — only 100 more generators were built in one year *(1 mark)*.

It's up to you exactly what data you use from the graph here — just make sure the figures you give support your answer.

c) Habitats like rainforest contain huge numbers of species, so when they are destroyed there is a danger of many species becoming extinct *(1 mark)*. This reduces biodiversity *(1 mark)*.

2   How to grade your answer:

0 marks:
No relevant information is given.

1-2 marks:
There is a brief mention of one or two ways in which human activities can cause water, land or air pollution.

3-4 marks:
There is a description of at least three ways in which human activities can cause water, land or air pollution. At least two different types of pollution are covered. The answer has a logical structure and spelling, grammar and punctuation are mostly correct.

5-6 marks:
There is a full explanation of at least four ways in which human activities can cause water, land and air pollution. All three different types of pollution are clearly covered. The answer has a logical structure and uses correct spelling, grammar and punctuation.

Here are some points your answer may include:
Sewage and toxic chemicals from industry may pollute ponds, rivers and oceans.
The chemicals we use to help grow crops on land (such as fertilisers, herbicides and pesticides) may be washed into waterways.
We can also pollute the land itself with the toxic chemicals (such as herbicides and pesticides) we use in farming.
We pollute the land by burying waste in landfill sites.
We pollute the air with smoke from cars and industry.
We burn fossil fuels, which releases gases such as sulfur dioxide into the atmosphere. Sulfur dioxide can cause acid rain.
Burning fossil fuels also releases carbon dioxide into the atmosphere. The increasing level of carbon dioxide is contributing to global warming.

3   a) i) $1.6 \times 52 = $ **83.2 L** *(1 mark)*.
    Remember: there are 52 weeks in a year, so you need to multiply 1.6 by 52.

    ii)   Any three from, e.g. it may cause other types of climate change (e.g. more extreme weather/ longer, hotter droughts) *(1 mark)*. / It may cause the sea level to rise *(1 mark)*. / It may cause changes in the distribution of organisms/where organisms are found (e.g. some may become more widely distributed, others less widely distributed) *(1 mark)*. / It may cause changes in the migration patterns of some animals/ birds *(1 mark)*. / It may lead to a reduction in biodiversity *(1 mark)*.

    b)   lost *(1 mark)*, fewer *(1 mark)*

    c)   Because the animals we farm for meat eat grain *(1 mark)*. If we eat less meat, we farm fewer animals and so use less grain feeding them *(1 mark)*.

d) i)   Any two from: e.g. some people think that forcing animals to live in unnatural and uncomfortable conditions is cruel *(1 mark)*. / The animals need to be kept warm and that often means using power produced by burning fossil fuels, which contributes to global warming *(1 mark)*. / The crowded conditions on factory farms create a favourable environment for the spread of diseases *(1 mark)*. / To try to prevent disease, animals are given antibiotics, which could lead to the antibiotics become less effective as human medicines *(1 mark)*.

    ii)   Intensive farming helps to improve the efficiency of food production, by reducing the amount of energy animals lose keeping warm and moving *(1 mark)*. This means they grow faster on less food, which makes the food cheaper for us and means the farmer should make more money *(1 mark)*. It also helps to feed an increasing human population *(1 mark)*.

Glossary

A

Abdomen (humans)
The lower part of the body, ending at the hips.

Accurate result
A result that is very close to the true answer.

Active transport
The movement of particles against a concentration gradient (i.e. from an area of low concentration to an area of high concentration) using energy released during respiration.

Adaptation
A characteristic that helps an organism to survive.

Addiction (drugs)
Being dependant on a particular substance.

Adult cell cloning
A method of cloning animals, which involves taking the nucleus from an adult body cell and inserting it into an unfertilised egg cell that has had its nucleus removed.

Aerobic respiration
The reactions involved in breaking down glucose using oxygen, to release energy. Carbon dioxide and water are produced.

Allele
An alternative version of a gene.

Alveolus
A tiny air sac in the lungs, where gas exchange occurs.

Amino acid
A small molecule that is a building block of proteins.

Amylase
A digestive enzyme that catalyses the breakdown of starch into sugars, in the mouth and small intestine.

Anabolic steroid
A type of performance-enhancing drug that increases muscle growth.

Anaerobic respiration
The incomplete breakdown of glucose, which produces lactic acid. It takes place in the absence of oxygen.

Anomalous result
A result that doesn't seem to fit with the rest of the data.

Antibiotic
A drug used to kill or prevent the growth of bacteria.

Antibiotic resistance
When bacteria aren't killed by an antibiotic.

Antibody
A protein produced by white blood cells in response to the presence of an antigen (e.g. on the surface of a pathogen).

Antigen
A molecule on the surface of a cell. A foreign antigen triggers white blood cells to produce antibodies.

Antitoxin
A protein produced by white blood cells which counteracts the toxins produced by invading bacteria.

Aorta
A blood vessel (artery) which transports blood from the heart to the rest of the body (excluding the lungs).

Artificial blood product
A product which is used as a substitute for normal blood.

Artificial heart
A mechanical device that's put into a person to pump blood if their own heart fails.

Artificial heart valve
A mechanical device that's put into a person's heart to control the direction of blood flow if they have a defective heart valve.

Artificial ventilator
A machine that moves air (often with extra oxygen in it) into or out of the lungs.

Asexual reproduction
Where organisms reproduce by mitosis to produce genetically identical offspring.

Atrium
A chamber of the heart into which blood enters from either the pulmonary vein or the vena cava.

Auxin
A plant hormone that controls the growth of a plant in response to different stimuli.

B

Bacterium
A single-celled microorganism without a nucleus. Some bacteria are able to cause disease.

Balanced diet
A diet that contains the right amounts of the different nutrients needed by the body.

Bias
Prejudice towards or against something.

Bile
A fluid that is made in the liver, stored in the gall bladder and released into the small intestine. It aids digestion by creating alkaline conditions in the small intestine and by emulsifying fats.

Biodiversity
The variety of species in a habitat (area).

Biofuel
Fuel made by the fermentation of natural products by microorganisms.

Biogas
A type of biofuel made by the anaerobic fermentation of plant material and animal waste containing carbohydrates, by microorganisms. It's usually about 70% methane and 30% carbon dioxide.

Biogas generator
A fermenter used to produce biogas.

Biological detergent
A detergent (e.g. washing powder) that contains enzymes to help break down stains.

Biomass
The mass of living material.

Blood
A tissue which transports substances around the body in the circulatory system.

Blood cholesterol level
The level of cholesterol (a fatty substance) in the blood.

Carbohydrase
A type of enzyme that breaks down starch into sugars.

Carbon cycle
The continuous cycle of carbon from the air, through food chains and back into the air.

Carrier
A person who carries the allele for a genetic disorder, but who doesn't have any symptoms of the disorder.

Catalyst
A substance that increases the speed of a reaction, without being changed or used up in the reaction.

Categoric data
Data that comes in distinct categories (e.g. blood type, eye colour, sex, etc.).

Cell elongation
The enlargement of a cell. Plant cells grow by cell elongation.

Cell membrane
A membrane surrounding a cell, which holds it all together and controls what goes in and out.

Cellulose
A molecule used to make strong cell walls in plants and algae.

Cell wall
A structure surrounding some cell types, which gives strength and support. In plant and algal cells, the cell wall is made of cellulose.

Central Nervous System (CNS)
The brain and spinal cord. It's where reflexes and actions are coordinated.

Chamber (of the heart)
An area of the heart (atrium or ventricle) through which blood is pumped.

Chlorophyll
A green substance found in chloroplasts which absorbs light for photosynthesis.

Chloroplast
A structure found in plant cells and algae, which contains chlorophyll. Chloroplasts are the site of photosynthesis.

Chromosome
A long molecule of DNA found in the nucleus, which carries genes.

Circulatory system
A system which uses blood to transport materials around the body.

Classification (of organisms)
The process of sorting organisms into groups based on their similarities and differences.

Climate change
A change in things like temperature or weather patterns in a part of the world or across the whole world. E.g. global warming is a type of climate change.

Clinical trial
A set of drug tests on human volunteers.

Clone
An organism that is genetically identical to another organism.

Cloning
Making a genetically identical copy of another organism.

Continuous data
Numerical data that can have any value within a range (e.g. length, volume or temperature).

Control experiment
An experiment that's kept under the same conditions as the rest of the investigation, but doesn't have anything done to it.

Control group
A group that matches the one being studied, but the independent variable isn't altered. It's kept under the same conditions as the group in the experiment.

Control variable
A variable in an experiment that is kept the same.

Core body temperature
The temperature deep within the body.

Coronary artery
A blood vessel which supplies blood to the heart muscle.

Coronary heart disease
A disease in which the coronary arteries are narrowed by the build up of fatty deposits.

Correlation
A relationship between two variables.

Culture (of microorganisms)
A population of one type of microorganism that's been grown under controlled conditions.

Cutting (plants)
A small piece of a plant (usually with a new bud on) that can be taken and grown into a new plant.

Cystic fibrosis
A genetic disorder of the cell membranes caused by a recessive allele.

Cytoplasm
A gel-like substance in a cell where most of the chemical reactions take place.

Decay
The breakdown of dead organisms.

Deficiency disease
A disease caused by a lack of a certain nutrient in the diet, e.g. a vitamin or a mineral.

Deforestation
The cutting down of forests (large areas of trees).

Dependent variable
The variable in an experiment that is measured.

Detritus feeder
An animal that feeds on dead material and breaks down animal waste products.

Dialysis fluid
A fluid that has a similar concentration of glucose and ions as blood plasma. It is used in kidney dialysis machines.

Diaphragm
The muscle separating the abdomen from the thorax. The contraction and relaxation of the diaphragm controls ventilation.

Differentiation
The process by which a cell becomes specialised for its job.

Diffusion
The spreading out of particles from an area of high concentration to an area of low concentration.

Direct proportionality
When a graph of two variables is plotted and the variables increase or decrease in the same ratio.

Discrete data
Numerical data that can be counted in chunks with no in-between value (e.g. number of people).

Distribution
Where organisms are found in a particular area.

DNA (deoxyribonucleic acid)
The molecule in cells that stores genetic information.

DNA fingerprinting
A technique used to identify an individual based on their DNA.

Dominant allele
The allele for the characteristic that's shown by an organism if two different alleles are present for that characteristic.

Double-blind trial
A clinical trial where neither the doctors nor the patients know who has received the drug and who has received the placebo until all the results have been gathered.

Drug
A substance that alters the chemical reactions in your body.

Ecological relationship
The interaction between organisms in the same environment.

Effector
Either a muscle or gland which responds to nervous impulses.

Embryo transfer (cloning)
A method of cloning animals, where an embryo is created and then split, before any cells become specialised, to produce clones. The clones are then transferred into the uteruses of host mothers.

Embryonic screening
Genetic analysis of a cell taken from an embryo before it's implanted into the uterus during IVF, in order to check that the embryo doesn't carry any genetic disorders.

Embryonic stem cell
A stem cell found in the early human embryo.

Enzyme
A protein that acts as a biological catalyst.

Epidemic
A big outbreak of disease.

Epidermal tissue
A type of plant tissue which covers the whole plant.

Epithelial tissue
A type of animal tissue which covers some parts of the body, e.g. the inside of the stomach.

Evaporation
The process by which a liquid turns into a gas.

Evolution
The gradual change in a species over time.

Evolutionary relationship
How organisms are related to other organisms through evolution.

Exchange surface
A specialised surface in an organism used for the exchange of materials, e.g. gases and dissolved substances.

Excretion
The removal of waste products from the body.

Extinction
The process by which a species dies out.

Extremophile
An organism that's adapted to live in seriously extreme conditions.

Factory farming
See intensive farming (of animals).

Fair test
A controlled experiment where the only thing that changes is the independent variable.

Family tree (genetics)
A diagram which shows how a characteristic (or disorder) is inherited in a group of related people.

Fermentation
The process by which bacteria and/or yeast break down sugars by anaerobic respiration.

Fertilisation
The fusion of male and female gametes during sexual reproduction.

Fertility
The ability to conceive a child.

Fishing quota
A limit on the amount of fish that can be caught in a certain time period in a certain area.

Follicle Stimulating Hormone (FSH)
A hormone produced by the pituitary gland involved in the menstrual cycle. It causes eggs to mature in the ovaries and stimulates the ovaries to produce oestrogen.

Food miles
A measure of the distance that food has been transported from where it was produced to where it is sold.

Fossil
The remains of an organism from many years ago, which is found in rock.

Fossil record
The history of life on Earth preserved as fossils.

G

Gamete
A sex cell, e.g. an egg cell or a sperm cell in animals.

Gene
A short section of DNA, found on a chromosome, which contains the instructions needed to make a protein (and so controls the development of a characteristic).

Genetic disorder
An inherited disorder that can be caused by an abnormal gene or chromosome.

Genetic engineering
The process of cutting out a useful gene from one organism's chromosome and inserting it into another organism's chromosome.

Genetically modified (GM) crop
A crop which has had its genes modified through genetic engineering.

Genotype
What alleles you have, e.g Tt.

Geological activity
The internal and external processes that affect a planet, e.g. the movement of tectonic plates.

Geotropism
See gravitropism.

Gland
The place where hormones are produced and secreted from.

Glandular tissue
A type of animal tissue which makes and secretes substances like enzymes and hormones.

Global warming
The rise in the average global temperature.

Glucagon
A hormone produced and secreted by the pancreas when blood glucose level is too low. It causes glycogen to be converted back into glucose, increasing the blood glucose level.

Glycogen
A molecule that acts as a store of glucose in liver and muscle cells.

Gravitropism
The growth of a plant in response to gravity. Also known as geotropism.

Greenhouse effect
When gases (called greenhouse gases) in the atmosphere absorb heat radiated by the Earth and re-radiate it back down towards the Earth, helping to keep it warm.

Guard cell
A cell found on either side of a stoma, which controls the stoma's size.

Habitat
The place where an organism lives.

Haemoglobin
A red pigment found in red blood cells which carries oxygen.

Hard drug
A drug that is believed to cause serious addiction and be more harmful to a person's health than a soft drug.

Hazard
Something that has the potential to cause harm (e.g. fire, electricity, etc).

Heterozygous
Where an organism has two alleles for a particular gene that are different.

Homeostasis
The maintenance of a constant internal environment.

Homozygous
Where an organism has two alleles for a particular gene that are the same.

Hormone
A chemical messenger which travels in the blood to activate target cells.

Hypothesis
A possible explanation for a scientific observation.

Immunity
The ability of the white blood cells to respond quickly to a pathogen.

Independent variable
The variable in an experiment that is changed.

Infectious disease
A disease caused by a pathogen.

Insulin
A hormone produced and secreted by the pancreas when blood glucose level is too high. It causes the body's cells to take up more glucose from the blood, reducing the blood glucose level.

Intensive farming (of animals)
When animals are grown inside and close together, so they waste little energy moving or keeping warm.

In Vitro Fertilisation (IVF)
The artificial fertilisation of eggs in the lab.

Isomerase
An enzyme that converts glucose into fructose.

Kidney
The organ responsible for producing urine. The kidneys play an important role in the regulation of water and ion content in the body, and in the removal of waste products such as urea.

Kidney dialysis
A way of artificially filtering the blood to remove waste products and keep the concentration of dissolved ions in the blood at normal levels. It is used to treat patients with kidney failure.

Kidney transplant
Where a damaged kidney is replaced with a healthy donor kidney in patients with kidney failure.

L

Lactic acid
The product of anaerobic respiration that builds up in muscle cells and can cause muscle fatigue.

Large intestine
An organ in the mammalian digestive system where water from undigested food is absorbed, producing faeces.

Limiting factor
A factor which prevents a reaction from going any faster.

Linear relationship
When a graph of two variables is plotted and the points lie on a straight line.

Lipase
A type of digestive enzyme that catalyses the breakdown of lipids into fatty acids and glycerol, in the small intestine.

Liver
An organ in the mammalian digestive system which produces bile.

Living indicator
An organism that is sensitive to changes in its environment, so can be used to study environmental change.

Lung
A gas exchange organ in mammals.

Luteinising Hormone (LH)
A hormone produced by the pituitary gland, which stimulates egg release around the middle of the menstrual cycle.

Malnourishment
A condition in which you don't have the right balance of foods to stay healthy.

Mean (average)
A measure of average found by adding up all the data and dividing by the number of values there are.

Median (average)
The middle value in a set of data when they're in order of size.

Meiosis
A type of cell division where a cell divides twice to produce four genetically different gametes. It occurs in the reproductive organs.

Menstrual cycle
The monthly sequence of events in which the female body releases an egg and prepares the uterus (womb) in case it receives a fertilised egg.

Mesophyll tissue
A type of plant tissue which is where photosynthesis occurs.

Metabolism
The chemical reactions in the body that keep you alive.

Metabolic rate
The speed at which the chemical reactions in the body occur.

Methane
A greenhouse gas produced by cattle and by microorganisms as they ferment waste.

Mitochondria
Structures in a cell which are the site of most of the reactions for respiration.

Mitosis
A type of cell division where body cells divide once to produce two genetically identical cells.

MMR vaccine
A vaccination against the diseases measles, mumps and rubella.

Mode (average)
The most common value in a set of data.

Monohybrid cross
Where you cross two parents to look at the inheritance of just one characteristic controlled by a single gene.

Motor neurone
A nerve cell that carries electrical impulses from the CNS to effectors.

MRSA (methicillin-resistant Staphylococcus aureus)
A strain of bacteria that is resistant to the powerful antibiotic methicillin.

Multicellular organism
An organism made up of more than one cell.

Muscle fatigue
Where muscles become tired and can't contract efficiently.

Muscular tissue
A type of animal tissue which contracts (shortens) to move whatever it's attached to.

Mutation
A change in an organism's DNA.

Mycoprotein
Protein produced by fungi, in particular *Fusarium*.

Natural selection
The process by which species evolve.

Negative correlation
When one variable decreases as another variable increases.

Nephron
The filtration unit of the kidney. The nephrons produce urine.

Nervous system
The organ system in animals that allows them to respond to changes in their environment.

Neurone
A nerve cell. Neurones transmit information around the body, including to and from the CNS.

Non-living indicator
Something that is not alive, but can be measured or monitored to give information about environmental change, e.g. temperature.

Nucleus (of a cell)
A structure in a body cell which contains genetic material in the form of chromosomes.

Nutrient
A substance needed by the body in order to survive and grow, e.g. protein.

Obesity
A condition defined as being 20% or more over the maximum recommended body mass.

Oestrogen
A hormone produced by the ovaries which inhibits the release of FSH during the menstrual cycle. It's found in some oral contraceptives.

Optimum dose (in drug testing)
The dose of a drug that is most effective and has few side effects.

Oral contraceptive
A hormone-containing pill taken by mouth in order to reduce fertility and therefore decrease the chance of pregnancy.

Organ
A group of different tissues that work together to perform a certain function.

Organ rejection
Where the antigens on a donor organ are attacked by antibodies produced by the recipient's immune system following organ transplantation.

Organ system
A group of organs working together to perform a particular function.

Osmosis
The movement of water molecules across a partially permeable membrane from a region of high water concentration to a region of low water concentration.

Ovary
An organ in the female body which stores and releases eggs. It is also a gland and secretes the hormone oestrogen.

Oxygen debt
The extra oxygen that needs repaying after anaerobic respiration in order to oxidise the lactic acid which has built up in the muscle cells.

Oxyhaemoglobin
A molecule formed when haemoglobin combines with oxygen.

Pancreas
An organ (and gland) in the mammalian digestive system which produces digestive juices.

Pandemic
A worldwide outbreak of a disease.

Partially permeable membrane
A membrane with tiny holes in it, which lets some molecules through it but not others.

Pathogen
A microorganism that causes disease, e.g. a bacterium or virus.

Peat bog
An area of land that is acidic and waterlogged, so plants don't fully decompose when they die, producing peat.

Penicillin
A type of antibiotic.

Performance-enhancing drug
A drug that can improve a person's performance in sport.

Permanent vacuole (plant cells)
A structure in plant cells that contains cell sap.

Phenotype
The characteristics you have, e.g. blue eyes.

Phloem
A type of plant tissue which transports sucrose around the plant.

Photosynthesis
The process by which plants and algae use light energy to convert carbon dioxide and water into glucose and oxygen.

Phototropism
The growth of a plant in response to light.

Pituitary gland
A gland located in the brain that is responsible for secreting various hormones, including FSH and LH.

Placebo (in drug testing)
A substance that's like the drug being tested but doesn't do anything.

Plasma
The liquid component of blood, which transports the contents of the blood around the body.

Platelet
A small fragment of a cell found in the blood, which helps blood to clot at a wound.

Polydactyly
A genetic disorder caused by a dominant allele where a sufferer has extra fingers or toes.

Positive correlation
When one variable increases as another variable increases.

Precise result
When all the data is close to the mean.

Prediction
A statement based on a hypothesis that can be tested.

Progesterone
A hormone produced by the ovaries, which is involved in the menstrual cycle. It's found in some oral contraceptives.

Protease
A type of digestive enzyme that catalyses the breakdown of proteins into amino acids, in the stomach and small intestine.

Protein
A large biological molecule made up of long chains of amino acids.

Pulmonary artery
A blood vessel (artery) which transports blood out of the heart to the lungs.

Pulmonary vein
A blood vessel (vein) which transports blood into the heart from the lungs.

Punnet square
A type of genetic diagram.

Pyramid of biomass
A diagram to represent the biomass at each stage of a food chain.

Quadrat
A square frame enclosing a known area which can be used to study the distribution of organisms.

Random error
A small difference in the results of an experiment caused by things like human error in measuring.

Range
The difference between the smallest and largest values in a set of data.

Receptor
A group of cells which are sensitive to a stimulus. E.g. light receptor cells in the eye are sensitive to light.

Recessive allele
An allele whose characteristic only appears in an organism if there are two copies present.

Recreational drug
A drug used for fun, e.g. alcohol, cannabis.

Red blood cell
A cell which forms part of the blood and contains haemoglobin to transport oxygen around the body.

Reflex
A fast, automatic response to a stimulus.

Reflex arc
The passage of information in a reflex from receptor to effector.

Relay neurone
A nerve cell that carries electrical impulses from sensory neurones to motor neurones.

Reliable result
A result that is repeatable and reproducible.

Repeatable result
A result that will come out the same if the experiment is repeated by the same person using the same method and equipment.

Reproducible result
A result that will come out the same if someone different does the experiment, or a slightly different method or piece of equipment is used.

Resolution
The smallest change a measuring instrument can detect.

Ribcage
A set of bones in the thorax, which protect the lungs.

Ribosome
A structure in a cell, where proteins are made.

Root hair cell
A cell on the surface of a plant root, which absorbs water and mineral ions.

Rooting powder
A powder containing plant hormones, which can be applied to plant cuttings to assist root development.

Salivary gland
An organ (and gland) in the mammalian digestive system which produces digestive juices.

Selective weedkiller
A weedkiller that contains plant hormones. It kills weeds (unwanted plants), without affecting the growth of crops.

Sense organ
An organ which contains receptors that detect stimuli, e.g. the eye.

Sensory neurone
A nerve cell that carries electrical impulses from the receptors in the sense organs to the CNS.

Sequestered
When something is stored up. For example, lakes sequester carbon dioxide.

Sex chromosome (humans)
One of the 23rd pair of chromosomes — together they determine whether an individual is male or female.

Sexual reproduction
Where two gametes combine at fertilisation to produce a genetically different new individual.

Small intestine
An organ in the mammalian digestive system where food is digested and soluble food molecules are absorbed.

Soft drug
A drug that is believed to be less addictive and less harmful to a person's health than a hard drug.

Specialised cell
A cell which performs a specific function.

Speciation
The development of a new species.

Species
A group of similar organisms that can reproduce to give fertile offspring.

Stable community
A community in which the materials taken out of the soil and used are balanced by those that are put back in — the materials are constantly cycled.

Standard of living
A measure of things like what access people have to food, education, health care and luxury goods like TVs, cars and computers.

Starch
An insoluble molecule used as a store of glucose in plants and algae.

Statins
A group of medicinal drugs that are used to decrease the risk of heart and circulatory disease.

Stem cell
An undifferentiated cell which has the ability to become one of many different types of cell.

Stent
A wire mesh tube that's inserted inside an artery to help keep it open.

Sterilisation (avoiding contamination)
The process of destroying microorganisms (such as bacteria) on an object.

Stimulant
A type of performance-enhancing drug that increases heart rate.

Stimulus
A change in the environment.

Stoma
A tiny hole in the surface of a leaf.

Stomach
An organ in the mammalian digestive system where food is digested.

Sulfur dioxide
A gas released by burning fossil fuels, which can cause acid rain if it mixes with rain clouds in the atmosphere.

Sustainable food production
Producing food in a way that means we have enough to eat now without using resources faster than they renew.

Synapse
The connection between two neurones.

Systematic error
An error that is consistently made every time throughout an experiment.

Target cell
A particular cell in a particular place, which is affected by a hormone.

Thalidomide
A drug that was developed as a sleeping pill in the 1950s, but that harmed babies when used untested on pregnant women to relieve morning sickness.

Theory
A hypothesis which has been accepted by the scientific community because there is good evidence to back it up.

Thermoregulatory centre
An area of the brain which controls and monitors body temperature.

Thorax (humans)
The upper part of the body, excluding the arms and head. Contains the lungs.

Tissue
A group of similar cells that work together to carry out a particular function. It can include more than one type of cell.

Tissue culture (plants)
A method of cloning plants in which a few plant cells are put on a growth medium containing hormones and allowed to grow into new plants.

Toxicity
How harmful something is, e.g. a drug.

Toxin
A poison. Toxins are often produced by bacteria.

Transect
A line which can be used to study the distribution of organisms across an area.

Transpiration stream
The movement of water from a plant's roots, through the xylem and out of the leaves.

Trial run
A quick version of an experiment that can be used to work out the range of variables and the interval between the variables that will be used in the proper experiment.

Trophic level
A stage in a food chain.

Type 1 diabetes
A condition where the pancreas produces little or no insulin, which means blood glucose can rise to a dangerous level.

Type 2 diabetes
A condition in which the body is unable to control blood sugar level.

Urea
A waste product produced from the breakdown of amino acids in the liver.

Uterus
The main female reproductive organ and where the embryo develops during pregnancy. (Another word for the womb.)

Vaccination
The injection of dead or inactive microorganisms to provide immunity against a particular pathogen.

Valid result
A result that answers the original question.

Valve (in the circulatory system)
A structure within the heart or a vein which prevents blood from flowing in the wrong direction.

Variable
A factor in an investigation that can change or be changed (e.g. temperature or concentration).

Variation
The differences that exist between individuals.

Vena cava
A blood vessel (vein) which transports blood into the heart from the rest of the body (excluding the lungs).

Ventilation
The movement of air into and out of the lungs.

Ventricle
A chamber of the heart which pumps blood out of the heart through either the pulmonary artery or the aorta.

Villus
A tiny projection on the inner surface of the small intestine in humans, through which nutrients are absorbed.

Virus
A disease-causing agent about 1/100th of the size of a bacterial cell. Can only replicate within host body cells.

White blood cell
A cell which forms part of the blood and part of the immune system, helping to defend the body against disease.

Wilting
The drooping of a plant due to lack of water.

Withdrawal symptom
A symptom, e.g. a headache, vomiting, which is caused by not taking an addictive drug.

Xylem
A type of plant tissue which transports water and mineral ions around the plant.

Yeast
A type of single-celled microorganism.

Z

Zero error
A type of systematic error caused by using a piece of equipment that isn't zeroed properly.

Acknowledgements

Data acknowledgements

Data used to construct the measles graph on page 38 from http://www.who.int/immunization_monitoring/diseases/big_Measles_global_coverage.JPG accessed March 2013.

Data used to produce the IVF table on page 54 from the Human Fertilisation and Embryology Authority (HFEA).

Data on pregnancy rates used in question on page 54 from the Human Fertilisation and Embryology Authority (HFEA).

Data used to create the aspirin study graph and table on page 73 reprinted from The Lancet, Vol 378, Prof John Burn et al. Long-term effect of aspirin on cancer risk in carriers of hereditary colorectal cancer: an analysis from the CAPP2 randomised controlled trial. Pages 2081-2087, © 2011, with permission from Elsevier.

Data used to construct the arctic sea ice graph on page 79 courtesy of the National Snow and Ice Data Center, University of Colorado, Boulder.

Data used to construct the big cat evolutionary tree on page 117 reprinted from Molecular Phylogenetics and Evolution, Vol 56. Brian W. Davis, Gang Li, William J. Murphy. Supermatrix and species tree methods resolve phylogenetic relationships within the big cats, Panthera (Carnivora: Felidae). Pages 64-76. © 2010, with permission from Elsevier.

Data used to construct the table on the use of stents on page 249 reprinted from the Journal of the American College of Cardiology, Vol 49/19. H Vernon Anderson et al. Drug-Eluting Stents for Acute Myocardial Infarction, pgs 1931-1933. © 2007, with permission from Elsevier.

Data used to construct the sea level graph on page 282 from Climate Change 2007: The Physical Science Basis. Working Group I Contribution to the Fourth Assessment Report of the Intergovernmental Panel on Climate Change, Figure 5.13. Cambridge University Press.

Photograph acknowledgements

Cover Photo **SciePro**/Science Photo Library, p 2 **Gustoimages**/Science Photo Library, p 3 **Philippe Plailly**/Science Photo Library, p 4 **Philippe Plailly**/Science Photo Library, p 5 **Frank Zullo**/Science Photo Library, p 6 **Andrew Lambert Photography**/Science Photo Library, p 7 **Robert Brook**/Science Photo Library, p 8 **Tony McConnell**/Science Photo Library, p 9 **Rosenfeld Images Ltd**/Science Photo Library, p 10 **Martyn F. Chillmaid**/Science Photo Library, p 15 **Pr. M. Brauner**/Science Photo Library, p 16 **Maximilian Stock Ltd**/Science Photo Library, p 17 **Ria Novosti**/Science Photo Library, p 19 **Biophoto Associates**/Science Photo Library, p 21 **Paul Rapson**/Science Photo Library, p 23 (left) **Paul Rapson**/Science Photo Library, p 23 (right) **Paul Rapson**/Science Photo Library, p 24 (top) **Eye of Science**/Science Photo Library, p 24 (bottom) **Ami Images**/Science Photo Library, p 25 (Fig. 3) **Juergen Berger**/Science Photo Library, p 25 (Fig. 5) **Biology Media**/Science Photo Library, p 28 **Saturn Stills**/Science Photo Library, p 30 **Scott Camazine**/Science Photo Library, p 31 **Michael Gabridge/Visuals Unlimited, Inc.**/Science Photo Library, p 33 Science Photo Library, p 39 **Kate Jacobs**/Science Photo Library, p 40 **Sovereign, ISM**/Science Photo Library, p 42 **Thomas Deerinck, NCMIR**/Science Photo Library, p 43 **PH. Gerbier**/Science Photo Library, p 46 **Mark Turnball**/Science Photo Library, p 47 **Scott Camazine**/Science Photo Library, p 49 **Professors P. M. Motta & J. Van Blerkom**/ Science Photo Library, p 52 **Cordelia Molloy**/Science Photo Library, p 53 **Zephyr**/Science Photo Library, p 55 **Martin Shields**/Science Photo Library, p 56 **Martin Shields**/Science Photo Library, p 57 **Martin Shields**/Science Photo Library, p 58 **Geoff Kidd**/Science Photo Library, p 67 **St. Bartholomew's Hospital**/Science Photo Library, p 70 (Fig. 1) **James Stevenson**/Science Photo Library, p 70 (Fig. 2) **Alex Bartel**/Science Photo Library, p 74 (Fig. 1) **Mark Phillips**/Science Photo Library, p 74 (bottom) **Leonard Rue Enterprises**/Science Photo Library, p 75 (Fig. 2) **Stephen J. Krasemann**/Science Photo Library, p 75 (Fig. 3) **Bjanka Kadic**/Science Photo Library, p 76 **Nature's Images**/Science Photo Library, p 77 **John Devries**/Science Photo Library, p 78 **Dr. John Brackenbury**/Science Photo Library, p 80 **Paul Rapson**/Science Photo Library, p 81 **Vaughan Fleming**/Science Photo Library, p 89 **Gustoimages**/Science Photo Library, p 90 **Dr Jeremy Burgess**/Science Photo Library, p 94 (Fig. 1) **Kate Jacobs**/Science Photo Library, p 94 (bottom) **Coneyl Jay**/Science Photo Library, p 96 (Fig. 2) **Dr Gopal Murti**/Science Photo Library, p 96 (Fig. 3) **Power and Syred**/Science Photo Library, p 97 **Manfred Kage**/Science Photo Library, p 98 **Eye of Science**/Science Photo Library, p 99 **Wim van Egmond/Visuals Unlimited, Inc.**/Science Photo Library, p 100 (top) **Sinclair Stammers**/Science Photo Library, p 100 (bottom) **Nigel Cattlin/Holt Studios**/Science Photo Library, p 101 **Gerard Peaucellier, ISM**/Science Photo Library, p 102 (Fig. 6) **James King-Holmes**/Science Photo Library, p 102 (Fig. 8) **Gustoimages**/Science Photo Library, p 103 **Tony Camacho**/Science Photo Library, p 106 (top) **Pasieka**/Science Photo Library, p 106 (bottom) **Bill Barksdale/Agstockusa**/Science Photo Library, p 108 **Gary Parker**/Science Photo Library, p 110 Science Photo Library, p 113 **Sheila Terry**/Science Photo Library, p 115 (top) **Tom & Pat Leeson**/Science Photo Library, p 115 (bottom) **Richard Herrmann/Visuals Unlimited, Inc.**/Science Photo Library, p 117 (Fig. 2) **Christopher Swann**/Science Photo Library, p 117 (middle) **Matthew Oldfield**/Science Photo Library, p 119 **Ken M. Highfill**/Science Photo Library, p 120 **Pasieka**/Science Photo Library, p 121 **Dr. Martha Powell, Visuals Unlimited**/Science Photo Library, p 122 **Steve Gschmeissner**/Science Photo Library, p 123 **Power and Syred**/Science Photo Library, p 125 **Andrew Lambert Photography**/Science Photo Library, p 128 **Steve Gschmeissner**/Science Photo Library, p 129 **Dr Keith Wheeler**/Science Photo Library, p 132 (Fig. 1) **B.W.Hoffman/Agstockusa**/ Science Photo Library, p 132 (Fig. 2) **Eye of Science**/Science Photo Library, p 135 **Eye of Science**/Science Photo Library, p 136 **Biophoto Associates**/Science Photo Library, p 138 **E. R. Degginger**/Science Photo Library, p 142 (Fig. 1) **Angel Fitor**/Science Photo Library, p 142 (Fig. 3) **36clicks**/iStockphoto, p 145 (Fig. 1) **Biophoto Associates**/Science Photo Library, p 145 (Fig. 2) **Wim Van Egmond/Visuals Unlimited, Inc.**/Science Photo Library, p 145 (left) **Angel Fitor**/Science Photo Library, p 145 (right) **Victor de Schwanberg**/Science Photo Library, p 146 **The Picture Store**/Science Photo Library, p 148 **Bob Gibbons**/Science Photo Library, p 149 **Martyn F. Chillmaid**/Science Photo Library, p 151 **Martyn F. Chillmaid**/Science Photo Library, p 157 **Clive Freeman, The Royal Institution**/Science Photo Library, p 162 **Martyn F. Chillmaid**/Science Photo Library, p 163 **Power and Syred**/Science Photo Library, p 164 **Eye of Science**/Science Photo Library, p 168 (Fig. 1) **Samuel Ashfield**/Science Photo Library, p 168 **Professors P. Motta & T. Naguro**/Science Photo Library, p 169 **BSIP, Laurent/B. Hop Ame**/Science Photo Library, p 171 **Gustoimages**/Science Photo Library, p 176 **David Parker**/Science Photo Library, p 177 **Tek Image**/Science Photo Library, p 178 (Fig. 1) **Sovereign, ISM**/ Science Photo Library, p 178 (Fig. 2) **Michael P. Gadomski**/Science Photo Library, p 179 **Herve Conge, ISM**/Science Photo Library, p 181 **Adrian T Sumner**/Science Photo Library, p 183 **Paul Gunning**/Science Photo Library, p 184 **Pascal Goetgheluck**/Science Photo Library, p 186 Science Photo Library, p 187 **kutipie**/iStockphoto, p 190 Science Photo Library, p 191 **Bob Gibbons**/Science Photo Library, p 194 **Wally Eberhart, Visuals Unlimited**/Science Photo Library, p 198 **Sovereign, ISM**/Science Photo Library, p 200 **Pascal Goetgheluck**/Science Photo Library, p 206 (Fig. 1) **Sinclair Stammers**/Science Photo Library, p 206 (Fig. 2) **Natural History Museum, London**/Science Photo Library, p 207 (Fig. 3) **Dirk Wiersma**/Science Photo Library, p 207 (Fig. 4) **John Reader**/ Science Photo Library, p 207 (Fig. 5) **Pasieka**/Science Photo Library, p 207 (Fig. 6) **Silkeborg Museum, Denmark/Munoz-Yague**/ Science Photo Library, p 208 (A) **Josie Iselin, Visuals Unlimited**/Science Photo Library, p 208 (B and C) **Herve Conge, ISM**/Science Photo Library, p 208 (D) **Philippe Plailly**/Science Photo Library, p 209 **Photo Researchers**/Science Photo Library, p 212 **kojihirano**/ iStockphoto, p 215 **Charles D. Winters**/Science Photo Library, p 219 (left) **E.R.Degginger**/Science Photo Library, p 219 (right) **Tom & Pat Leeson**/Science Photo Library, p 220 **Biophoto Associates**/Science Photo Library, p 221 **Eye of Science**/Science Photo Library, p 222 **Zephyr**/Science Photo Library, p 224 (Fig. 5) **Science Source**/Science Photo Library, p 224 (Fig. 6) **Dr P. Marazzi**/ Science Photo Library, p 226 (Fig. 3) **Dr Jeremy Burgess**/Science Photo Library, p 227 **Dr Keith Wheeler**/Science Photo Library, p 235 **Steve Gschmeissner**/Science Photo Library, p 236 **CNRI**/Science Photo Library, p 237 **Steve Gschmeissner**/Science Photo Library, p 238 (Fig. 3) **Power and Syred**/Science Photo Library, p 238 (Fig. 4) **Susumu Nishinaga**/Science Photo Library, p 238 (Fig. 5) **Antonia Reeve**/Science Photo Library, p 240 (Fig. 1) **Hank Morgan**/Science Photo Library, p 240 (Fig. 2) **CNRI**/ Science Photo Library, p 241 (Fig. 3) **Dr P. Marazzi**/Science Photo Library, p 241 (Fig. 5) **Sovereign/ISM**/Science Photo Library, p 242 **Jim Varney**/Science Photo Library, p 244 (Fig. 2) **Dr. Richard Kessel & Dr. Gene Shih/Visuals Unlimited, Inc.**/Science Photo Library, p 244 (Fig. 4) **Biophoto Associates**/Science Photo Library, p 256 **Life in View**/Science Photo Library, p 257 **Cordelia Molloy**/ Science Photo Library, p 258 **Dr. Barry Slaven/Visuals Unlimited, Inc.**/Science Photo Library, p 260 **toos**/iStockphoto, p 261 **Robert Markus**/Science Photo Library, p 264 **Coneyl Jay**/Science Photo Library, p 271 **Michael Marten**/Science Photo Library, p 273 **Robert Brook**/Science Photo Library, p 274 **John Heseltine**/Science Photo Library, p 276 (Fig. 3) **Mark A. Schneider**/Science Photo Library, p 273 (Fig. 4) **Ailsa M Allaby**/Science Photo Library, p 279 **NASA**/Science Photo Library, p 280 **Dr. John Brackenbury**/Science Photo Library, p 281 **Martin Bond**/Science Photo Library, p 283 **Pascal Goetgheluck**/Science Photo Library, p 285 (Fig. 2) **James King-Holmes**/Science Photo Library, p 285 (Fig. 3) **Prof. David Hall**/Science Photo Library, p 290 **Alex Bartel**/ Science Photo Library, p 291 **Cordelia Molloy**/Science Photo Library, p 292 (Fig. 2) **Jim Varney**/Science Photo Library, p 292 (Fig. 3) **Victor de Schwanberg**/Science Photo Library, p 298 Science Photo Library, p 304 **Andrew Lambert Photography**/Science Photo Library, p 306 Science Photo Library, p 314 **Photostock-Israel**/Science Photo Library.

Every effort has been made to locate copyright holders and obtain permission to reproduce sources. For those sources where it has been difficult to trace the originator of the work, we would be grateful for information. If any copyright holder would like us to make an amendment to the acknowledgements, please notify us and we will gladly update the book at the next reprint. Thank you.

Index

BATB41